Declaration of Conscience

Declaration of Conscience

Margaret Chase Smith

Edited by

William C. Lewis, Jr.

Doubleday & Company, Inc., Garden City, New York, 1972

Contents

Editor's Preface

There has long been, with some reason, considerable cynicism about speeches—their degree of sincerity, their motivation, their purpose, their value, and their impact. Perhaps it is more accurate to say that this cynicism is about speakers rather than speeches—especially if the speakers are politicians.

Rarely is there a speech of lasting impact. In American history, Washington's Farewell Address, Lincoln's Gettysburg Address, Wilson's "Save the World for Democracy," and Franklin D. Roosevelt's "The Only Thing We Have to Fear Is Fear Itself" are remembered, in part perpetuated in the classrooms through required reading of the history books. But these are the exceptions. And in an age marked by a desperate need for communication among peoples—to talk instead of fight, in Vietnam or in the ghettos or on the campuses—it is strange that there are so few significant speeches, or books which tell what led up to them and what resulted from them.

For in the great emphasis placed upon the need for communication, there is greater need to recognize the fundamental truth that the greatest means of communication is in speech. We talk and write much about the importance of articulation. Yet we rarely take a real close look at what causes that articulation and what results from it.

More often, people are more impressed with the style of a speaker than with the content of what he says—*how* rather than *what* he says. And even less, in *why*. Seldom at all do we interest ourselves in *what resulted* from what was said.

The purpose of this book is to recount several of the more significant statements of a Quiet Woman; to set forth *why* she

made such statements, what led up to them, *what resulted* from
them—as repercussions, reprisals, recognition, headaches, heart-
aches, humiliation, or honors.

Most of us soon forget a speech we have heard or read.
But the political speaker has to live with every word of that
speech for the rest of his or her life. Any public official is fair
game on "Meet the Press" or "Face the Nation" or "Issues and
Answers" or "Firing Line" for the panelist's needle: "Well, Senator, how do you justify this statement you made ten years ago
in light of today's developments?"

Most everyone can recall hearing the wise counsel of such
adages as "You never have to be sorry for, or explain, or
apologize for the unspoken word" or "Don't speak unless to do
so improves upon silence." But anyone who unbrokenly follows
such caution also studiously avoids involvement. Such a person
is lacking in leadership.

Margaret Chase Smith, the author of this book, is currently
the only woman member of the United States Senate and the
only woman to have been elected to, and served in, both the
United States House of Representatives and the United States
Senate. To call her a Quiet Woman is accurate because she rarely
speaks in the Senate. Yet to call her quiet can be seriously misleading, for she does not shun or avoid involvement.

This book documents that involvement and the price she has
paid for it. She has been at the center of conflict and controversy.
Quiet? Yes, but she is the one Senator who spoke out most
forcefully year after year against the McCarthyism that gripped
our nation in the early and mid-fifties. It is the speech given by
the only woman in the Senate to her male colleagues, most of
whom remained politically tongue-tied throughout the siege, that
constitutes the heart of this book—the Declaration of Conscience. If historians attach any significance to the McCarthy
era, then surely Margaret Chase Smith's Declaration of Conscience of June 1, 1950, will be to that conflict what Lincoln's
Address at Gettysburg was to the Civil War.

The author herein is the Quiet Woman. Her deeds and speeches
are the heart, brain, and backbone of the book. The editor and

annotator has merely filled in, adding flesh to the body of the book. In doing so, I have made observations and expressed opinions about Senator Smith that she would never make about herself. My qualification to do so is the fact that I have had the good fortune to be associated with her on all the episodes in this book save the Navy Day talk, which she made five years before we met.

Margaret Chase Smith makes no claim for infallibility and her editor has no illusions about his objectivity. I confess to considerable subjectivity and a desire to leave criticism and detraction to others. Still, Senator Smith and I have made every effort to be factual throughout.

William C. Lewis, Jr.

*"My creed is that public service must be
more than doing a job efficiently and honestly. It
must be a complete dedication to the people and to
the nation with full recognition that every human
being is entitled to courtesy and consideration,
that constructive criticism is not only to be expected
but sought, that smears are not only to be expected
but fought, that honor is to be earned but not bought."*

—November 11, 1953

Declaration of Conscience

Declaration of Conscience I

JUNE 1, 1950

"I wouldn't want to say anything that bad about the Republican Party."

—President Harry S. Truman
June 1, 1950

"If a man had made the Declaration of Conscience, he would be the next President of the United States."

—Bernard M. Baruch
June 2, 1950

I first met Senator Joseph McCarthy through a very good and close friend, May Craig, the peppery little newshen with the quaint little hats. Millions of television viewers watched May needle Presidents and Senators and top government officials on the "Meet the Press" TV program and at White House press conferences. She was characterized as the "hair shirt" of the women's press corps, not only because of her questioning of the great and near great but because of her militant demands for equal rights for women—particularly for recognition and facilities for women in the press corps.

When May's husband died, she inherited his place as the Washington correspondent for the Guy Gannett newspapers of Maine. Because of her chatty daily column for those papers, thousands thought that she was from Maine. Almost nobody knew she was a Yankee from South Carolina.

When my husband began his first term as United States Representative for the Second Congressional District of Maine in 1937, I made a special effort to accommodate Mrs. Craig on potential news out of Clyde's office—even going to the extent of letting her read the mail to get material for her daily column. Having done some work for a newspaper myself, I had a real empathy for May Craig's work. At the same time, I recognized that cooperation would help Clyde when re-election time came up.

May got her first on-the-spot introduction in Maine to Maine people as our house guest in Skowhegan, Maine. We gave a large party honoring her and asked her to speak on Washington, her work and her relations with President Franklin D. Roosevelt and Mrs. Eleanor Roosevelt, a close friend of May Craig's. Her remarks to the group were well received. Publisher Guy Gannett was so pleased that he suggested that I invite May up again, and Gannett would make arrangements for May to make three or four speeches. This was done— and thus strong personal ties were formed between the South Carolina gal and the Maine Yankees, through a little act of courtesy.

Our friendship grew closer and stronger as the years passed.

When I succeeded Clyde in the House, May was regarded by her colleagues in the Congressional press galleries as my mentor and ghost writer. While I did value May's advice greatly, May never wrote a speech for me.

Good friends as we were, May was quite frank. She did not foresee any great future for Margaret Smith. She said as much once, without using the blunt words, at lunch in 1946 in the House restaurant. She told me: "Margaret, you have reached your peak—you can go no further—so you must adjust yourself to going downhill from now on."

The turning point in my career was when I decided to run for Senator. I think that May, perhaps unknowingly, accomplished the opposite result of what she intended. Instead of resigning myself to going downhill, I determined to go up.

Others, like Senator Leverett Saltonstall, felt that I had reached my peak. He revealed this in a table conversation with Bill Lewis at a Reserve Officers banquet honoring Defense Secretary Forrestal in February 1948. Bill, who at that time was my campaign manager, was unknown to Senator Saltonstall and so when he asked the Senator about Congresswoman Smith's chances of winning the Senate race, Saltonstall replied that Margaret didn't have the slightest chance of beating Governor Hildreth. "Why then would she run in the face of certain defeat?" Bill asked. Saltonstall answered that it was because a young veteran (Charles Nelson) was going to run against me and I would rather retire from Congress being defeated for reaching higher to the Senate than to be ousted from my House job. Taking issue with Saltonstall was Congressman L. Mendel Rivers of South Carolina, later to be Chairman of the House Committee on Armed Services. Rivers flatly predicted that Margaret Chase Smith would be elected to the Senate by a big margin.*

At an informal dinner, May introduced me to Joe McCarthy. I found him to be pleasant but I was not as impressed with

* Eighteen years later Margaret was to succeed Saltonstall as the Chairman of the Senate Republican Conference and as the top Republican on the Senate Armed Services Committee.

him as May obviously was. May said that the new Senator was a comer with a great future. (This was not long after May had, in effect, told me that my future had passed.)

When I became a member of the Senate in January 1949, no one challenged the sanctity of the seniority system. Nor did anyone propose that any special consideration be given to the only woman in the Senate. Consequently, I drew the lowest ranking Senate assignments—the District of Columbia Committee and the Executive Expenditures Committee. Not until I had served four years in the Senate did I receive a major committee assignment. So I smile now when I watch special committee consideration given freshman Senators to insure that they get at least one major committee assignment at the outset of their service.

Of the two committee assignments, Executive Expenditures (later the name was changed to Government Operations) was the more interesting. Joseph McCarthy was the top Republican on Executive Expenditures and, as such, he made the Republican assignments on the subcommittees. I asked for the Permanent Investigations Subcommittee. When Joe appointed me and Karl Mundt (who had been elected in 1948 also) to join him as the three Republicans on this subcommittee, I was sure that May Craig's friendship had been an important factor.

In that year of 1949, Joe even spoke of me as being his choice for Vice President. In January 1950 he urged me to go to Milwaukee to speak to the journalism sorority, Theta Sigma Phi. In expressing regret to that organization, I referred to our subcommittee work, writing, "We have served on the Senate Investigating Committee, an excellent assignment for him because of his experience and ability to get things done."

Relations between Joe and me on that Permanent Investigations Subcommittee were reasonably good. The work had been principally investigating "five percenters" and had not dealt with communism and subversion. One "five percenter" investigated and exposed by the subcommittee was a man named Hunt. His appearance before the subcommittee was repeatedly delayed because of heart trouble. I took a very strong stand in pressing for Hunt to appear before the subcommittee. His case proved to be embarrassing after I had demanded his appearance.

The subcommittee Counsel, Bill Rogers (later to be Attorney General and Secretary of State), came to me with the news that the investigating staff had found a letter of mine in Hunt's file. The letter forwarded an autographed picture of me to him. Although I did not know Hunt, I had sent him the photograph at the request of a mutual friend, Miss Marion Martin.

When Rogers showed me the photocopy of my letter, I found that I had forgotten all about it. The request was only one of hundreds of such instances. I told Rogers that this letter made no difference; Hunt should be made to appear before the subcommittee and answer the charges against him. Later, the newspapers carried a picture of Hunt's office wall on which one of the pictures was mine. I took quite a ribbing over it.

It was this "five percenter" investigation that caused me to have my first doubts about Joe McCarthy. I was pressing for the Republican minority on the subcommittee to demand a very strong and hard-hitting report. Joe held a closed meeting with Karl Mundt and me and we agreed that our discussion on the final report of the investigation would not be discussed with the press. Joe then turned around and, without any notice, told the reporters that I would hold a press conference on the closed meeting.

McCarthy and Mundt were willing to accept a comparatively softer report than I would accept. Only in view of my threat to file an individual minority report was it ultimately agreed to incorporate in the report the strong excerpts that I had drafted.

In the Lincoln Day Republican speechmaking period of February 1950, Joe McCarthy launched his charge of card-carrying Communists in the State Department and started playing the numbers game as to just how many there were. Many thought that his Wheeling, West Virginia, speech was actually a political accident and that Joe had had no idea that it would catch on as it did.

In the following weeks and months, he expanded and intensified his State Department card-carrying Communist charges.

At first, I will admit, I was impressed with what he was saying. That "I hold in my hand a photostatic copy" had a most impressive tone and ring of authenticity. It looked as if Joe was onto something disturbing and frightening.

When several liberals, one after another, came to me, they urged me very earnestly, even emotionally, to take issue with McCarthy, I frankly told them that I thought he had something in his charges. I made it a point to go to the Senate Floor repeatedly to listen to his speeches.

Then I asked to look at "the photostatic copies" he held as he detailed his charges on the Senate Floor. At first glance, I thought they were impressive; they appeared to be authentic. When I did not readily see their relevancy to what Joe was charging or quickly perceive how they clearly proved his charges, I first concluded that this was because of my own deficiency—I am not a lawyer. After all, Joe was a lawyer and any lawyer Senator will tell you that lawyer Senators are superior to non-lawyer Senators and more quickly grasp and perceive issues and their relevancies.

But the more I listened to Joe and the more I read the papers he held in his hand, the less I could understand what he was up to. And more and more I began to wonder whether I was as stupid as I had thought. It was then that I began to wonder about the validity, accuracy, credibility, and fairness of Joseph McCarthy's charges.

As I listened to him, increasingly, I am afraid, my bewilderment and doubt began to show on my face. Several times I indicated to Senator McCarthy in a friendly manner that I was concerned because he did not produce evidence to back up his serious charges against people. One day Joe said, "Margaret, you seem to be worried about what I am doing." I said, "Yes, Joe. I want to see the proof. I have been waiting a long time now for you to produce proof."

"But I have shown you the photostatic copies, Margaret."

"Perhaps I'm stupid, Joe. But they don't prove a thing to me that backs up your charges."

Among the earnest liberals who called on me to speak out

against Joe McCarthy was the radio commentator Ed Hart. I first met Ed Hart in 1949, when we did a radio interview of his program for Easter Sunday, April 17. The subject of our discussion in that interview was peace and the role that women could play in effecting peace. That interview apparently made a lasting impression on Hart.

Repeatedly, during the period of March through May, Hart went to Bill Lewis. "Margaret Chase Smith is the ideal person to speak out and challenge Joe McCarthy," he told Bill. Ed Hart stressed the theme of the right to hold unpopular beliefs.

Another who urged me to speak up—and who bemoaned the paralysis of silence that seemed to grip the Senate—was liberal columnist Doris Fleeson. Doris was heavily partisan, a Democrat, and she made no bones about it. But she had written that she admired my "political independence and courage." Doris excoriated the Democrats in the Senate for not standing up to McCarthy. She was particularly critical of the Democratic Leadership.

Interestingly, Doris Fleeson shared an office in the National Press Building with her good friend May Craig. They differed sharply over Joe McCarthy. May continued to admire and support him for what she was convinced was a great patriotic service to his country. Doris had an intense dislike of Joe for what she considered to be grave irresponsibility.

It was this difference about McCarthy that brought May and Doris to a parting of the ways, some thought, and to a termination of their joint office arrangement. And it was a difference on Joe McCarthy that made a serious, if not irreparable, rupture in the friendly relations between May Craig and me.

Week after week went by with charge after charge by Joe McCarthy which remained unproved. My doubts increased. Finally I became convinced that he simply was not going to come up with any proof to substantiate his charges.

To those of us, especially in Washington, who lived through this period of political nightmare of McCarthyism, I need not summarize the situation Joe had produced. But to those now too young to have known or to recall, I would point out that

McCarthy had created an atmosphere of such political fear that people were not only afraid to talk but they were afraid of whom they might be seen with.

Dozens of State Department employees were pilloried by McCarthy under the cloak of senatorial immunity with unproved accusations and smeared with guilt-by-association and guilt-by-accusation tactics. This great psychological fear even spread to the Senate where a considerable amount of mental paralysis and muteness set in for fear of offending McCarthy. Distrust became so widespread that many dared not accept dinner invitations lest at some future date McCarthy might level unproved charges against someone who had been at the same dinner party. I was also to become one of his targets because subsequent to my Declaration of Conscience I met for the first time, and had no subsequent contact with, a State Department official against whom he leveled unfounded and unproved charges.

But I was reluctant to respond to the requests that I speak up and challenge McCarthy. In the first place, I was a freshman Senator—and in those days, freshmen Senators were to be seen and not heard, like good children. In the second place, it was clear that he should be challenged by Democratic Senators speaking in defense of a Democratic Administration, a Democratic President, and a Democratic Secretary of State. Surely one of the Democrats would take the Senate Floor and make a major challenge to Joe. Increasingly, it became evident that outside the Tydings Committee* this challenge simply was not to be. Increasingly, it became evident that Joe had the

---

* The Tydings Committee was a subcommittee of the Senate Foreign Relations Committee appointed by Chairman Tom Connally to investigate McCarthy's charges of card-carrying Communists in the State Department. Members of the subcommittee were Chairman Millard E. Tydings (D., Md.), Brien McMahon (D., Conn.), Theodore Francis Green (D., R.I.), Henry Cabot Lodge, Jr. (R., Mass.), and Bourke B. Hickenlooper (R., Iowa). Of these five, only Hickenlooper was friendly to McCarthy and what McCarthy was doing. In Senator Smith's opinion (and that of many other well-qualified observers), the Tydings subcommittee made the fatal error of subjectively attempting to discredit McCarthy rather than objectively investigating and evaluating his charges. This criticism of the Tydings subcommittee was indicated in Senator Smith's Declaration of Conscience.

Senate paralyzed with fear. The political risk of taking issue with him was too great a hazard to the political security of Senators.

Ed Hart suggested to Bill Lewis that I talk with columnist Walter Lippmann. When Bill relayed this suggestion, I talked with Lippmann in his Washington home at 11:15 A.M. on May 23, 1950. I told him of my concern, that I was contemplating taking issue with McCarthy in a speech on the Senate Floor, and asked for his reaction, observations, or comments. Lippmann expressed strong approval but he did not suggest any theme or wording for my potential speech.

I decided to draft a short statement and invite a few Republican Senators to join me in it. I asked Bill Lewis to prepare a draft. Lewis asked Ed Hart for his suggestions. Then I went over the suggested draft and made my personal revisions. I boiled down the draft for it was too wordy and too grandiose.

Then I showed it to Senator George D. Aiken one afternoon in the Senate restaurant. We sipped coffee while taking a break from a Senate debate. Aiken said he thought it was good and had no changes to suggest. I asked him whom he would recommend I invite to join in on the statement besides himself. Between us, we decided on Charles W. Tobey of New Hampshire, Wayne L. Morse of Oregon (then a liberal Republican), Irving M. Ives of New York, Edward J. Thye of Minnesota, and Robert C. Hendrickson of New Jersey.

We considered other liberal or moderate Republican Senators but finally agreed that no others had to be invited. Some we ruled out because of a tendency to nit-pick on language—some because it was doubtful that they would keep the matter in strict confidence until the statement was issued—some because of the possibility that they might go to the influential Senator Robert Taft for advice, which could result in pressure against issuing the statement—and some simply because there was doubt that they could stand firm against criticism after the statement had been issued. So only five in addition to Aiken were invited. They all accepted. Of the five, only Wayne Morse was to hold his ground and not show any subsequent misgivings about the statement or signs of retreat and partial repudiation of it.

I had called each of the five and read the statement to them over the telephone. Each cordially expressed approval of the text as read to them. The only one who suggested any change was Irving Ives who thought that in the last sentence the word "tactics" should be changed to "techniques." This was acceptable to me.

Accompanied by Bill Lewis, I went to Maine on Friday, May 26, 1950, for the Memorial Day holiday weekend. At my home in Skowhegan, on Monday evening, May 29, we wrote the draft of a full speech to be made in presenting the statement of the seven Republican Senators to the Senate. No one else participated in the drafting. The only other credit line for any portion of the full speech would have to go to conservative columnist David Lawrence. He had written a column lamenting the lack of national leadership and a couple of his expressed thoughts in that column were incorporated in the draft of the full speech.

I returned to Washington on the evening of Memorial Day, Tuesday, May 30, with the final draft. Early on Thursday morning, June 1, one of my secretaries cut a stencil of the speech. It was taken to the Senate Service Department and two hundred mimeographed copies were made. I insisted on tight security because I did not want the speech to get out ahead of its delivery on the Floor because the Republican Leaders in the Senate might try to dissuade me.

Shortly after lunch, Bill Lewis and I left my office and headed for the Senate Floor. Bill carried the mimeographed copies. I instructed him to withhold release of any copy to anyone until after I had actually begun my delivery of the speech on the Senate Floor.

As we approached the little Senate subway train, Senator McCarthy appeared.

"Margaret," he said, "you look very serious. Are you going to make a speech?"

I said, "Yes, and you will not like it."

He smiled, "Is it about me?"

"Yes, but I'm not going to mention your name."

Then he frowned, "Remember Margaret, I control Wisconsin's twenty-seven convention votes!"

"For what?" I said. Apparently this was his way of threatening me, an implication that he would keep me from getting Wisconsin support for the Republican Vice Presidential nomination. No further conversation was exchanged between us.

At my desk on the Senate Floor, I waited for recognition by the presiding officer. As I awaited my turn to speak, I listened to Senator William F. Knowland of California deliver a speech about the Amerasia spy case. Because of his remarks, and to avoid any appearance that I was taking issue with him, I made a last addition to the prepared speech.

Bill Lewis stood next to the wall near the desk holding the mimeographed copies. Joe McCarthy sat two rows behind me. When I stood and was recognized by the presiding officer, Bill gave the mimeographed copies of the speech to a young Senate Page to take to the press galleries for distribution.

Newspapermen and women in the Senate Press Gallery section leaned over the edge of the balcony to watch. Because many of them thought that May was my mentor and ghost writer, several reporters asked May what was going on. This must have been awkward and embarrassing to May because I had not consulted or confided in her. I was well aware of May's admiration and approval of Joe McCarthy and our deep difference of opinion on him.*

"Mr. President," I said, and then I began:

I would like to speak briefly and simply about a serious national condition. It is a national feeling of fear and frustration

---

* EDITOR'S NOTE: Many of their mutual friends feel that this was literally the moment of truth between May and Margaret when they truly came to a parting of the ways not only because of their disagreement on McCarthy but as well because the incident removed any possible impression or idea that May was Margaret Chase Smith's mentor.

that could result in national suicide and the end of everything that we Americans hold dear. It is a condition that comes from the lack of effective leadership in either the Legislative Branch or the Executive Branch of our Government.

That leadership is so lacking that serious and responsible proposals are being made that national advisory commissions be appointed to provide such critically needed leadership.

I speak as briefly as possible because too much harm has already been done with irresponsible words of bitterness and selfish political opportunism. I speak as simply as possible because the issue is too great to be obscured by eloquence. I speak simply and briefly in the hope that my words will be taken to heart.

I speak as a Republican. I speak as a woman. I speak as a United States Senator. I speak as an American.

The United States Senate has long enjoyed worldwide respect as the greatest deliberative body in the world. But recently that deliberative character has too often been debased to the level of a forum of hate and character assassination sheltered by the shield of congressional immunity.

It is ironical that we Senators can in debate in the Senate directly or indirectly, by any form of words, impute to any American who is not a Senator any conduct or motive unworthy or unbecoming an American—and without that non-Senator American having any legal redress against us—yet if we say the same thing in the Senate about our colleagues we can be stopped on the grounds of being out of order.

It is strange that we can verbally attack anyone else without restraint and with full protection and yet we hold ourselves above the same type of criticism here on the Senate Floor. Surely the United States Senate is big enough to take self-criticism and self-appraisal. Surely we should be able to take the same kind of character attacks that we "dish out" to outsiders.

I think that it is high time for the United States Senate and its members to do some soul-searching—for us to weigh our consciences—on the manner in which we are performing our duty to the people of America—on the manner in which we are using or abusing our individual powers and privileges.

I think that it is high time that we remembered that we have sworn to uphold and defend the Constitution. I think that it is high time that we remembered that the Constitution, as amended, speaks not only of the freedom of speech but also of trial by jury instead of trial by accusation.

Whether it be a criminal prosecution in court or a character prosecution in the Senate, there is little practical distinction when the life of a person has been ruined.

Those of us who shout the loudest about Americanism in making character assassinations are all too frequently those who, by our own words and acts, ignore some of the basic principles of Americanism:

The right to criticize;

The right to hold unpopular beliefs;

The right to protest;

The right of independent thought.

The exercise of these rights should not cost one single American citizen his reputation or his right to a livelihood nor should he be in danger of losing his reputation or livelihood merely because he happens to know someone who holds unpopular beliefs. Who of us doesn't? Otherwise none of us could call our souls our own. Otherwise thought control would have set in.

The American people are sick and tired of being afraid to speak their minds lest they be politically smeared as "Communists" or "Fascists" by their opponents. Freedom of speech is not what it used to be in America. It has been so abused by some that it is not exercised by others.

The American people are sick and tired of seeing innocent people smeared and guilty people whitewashed. But there have been enough proved cases, such as the Amerasia case, the Hiss case, the Coplon case, the Gold case,* to cause nationwide distrust and strong suspicion that there may be something to the unproved, sensational accusations.

As a Republican, I say to my colleagues on this side of the aisle that the Republican Party faces a challenge today that is

---

* The listing of these cases was the addition I made to my speech while Senator Knowland finished his.

not unlike the challenge that it faced back in Lincoln's day. The Republican Party so successfully met that challenge that it emerged from the Civil War as the champion of a united nation—in addition to being a Party that unrelentingly fought loose spending and loose programs.

Today our country is being psychologically divided by the confusion and the suspicions that are bred in the United States Senate to spread like cancerous tentacles of "know nothing, suspect everything" attitudes. Today we have a Democratic Administration that has developed a mania for loose spending and loose programs. History is repeating itself—and the Republican Party again has the opportunity to emerge as the champion of unity and prudence.

The record of the present Democratic Administration has provided us with sufficient campaign issues without the necessity of resorting to political smears. America is rapidly losing its position as leader of the world simply because the Democratic Administration has pitifully failed to provide effective leadership.

The Democratic Administration has completely confused the American people by its daily contradictory grave warnings and optimistic assurances—that show the people that our Democratic Administration has no idea of where it is going.

The Democratic Administration has greatly lost the confidence of the American people by its complacency to the threat of communism here at home and the leak of vital secrets to Russia through key officials of the Democratic Administration. There are enough proved cases to make this point without diluting our criticism with unproved charges.

Surely these are sufficient reasons to make it clear to the American people that it is time for a change and that a Republican victory is necessary to the security of this country. Surely it is clear that this nation will continue to suffer as long as it is governed by the present ineffective Democratic Administration.

Yet to displace it with a Republican regime embracing a philosophy that lacks political integrity or intellectual honesty would prove equally disastrous to this nation. The nation sorely needs a Republican victory. But I don't want to see the Republican Party ride to political victory on the Four Horsemen of Calumny—Fear, Ignorance, Bigotry, and Smear.

I doubt if the Republican Party could—simply because I don't believe the American people will uphold any political party that puts political exploitation above national interest. Surely we Republicans aren't that desperate for victory.

I don't want to see the Republican Party win that way. While it might be a fleeting victory for the Republican Party, it would be a more lasting defeat for the American people. Surely it would ultimately be suicide for the Republican Party and the two-party system that has protected our American liberties from the dictatorship of a one party system.

As members of the Minority Party, we do not have the primary authority to formulate the policy of our Government. But we do have the responsibility of rendering constructive criticism, of clarifying issues, of allaying fears by acting as responsible citizens.

As a woman, I wonder how the mothers, wives, sisters, and daughters feel about the way in which members of their families have been politically mangled in Senate debate—and I use the word "debate" advisedly.

As a United States Senator, I am not proud of the way in which the Senate has been made a publicity platform for irresponsible sensationalism. I am not proud of the reckless abandon in which unproved charges have been hurled from this side of the aisle. I am not proud of the obviously staged, undignified countercharges that have been attempted in retaliation from the other side of the aisle.

I don't like the way the Senate has been made a rendezvous for vilification, for selfish political gain at the sacrifice of individual reputations and national unity. I am not proud of the way we smear outsiders from the Floor of the Senate and hide behind the cloak of congressional immunity and still place ourselves beyond criticism on the Floor of the Senate.

As an American, I am shocked at the way Republicans and Democrats alike are playing directly into the Communist design of "confuse, divide, and conquer." As an American, I don't want a Democratic Administration "whitewash" or "cover-up" any more than I want a Republican smear or witch hunt.

As an American, I condemn a Republican "Fascist" just as much as I condemn a Democrat "Communist." I condemn a Democrat "Fascist" just as much as I condemn a Republican "Communist." They are equally dangerous to you and me and to our country. As an American, I want to see our nation recapture the strength and unity it once had when we fought the enemy instead of ourselves.

It is with these thoughts that I have drafted what I call a "Declaration of Conscience." I am gratified that Senator Tobey, Senator Aiken, Senator Morse, Senator Ives, Senator Thye, and Senator Hendrickson have concurred in that declaration and have authorized me to announce their concurrence.

*   *   *

STATEMENT OF SEVEN REPUBLICAN SENATORS

1. We are Republicans. But we are Americans first. It is as Americans that we express our concern with the growing confusion that threatens the security and stability of our country. Democrats and Republicans alike have contributed to that confusion.

2. The Democratic Administration has initially created the confusion by its lack of effective leadership, by its contradictory grave warnings and optimistic assurances, by its complacency to the threat of communism here at home, by its oversensitiveness to rightful criticism, by its petty bitterness against its critics.

3. Certain elements of the Republican Party have materially added to this confusion in the hopes of riding the Republican Party to victory through the selfish political exploitation of fear, bigotry, ignorance, and intolerance. There are enough mistakes of the Democrats for Republicans to criticize constructively without resorting to political smears.

4. To this extent, Democrats and Republicans alike have unwittingly, but undeniably, played directly into the Communist design of "confuse, divide, and conquer."

5. It is high time that we stopped thinking politically as Republicans and Democrats about elections and started thinking patriotically as Americans about national security based on in-

dividual freedom. It is high time that we all stopped being tools and victims of totalitarian techniques—techniques that, if continued here unchecked, will surely end what we have come to cherish as the American way of life.

> Margaret Chase Smith, Maine
> Charles W. Tobey, New Hampshire
> George D. Aiken, Vermont
> Wayne L. Morse, Oregon
> Irving M. Ives, New York
> Edward J. Thye, Minnesota
> Robert C. Hendrickson, New Jersey

EDITOR'S NOTE:
Senator Joseph McCarthy sat at his desk behind Margaret Chase Smith throughout her fifteen-minute speech. When she finished she sat down, fully expecting that he would make an answering speech. She waited but he did not say a word. Instead, he quietly left the Senate Floor. In fact there was very little response of the Floor to her speech. Only Senators H. Alexander Smith and Robert Hendrickson of New Jersey, Herbert H. Lehman of New York, and Millard Tydings of Maryland seemed to take any notice. They all praised her statement, but Tydings' praise was qualified. He remarked that he was not in complete agreement with what she had said. He recognized very clearly her criticism of the manner in which he and other Democratic leaders had reacted to McCarthy.

The aftermath of that Declaration is essentially the story of Senator McCarthy's campaign of retaliation against Senator Smith. But before turning to that, it is well to speak of some interesting post-speech developments. The politically risky speech produced the heaviest mail Margaret Chase Smith ever received. It was an 8 to 1 favorable ratio. Editorial comment was overwhelming in support of the speech. Some papers like the Chicago *Daily Tribune* excoriated Margaret, both by editorial text and editorial cartoon. But this was to be expected. After all, the *Tribune* had raked her over the coals before, when she was in the House of Representatives. At that time the editorial writer revealed his ignorance by referring to Representative Smith in the masculine gender.

Awards and citations from groups and associations ranged from the Americans for Democratic Action on the Left to the Freedoms Foundation on the Right. The following Washington's Birthday, February 22, 1951, Senator Smith received a Freedoms Foundation Award for the Declaration of Conscience. Not long thereafter conservative columnist George Sokolsky at lunch took the chief executive officer of Freedoms Foundation, Doctor Kenneth Wells, severely to task for this. That organization never repeated the mistake. And the ADA has long been disaffected of Margaret Chase Smith for what they consider to be too strong and too frequent deviations from their standards. Perhaps Margaret Smith fell into the ideological pattern in which yesterday's liberal is today's moderate and tomorrow's conservative.

Among those in the press who chastised Margaret were columnist John O'Donnell (to whom Franklin Delano Roosevelt once said the German Iron Cross should be awarded); *The Tablet,* a weekly Catholic newspaper of Brooklyn; the *Saturday Evening Post,* calling her and the six cosigners "the Soft Underbelly of the Republican Party"; *Life* magazine which termed them "Quixotic"; and columnist Westbrook Pegler. (The Nashville *Tennessean* ribbed Pegler in an editorial cartoon showing Margaret crying at her desk, moaning, "Pegler Doesn't Approve of Me!") Bernard Baruch said that if a man had made the Declaration of Conscience, he would be the next President of the United States.

Frank Altschul of Stamford, Connecticut, reprinted the speech in a handsome small booklet through his Overbrook Press and distributed copies to members of Congress and his friends. One Republican Representative (now part of the

Republican Leadership in the House) responded with the charge that Mr. Altschul was doing a disservice. Specifically, the Republican critic wrote:

It is an attractive appearing publication and the thoughts therein are expressed in the finest rhetoric. It is a model in literary eloquence, employing a quality of phraseology and sentence structure rarely heard anywhere. In fact, never previously nor since have I seen this same style used by Mrs. Smith.

Save for this acknowledged literary value, I personally find it difficult to understand why any real Republican would feel he was in any way making a contribution to the Party to which he professes adherence by distributing the speech. By doing so he is unwittingly, maybe even knowingly, aiding and abetting the cause of the radical New Deal elements who were able to get the speech delivered. Some allege it was prepared by someone high in government position, and probably the product of several minds skilled in strategy and accomplished in rhetoric.

While Mr. Altschul gave Senator Smith the name of the Republican Congressman who wrote this letter, he refused to let her contact the man or to identify him. Recently, the same Congressman asked Senator Smith to come into his state to make a speech for him and help his re-election.

At his press conference the afternoon of June 1, 1950, President Truman ridiculed the speech and made light of it when the press asked for his reaction. William S. White, then of the New York *Times,* reported that "President Truman replied, with a broad smile, that he wouldn't want to say anything that bad about the Republican Party."

Several days later, Harry Truman came up to the Senate, where he had served while Margaret was in the House, to attend a small luncheon in the office of Les Biffle, Secretary of the Senate. Margaret was one of the few Senators invited to the luncheon and she was seated next to the President. At the table, he turned to her and said, "Mrs. Smith, your Declaration of Conscience was one of the finest things that has happened here in Washington in all my years in the Senate and the White House." His public ridicule of the speech and his private praise of it were perhaps understandable by partisan political codes even if clearly conflicting by other standards.

That the Declaration of Conscience put the national spotlight on Margaret Chase Smith was evident. *Newsweek* did a cover story on her, further speculating on her potential future as a Vice President. There were many such speculative pieces. And other odd adornments. She was selected as one of the Ten Best Tailored Women of the world, the best tailored in Government. She was selected as one of the Six Best Dressed Little Women (under five feet five inches).* She was offered a commission as a Lieutenant Colonel in the Air Force Reserve.

———————————

Senator McCarthy's first tactic in retaliation was not the usual heavy-handed approach. Instead he applied a deft touch of ridicule, which he then spoiled by overuse. He labeled me and my cosigners as "Snow White and the Seven Dwarfs." There were really only six cosigners but he included H. Alexander Smith of New Jersey because he was one of those who had arisen on the Senate Floor to state that he was in agreement with my speech.

McCarthy's first open act of revenge came seven months later. In January 1951, in violation of all Senate custom, procedure, and tradition, he kicked me off the Permanent Investigations Subcommittee. My replacement was the newly elected Junior Senator from California, Richard Milhous Nixon.

McCarthy waited until the last minute to send notice that he was eliminating me from the Investigations Subcommittee. He did it by having a member of his staff deliver to my office,

* The Russian press was later to call her an "Amazon warmonger."

after 6 P.M. on the eve of the full committee meeting on sub-committee assignments, a copy of a memo which he had pre-pared for all Republican members with respect to subcommittee assignments. The door of my office was locked. McCarthy's staff member put the letter under the door.

However, I was in that office. I was preparing to join Repre-sentative Frances P. Bolton who was waiting downstairs in her car to take us to Constitution Hall where there was a fund-raising event for the U.S.O. Upon reading the notice, which otherwise I would not have seen until the next morning, I called McCarthy's office. The girl answering the phone said McCarthy could not talk to me; he was busy on another phone. I said: "Then give him this message—tell him that I called and that I fully realize that kicking me off of the Investigations Subcommittee is an act of vengeance to retaliate for my Dec-laration of Conscience."

The next morning, accompanied by Bill Lewis, I went to the executive meeting of the Executive Expenditures Committee. I said at the outset of the meeting that I had made a radio commitment some time ago, prior to the date set for the committee meeting, which I would have to keep downtown in a few minutes. Therefore, I asked Senator McClellan, the Chair-man, to take up the matter of my removal by McCarthy from the Investigations Subcommittee. McCarthy broke in and said that he felt that his action was misinterpreted by Senator Smith, that it was not an unfriendly act toward me but simply that he wanted to put the most experienced Senators on the sub-committee and that he felt that Senator Nixon, because of his work on the House Un-American Activities Committee, had more investigative experience than I did. He also felt that Senator Mundt had more experience.

At this point, I said, "Mr. Chairman, I should like to make some observations—"

But McCarthy, characteristically, butted in, saying, "Just a minute, just a minute, let me finish."

To this I replied, "Joe, you keep quiet for a minute. I haven't said anything while you were talking—now I am going to have my say and you keep quiet!"

I said I would address myself to two points—the first, the matter of investigative experience, and the second, the custom and precedent with respect to subcommittee assignments. I turned to McCarthy. "Joe, now that you have raised the standard of service on investigating committees and experience, I want to point out to you the fact that my service on congressional investigating committees is longer than yours or Senator Mundt's or Senator Nixon's. I was a member of a congressional investigating committee four years before you ever came to Congress, four years before Senator Nixon was a member of Congress, and one year before Senator Mundt ever served on a congressional investigating committee. I was first a member of a congressional investigating committee back in 1943—the Naval Affairs Investigating Committee. So you have not only disregarded custom, precedent, and common courtesy, but you have even disregarded experience on investigating committees."

I turned to Chairman McClellan—to ask only one question —whether once a member had been assigned to a subcommittee that member could be removed over the member's protest. McClellan responded that he thought it was a rather serious matter and he thought the committee should think it over for a week and act on it at the next meeting. Virginia's Senator Willis Robertson said he felt that it was a rather dangerous thing to remove a member from a subcommittee and that if it went through, what happened to Senator Smith could happen to him and any other member of a subcommittee in the future.

At this point, McCarthy protested vigorously, accusing McClellan of usurping his (McCarthy's) authority as the ranking Republican member with respect to subcommittee assignments for Republicans. McClellan receded and said to me that he guessed it was a matter in which the Democrats did not have any voice. They would have to accept the decision of the ranking Republican member of the committee.

Apparently, that settles the issue, I said; there was nothing further to be gained in protesting McCarthy's action as long as the Chairman had made such a ruling. Besides, I was late for the engagement downtown and would have to leave. I left for radio station WOL to do a morning radio broadcast with Mrs. Eleanor Roosevelt.

In a letter dated February 20, 1951, Senator Clyde R. Hoey, Chairman of the Senate Investigations Subcommittee, indirectly commented on McCarthy's action:

> Let me say how much I miss you on the Committee. I am still greatly disappointed that my Committee has been deprived of your valuable service.

A few days later I became a member of the Senate Rules Committee, leaving the District of Columbia Committee. The most avoided assignment on this new committee was its Privileges and Elections Subcommittee. New members were almost automatically assigned P & E as freshman duty and I was no exception. So the ranking Republican on the Rules Subcommittee (Senator Kenneth Wherry of Nebraska) assigned me to the Privileges and Elections Subcommittee without consulting me. This he was later to regret.

At the first meeting of the subcommittee, I was assigned to help investigate the Maryland election—a two-man task for Senator Mike Monroney and me. We both protested. Neither of us was a lawyer and an investigation of an election should include lawyer-Senators. But we were overriden by the other members of the subcommittee who said it was not necessary to have lawyer-Senators on the investigation. Actually they were exerting their seniority and attempting to dodge a most unpleasant task. Senator Hendrickson, who outranked me on the subcommittee, chose the investigations on Pennsylvania and New York in preference to Maryland, because work on them would give him an opportunity to go home to adjacent New Jersey weekends on official business. The complaints that were to be investigated in Maryland stemmed from the smear campaign masterminded by McCarthy against Senator Tydings in the 1950 general election. To create doubt about Tydings' loyalty such tactics were used as the famous composite picture which represented Tydings and Earl Browder, head of the American Communist Party, to be in intimate conversation. Separate pictures of Tydings and Browder had been pasted together and the resulting composite picture was reproduced in a smear tabloid representing Tydings as a pal of Browder when, in fact, Tydings, a World War combat hero, hated Browder because of his Communist activities. Other similar tactics were used by the McCarthy group to defeat Tydings and consequently complaints were filed with the Senate Privileges and Elections Subcommittee.

The next day Senator Wherry, ranking Republican on the full Rules Committee, called me and said that he would be glad to have me transferred to another subcommittee and off the Maryland election investigation—since it involved Senator McCarthy and might embarrass me.

I said that Senator Wherry could do as he pleased, that I had not asked for nor been consulted by him on either the Elections Subcommittee assignment or on the Maryland investigation sub-subcommittee assignment, I had taken on the chores realizing that they were a sort of freshman duty, but that now that I had been given the assignments without consultation I would not shirk my duty. It was for Senator Wherry himself to decide whether he would take me off the Maryland investigation.

Shortly thereafter, Hendrickson called and said that he had been selfish in taking the Pennsylvania and New York investigation assignments and would be happy to trade them for the Maryland investigation assignment. I replied that I was not seeking a change in assignments and would abide by whatever Senator Wherry or the Chairman of the Elections Subcommittee decided.

At the next meeting of the Elections Subcommittee, Chairman Gillette announced that he was increasing the Maryland sub-subcommittee to four, adding Senators Hennings and Hendrickson. Why? Because they were lawyers and the investigation needed lawyer-Senators and Senators Monroney and I were not lawyers. Significantly, he reversed himself as well as the position of Hennings and Hendrickson, who had overruled Monroney and me at the previous meeting. Thus, Gillette became the only member to escape Maryland duty.

On January 30, 1951, an Associated Press article by Jack Bell reported that I had refused to speak at a Lincoln Day Box Supper in Washington because McCarthy was to speak also—and that I had refused to sit on the same platform with him. This was inaccurate. Bell had checked with Bill Lewis who had corrected the rumor Bell had received. Yet Bell insisted on writing the rumor as fact. I wrote Bell a letter of protest. I had received several letters about the Bell story and replied that: (1) I was not invited to speak; (2) I was in no position to refuse invitations which I do not receive; (3) I had attended the Box Supper with my staff and our guests—bringing to the supper fifty people and $110.

On June 14, 1951, Senator McCarthy made a sixty-thousand-word attack on General George C. Marshall, accusing him of a "conspiracy of infamy." On June 18, 1951, I registered my disagreement with that attack by reaffirming my Declaration of Conscience of the year before. In contrast, Senator Hendrickson (one of the six originally who had joined me in the 1950 statement against McCarthy) commended McCarthy when he made the anti-Marshall speech.

A few nights later, the Senate session lasted into the evening. Bill Lewis and I sat at the long table in the Capitol's old Senate dining room for dinner. The table was one where Senators and their aides could go without grouping at the small tables. As we were waiting for our food, a bubbly and ebullient freshman Democratic Senator came to the table and sat down across from us. "Margaret," he said, "what you did the other day to express your disapproval of Joe's attack on General Marshall was wonderful. You're doing a wonderful thing in the way that you continue to stand up on the Senate

Floor against Joe. I'm proud of you—and practically everyone on my side of the aisle is proud of you and with you!"

I looked at him and said quizzically, "Do you really mean that?"

"Of course I mean it. Why would I say it if I didn't?"

There was a short silence as I looked at him. Then I asked quietly, "Then why don't you and those on your side of the aisle get up and do what I do?"

With this his hands went up over his head and his eyebrows raised and he said, "My God, Margaret, that would be political suicide!"

I was convinced that he was completely and unabashedly honest and frank. He reflected the policy of Majority Leader Lyndon Johnson that McCarthy was the Republicans' problem and the Democrats shouldn't get involved in it.

In early June 1951, Jean Kerr (then secretary to Senator McCarthy and later his wife) called at my office to discuss the controversial sheet (with the famous composite picture) Miss Kerr had worked on in the Maryland election. She tried to convince me that there was nothing wrong with it.

During the latter part of June, Mike Monroney told me that he was having great difficulty writing the Maryland report, that he was not satisfied with what the staff had written, and that no one of his personal staff seemed to be able to do a good job of it. He wanted my help and Bill's. He then turned over the material he had worked on to Bill, who wrote a new report.

That new report was given to Senator Monroney without anyone but Monroney, Bill Lewis, and myself knowing who had written it. Weeks passed without the subcommittee facing up to its job of making a report. Finally I submitted to the subcommittee my own draft of a report (very similar to Bill's) and notified them that I had promised Senator Wherry that if he would hold off his pressure for an early report, a report would be made by June 1. I also stated that I was tired of waiting and that unless the subcommittee made its report by August 1, I would file my report (copies of which I gave every member of the subcommittee) with Chairman Gillette and announce to the press that I had done so. But I would not give my report to the press. In the face of this ultimatum, the subcommittee made its report by August 1 and for the most part adopted our Smith version. Senator Hennings boycotted the meetings because of his displeasure and his feeling that as a minority member I was usurping the prerogatives of the Chairman of the subcommittee. Apparently Senator Hennings considered my position to be an unreasonable ultimatum. He responded by boycotting subcommittee meetings for a week during a time when the subcommittee was meeting constantly, day and night.

The committee report tied the smear tabloid to McCarthy, characterizing it as false, malicious, devoid of simple decency and common honesty, and a shocking abuse of the spirit and intent of the first amendment to the Constitution. It highlighted the unchallenged testimony that the idea for the tabloid was the suggestion of McCarthy.

Apparently McCarthy was shocked when the subcommittee report came out—shocked that the subcommittee would so frankly criticize him. On August 3 he issued a public statement in which he said that he was not surprised at the two "Republicans" and called us "puny politicians."

On August 6, 1951, Senator Benton introduced S. Res. 187 to consider expulsion of McCarthy on the basis of the Maryland report. I disapproved of this and resented it. First, the Maryland report stressed the fact that our recommendations were keyed to the future and not to the past—yet Benton sought to use the report to punish for the past instead of preventing in the future. Second, I felt Benton should propose censure, which would require only a simple majority and would have been possible, whereas expulsion required a two-thirds vote of the Senate. The more drastic action obviously could not get that many votes because of the precedent it would set and the future danger it would present to other Senators. It was reported that some Senators (not I) suggested to Bill Benton that he amend his resolution to make it censure instead of expulsion and that he refused to do so, saying that such a change should be made by the Elections Subcommittee considering his resolution. This further irritated us. We felt that Benton was trying to unload on us the responsibility for correcting his tactical and strategic error instead of doing so himself.

McCarthy sought and obtained the permission of the Rules Committee (of which he was then a member) to file a minority report without the committee even seeing it before it was printed and given to the full Senate. Turnabout, as usual with McCarthy, was not fair play; he had been able to force two or three changes in the majority report before it was sent to the Senate.

When he saw he was unable to get any other Republican to join him on the minority report, including Wherry and Jenner, he then wrote a memorandum to them stating that he would not ask them to join him because he didn't want them to be subjected "to all of the left-wing smear and character assassinations."

In his typical fashion McCarthy talked to the press about what he was going to say on the Floor of the Senate—implying but not stating specifically—and so a speculative story appeared in the press a few days before his Senate speech. It was extremely helpful to me in preparing a reply.

On August 20, 1951, McCarthy made a two-hour attack on the Maryland report, specifically on Senator Hendrickson and me. His basic arguments against us were (1) that we were disqualified because we had signed the Declaration of Conscience and (2) we lacked ability to judge facts and evidence because we were not lawyers. During this time, I asked no questions. But Hendrickson made observations and comments defensive in character, implying that his arm had been twisted to make him sign the report. He said that he did not approve of some of the language and conclusions in the report but that he had compromised, agreeing to them in order to get a report out to clear Maryland Senator Butler's status in the Senate, as he had promised Senator Wherry. The only thing that angered Hendrickson or caused him to take issue with

Senator McCarthy was when McCarthy stated that Hendrickson was not a lawyer. Significantly no Democrat defended the report.

I was the only Senator to reply directly to McCarthy. When he had finished, I took the floor and delivered a two-minute answer to his two-hour attack: "Opposition to communism," I began, "is surely not the exclusive possession of Senator McCarthy. Nor does differing with him on tactics automatically make one a Communist or a protector of communism."

I said that it was strange for Senator McCarthy to raise the question on disqualification seven months after my appointment to the subcommittee and fourteen months after the Declaration of Conscience which he claimed to be the basis for disqualification. "It would appear that the McCarthy standard basis for disqualification was disagreement with Senator McCarthy," I said. He should ask Senator Wherry to remove me from the subcommittee as McCarthy had from the Investigations Subcommittee in January. The most direct answer to him, I suggested, was that he hadn't been able to get another Republican to join him in his minority report.*

On that same day of August 20, 1951, I tangled with Republican Leader Wherry on the Senate Floor in debate and drew from him the admission that he thought the Elections Subcommittee had "done a whale of a job" on the report. Wherry's assistant edited that out in the revised remarks for the Record. Senator Wherry became so rattled in our debate that he said at one point, "I don't think two rights make a wrong."

On September 18, 1951, McCarthy wrote Senator Hennings that he should disqualify himself on the Benton resolution because Hennings' law partner had agreed to be counsel for the editor of the *Daily Worker* in a case before the Supreme Court. Hennings replied that his law partner had done so only because

---

* EDITOR'S NOTE: After her remarks, W. McNeil Lowry, Washington Chief of the Cox Newspapers, wrote Senator Smith: "In my newspaper coverage, in my contacts with the White House, and through my friendship with many colleagues of yours, I have made very slow progress in trying to elicit the quality of courage you displayed today, which under the circumstances surpasses that you showed a year ago in June."

he had been assigned to do so by the Court on a question of constitutional law and individual freedom. When Hennings finished his speech, I was the only Republican to cross the Senate Floor and congratulate him.

On September 24, 1951, I wrote Chairman Hayden of the Senate Rules Committee, recalling that in my answer to McCarthy's "disqualification" attack on August 20, I had challenged him to press the matter with the ranking Republican on Rules (Senator Wherry) and the Republican Conference; I pointed out that Senator McCarthy had raised a very basic issue which should be resolved as soon as possible; that since Senator McCarthy had failed to press the issue or to seek a decision, I was calling upon the Senate Rules Committee to decide whether I should be disqualified or not. Until it did, I added, I would refrain from sitting as a member of the Elections Subcommittee on any matters involving Senator McCarthy.

On September 26, 1951, the Rules Committee met with thirteen members present, all except Senator Wherry who was absent because of illness. Before getting to my request for a decision, McCarthy left the meeting. Chairman Hayden read my letter and a letter written that same day, September 26, by McCarthy in which he asked that the committee not vote to disqualify me. He claimed that I should do that myself. It was then voted unanimously that I was not disqualified. The vote was 11 to 0 (including McCarthy's proxy). I abstained from voting and Senator Wherry did not leave a proxy on this issue (the only vote on which he did not give a proxy that day).

Wherry died in December 1951, leaving a Republican vacancy on the Rules Committee and the Appropriations Committee and their subcommittees. McCarthy was appointed to Senator Wherry's vacancy on Appropriations and left the Rules Committee. This left two Republican places on Rules and Senators Dirksen and Welker (both strong McCarthyites) were appointed to those vacancies.

Under operating procedure of seniority, this would have meant almost automatically that Senator Hendrickson and I would leave the Elections Subcommittee and that the two new

Republicans (Dirksen and Welker) as "freshmen" would have that duty. However, this prospect disturbed both the Democrats, who wanted the burden of handling McCarthy to continue to fall on the shoulders of the Republicans, and the McCarthyites who didn't like the idea of having some of their own shouldered with the responsibility of investigating McCarthy. Also, the Senate's McCarthyites did not want the limitations of such responsibility—they preferred being free to continue in the luxury of constant criticism and attack on those investigating or disagreeing with McCarthy.

A further tactical consideration: if Dirksen and Welker were kept off the Elections Subcommittee, they could still sit in review and judgment (as members of the parent Rules Committee) on our subcommittee's actions, particularly on Hendrickson and me. They would be in a vetoing position over us.

Two subcommittee vacancies created by Senator Wherry's death and by McCarthy's leaving the Rules Committee were those on the Library Subcommittee (McCarthy's subcommittee) and the Rules Subcommittee (Wherry's). Of these two, the more desirable was the Rules Subcommittee. Actually it was the Executive Committee of the full Rules Committee. This was evident from the fact that Senator Hayden as the ranking Democrat and Senator Wherry as the ranking Republican had always assigned themselves to this subcommittee.

To me the Rules Subcommittee was attractive from another standpoint. It was composed of only three members—two majority party (then Democrat) and one minority party—and if the Republicans should win the 1952 election whoever was the sole Republican on the Rules Subcommittee in 1951 would automatically become the Chairman of this powerful subcommittee. It literally ran the full committee. Thus, if I could get the Republican vacancy on the Rules Subcommittee, I'd become Chairman of it if the Republicans won control of the Senate. (I couldn't do that on the Elections Subcommittee because Hendrickson had seniority—seniority he gained only when I had been passed over for appointment to the full Rules Committee.)

On January 11, 1952, I wrote Senator Lodge (who became ranking Republican of the Rules Committee when Senator Wherry died) requesting the Rules Subcommittee assignment. Before doing so, I talked with Senator Hendrickson. I felt he should know. Bill Lewis talked to Senator Hendrickson's assistant, Paul Williams, pointing out some of the tactical considerations. Both men reacted by saying that Hendrickson would seek the Library Subcommittee assignment.

Lodge stepped aside. Instead of taking the Rules Subcommittee assignment for himself as ranking Republican, he gave it to me—the first time that any Republican had shown any consideration to me on committee assignments.

Then the pressure started. Jack Anderson, leg man for Drew Pearson, called Bill Lewis on the phone and said that Pearson was disappointed that I was going off the Elections Subcommittee. He wished I would reconsider—that if I didn't Pearson would comment adversely on his radio program about it. Lewis said: "Implied threats usually drive Senator Smith to defy them." Later, Pearson did attack me on his program.

On January 17, 1952, Hendrickson called to say that he had intended to go off Elections Subcommittee but that McCarthy had come to him on the Senate Floor that day and said that it was a good thing Hendrickson was leaving. Hendrickson felt that McCarthy was in substance saying that Hendrickson had been scared off. Because he didn't want McCarthy to be able to say that, he was going to stay on the Elections Subcommittee.

Late that afternoon, at around 6 P.M., the Elections Subcommittee Counsel, John Moore, made a desperate effort to get into my hands the staff's confidential field investigation report on the Benton charges against McCarthy. Strangely, it was discovered the next day that no such attempt had been made to get a copy of that report to any other member of the subcommittee, including Chairman Gillette. The report had been expected for months but until that time the staff had made no report to the investigating subcommittee. Suddenly, when it appeared that I was going off the Elections Subcommittee, a frantic attempt was made to write a report and get it in my hands. Why? So that I would be obligated to stay on the Elections Subcommittee and give up the Rules Subcommittee. The theory, you see, would be that I was a judge and juror who had received information that was not public. So I deliberately avoided seeing John Moore and receiving the report.

On the following day an Elections Subcommittee meeting was held. At the seat of each member was a copy of the report. However, the subcommittee did not read or discuss the staff's report but rather spent most of its time trying to argue that I should not leave the subcommittee. When the meeting ended each member took his copy of the report with him. When I got to the office with a copy, Bill Lewis advised me to return it immediately with a letter of transmittal. We sent it down to Gillette's office with a note:

In view of the developments at the Subcommittee Meeting this morning and the delay on action, I prefer not to have the enclosed staff report on the Benton Resolution in my possession.

The Democrats—notably Benton, Monroney, and Gillette—publicly put up a hue and cry. I should not be permitted to leave the Elections Subcommittee because it was like changing the jury in the middle of a trial. They threatened to block my appointment to the Rules Subcommittee. Chairman Carl Hayden said nothing publicly but rather, in his typical back-of-the-scenes, don't-stick-your-neck-out manner, sent an aide to Bill Lewis. Senator Smith should know, the aide said, that the Democrats were going to vote against her getting the Rules Subcommittee assignment—and that they had more votes on the committee than the Republicans.

Our reply was prompt—and Bill spelled things out plainly. Senator Smith recognized, he said, in his quiet, unruffled manner, that the Democrats could do this—but that she would remind Chairman Hayden that what the Democrats could do then with their majority it would be possible for the Republicans to do in the future when *they* got a majority. If the Democrats set a precedent by rejecting Republican assignments made by ranking Republican Senator Lodge, the Republicans might follow such precedent in the future and reject subcommittee nominations made by Senator Hayden—at a time when he might not be Committee Chairman but only the ranking minority member.

That apparently ended any serious Democratic thought of blocking my transfer from Elections to Rules. Within a day or so, I found on my desk on the Senate Floor an anonymous typed note on plain paper which warned against taking the advice of my assistant.

On January 22, 1952 (the day before the committee meeting to act on the subcommittee transfer), I wrote Chairman Hayden that I was perfectly willing to serve on the Benton Resolution hearings but that I did not intend to permit my willingness to prevent me from getting the assignment to the Wherry vacancy on the Rules Subcommittee. To accomplish both objectives, I proposed three alternatives to Chairman Hayden—(1) the Benton Resolution matter be taken away from Elections and assigned to Rules (the other two members of this subcommittee were Hayden and Monroney—Monroney was also on the Elections Subcommittee and he and I had done most of the work of that subcommittee—but Hayden didn't want to tangle with McCarthy); or (2) a special subcommittee be appointed on the Benton Resolution; or (3) transfer the Resolution from the subcommittee to the full Rules Committee. I pointed out that in any of these proposals, I would continue to serve on the "jury" or "tribunal."

On January 23, 1952, I went to the committee armed with a brief memorandum that enumerated some of the previous changes that had occurred on the Elections Subcommittee.*

---

* A jury of Gillette-Stennis-Schoeppel had started investigations into the Maryland, Pennsylvania, and New York elections and had been changed in the course of the investigations, with Monroney-Hennings-Hendrickson-Smith on the Maryland elections and Hennings-Hendrickson on the Pennsylvania and New York elections. Senator Gillette who had talked so much about changing

It was not necessary to present the memorandum for no opposition was offered by the Democrats to my assignment to the Rules Subcommittee. To my surprise, Chairman Hayden did not even read my letter. And so the next day I wrote Hayden again, saying that my letter of January 22, 1952, was a "standing and continuing offer." On January 25, 1952, Hayden declined to accept my offer.

I wrote on February 19, 1952, pointing out to Chairman Hayden the many bills of importance that had been pending for several months before the Rules Subcommittee (of which Hayden was also Chairman) and of which I had become a member. I was anxious to see this subcommittee act on its assignments. I was sincere in wanting the Rules Subcommittee assignment. Again I pointed out to Hayden that my three-alternative proposal to serve on the Benton Resolution was still before him for action and decision. Again on February 21, 1952, Hayden declined to accept my offer.

On January 17, 1952, Father James P. Finucan of LaCrosse, Wisconsin, wrote a letter attacking me for my attitude on McCarthy and asking when McCarthy had hidden behind his Congressional immunity. I replied, suggesting that he write Hornell Hart, Professor of Sociology at Duke University, and ask for a copy of an analysis he had made on the subject.

Finucan sent McCarthy my letter. McCarthy said that the Hart analysis was the Communist Party line and "It is almost impossible for me to believe that a Senator who claims to be a Republican would adopt the words of a man like Hornell Hart as her words."

The next clash with Senator McCarthy came in April 1952 on the Monroney Resolution, S. 187, which proposed that the

---

the jury had removed himself from the jury on these investigations. Senators Dirksen and Welker as eminent lawyers were both well qualified to replace Senator Smith. The history of the Elections Subcommittee showed in only one instance had a Republican served on that subcommittee for more than two years. Senators Benton and Monroney had not voted against Senator McCarthy when he removed Senator Smith from the Investigations Subcommittee. It would be strange for them to do exactly the opposite by voting to veto Senator Lodge's nomination of her for the Rules Subcommittee.

Elections Subcommittee be discharged from hearing the Benton Resolution and investigating McCarthy because McCarthy had challenged both the jurisdiction and the integrity of the members of the subcommittee on the matter. Monroney thus proposed to call McCarthy's bluff on a *subcommittee* basis just as I had earlier called his bluff on an *individual* basis. It amounted to asking the Senate for a vote of confidence and to reject McCarthy's accusation against the subcommittee when he said that they were picking the pockets of the taxpayers.

At a meeting of the full Rules Committee on March 7, 1952, I said that while I was no longer a member of the Elections Subcommittee I was supporting the move to report the Monroney Resolution out of committee to the Senate for a vote and to confront McCarthy with his reckless accusations. The committee voted 8 to 3 to report the Resolution out—only Dirksen, Welker, and Jenner voting against it. Then Jenner whispered to me: "Joe has gone too far this time."

The Monroney Resolution came before the Senate for debate and vote on April 10, 1952. During the debate on the Monroney Resolution, I stood up:

> . . . I say to the Members of the Senate that Senator McCarthy has made false accusations which he cannot, and has not had the courage even to try to, back up with proof . . . Regardless of the face-saving attempts and words of Senator McCarthy at this time in trying to soften the rebuff and confuse the issue . . .

Before the debate was concluded Senator McCarthy asked the Senate not to vote to discharge the Elections Subcommittee. As he prepared to run out, he left word that he was against a vote of no confidence for the subcommittee. As before, he saw he couldn't win and so he tried to soften the blow by voting with those who were calling his bluff. We had defeated him earlier 11 to 0 and now defeated him 60 to 0.

What attracted more attention than my words above was a debate with Senator Hickenlooper who accused me of being unduly sensitive. Several years later Senator Hickenlooper and I were to become good friends working in full harmony and as a team in his position as Chairman of the Senate Republican Policy Committee and in mine as Chairman of the Senate Republican Conference.

In early 1952, Joe McCarthy made his most serious attack on me—indirectly. This attack came through the publication of a book *U.S.A. Confidential* by Jack Lait and Lee Mortimer. In that book I was said to be a "pal" and fellow traveler of Mrs. Esther Brunauer, one of the State Department officials McCarthy had attacked.

I was represented as pro-Communist; a fellow traveler; a "stunted visionary"; "making . . . boneheaded speeches." A Senate doorman was reported to have said that "there's too many women in the Senate!" I was "a lesson why women should not be in politics"; lay "awake nights scheming how to 'get even'"; "reacted to all situations as a woman scorned, not as a representative of the people"; was "under the influence of a coterie of left-wing writers"; was "a left-wing apologist"; and other compliments.

On May 7, 1952, I filed a libel suit against the authors and the publishers of the book—the only one of several Senators attacked in the book to sue. It took four and a half years to get the defendants down to trial in Federal Court in New York City.

Later that month, on May 26, 1952, Senator McCarthy said in the Senate:

Incidentally, a rather humorous incident occurred in connection with this case. Jack Lait wrote a book in which he pointed out that one of the Senators traveled to Italy with Mrs. Brunauer, and the Senator, who has defended these innocent people constantly, has sued Lait for $2,000,000 because she thought her character was injured to that extent by the story that she had known the Brunauers. Mrs. Brunauer has been suspended.

This was vintage McCarthyism. *Falsehood example*—I never defended Mrs. Brunauer—I had never met Dr. Brunauer. *Distortion example*—I sued not because I had only slightly known Esther Brunauer but because references in the book painted me as pro-Communist. *Half-truth example*—I sued for one half of the amount McCarthy stated. Also, the book was actually written by Lee Mortimer. McCarthy knew as much for Mortimer had conferred with him in the preparation of the book. Lait's name was on as coauthor because Mortimer worked for Lait and Lait was better known. McCarthy had avoided reference to Mortimer. Later, it was definitely established that the motivation for the assault on this bone-headed woman was Mortimer's and McCarthy's bitterness about my Declaration of Conscience.

A further bit of evidence of the tie-up between McCarthy and Mortimer came in a letter written to Mrs. Brunauer by Mortimer's attorney, Hyman I. Fischbach, on May 29, 1952, in which he called Mrs. Brunauer's attention to Senator McCarthy's statement on page 6058 of the temporary Congressional Record of May 26, 1952.

In the intervening four and a half years, Mortimer had acrimonious disagreement with his attorneys, first Hyman Fischbach, then Godfrey Schmidt. He fired them or they severed their relations with him in counteractions. They sued him for attorney fees and he petitioned the New York Bar Grievances Committee to have each of them disbarred. Mortimer, not an attorney but a cafe society gossip columnist, became his own counsel. He filed an amazing series of pleadings thanks to the Federal Judges who were lenient to a point they never would have been with a lawyer. As one of my attorneys in the case, Bill Lewis prepared the trial brief. He documented more than 150 misrepresentations made by the authors in the book and in the pleadings filed preparatory to trial.

Mortimer reached his peak when, on September 21, 1956, in his motion for dismissal, he charged me, Bill Lewis, and my principal attorney, Richard H. Wels, with causing four deaths by the suit:

> As a result of this evil conspiracy by Plaintiff and others to destroy this Defendant through the bringing of fraudulent law suits and other illegal means, Defendant's 28-year-old wife, his mother, his father and his collaborator and literary partner, Jack Lait, fell ill and all four of them died within a period of nine months of one another.

The facts were that Mortimer's wife and Jack Lait both died of cancer. What his parents died of is not recalled.

After four and a half years of an ordeal of lies and misrepresentations given great publicity, we finally got the defendants to trial on October 17, 1956. When the judge directed the beginning of the impaneling of a jury, Mortimer stood and said that there was no need for the case to be tried because defendants were willing to admit their statements about me were false. Up until that second, Mortimer had vowed that he would fight to the end and had made grave threats against my reputation.

They folded completely, retracted their statements, made a public apology and retraction that was published in a large advertisement in New York and Maine papers, and paid damages. The advertisement:

A CORRECTION

Several years ago Lee Mortimer and Jack Lait wrote the book *U.S.A. Confidential,* which was published by Crown Publishers, Inc.

This book made certain statements concerning Senator Margaret Chase Smith of Maine.

More thorough investigation since the publication of the book has convinced Lee Mortimer, the Estate of Jack Lait, Crown Publishers, Inc., and their attorneys that these statements con-concerning Senator Margaret Chase Smith were mistaken and should not have been made. Senator Smith enjoys an excellent and enviable reputation. Nothing in the book was meant to reflect on the patriotism, honesty, morality or good citizenship of Senator Smith, nor was anything meant to say or imply that she was an apologist for or sympathizer of Communists or Reds.

We regret very much these mistaken statements concerning Senator Smith. We are now convinced that they were untrue although made unintentionally.

In fairness to Senator Margaret Chase Smith, we are happy to make this correction.

Crown Publishers, Inc.
Lee Mortimer
Estate of Jack Lait

Attempts were made to get me to go to Wisconsin to campaign against Senator McCarthy in the 1952 Republican Senatorial primary. I refused. It was not for me to tell the people of Wisconsin what to do about Senator McCarthy. They knew full well my attitude toward him by the many statements and stands I had taken and it would be bad political psychology as Wisconsin voters would resent an outsider trying to tell them how to vote.

In January 1953, with the opening of the first session of the 83rd Congress, another episode developed. Prior to this time the only victory over me that McCarthy had enjoyed was when he kicked me off the Investigations Subcommittee in January 1951, two years earlier.

McCarthy again bragged to the press that he was going to get me kicked off a committee—this time the full Government Operations (formerly Executive Expenditures Committee). He started his off-the-record bragging right after the Senate reconvened and again some two weeks before the committee assignments were to be made.

As he wanted, word of his bragging got to me. Having been discriminated against before by Senator Hugh Butler, Chairman of the Republican Committee on Committees, when he violated any seniority and put Senators Schoeppel and Hendrickson (junior to me) on the Rules Committee, and doing it secretly without saying a word to me—and not having been given a major committee assignment during four years in the Senate—I talked with Senator Butler. He assured me that he would go over all committee assignments with me before any were made and convince me that I was not being discriminated against again.

On the day the Republican committee assignments were to be made, Joe Hall of the Associated Press called Bill Lewis in the morning to congratulate me on getting new committee assignments—Appropriations and Armed Services—saying that he noticed that I was giving up Government Operations. I called Butler and said that I had *not* agreed to give up that committee, was entitled to it as one of the few committees that could be kept as a third committee, and was surprised because Butler assured me that he would go over the committee assignments with me.

When Senator Butler replied that it had been decided that *all* of the present Republicans, with the exception of McCarthy, who would be the new Chairman, would go off the Government Operations Committee to make places for the freshmen Republicans, I felt that I could not object to getting the same treatment as my fellow Republicans—even if McCarthy was, through this move, going to realize his bragged-about ambition to get me off the committee.

Bill Lewis advised me to call Butler back and ask specifically if Senators Mundt, Dworshak, Dirksen, and Potter each were going off the Government Operations Committee. Senator Butler said that I must have misunderstood him—only *some* of the Republicans were giving up that committee. While Dirksen and Potter (who were two years junior to Senators Mundt, Smith, and Dworshak) were giving it up, Senators Mundt and Dworshak were staying on. I replied that I had not been consulted; I had not agreed to go off as Senators Dirksen and Potter, who were junior to me, had; I could not understand why it had been decided to reach in *between* Mundt (two *days* my senior) and Dworshak (my junior) and take me off when leaving them on; and I intended to make an issue of it. Senator Butler said that I had better come right over to talk with the Committee on Committees as it was planning to announce the assignments that afternoon.

Because there was no Senate session that day I had been cleaning out old dusty files. But I dropped everything and, dressed in an old red-plaid cotton dress, headed straightaway for the committee. It did not take long to find out that two members were trying to accommodate McCarthy in getting me off—Senator Hugh Butler and Senator Francis Case (who later was to defend McCarthy and be the only Senator to decline to vote for or against censure of Senator McCarthy on the final vote of 64 to 24 on December 2, 1954). I started off by stating to the committee that I was not asking for any special privileges but rather standing on my rights as a Senator and refusing to be discriminated against. Under the rules of the Senate, the Government Operations Committee was one of the four or five committees that members were permitted to hold as a third committee—this was the case in spite of the fact that Senator Taft and I had argued earlier that this committee was not a minor, but rather a major, committee and should not be permitted under the third committee category. We contended that a committee like Rules should be substituted for it in that category. But Senator Francis Case and others had opposed me and Senator Taft successfully on this.

Senator Butler said that it was felt that the older members should step aside for the freshman Republicans to get appointments to this committee; that by taking such an attitude I was preventing Senator Payne from getting a place on the committee.* I should give more consideration to my colleague, he

---

* EDITOR'S NOTE: The McCarthy desire for this became evident later when, in November 1953, Senator Payne welcomed McCarthy into Maine. McCarthy could put Payne on the Investigations Subcommittee and try to show up Senator Smith.

said, adding that it would be embarrassing to Butler since he had already given out the committee assignments to western newspapers.

I replied: (1) Senators Mundt and Dworshak were not being taken off the committee; (2) as far as consideration of my colleague Fred Payne was concerned, he was doing all right since he was not only getting a major committee but the very committee he wanted the most—Banking and Currency; (3) when Senator Butler's very good friend Owen Brewster had been in the Senate for the four years I had, no consideration had been shown me on committee requests but rather that I had been discriminated against in favor of Senators Schoeppel and Hendrickson on the Rules Committee assignment; (4) that in all of my four years I had not been given a major committee assignment and now was getting them only after my former colleague and close friend of Senator Butler had been defeated by Payne and removed from the Senate; and (5) I had no responsibility for Senator Butler's embarrassment in giving the committee assignment to western newspapers before they had been submitted to the Republican Conference for acceptance.

At this point Francis Case (who was two years junior to me) stepped in and said that I was being selfish, that I was getting two major committees at one time and that should be enough, that after all, Senator Mundt was not really getting a major committee in the Agriculture assignment in addition to his Appropriations and Government Operations assignments; and, after all, Senator Dworshak likewise was not getting a major committee assignment on Interior in addition to his Appropriations and Government Operations assignments.

I was getting two major committees at this time, I said, only because I had gone four years without a major committee assignment and because they couldn't prevent it any longer. I was no more selfish than Senator Mundt, who was getting Appropriations and Agriculture at the same time and still being permitted to keep Government Operations. I was no more selfish than Senator Dworshak, who was getting Appropriations and Interior at the same time and still being permitted to keep

Government Operations. It didn't make sense to let Mundt and Dworshak do this and to prevent me from staying on Government Operations merely because I was getting Appropriations (the same committee Mundt and Dworshak were getting) and Armed Services at the same time. It was ridiculous for Senator Case to say that Mundt, from South Dakota, was really getting a minor committee in Agriculture when agriculture was so important to Senator Case's own people of South Dakota. Would Senator Case be willing to say the same thing to his people back home? It was equally ridiculous for Case to say that Interior was really a minor committee assignment for Senator Dworshak when actually the most important committee to Dworshak's State of Idaho was the Interior Committee (it had jurisdiction over such matters so vital to Idaho as Mining and Public Lands). I couldn't believe that Senator Case meant what he had said. Case retreated in defeat.

At this point, Senator Butler came back into the discussion with the final comment—a comment that revealed what actually had been under way—that he wouldn't think I would want to be on a committee on which I was not wanted by the Chairman. I said that I did not intend to permit Senator McCarthy's dislike to impair any of my rights as a Senator. He had bragged that he was going to get me off Government Operations, I would fight his doing so, and I would carry the fight to the Senate Republican Conference and to the Floor of the Senate, if necessary.

When the committee assignments were announced that afternoon, I was still on Government Operations. It was reported that when someone said something to McCarthy about his boast not coming true that he replied angrily, "There's too damn many women in the Senate!"—oddly similar to the alleged doorkeeper's remark quoted in *U.S.A. Confidential.*

But this was not to end our fight. Because I remained on the Committee on Government Operations, I automatically became the Chairman of the Reorganization Subcommittee. And that was a bitter pill for Joe. Back in 1951 when he kicked me off the Investigations Subcommittee he had claimed, in denying that he had done so, that he had merely promoted me to the ranking Republican position on the Reorganization Subcommittee. Joe's "cute" statement had now come up to haunt him two years later. If he kept me from becoming Chairman of Reorganization then he would obviously be admitting that he lied in 1951. So, faced with being caught red-handed, he did not oppose me. In two years, he had completely outsmarted himself.

Not only did Joe's heavy-handedness and bragging-in-advance ironically result in personal defeat, it also resulted in rather poetic justice. Actually, I had grown weary of service on the Executive Expenditures (Government Operations) Committee and had decided to leave it when I got two major committee assignments. I was prepared to leave it gracefully. But when Joe snorted to the press that he was going to kick me off Government Operations as he had kicked me off the Investigations Subcommittee, my self-respect left no choice but to accept the challenge.

So I stayed on the committee and ultimately to my own best interest, as distinguished from self-respect. By doing so, I became the top Republican on the Senate Space Committee.

After the shock of Sputnik in 1958, Lyndon Johnson set up the temporary Senate Space Committee. The membership was formed from the top Democrats and top Republicans on certain standing committees, including Government Operations. This committee became a standing (instead of temporary) committee the next year. Karl Mundt had become the top Republican on Government Operations when Senator McCarthy died on May 2, 1957. Since Senator Mundt was also on the Space Committee, he had to choose one of them to leave because he was also on two other standing committees (Appropriations and Agriculture). Because he was the top Republican on Government Operations, he chose to give up Space.

After McCarthy's death, I had become the second ranking Republican on Government Operations and was then given the choice of going on the Space Committee and leaving Government Operations. I chose to do just that. I had long lost my interest in the Government Operations Committee and this was not only a graceful way of leaving it, but the Space Committee easily promised to be the most exciting Senate committee at that time.

In short, Joe McCarthy had indirectly caused me to be appointed to the Senate Space Committee and later to be the top Republican on it.

EDITOR'S NOTE:
Some political reporters claimed that the two most direct pieces of evidence that Senate Republicans punished Margaret Smith for her Declaration of Conscience were her being kicked off the Investigations Subcommittee and removed from the Senate Republican Policy Committee. They said that both of these actions were approved by "Mr. Republican," Senator Robert A. Taft. It was a disservice and unfair to Taft to claim that she had been punitively removed from the Senate Republican Policy Committee. The truth was that she removed herself in order to let her Maine colleague, Senator Owen Brewster, go on the Policy Committee since he was up for re-election in 1952. It was an act of courtesy on her part—not an act of discourtesy on the part of Taft, Brewster, or McCarthy. In fact, in 1953 Taft put her right back on the Policy Committee on which she has served all of her twenty-three years in the Senate except for the two-year, 1951–52, interval.

The charges against Taft were not believed by Senator Smith for they had been very good friends. To the surprise of the press and contrary to their prediction, on January 3, 1949, she had voted for him to remain Chairman of the Senate Republican Policy Committee when her good friend Henry Cabot Lodge,

Jr., ran against him. Later, with respect to a crucial vote on the Taft-Hartley Act, the July 2, 1949, issue of *Business Week* had written:

> Margaret Chase Smith, the Senator from Maine, provided the margin for Taft's victory on Emergency Injunctions—the closest spot he has had to face.
>
> She did it on the Lucas Amendment with which the Truman forces hoped to rip injunctions out of Taft's Injunction-Seizure proposal.
>
> Before the vote, Taft counted Mrs. Smith as one of the Republicans lined up against him. Taft's labor expert, Tom Shroyer, put this plea to her: "We figure the vote as a 45–45 tie, with Vice President Barkley deciding against us; if Taft is licked, he is through politically."
>
> Mrs. Smith replied: "Tell Taft the vote will be 46 to 44."
>
> It was.

On December 31, 1951, Taft wrote Senator Smith: "I shall always be grateful for what you have done in connection with our Ohio Election Investigation."

Senator Taft denied that he had anything to do with McCarthy's removal of Senator Smith from the Investigations Subcommittee in 1951. The impression that he had, came from McCarthy's quote in the Chicago *Daily Tribune,* stating that he had consulted with other GOP leaders before taking the action. On February 21, 1951, Taft told Senator Smith that he had "accosted" McCarthy about this the day before at lunch and that McCarthy denied that he had made such a statement and said he had consulted all Republican members of the Executive Expenditures Committee. On February 28, 1951, Senator Taft wrote Senator Smith a letter in which he said: "I had nothing whatever to do about this action and was never consulted."

On June 15, 1953, Senator McCarthy made a speech in Madison, Wisconsin, in which he quoted from the report of Senator Smith's Ammunition Shortages Subcommittee and in which he said: "That Committee did a good job." He sent a copy of his speech to her.

The next chapter in the Smith-McCarthy story unfolded during the closing days of the first session of the 83rd Congress. The first development was when Senator Smith received a report that the McCarthy-Greek Shipowners matter which had developed early in 1953 was the result of a deal. An attorney for one of the Greek shipowners, the report was, against whom the Federal Government had a tax lien of a million dollars for back taxes and who had been refused an exit visa to go back to Greece, proposed a deal to McCarthy whereby the attorney's client and other Greek shipowners would sign an agreement with McCarthy to stop their ships from transporting materials to Communist countries if McCarthy would get the Federal Government to drop the tax matter against the attorney's client and give him an exit visa.

In the latter part of July, Investigations Subcommittee Counsel Francis Flanagan sent Senator Smith, as a member of the Government Operations Committee, a copy of the Investigations Subcommittee's proposed report on the Greek shipowners trading with the Communists and asked her to sign a poll authorizing the filing of the report. Prior to this, such practice had not been followed because the Investigations Subcommittee with seven members constituted a majority of the thirteen-member parent Government Operations Committee and thus could give the necessary seven majority approval of filing the subcommittee's reports without having consulted the remaining six members of the full committee, who were not on the Investigations Subcommittee. But when the three Democrats (McClellan, Jackson, and Symington) boycotted the Investigations Subcommittee, that narrowed its membership to only four Republicans and thus made it necessary to get at least three *other* members of the full committee to approve the filing of the report in order to comply with the majority approval of the thirteen-member full committee.

Senator Smith replied by letter to Mr. Flanagan that she could not sign the approval to file the report because of the word she had received about the Greek-McCarthy deal. Both Flanagan and McCarthy then wrote Senator Smith denying any such deal and demanding that she give them the name of her informant. She replied to Flanagan that, as a former FBI man, he was fully aware and appreciative of the fact that names of informers were often withheld (the FBI never reveals the identity of its informers) and that no purpose would be served since the best sources of information on the matter were the attorney for the Greek shipowners and Senator McCarthy. She sent a copy of her letter to Flanagan to McCarthy. She never heard any further word from either Flanagan or McCarthy.

On the closing night of the first session of the 83rd Congress (August 3), Senate Republican Leader William Knowland asked unanimous consent of the Senate that the Investigations Subcommittee be authorized to file reports during the Congressional recess (after the Senate adjourned and the Senators had left Washington) for the rest of the year. Since the three Democrats had boycotted the Investigations Subcommittee and refused to take any responsibility for it, and since three of the four Republican members had unofficially disassociated themselves from it, the Investigations Subcommittee had actually become a one-man show composed only of Senator McCarthy. Had the Senate given its consent to the Knowland request, made in behalf of McCarthy, since McCarthy was not present at the closing of the session, it would have meant that McCarthy as a one-man Investigations Subcommittee could have filed anything he wanted to in reports from August 1953 to January 1954.

Because she felt that McCarthy should not have such sweeping power, that the Democrats should not be permitted to shirk their responsibility, that it was better for everyone (including McCarthy) and would actually help him if he was doing anything constructive, Senator Smith objected to the Knowland request unless it were modified to follow the same procedure that Senator McCarthy had some two or three weeks prior adopted. Illustrative of this was the Flanagan poll request to members of the parent Government Operations Committee asking them to approve the filing of one of the subcommittee reports. She insisted upon the normal requirement that no subcommittee report could be filed until after the full thirteen-member parent Government Operations Committee had been polled to determine if there were any objection to the filing of the subcommittee report.

Knowland said that since his request required unanimous consent, he had no choice but to accept the Smith modification of the McCarthy request. The following day McCarthy said that Senator Smith had thrown up another block to his efforts to get the truth and information on the Communist threat to the people. Senator Smith's reply was that her modification helped McCarthy by requiring Democratic participation and responsibility—and that she had proposed only the very same procedure that McCarthy himself had adopted at least two or three weeks prior.

This apparently set the stage for McCarthy's supreme effort to destroy Senator Smith politically and to remove her from the Senate. Shortly thereafter in the latter part of August, he placed a long distance call to former Senator Owen Brewster in Maine asking Brewster if anyone had been found to run against Margaret Smith in 1954. Brewster replied that no one seemed to want to take her on. McCarthy then said to Brewster that he could get plenty of money and financial backing outside of Maine for anyone who would run against her.

During this same time, McCarthy's collaborator Lee Mortimer, substituting for Walter Winchell while Winchell was on vacation, wrote in the nationally syndicated column on August 25, 1953:

> . . . Joe will fight back, taking to the hustings in the states of his opponents, and especially in Maine where La Smith is up for re-election in 1954. (Remember what happened to Tydings?)

Mortimer's reference to Tydings, and McCarthy's telephoning Brewster, recall the belief of many that it was McCarthy and Brewster who chose John Marshall Butler to run against—and defeat—Tydings in Maryland. That is particularly interesting for during this period of late August and early September, Joe McCarthy, after finding that no one in Maine was willing to run against Margaret Smith, desperately chose Robert L. Jones (who had been put on Brewster's staff in 1952 for campaign purposes and who did much of the managing of Brewster's unsuccessful campaign) to be the McCarthy candidate against Margaret Smith.

On September 1, 1953, Jones started traveling with McCarthy's one-man Investigations Subcommittee (representing his new boss, Senator Charles Potter of Michigan), ultimately getting involved in the Fort Monmouth and General Zwicker fiascos. In the latter part of August while Senator Potter was overseas in Korea, Senator McCarthy called Ray Anderson, Senator Potter's Administrative Assistant, and asked that Jones be permitted to go to New York and New Jersey to audit the hearings and report back to Senator Potter. Anderson agreed to let Jones go but only for the purpose of listening and not for asking questions or acting in any capacity as though he were Senator Potter.

From that point on, McCarthy started letting Jones participate at these hearings as though he was a Senator—asking questions and making statements to the press. The build-up was on.

In mid-November McCarthy invaded Maine making two speeches sponsored by the VFW—one in Portland and one in Bangor. His entourage included Jones; Lloyd Stover who later was openly to become Jones's campaign manager; and Congressional Medal of Honor hero Captain Lewis Millett whose wife was in January to start the first circulation of Jones-for-Senate primary papers.

McCarthy's strategy was not to attack Margaret Smith directly but rather to praise Jones on the speaking platform as a fighter of Communists and as the kind of young man the people of Maine should send to Washington. Perhaps he decided to do this after he had asked at a press conference in Portland if there was anyone stronger politically with the people of Maine than Senator Smith. His eyes brightened up and a smile covered his face when one reporter finally said, "Yes. There is one who is stronger with Maine people than Margaret Smith." With eager anticipation, Joe asked, "Who?" Solemnly and slowly the reporter replied, "Almighty God." With a dark face, Joe dropped the subject.

Part of McCarthy's strategy was to align himself with Senator Fred Payne. He praised Payne's voting attendance record which was good at that time although not as good as Senator Smith's (which was perfect for both 1953 and 1954). This was significant because later, when told by former Senator Owen Brewster that Jones had no chance to defeat Margaret Smith, McCarthy said he knew that but by getting Jones to run against her he would do three things—(1) ruin her perfect attendance record, (2) bankrupt her, and (3) harass her.

Although Payne had campaigned against Brewster on the claim that he would cooperate with Senator Smith instead of fighting her, as he claimed Brewster had, and although Payne had been a friend and supporter of Margaret Smith, he made a long distance call from his home in Lincoln County to McCarthy in Portland prior to his evening speech and warmly welcomed Joe into Maine at a time when everyone knew that Joe was coming in to defeat Margaret Smith—and when all other prominent Republicans studiously avoided being seen with McCarthy. Joe announced Payne's welcome to him in his Portland speech.

When Joe went to Bangor to speak, Fred and Ella Payne sent Joe and Jean McCarthy flowers which were put on public display. A week or so prior to the time that Joe went into Maine to launch the drive to destroy Margaret Smith through the Jones candidacy, Fred Payne made a public statement in Lewiston in which he said that Joe McCarthy had not done any injustice to anyone, that he had performed a great public service for the American people and his country, and that he deserved the full support of every American.

And on a matter concerning a Biddeford, Maine, veteran on which the Federal District Court Judge had instructed the U. S. Attorney to contact Senator Smith and get her to introduce a bill, Payne joined with McCarthy to take such a bill away from Margaret Smith and to plan joint introduction by McCarthy and Payne.

Added to this was the fact that a Senate Gallery doorman appointed by Senator Payne, Harry Charles Koutalidis, became Jones's Assistant Campaign Manager. But, in fairness to Payne, it must be acknowledged that Payne never gave the slightest endorsement or indication of personal support or approval of Jones—despite Jones's claim that Payne preferred him. Further it is to be noted that Payne fully supported Margaret Chase Smith in the general election after she defeated Jones in the primary, although Payne refused to support Burt Cross, the GOP nominee for Governor that year. It is to be further noted that Payne and Margaret Smith were and remain good friends. His actions were not pro-Jones but instead were friendliness to McCarthy at a crucial time.

McCarthy took his next step against Senator Smith on January 17, 1954, at a meeting at the Mayflower Hotel attended by Jones, McCarthy, and others. It was reported to Senator Smith by one of those attending the meeting (Charlie Kress, former Mayor of Binghamton, New York) that there was general discussion on how Jones would conduct his campaign and how it would be financed. He further reported that among those present at the meeting were Ham Fish (former New York conservative Congressman who later withdrew from the group upon the advice of Kress), former Senator Owen Brewster, New York investment banker Robert Harriss, and former New Jersey Governor Charles Edison.

When McCarthy went on a Lincoln Day speaking tour in February he returned by way of Texas and in Houston he enlisted the financial support of Hugh Cullen and Cullen's son-in-law Douglas B. Marshall who then wrote Jones pledging their financial support.

When Robert Jones formally announced his candidacy, he

gave priority on the story to John Kelso, Washington correspondent of the Boston *Post* and a rabid McCarthyite. In his story on the announcement of the Jones candidacy, Kelso reported that McCarthy would make at least three speeches for Jones in Maine in March—one in Sanford, one in Biddeford, and one in Lewiston.

Shortly thereafter McCarthy announced that he had no speaking commitments in either Sanford or Biddeford—and that he was canceling his speaking engagement in Lewiston which he denied was to be for Jones and claimed it was only a patriotic speech sponsored by the VFW. He gave three reasons for canceling the Lewiston speaking date—(1) a sore throat, (2) his wife's illness, and (3) the pressure of committee business. That these were false reasons became evident. On the date he was to speak in Lewiston he was fishing in Florida. A few days later he spoke in Chicago and Oklahoma City with what doctors described as a very bad sore throat and he said that he had never run out on a speaking engagement and wouldn't let a sore throat stop him.

He also stated at the time that he was not going to get involved in the Maine primary. Perhaps this was because Jones's supporters had told him that he would hurt Jones if he openly came into the campaign. But he was already involved, for he had chosen Jones as his candidate, had informally launched his candidacy in the November speaking tour, and had obtained financial backing for him. A day after he disclaimed any participation in the campaign he was seen lunching at the Carroll Arms Hotel dining room in Washington with Lloyd Stover, Jones's campaign manager, poring over a thick pile of papers.

The plain fact was that McCarthy again ran away from a fight out in the open, preferring to work behind the scenes.

During the Army-McCarthy hearings, Joe once referred to Jones as "Senator Jones" in connection with the subcommittee visit to Fort Monmouth. If Joe said it deliberately, he betrayed his true colors. If he said it inadvertently it was a Freudian slip and he revealed what he was thinking subconsciously. (Jones in a January clandestine campaign planning meeting had stated that in the November visit McCarthy had introduced Jones to publisher Guy Gannett as the next Senator from Maine.)

But it was not to be Senator Jones. Margaret Smith on June 21, 1954, beat Joe's boy 5 to 1 and by almost eighty thousand votes, setting a new record total in votes in a Maine state primary.

Before the Army-McCarthy hearings were over, Senator Flanders of Vermont introduced a resolution to censure McCarthy. Prior to that he had planned to propose that McCarthy be stripped of his committee Chairmanship. When he consulted Senator Margaret Smith and Senator William Fulbright (whom McCarthy had called "Halfbright"), they advised him that the Senate would never vote to do this because it would violate the seniority system and many Senators who were either Chairmen or near being Chairmen would regard it as a precedent that might keep them from being Chairmen. Senator Alexander Smith urged Flanders to drop any action against McCarthy and assured Flanders that he, Alex Smith, could handle McCarthy. In contrast, Senators Margaret Smith and Fulbright told Flanders that though they would not support him on the proposal to remove the Chairmanship, they would support him on a censure resolution.

Flanders then introduced a resolution. It was proposed that prior to the Senate's vote a special select committee be appointed to study the charges and to give Senator McCarthy a chance to answer them. The appeal that was made was that McCarthy, under our American system of justice, was entitled to a fair trial.

The Payne-McCarthy alignment showed up on the voting on the Censure Resolution. Payne voted for the Mundt proposal to defeat the censure of McCarthy and to substitute for it a general censure of anyone who indulged in the alleged indiscretions McCarthy had, without naming McCarthy.

There were basically two things that destroyed McCarthy's political power and the paralysis of fear that he exerted on the

Senate. One was the televised Army-McCarthy hearings. The other was the result of the 1954 Maine Republican Senatorial primary. The televised hearings damaged McCarthy's image nationally. But a more specific measurement was the Maine Republican primary. Ever since Joe had successfully purged Maryland Senator Millard Tydings from the Senate in the 1950 Maryland Senatorial election, most United States Senators feared for their own political lives lest they cross Joe's path and offend him.

When Margaret Chase Smith chose to stand up to Joe in 1950, again in 1951, again in 1952, again in 1953, he then put up his proxy candidate to try to purge her from the Senate in 1954—the first and only Republican Senator he attempted to purge. His proxy candidate, Robert L. Jones, not only echoed fully Joe's views and tactics but he even aped Joe in mannerisms, hesitant and repeated phrases, tonal inflections, scowls, smiles, and other gestures. He could have been considered literally, physically, vocally, and politically a junior-grade Joe McCarthy. How well he acted the role was revealed in an Edward R. Murrow "See It Now" CBS television program. That program merely took clips of Jones campaigning and Margaret Smith campaigning, pasted the clips together ironically in composite style (since Joe had led the way in the composite picture used against Tydings in 1950) to effect the appearance of Jones and Smith debating. While there was no significant commentary by Murrow, the filmed contrast of only thirteen minutes was devastating. It revealed Jones as the Army-McCarthy hearings had revealed McCarthy and others.

Margaret Chase Smith's trouncing of the proxy candidate against her was devastating to Joe McCarthy in the United States Senate. Suddenly his paralytic power over the United States Senate was lifted and destroyed. No longer was it "political suicide," as a Democratic Senator had said three years prior to Senator Smith, to stand up to Joe McCarthy. For if a mere woman could beat Joe McCarthy by a 5 to 1 margin, then why should the men Senators have any further fear of him? It was as simple as that—Senator Smith not only defeated the candidate that Joe had fielded against her, she had defeated Joe, and, in doing so, she had destroyed his power in the United States Senate. Even Dwight D. Eisenhower, who had shunned her during these McCarthy years, sent her a telegram of congratulations and had the White House press secretary issue a statement expressing his delight with her primary victory.

In the middle of July 1954 after the primary, former Senator Owen Brewster called at the office of Senator Smith in behalf of her defeated opponent, Robert L. Jones. He said that a few days before he had called Jones's Silver Spring home and talked with him. The following day Jones had come with two of Jones's children to Brewster's room at the Mayflower Hotel. In those meetings Brewster said that he had heard that Jones had gotten quite a bit of money from Texas oil men for his campaign and that since it appeared that Jones hadn't spent too much money in his campaign, Brewster would appreciate it if Jones would repay Brewster the $2000 he had loaned him in 1952 and which Jones had never repaid. He said that Jones stated that he didn't have the money, didn't have a job or the prospect of a job (although he had previously told Carlton Brown in Maine that McCarthy had promised him a big job if he would run against Margaret Smith), and that he owed $750 on his campaign expenses.

Brewster said that he felt sorry for Jones and that the next night they went to McCarthy's house near the Senate Office Building and told Joe that since Jones had performed his chore McCarthy owed it to Jones to get Jones a job. Brewster said that McCarthy replied that there was a vacancy on the professional staff of the Government Operations Committee that he would give to Jones if Jones and Brewster could get Margaret Smith to ask McCarthy to appoint Jones to that vacancy.

Brewster said that he wished Senator Smith would so request because it would not only help Jones and his family, but it would help Brewster. Jones could then pay Brewster the $2000 he owed him.

Senator Smith merely looked at Brewster and made no comment. Brewster repeated his hopes twice and Senator Smith made no response. Brewster then said that he guessed he would just have to tell Bob and Joe that he had done their errand and that the response was negative. Senator Smith made no comment.

About a week or ten days later, Brewster called on Senator Smith again and asked her if she would have any objection to his becoming Chief Counsel to the Government Operations Committee, replacing Roy Cohn who had resigned. Apparently this was the beginning of a maneuver on the part of certain Republicans who were politically indebted to Brewster and who disliked Margaret Smith. By this move they would discharge their indebtedness to Brewster and at the same time put Margaret Smith on the spot. They were confident that she would object to Brewster.

Apparently McCarthy and Company were taken by surprise when Margaret Smith did not say no to Brewster. So McCarthy's next move was to get Margaret Smith in a committee meeting and to try to maneuver her into the position of proposing Brewster for the position. But he added a new twist to it by proposing that Brewster's work be with the Reorganization Sub-committee of which Senator Smith was Chairman and to bar him from all work on the Investigations Subcommittee.

But again he, and his associates, underestimated Margaret Smith. Several meetings of the full committee were held but Margaret Smith was absent from every one of them, being busy at other committee meetings of Appropriations and Armed Services and the subcommittees of which she was a member. Desperate to get Senator Smith on record proposing Brewster for the position (when, in a letter of July 31, 1954, she said she had no objection to him but that she didn't need any counsel for her Reorganization Subcommittee) McCarthy finally had Committee Chief Clerk Walter Reynolds take a typed poll around to the members. They were asked to signify their approval of the appointment of Owen Brewster as the Chief Counsel of the Government Operations Committee.

Walter Reynolds first took the poll to Senator Mundt. Then

Walter came to me with it to get Senator Smith's signature. Upon questioning I found that Mundt had stated that he would sign it only if Senator Smith did. After talking with Senator Smith, I told Walter Reynolds that the Senator had stated that since oral statements were subject to misunderstanding it would be best to get Senator Mundt's stated conditions of signing in writing. When that was accomplished she would sign with conditions of her own. Reynolds went to Senator Mundt who signed and attached his written condition that he was signing only with the understanding that Senator Smith and at least three Democrats would sign.

Faced with this obvious attempt to put the burden on her, Senator Smith signed. But to the left of her signature was typed in one condition: her signature was valid only if all other Republican and at least three Democratic members of the committee signed.

The poll was then taken to Senator Dirksen who refused to sign. When Brewster heard of this he went to Dirksen and laid down the law and Dirksen signed—but, like Senator Smith, he had conditions typed in to the left of his signature stating that his signature was valid only if at least three Democratic members signed.

Thus, the attempt by McCarthy and associates to embarrass Senator Smith backfired. This was not only to their disappointment and chagrin, but to the discomfort of the Democrats as well. They had hoped they would be spared having to take any action by the expediency of having Margaret Smith block the Brewster appointment. Brewster claimed to Senator Smith that Senators McClellan and Symington had pledged to him that they would agree to his appointment, that Symington considered Brewster and Steve Leo to be his two best Maine friends. Both McClellan and Symington separately went to Senator Smith urging her to object to Brewster, saying that they didn't want him around to embarrass her. She told both of them that she had no objection to Brewster getting the job. The final result was that all six Democrats refused to sign the poll or take any part in the appointment of Brewster and thus blocked his appointment. Both the McCarthyites and the Democrats failed to maneuver Senator Smith into blocking Brewster.

The aftermath of the June 1, 1950, Declaration of Conscience was predominantly McCarthy's efforts to retaliate against, punish, and politically destroy Margaret Chase Smith for daring to differ publicly with him and criticize him. Where most all other Senators either retreated from the battle against him after initial forays of courage, or sought to avoid battle with him and kept their political distance from him, Margaret Chase Smith stood up against him year after year. With the sole exception of his successful expulsion of her from the Investigations Subcommittee, she baffled, outwitted, outmaneuvered, and defeated him at every turn. She not only won the war, but every battle save the one. And McCarthy, in attempting to kill Margaret Chase Smith politically, had dug his own political grave. The ill-fated McCarthy campaign against Margaret Chase Smith began and ended on the little subway train between the Senate Office Building and the Senate wing of the Capitol Building. It had begun when Margaret and Joe accidentally boarded the train together as she went over to deliver her Declaration of Conscience. And it ended ironically on the train sometime after the 1954 primary when again on one day there were several quorum and roll calls. Margaret ran into Joe several times that day at the train—he the crusader against the Communists and she the woman he labeled as a sympathizer, fellow traveler, and apologist for Communists. Finally, after riding together several times, Joe said rather uneasily, and as though he wondered if people had noticed, "Margaret, we seem to be following each other and riding together."

Margaret looked at him and said, smiling: "Yes, Joe. If you don't watch out, people will say we are fellow travelers."

Navy Day

OCTOBER 27, 1938

". . . the real attack . . . will be by the way of the sea."

—Margaret Chase Smith
October 27, 1938

—Pearl Harbor
December 7, 1941

A speech to a woman's club may well have been the initial key to my chance to serve in Congress.

At the time I had no thought of every becoming a Member of Congress. My husband, Clyde H. Smith, was the Representative from the Second Congressional District of Maine, serving his first term, and he had been elected to his second term, which was to start on January 3, 1939.*

I seldom got out front on my own. My role was to be at Clyde's side as his right hand. I had no desire to attract attention—and Clyde like most officeholders was not receptive to any staff member competing with him. In any case, the voter would be looking for Clyde's name rather than mine.

There were rare exceptions. One of those exceptions was an invitation from the Kennebec County Women's Republican Club to address the members on October 27, 1938. They wanted to hear about our social life in Washington. In fact, the title of my talk was to be "The Experiences of a Congressman's Wife in Washington."

Though I knew my place as Clyde's wife, and though I knew that it was important to Clyde to cultivate the women's vote for him, I had never been a feminist. But I was somewhat rebellious to the idea of restricting the talk to the social life of Washington, D.C. I was quite willing to talk on that subject but I also wanted to convey a more serious message. Because I believed that women could made a greater contribution to government on the local level, I wanted to include something in the speech that would encourage women to work for im-

* EDITOR'S NOTE: Margaret was an active wife, in fact Clyde Smith's top staff member. This had come at the insistence of his constituents. Representative Smith had vetoed the suggestion that Margaret be appointed to his staff. He was opposed to nepotism. But a petition was started in Knox County and circulated throughout the Congressional district. Several thousand people stated that they had voted for Margaret as much as for Clyde when they cast their ballots. Clyde gave in to their strongly worded petition.

They campaigned as a team. Clyde was the candidate, Margaret the manager. She drove the car and she maintained a current blackbook of maps of all the routes in the district with the names of key people and their residences and offices along the routes. In Washington she handled the correspondence, which was the backbone of the office operation, keeping the political fences mended back in Maine. Many times she typed until midnight or later.

provement of their communities. I had often said that the Federal Government is only as strong as are the local governments.

I asked Clyde to make suggestions and to help in the preparation of the speech. He refused. He said that I was on my own. Whatever the reason or motivation for his refusal to help, it was probably one of the luckiest things that ever happened to me. Probably he never would have suggested that I talk about the United States Navy.

In searching for an appropriate subject of serious consideration, I finally decided to talk about the importance of the United States Navy because the date of the appearance before the Republican women would be Navy Day, October 27, 1938.

After completing a few observations about Washington's social life, I then launched into certain remarks about the Navy. Among the things I said were: "Those who oppose naval protection fail to perceive that the real attack, if any, will be by way of the sea. Development of our Navy is necessary self-preservation." The founders of this Republic, I noted, had advocated preparedness when it took literally months to cross the ocean, adding that "now, when barely hours are required, preparedness is doubly imperative." Our first Presidents had been aware of the necessity of being prepared. If their advice was good in those days, how much more important was it for us to be fortified especially in days of fast travel and worldwide commerce, and at a time when nations were seemingly war crazy.

EDITOR'S NOTE:
Whether her remarks about the Navy made much of an impression on the Republican women is not known. It is very doubtful that Clyde Smith was impressed—or even interested. In fact, it is doubtful that anyone paid much attention. However,

some years later two important men were to become crucially impressed—crucial from the standpoint of Margaret Chase Smith's career. Those two men were Guy P. Gannett, owner of the only newspaper chain in Maine (and subsequently of radio and television stations), and Carl Vinson, Chairman of the House Naval Affairs Committee, who at that time was waging a losing battle in Congress for the fortification of an island named Guam as an American naval base.

Less than two years later, in April 1940, Clyde died of a heart attack. Margaret ran to succeed him as the Representative of the Second District after he died. When she sought the support of Guy Gannett and his news media, Gannett asked her how she stood on the issue of national defense, and especially on the Navy.

Margaret replied, "Don't take my word for it. I'll send you a clipping from the Waterville *Sentinel* and Kennebec (Augusta) *Journal* (Gannett's papers) of my public stand two years ago on Navy Day." Her October 27, 1938, speech won his enthusiastic support. She was elected by an overwhelming margin.

Nearly five years after that Navy Day Speech, it was to become a decisive factor in her request for assignment to a certain committee of the House. Although she was a Republican and Republican Leaders had decided that it was all right with them for her to go on a committee as important as Naval Affairs (in order to keep her off Appropriations), it was the "Admiral" —Democratic Chairman Carl Vinson—who was to decide whether she could join his Naval Affairs Committee.

Her 1938 Navy Day speech convinced him. It was not just the speech itself. It was the timing of the speech. For in 1942–43 he well remembered how in the late thirties the House had turned him down on his plea for fortification of Guam. Margaret and the "Admiral" had been talking the same language at the same time. He welcomed her to his committee in January 1943. And it was on Naval Affairs that Margaret Chase Smith first made her mark, drawing respect and recognition not only from her colleagues but from Franklin D. Roosevelt as well. Later, he issued a Presidential commendation of her work on that committee.

Perhaps when Carl Vinson read her 1938 speech, he had nodded his head at that one sentence: "Those who oppose naval protection fail to perceive that the real attack, if any, will be by way of the sea." Japanese naval sea-air forces had attacked Pearl Harbor on December 7, 1941, by way of the sea.

Unification-Air Force Debate

"Maggie, you made a God-damned fool out of me!"

—Colonel Melvin J. Maas, USMCR
July 8, 1947

When I joined the House Naval Affairs Committee in January 1943, I had already been on record for two years in support of Unification and a separate Air Force. And now I found myself in a hotbed of anti-Unification forces. Chairman Carl Vinson, known respectfully and affectionately as the "Admiral" because of his militant advocacy and supervision of the Navy, had successfully prevented Unification bills from ever reaching the Floor of the House or the Senate for a vote.

His unrivaled Congressional cunning was widely admired and respected. Also a part of his effectiveness against the merger of the Army and Navy was generally attributed to the solid backing that his House Naval Affairs Committee gave him. No one apparently had paid any attention to my 1941 statement in behalf of Unification. For three years I did not assert my difference with the committee view. But when I did, in 1946, it marked the first break within that strongest of all Navy strongholds.

The next break came at the beginning of the 80th Congress in 1947 with the merger of the Military Affairs and Naval Affairs Committees into the Armed Services Committee. Unification on the legislative side added impetus for unification on the executive side, that is, the departments themselves. Merger of the two committees was fought to the bitter end by W. Sterling "Stub" Cole, a Naval Reservist and ranking Republican of the House Naval Affairs Committee, who would have been the new Chairman of that committee if it were not merged out of existence.

I complimented him on the personal sacrifice he was making in his one-man campaign and deplored the unfair accusations of selfishness made against him. But I told him very simply that I thought that since merger of the committees had been voted for by the Congress and supported by the Republican Party which used its support to help elect a Republican Congress in 1946 that failure to merge the two committees would be a breach of trust to the electorate by Republicans. Speaker Joe Martin agreed and the two committees were merged.

A short time later it looked as though the Republican Congress was well on its way to passing the Unification Bill, H.R. 4214. But instead of going to the Armed Services Committee as it had in the Senate, the House bill was referred to the Executive Expenditures Committee. The House Executive Expenditures Committee claimed jurisdiction on the basis that the Unification Bill proposed a reorganization in the executive Departments of War and Navy. This was definitely a setback for Unification advocates for the new merged House Armed Services Committee was known to be heavily in favor of Unification. Some suspected that the referral to the Executive Expenditures Committee stemmed from the fact that Speaker Joe Martin, who made the committee assignment, was from the traditionally naval state of Massachusetts.

The Chairman of the Executive Expenditures Committee, Clare Hoffman of Michigan, exhibited determined opposition to the bill from the start. Because Hoffman had concentrated in the past on labor matters and revealed no special interest in military or naval legislation, it was surprising that he should suddenly become an advocate for the Navy's position. What very few people knew was that Chairman Hoffman's son, who was the General Counsel of his father's committee, was a Naval Reserve officer, and that another top member of the professional staff was a Naval Reserve officer. Still another key Republican member, who opposed the bill, had a son who was a Marine Reservist.

After a while the strategy of Chairman Hoffman and his anti-Unification members of the committee became evident. They took a leaf from "Admiral" Vinson's log and prolonged the hearings hoping to bottle up the bill in committee until after Congress adjourned. It had been expected that Congressman James Wadsworth, former United States Senator from New York, as a member of the Executive Expenditures Committee would be able to push the bill through the committee. Wadsworth was regarded by many as the strongest man in the House. He had been the spearhead of the proposal to merge the Naval Affairs and Military Affairs Committees. But Wadsworth did not initially prove as effective as had been anticipated. He felt that he could not press for the bill because his son-in-law, W. Stuart Symington, who was then the Assistant Secretary of War for Air, undoubtedly would be appointed Secretary of the Air Force if the bill were passed. In addition to unifying the War and Navy Departments, the bill also provided for a new Department of the Air Force. The leadership of the fight for the bill within the committee therefore fell to freshman Congressman W. J. Bryan Dorn who had served in World War II as an enlisted man in the Army Air Forces. What Dorn lacked in political sophistication, he made up for with his political courage. His vigor unfortunately was no match for the prolonged hearings and dilatory postponements that were eating up precious Congressional time. Adjournment time was rapidly approaching.

It was early in May 1947 and I was enjoying a weekend with old friends in Oklahoma City. When a phone call came from Washington that abruptly changed the course of the Unification Bill, I was visiting at the home of Army Air Corps Reserve Colonel and Mrs. William C. Lewis, Sr. Colonel Lewis (later Brigadier General) was the Executive Director of the Air Reserve Association and the call was an urgent one for him to come to Washington to see what he could do to resurrect the Unification Bill. The two of us went to bat immediately.

Upon my return to Washington, I consulted my best friends on the Executive Expenditures Committee, including Representative R. Walter Riehlman of New York. The most important thing I learned was that Wadsworth's silence was hurting the bill with those committee members who were inclined to be in favor of it; their enthusiasm was dwindling. I also learned that the only way that the bill could be forced out of the committee was for Speaker Joe Martin to tell Chairman Clare Hoffman that the bill must be reported out. On the Senate side Republican Senator Edward V. Robertson of Wyoming, the most vigorous advocate of the Navy in the Senate, was effectively blocking the bill in the Senate Armed Services Committee. It appeared that Senator Robert Taft, Chairman of the Republican

Policy Committee, would have to say the word before the Senate Committee would report the bill out.

This information was relayed to Bill Lewis, Jr.,* and he and his father then galvanized the Air Reserve Association into immediate action. ARA called on its members throughout the country to bombard Speaker Martin and Senator Taft with letters. The ammunition of the "letter bombs" was that the Republicans had campaigned on the promise of passing the Unification Bill and that if the Republican Congress failed to live up to that promise, it would be nothing less than a betrayal of the electorate which would not be forgotten. ARA also let its friends in the Army Air Forces know so that they could pass the word on to other groups.

Their strategy reached a climax in June when Colonel Lewis, Sr., wrote an open letter to Chairman Hoffman insisting that the national security should no longer be jeopardized by in-

* Bill Lewis, Jr., had been the General Counsel of the Old House Naval Affairs Committee first as a Naval Reserve officer and then in civilian status. In September 1946, while he was still with the House Naval Affairs Committee, the Army Air Forces informally offered him a commission in the Army Air Corps Reserve in the rank of Lieutenant Colonel, the rank commensurate with his rank as full Commander in the Naval Reserve. He declined the offer stating that he felt an obligation to stay with the Navy.

When the Naval Affairs Committee was merged with the Military Affairs Committee in January 1947 and the Republicans took control of the House, "Admiral" Carl Vinson (deposed as Chairman because he was a Democrat) had, without Bill's consent or knowledge, proposed that he be made a professional staff member of the newly formed House Armed Services Committee. Republican Representatives W. Sterling Cole and George J. Bates opposed the appointment of Lewis. They had been urged to oppose Lewis by the Navy Judge Advocate General and the Navy Legislative Counsel on the grounds that his father was a Colonel in the Army Air Corps Reserve.

Vinson was shocked at their opposition and even more at the basis of their opposition. He asked why they had not raised the question about Lewis during the time that he had served as General Counsel of the House Naval Affairs Committee. It was not until two months later in early March that Vinson revealed to Lewis what had happened. Lewis then asked Vinson if he should accept the offer of the commission as a Lieutenant Colonel in the Army Air Corps Reserve. Vinson told him he would be a fool if he didn't because it was quite clear that Lewis wasn't going anywhere in the Naval Reserve with the Navy evidencing such prejudice against him. Lewis then notified the Army Air Forces he would accept the offer that he had declined six months before; his sense of loyalty, he explained, seemed to have been misplaced. On April 28, 1947, Lewis resigned as a Commander in the Naval Reserve in the morning and in the afternoon was sworn in as a Lieutenant Colonel in the Army Air Corps Reserve.

decision and calling on the committee to make a straight "yes or no" vote without further delay. About the same time, Speaker Joe Martin bore down on Hoffman and Senator Taft called for quick passage of the Unification Bill by the Senate. With a little prodding from me, the press started pressing Speaker Martin for an answer as to whether the House was going to act on Unification before it adjourned. And I kept lobbying away quietly though intensely in the daily sessions of the House. My participation in the Unification battle came to the public's attention in a dramatic way when I appeared with two colorful war heroes in a radio debate on the "American Forum of the Air": Lieutenant General Jimmy Doolittle, the famed Air Force leader of the bombing of Tokyo, by then a civilian, and Colonel Melvin J. Maas, a Marine combat ace aviator, my former ranking Republican colleague on the Naval Affairs Committee and cosponsor of WAVE legislation. The subject of the forum was "Should the Present Army-Navy Unification Bill Be Passed?" Doolittle and I took the affirmative and Mel Maas upheld the negative with Congressman Harry R. Sheppard, past Chairman of the House Naval Appropriations Subcommittee. My inclusion in the forum was not the recognition for the fight I had been making that it might appear. As a matter of cold fact, I was chosen for the forum only after two other Unification advocates had dropped out. I was chosen merely as a result of dire expediency a very few days before the time of the debate. It was the deputy to Major General "Rosie" O'Donnell, then Public Information Director of the Army Air Forces, who called me and asked if I would go on the forum with Doolittle to argue for Unification. I said I would be glad to and then immediately put in a call to Bill Lewis, my principal collaborator on Unification. "Admiral" Vinson had once told me that Bill, his former General Counsel, knew more about the pros and cons of Unification than anyone. And Vinson ought to know in view of his successful defeat of Unification up to that time.

Bill coached me in every detail of the subject and helped me prepare both an opening and closing statement. He had answers to nearly all of the anti-Unification arguments, particularly those of Mel Maas whose thinking he knew like the back of his hand. But there were a few points to which he didn't have the answers. On these he advised me to ask the Army Air Forces for the best possible answers. He said that it was almost a certainty they would be brought up by Mel Maas, because they were the best points the other side could make. The two questions that I asked the Army Air Forces were these: (1) "How can the bill be called real Unification when it doesn't require unifying such functions as procurement, medical services, transportation, and other noncombat common activities of the Army, Navy, and Air Force?" and (2) "How will Unification provide economy and specifically what will it save in dollars and cents?"

The Army Air Forces sent me no material until the afternoon of the day of the broadcast. About the best that could be said of the material was that it had quantity. Bill blew his top when he realized that the Army Air Forces had not provided any answers to the two main questions. Their excuse was that there *wasn't any answer* to them, most particularly to the question of how much money Unification would save. By the time Bill had read the Army Air Forces' suggested opening statement for me, he was so disgusted he hurled it at the wastebasket, and made a direct hit.

So at the last minute we tried to work out the answers that the Army Air Forces hadn't provided. We decided that the best answer to the point about the bill's failing to merge the procurement, medical, and other noncombat services of the Army, Navy, and Air Force, was that the bill had not been presented in final form and that it remained to be seen what the bill would be like when amended. The only answer we could conjure up to the question of how much money Unification would save was that efficient national security was more important than saving pennies.

At a luncheon conference earlier in the day with General Doolittle, I had suggested that the General should carry most of the debate and answer most of the questions for our team, and I would make the closing summation. General Doolittle, as a war ace, could better handle the aviator star of the other team, Mel Maas, I said. General Doolittle said it suited him fine. My suggestion was readily accepted because, to be completely frank about it, there was some question as to whether I could hold my own. Something was said about a closing summation being a tough job. I replied, "Don't worry. I'll hold all right on that."

And I did—to the surprise of everyone, including me. I had answers for all of the questions asked me except one. And that was the anticipated one that Mel Maas asked me about Unification of the noncombat common services of the Army, Navy, and Air Force. I gave the answer that Bill and I had agreed upon. And Mel really scored against me with his reply, "I used to say that same kind of thing when I was a Congressman, but that is no answer." General Doolittle came immediately to my rescue. "I would like to answer that question, Mel," he said. "The bill makes possible the accomplishment of all of these things. It doesn't yet make it mandatory."

While not doubting in the slightest General Doolittle's knowledge and ability, I immediately recalled that General Doolittle had spent the afternoon with the Public Information section of the Army Air Forces in preparing for the forum and that it was this same section that had told me there *was no possible answer* to this particular question.

I was still thinking about that Army Air Forces section, when Harry Sheppard asked General Doolittle to show how Unification would save any money and General Doolittle pulled out a detailed and prepared answer of cost figures. This was the discussion that followed:

GENERAL DOOLITTLE: I am going to have to ask your tolerance, because you have asked a question that takes a few minutes to answer. I won't answer any more questions after this, if I take too much time.

CHAIRMAN GRANIK: Not too many figures, General.
GENERAL DOOLITTLE: This is one I was hoping someone would ask.

And then he proceeded to present a financial cost analysis of what Unification would cost in additional salaries, housing and other items—and what would be saved in cost. Citing a string of figures, he estimated the additional cost at two million dollars annually and the estimated savings at far more than one hundred million dollars annually.

This was the answer that the Army Air Forces told me they did not have! The only chance at a punch I got was in my summation. Luckily I had won the toss of the coin giving our side the right to make its closing statement last. It was a decided break because after Mel Maas impressively summed up for his side, he and Harry Sheppard had no opportunity to come back at me. This is what I said:

Mr. Granik, I would sum up our discussion with three simple observations.

1. The making of the decision on merger is more important than what that decision is, because until Congress votes "Yes" or "No" on the proposal, whether it be S. 758 or any other bill, the United States cannot even begin to plan its Army, Navy, and Air Force. In a world rapidly choosing sides for another war, as you say, Colonel Maas, we have dangerously delayed the postwar organizing of our Armed Services in waiting for a decision on the merger.

2. Merger opponents are not merely opposed to the present bill. They want no change at all. Their strategy is delay, delay, delay. Their tactics have been dilatory and specious arguments that have shifted from military dictatorship to threats to Naval Aviation and the Marine Corps to, finally, the theory of a "sea lawyer" that a separate Air Force is unconstitutional.

3. Merger opponents successfully stifled last year's bill in committees by offering the Navy-Eberstadt plan. In essence the

Navy-Eberstadt plan has been made the very heart of the present merger bill, and yet they now oppose it. They no longer want what they offered last year. In other words, don't be fooled by those pious words of "true unification." Their actions show that they simply just don't want any change at all.

EDITOR'S NOTE:
At the end of the broadcast, Mel Maas leaned over the table and said, "Margaret, that was the most devastating thing I ever had thrown at me and I didn't even have a chance to answer you." Coming from one of the best informed, most articulate and colorful personalities ever to grace the Washington scene, that was some tribute. Jimmy Doolittle later was to recall: "Mel Maas, who summed up for his team, came over to her after the debate and put it very succinctly by saying, 'Maggie, you made a God-damned fool out of me.' There was no one, including Congressman Sheppard, to say him nay. She did a superb job of summing up for our side and comfortably won the debate."

Representative Smith immediately became quite popular with the Army Air Forces. Her surprising performance highlighted conversations in Congressional and military circles for several weeks. The Portland (Maine) *Press Herald* of July 11, 1947, had a page-length column editorial on the excellence of her performance, concluding that "Maine can be proud of her."

The National Commander of the American Legion, Paul Griffith, who was testifying before the House Armed Services Committee on Universal Military Training legislation, departed from his prepared statement to say:

I would like just at this time to congratulate the lady of the committee for her fine presentation on the subject of Unification on the air last night. It was a very intelligent presentation and as National Commander of the American Legion, I am very happy to know that she is serving as a member of this committee.

What significant psychological effect, if any, the debate had is anyone's guess. But chronologically, a strong case can be made that the effect was immediate, decisive, and crucial. The very next day, following the debate, on Wednesday, July 9, 1947, the Senate passed its own Unification Bill by a voice vote. Eight days after the debate, on July 16, the House Executive Expenditures Committee, where the Unification Bill had been bottled up, reported out its bill. Eleven days after the debate, on July 19, the House passed the Unification Bill by a voice vote. President Truman signed the Unification Bill on July 26, 1947. And the next day the Congress recessed until late in the fall. An interesting facet in these developments was the fact that the heretofore leading opponent of Unification legislation, "Admiral" Carl Vinson, did not raise his voice in the debate on the legislation and was absent from the House when the Unification Bill was passed by a voice vote. He was recorded as absent on the two quorum calls of the House that day.

After the stunning victory, Commanding General of the Army Air Forces, Carl Spaatz, wrote this letter:

July 22, 1947

Honorable Margaret Chase Smith
Representative from Maine
House of Representatives

Dear Mrs. Smith:
This note is to congratulate you on the effective work you have done during the present and previous sessions of the Congress in improving the military establishment and in according to air power its appropriate place in that establishment.

Your participation recently with General Doolittle in the radio debate on Unification came at a very important time and drew the issues so clearly that there was little to be said in opposition.

Sincerely,
Carl Spaatz
General, U. S. Army
Commanding General, Army Air Forces

The repercussions of her championship of the Air Force were to continue for years. Three years after the radio debate, Margaret Chase Smith was commissioned as a Lieutenant Colonel in the United States Air Force Reserve on July 14, 1950. Seven years after the radio debate, she was accused by her Democratic opponent in the 1954 Maine Senatorial General Election of having acted to undermine and weaken the Air Force and the national security. Ten years later she was locked in bitter controversy with Lieutenant General "Rosie" O'Donnell on the Jimmy Stewart nomination for Brigadier General in the Air Force Reserve, and at the end of that year she was to retire from the Air Force Reserve without pay. Twenty-four years later, the Chief of Staff of the Air Force was to call upon Senator Smith to get her clearance and approval of the Air Force's selection for Chief of the Air Force Reserve before making the official appointment.

Fight for WACS, WAVES, WAFS

". . . 8 percent of all the women while they were in the service became pregnant . . . when they reach the age of menopause or go through the change of life, with the physical disabilities or illnesses that result, the cost of the program would be stupendous if not prohibitive."

—Representative Dewey Short
April 21, 1948

"It took women years and years and years of a very hard struggle to achieve economic security and freedom. But it did not take such a hard struggle to have the physical and biological security and freedom that the pill has so suddenly and explosively brought . . . such power should be very carefully exercised lest it ultimately be the self-destruction of woman and her rightful and responsible place in civilization rather than 'man-kind.'"

—Senator Margaret Chase Smith
July 16, 1969

In my service in the U. S. House of Representatives, I was perhaps identified more with WAVE* legislation than any other. It left the impression, I'm afraid, that I was a feminist concentrating on legislation for women. And if there is any one thing I have attempted to avoid it is being a feminist. I definitely resent being called a feminist.

I always felt and said so repeatedly to the women themselves, as well as to top Armed Services officials and members of the Naval Affairs and Armed Services Committees of the House, that I did not want to see women in the services after the war unless there was a definite need for them.

I opposed retaining women's organizations in the Army, Navy, and Air Force merely as a noble gesture for their splendid war service. And I did not think they should be kept as Reservists on inactive duty indefinitely. Either there was a permanent need for them or there wasn't. If there was, then they should be made Regulars as well as Reservists. If there wasn't a need, then they should not be kept on active duty—and the only justification for a women's Reserve was for call in the event of another war. I challenged the services to prove that they needed the women in specific jobs before I would support legislation to give them peacetime status.

Overseas service was the first WAVE legislation that I sponsored and made a successful fight for. Later, in November 1944, I made an official inspection of WAVE establishments and in my report expressed interest in the role to be played by women in the peacetime Navy, Marine Corps, and Coast Guard.

When the Navy Department asked the Naval Affairs Committee in 1945 for legislation authorizing permanent status for women in the Navy and for a permanent Women's Naval Reserve, their representatives came to tell me that Chairman Vinson favored providing for Reserve status but did not want to give the women permanent status for a while. They were afraid

* Acronyms for women in the armed services: WAC—Women's Army Corps; WAVES—Women Accepted for Volunteer Emergency Service (Navy); WAF —Women in the Air Force; SPARS—Women's Reserve of the Coast Guard Reserve. There is no acronym for Women Marines.

that I would insist on permanent status for the women and that might kill the bill.

They were only half right. I said I would fight for permanent status for women in the Navy *if the Navy really needed them.* But I warned that I was opposed to giving them only Reserve status and keeping them on active duty indefinitely. Finally, I said they would have to prove the specific need for the women before I would back the measure.

During the hearings, I repeated what I had told the Naval representatives and I placed in the hearing record a questionnaire that I asked the Navy Department to answer in detail. If the answers were satisfactory, I promised to support the legislation. The answers were not. The legislation did not pass.

By 1948 the entire Armed Services was vigorously urging both permanent and Reserve status for women. Defense Secretary Forrestal, Army General Eisenhower, Admiral Denfeld, Air Force General Spaatz, and the Secretaries of Army, Navy, and Air Force all appeared before the House and Senate Armed Services Committees stating that there was a critical need for the women. Though in the past it had always waited for the House Committee to act first on personnel legislation, this time the Senate Armed Services Committee responded first —and fairly fast. It reported out S. 1641 giving both permanent and Reserve status to women in the services on July 23, 1947.

When S. 1641 went to the House Armed Services Committee, however, it languished for eight months in Organization Subcommittee No. 3. The members alternately adopted and rejected the permanent status provision and couldn't come to an agreement.

Finally Policy Subcommittee No. 12, which was composed of the four top-ranking Republicans and the three top-ranking Democrats, took the matter in hand and decided that the permanent status should be eliminated. This subcommittee, which was dominated by Chairman "Ham" Andrews and Ranking Democrat Carl Vinson, concluded that the granting of permanent status should be deferred for two years and given further study.

Meantime, I was getting almost hourly communiques on the subcommittee developments on the bill by WAVES, WACS, WAFS, and others interested. The servicewomen leaders indicated that they would reluctantly accept the elimination of permanent status because they feared that insisting on it would kill the bill and they would thus lose their Reserve status as well. They hoped I would accept their reasoning. But I could not.

When I learned that Policy Subcommittee No. 12 had dropped the permanent status from the bill as a result of "off-the-record executive session" statements made by representatives of the Navy, I was ready to fight, and I made it clear in a letter to Chairman "Ham" Andrews:

February 14, 1948

Honorable W. G. Andrews, Chairman
Committee on Armed Services
House of Representatives
Washington, D.C.

My Dear Mr. Chairman:

I have been told that Subcommittee No. 12, the Policy Subcommittee, has cleared S. 1641, the Women's Armed Services Integration Bill, for hearing and action by Subcommittee No. 3, the Organization Subcommittee, only at your urgent personal intervention. May I commend you for your forthright action.

However, I have also been told that the Policy Subcommittee took this action on the strict condition and understanding that the bill be amended to prevent women from being given Regular status in the Armed Services keeping them on active duty indefinitely. I have also been told that this compromise agreement results from "off-the-record executive session" statements of duly authorized officer representatives of the Navy Department.

Such a compromise would definitely dodge the issue. The issue is simple—either the Armed Services have a *permanent* need of women officers and enlisted women or they don't. If they do, then the women must be given a permanent status. The only possible permanent status is that of Regular status— not Reserve status, which *at most* is temporary. There is no such thing as a service career for a Reservist.

This issue was squarely met by the Senate, which granted the request of the Armed Services to give women Regular, as well as Reserve, status in the Armed Services—and rejected the attempts to deny women Regular status.

I hope the House Armed Services Committee will match the forthright manner of the Senate and give a direct "Yes or No" answer and not a dodging "maybe" as has been reported to have been agreed upon by the Policy Subcommittee.

I sent a copy of this letter to Congressman Paul W. Shafer, Chairman of Subcommittee No. 3, which was holding hearings on the bill, so that there would be no question of my position and so that Subcommittee No. 3 might consider the points I had raised. My plea fell on deaf ears.

But the Legislative Counsel of the Navy Department, Captain Ira H. Nunn, quickly came to see me. He assured me that, the report to the contrary, the Navy Department was fully behind permanent Regular status for women in the Navy, and that no cognizant Naval officer had opposed such a provision in either open or closed meetings with the committee. (It had been reported that the Navy opposed women in the Regulars because they didn't want them serving aboard ships and restricting them to shore billets would mean slowing up the rotation of men from ship duty to shore duty.)

The Shafer Subcommittee did report out the bill and when the full Armed Services Committee met on March 23, 1948, to vote on it, I could not be present. I asked my good friend Leroy Johnson of California to cast my proxy votes. He carried my letter to Chairman Andrews stating that I desired my proxy votes to be cast as follows:

(1) *For*—integrating women into the Armed Services in permanent Regular status and Reserve status;

(2) *Against*—integrating women into the Armed services only in a Reserve status and on extended active duty indefinitely, and barring them from permanent Regular status; and

(3) *For*—restricting the assigned duties and number of Women Reservists on active duty to the bare minimum necessary for the administrative "housekeeping" of a skeleton Women's Reserve organization to be expanded in wartime—and exclusively for this purpose and not for any other duty.

But just as I had lost with Chairman Andrews, with Policy Subcommittee No. 12, and with the Shafer Organization Subcommittee No. 3, so I lost that day with the full committee. The full committee voted for the Shafer Subcommittee bill and against permanent Regular status for women by the margin of 26 to 1. It was everybody against me—with the possible exception of Charles Clason of Massachusetts who abstained from voting. He didn't vote with me but he didn't vote against me, and I showed my appreciation by campaigning for his re-election seven months later.

A few days later Captain Ira H. Nunn, the Navy's Legislative Counsel, called again. In his usual disarmingly quiet and smiling manner, he said that he supposed I knew that the bill was coming up on the Consent Calendar* the following Tuesday and that I would not oppose it after the committee had voted as it had. I told him I was greatly indebted to him for I had not known that the bill had been put on the Consent Calendar and would be up for vote. Had he not told me, I would not have had the chance to oppose the bill, I said, and that was what I intended to do.

Putting the bill on the Consent Calendar not only meant that Chairman Andrews and the committee were steamrolling my opposition, but it also meant that the House Armed Serv-

* Bills placed on the Consent Calendar are never controversial bills. They are practically always bills that have been approved unanimously by the committee reporting them. When the committee gets a bill on the Consent Calendar, it is not open for debate or amendments.

ices Committee Chairman was utterly disregarding the basic difference between the bill passed by the Senate and the House committee's version which deleted the permanent Regular status provision. It was a surprising defiance of normal parliamentary procedure to put a controversial bill on the Consent Calendar. Fortunately there was one rule which prevented their getting away with it. Any bill called up on the Consent Calendar can be blocked by one objection. In other words, bills on the Consent Calendar must pass unanimously. They must have felt that in the final crunch, I wouldn't dare to object.

Thanks to the tactical error of Captain Nunn, I was seated at my desk as the time approached for the bill to be called up on the Consent Calendar. Members of the Armed Services Committee kept a steady eye on me, some of them coming up to me to plead or argue, a few almost threatening reprisals.

Then the bill was called up and I rose, and in a firm voice I stated that I objected. Here is the Congressional Record's verbatim report of the proceedings:

Congressional Record
April 6, 1948

The Clerk called the bill (S. 1641) to establish the Women's Army Corps in the Regular Army, to authorize the enlistment and appointment of women in the Regular Navy and Marine Corps and the Naval and Marine Corps Reserve, and for other purposes.

The SPEAKER. Is there objction to the present consideration of the bill?

Mrs. SMITH of Maine. Mr. Speaker, I object.

Mr. SHAFER. Mr. Speaker, if the gentlewoman will yield, does the gentlewoman insist upon her objection?

Mrs. SMITH of Maine. Yes, sir.

Mr. SHAFER. Mr. Speaker, it is difficult to understand the gentlewoman's objection. She has always been a great friend of women in service. Her objection may mean the ultimate defeat of this legislation which was reported favorably to the House by the Armed Services Committee. Should there be adverse action as the result of the gentlewoman's objection, she must assume full responsibility.

The SPEAKER. Is there objection to the present consideration of the bill?

Mrs. SMITH of Maine. Mr. Speaker, I object.

It was as simple as that. Only two words, "I object." There was no need for debate for Representative Shafer well knew my reasons for objecting. But later in that day's Congressional Record, I made a full reply to Congressman Shafer's charge that I would have the full responsibility for the defeat of the bill.

Mr. Speaker, the gentleman from Michigan [Mr. Shafer] has charged me with the responsibility of killing S. 1641.

If a bill as important as this is to be considered only on the Consent Calendar, then I unhesitatingly accept that responsibility.

In the first place, I would call the attention of the House to page 48 of the Consent Calendar, for Tuesday, April 6, 1948—today's calendar—wherein it describes S. 1641 as "An act to establish the Women's Army Corps in the Regular Army, to authorize the enlistment and appointment of women in the Regular Navy and Marine Corps and the Naval and Marine Corps Reserve and for other purposes."

The Members of the House will note that the words "Regular Army" and "Regular Navy" are predominant in the description of the bill. This is grossly misleading as this bill in the form it was reported out by the Committee on Armed Services in no respect establishes Women's Corps in either the Regular Army or the Regular Navy. Make no mistake about it, it is a temporary one-year Reserve bill.

The Senate voted to give women Regular status as well as Reserve status in passing S. 1641.

The House Armed Services Committee refused to give Regular status.

The House bill definitely dodges the issue. The issue is simple—either the armed services have a permanent need of women officers and enlisted women or they do not. If they do, then the women must be given a permanent status. The only possible permanent status is that of Regular status—not Reserve status, which at most is temporary. There is no such thing as a service career for a Reservist.

This issue was squarely met by the Senate, which granted the request of the armed services to give women Regular, as well as Reserve, status in the armed services—and rejected the attempts to deny women Regular status.

This legislation does not give women any security in their military service because it discriminates against women, and will result only in not getting women of desirable caliber for the armed services.

I am convinced that this is extremely unwise legislation. I am further convinced that it is better to have no legislation at all than to have legislation of this type. I am, therefore, unalterably opposed to it and I objected.

I would point out in answer to the charge of the gentleman from Michigan [Mr. Shafer] that I have killed the bill, that there is nothing to prevent the Committee from seeking a rule on the bill so that the House can fully discuss the bill—and so that amendments to the bill may be offered. Therefore the responsibility is clearly that of the House Armed Services Committee—for it is up to the Committee to request a rule—and that means specifically the chairman of the subcommittee, the gentleman from Michigan [Mr. Shafer], and the chairman of the full committee, the gentleman from New York [Mr. Andrews].

When there is such a radical difference between the Senate version and the House version, it is extremely surprising that an attempt would be made to get this legislation railroaded through on the Consent Calendar.

Two days later Congressman John W. McCormack, for several years the Democratic Majority Leader of the House and later to become Speaker, took the floor in my behalf. In his several years as Majority Leader, he had become an expert on parliamentary procedure, and so it meant a great deal when he said:

> When a bill appearing on the Consent Calendar is called, and consent for its consideration is granted, every Member of the House is justified in assuming that no amendments will be offered to the bill after unanimous consent is granted for its consideration, certainly no amendment of a serious nature, and probably none other than an amendment which might come from the committee itself. Unanimous consent being granted for consideration of a bill appearing on the Consent Calendar carries with it the implication and the implied promise, if not express, that the bill is going to be passed in the form reported by the committee. Of course, with a bill of this kind the gentlewoman from Maine, recognizing the situation, could not place herself in that position, and I admire her. When the gentleman from Michigan undertook to place the responsibility upon her, he should have taken a little look at the gentlewoman's chin, and he would know that he could not bluff her, because the gentlewoman from Maine is not the type that can be bluffed very easily from my observation of her during the years that both of us have served in this body.
>
> . . . For anyone to undertake to prevent this bill coming up under the rules of the House, so that the House can pass upon either the Senate bill or the House substitute, would be a grave mistake. The gentlewoman from Maine did the right thing, in my opinion, so that the House could have an opportunity of voting upon the substitute reported out by the Committee on the Armed Services, and she is to be congratulated . . . Certainly the leadership of the House should not take any course of action adverse to this bill coming up under the regular rules of the House.

"That is my intention," came the reply from the committee's Chairman, "Ham" Andrews. "We have made arrangements to apply for a rule on the bill."

Forcing the Andrews-Shafer-Short opposition to bring the bill up under the regular rules of the House was a sweet victory after the three previous overwhelming setbacks. By the time the bill came to the House Floor two weeks later on April 21, 1948, for full debate and vote, several Congressmen had come over to my side. Nevertheless, "Ham" Andrews warned me that I wouldn't get more than four votes for my amendment. I might not have, had I accepted the draft of my amendment written by the Committee Staff Counsel assigned to assist me. A patronage appointee of my adversary Dewey Short, the Counsel did not furnish the draft until the last minute—and it was a maze of separate technical amendments that would take hours to introduce one by one. As I had had to do before, I called on Bill Lewis, and he prepared the draft for the simple, overall single amendment which would restore the permanent Regular status to the bill. Even before I had officially offered the amendment, several Congressmen made strong appeals to support it. For a while it looked as though a majority of the House Armed Services Committee would reverse themselves and vote for the Smith Amendment. The debate was going so badly against them that a frantic call went out from the Republican Leadership to get the Andrews-Shafer-Short followers in on the Floor. Representative Dewey Short, Republican of Missouri, involuntarily revealed his desperation when he made his final plea for defeat of my Amendment:

Mr. Chairman, the gentleman from South Carolina has truthfully pointed out certain biological differences between the sexes. He says that the female is more deadly than the male. I agree to that. "Hell hath no fury like a woman's scorn" [sic].

There are several aspects to this bill that I do not care to discuss here publicly. We discussed them in detail and rather intimately in our committee. Realizing those biological differences, we were told that 8 percent of all the women while they were in the service became pregnant. I do not cast aspersions. I tell facts. We were told that because of certain biological differences in the sexes when they reach the age of menopause or go through the change of life, with the physical disabilities or illnesses that result, the cost of the program would be stupendous if not prohibitive. Those are a few of the fundamental and essential facts, unpleasant as they might be, which we must as legislators wisely and soberly consider. [Page 4717, Congressional Record, April 21, 1948, Volume 94, Part 4.]

Congressman George J. Bates roared back:

Mr. Chairman, the argument of my good friend from Missouri in opposition to this amendment really amazes me, as it does every Member of this House. Said he, "If we only could discuss publicly on the Floor of the House those things that we discussed behind closed doors."

A voice vote was called. And it was so close that the presiding officer called for a division, that is, a stand-up vote. We lost 54 to 42. But it was a long way from the 26 to 1 vote in my own committee. And ten times better than "Ham" Andrews' prediction.

EDITOR'S NOTE:
Having almost singlehandedly defeated her own committee on the Floor of the House and having strengthened the hand of the Senate conferees who would be ironing out the differences between the House and Senate versions, Senator Smith could have rested on her laurels. But getting permanent Regular status for women in the services had literally become a crusade with her. And because she knew how things can slip in conferences,

she wasn't taking any chances. Dewey Short had revealed his hand, and now she played her trump card. She did it in this letter to Secretary of Defense Forrestal.

April 22, 1948

Honorable James V. Forrestal,
The Secretary of Defense
Washington, D.C.

My dear Mr. Secretary:

Yesterday the Honorable Dewey Short in opposing the proposal to grant women Regular Status in the Armed Services stated:

"We were told that because of certain biological differences in the sexes when they reach the age of menopause or go through the change of life, with the physical disabilities or illnesses that result, the cost of the program would be stupendous if not prohibitive. Those are a few of the fundamental and essential facts, unpleasant as they might be, which we must as legislators wisely and soberly consider." (Page 4717, Congressional Record, April 21, 1948, see enclosed clipping.)

This statement, coupled with reports that I have received, that although the civilian and military heads of the respective Armed Services had unanimously urged Regular status for women in the Armed Services, the Legislative and Liaison officer representative of the Armed Services had "behind closed doors and in executive session" opposed Regular Status for women.

Mr. Short's statement on the floor of the House confirms these reports that the Armed Services had officially through their legislative and liaison representatives opposed Regular Status for women at least on a cost basis.

This, to say the least, is duplicity that gravely questions the integrity of the administration of the National Military Establishment. I believe that it is incumbent upon you as the head of your department to determine and identify the Armed Services representatives whose statements were the basis for

Mr. Short's statement. The basic question is whether we are to accept the official "on the record" statements of the executive and military heads of the Armed Services or the "behind closed doors" statements of your legislative representatives to individual members of the Committee.

Since S. 1641 is now in conference, I believe that immediate action and reply on your part is imperative.

> Sincerely yours,
> Margaret Chase Smith, M.C.

Her letter got results. Forrestal immediately told the conferees, headed by Senator Chan Gurney and Congressman Shafer, that the National Military Establishment felt it imperative that women be granted permanent Regular status in the Armed Services. The House conferees gave in and the substance of the Smith Amendment was incorporated in the bill and it was then passed by both the House and Senate. The women got their permanent Regular status because one woman Representative had refused to give up in the face of overwhelming odds against her.

Dewey Short was defeated for re-election to Congress in the 1956 election when President Eisenhower was re-elected. Eisenhower, who had vigorously supported permanent status for women in the Armed Services, appointed Short to be one of the Assistant Secretaries of the Army. When Short appeared before the Senate Armed Services Committee that was considering confirmation of his appointment, he faced his former adversary across the hearing table.

Recalling his opposition to a permanent status for women in the Armed Services nearly a decade past, Senator Smith asked him if he still felt that way. Short had obviously anticipated her questioning for he had brought with him the Congressional Record of April 21, 1948, and he read from it at length. Short had given little ground. "I am not against giving them Regular status," he said. But then, as he had done nine years before, he harped again on the biological differences between women and men. And this time he got pointedly personal with Senator Smith. "Of course we all recognize those biological differences. I think perhaps you did yourself." He reaffirmed his beliefs that "the female is more deadly than the male" and that "Hell hath no fury like a woman scorned."

Senator Smith was tempted to vote against his confirmation. She still wonders whether she should have registered a protest against his views by voting against him.

If Short had thought that he could embarrass Margaret Smith by bringing up biology, he had not learned much about her in their eight years of mutual service in the House. She has never flinched from open discussion of any subject. In fact, she may have been too frank for some members of her own sex in a speech she was to give much later on July 16, 1969.

A long-time member of the Business and Professional Women's Club (she served as State President in Maine four decades earlier), she was invited to speak at the District of Columbia's celebration of the BPW's fiftieth anniversary. The topic assigned her was "In Pursuit of the Golden Age for Women":

The title of my remarks is almost a blank check and unlimited hunting license for any subject concerning women. It certainly is timeless—for I think that ever since the beginning with Eve woman has, or women have, been in pursuit of a Golden Age.

Until recent times, we of the so-called weaker sex have been relegated to the secondary position of serving man. We haven't even been given an independent status of our own as far as designation or nomenclature is concerned. Instead our derivation has always stemmed from the opposite sex.

We are "wo-men"—a derivation of the term "men." We are "fe-male"—a derivation of the term "male." Of course, we do have some exceptions like "lady" instead of "wo-gentleman" or "fe-gentlemen." But such exceptions are limited in their application because the designation "lady" is for a special kind of woman and not for all women.

Until recent times, we could greatly blame ourselves for such secondary or derivative status as we were relatively content with it. For example, we were content with the role of being pursued—at least making it appear that we were being pursued. Heaven forbid that we be guilty or even accused of pursuing.

But ultimately women started openly pursuing—yes, engaging in the pursuit of the Golden Age by pursuing suffrage, the right to vote, the right to hold public office—overall the right to equal rights with men.

And yes, we women now openly and aggressively pursue the men. Bachelor girls are becoming as prevalent as bachelor boys. Perhaps women now have captured that Golden Age which they have pursued so long.

Perhaps we are now in the Golden Age of full emancipation. But if we are, I am not so sure that it is because of our militant drives for suffrage and equal rights.

I think that we can take credit ourselves for some achievement of the relative emancipation—for the economic and financial strength that we have developed for ourselves—for the growing economic and financial independence that we have.

There has been growing recognition of the fact that women not only are the majority of the population even though they have been treated like a minority—but that women actually possess and control most of the economic and financial resources of our country.

Paradoxically, some of those who call us the weaker sex say that we possess such financial and economic control because we outlive the men and thus inherit the money. Did someone say something about "survival of the fittest"?

I would not deny that there is factual basis for the inherited control allegation. But I would observe that it is rather derogatory to us and deprecates our own ability.

Instead I believe that recognition should be given to the accomplishments of women like those of your organization—of my organization of which I am so proud—the BPW. For the women of the BPW did not inherit financial and economic pre-eminence—they earned it—they worked for it—and yes, they had to fight for it over the opposition not only of men generally but as well of some women.

Yes, women are more emancipated today than ever before. Less and less are they dependent upon men for their sustenance and their survival. This is greatly because of their own doing—and because of the leadership of such groups as yours.

But in giving this richly deserved credit to women for their own emancipation and the greatest freedom of action that they have ever enjoyed, let me be frank enough to recognize a second dominating factor of emancipation.

The first factor of emancipation has been a gradual development. It has been a matter of gradual evolution. For the acquisition of financial and economic security by women and their growing financial and economic independence from men has been gradual and evolutionary—and has been over the persistent opposition of men.

But for the second factor—the most recent and sudden factor—the explosive and revolutionary factor—the pill—this is not an achievement of women—rather it is an achievement of medical science.

It took women years and years and years of a very hard struggle to achieve economic security and freedom. But it did not take such a long time and such a hard struggle to have the physical and biological security and freedom that the pill has so suddenly and explosively brought.

I don't propose to evaluate the pill in terms of moral standards. I leave that to others to do—to others who are far more competent on either moralizing or demoralizing.

Instead I speak of the pill objectively—and at the risk of a pun—as an inescapable, even if suddenly new, fact of life.

Some of its consequences are bluntly clear—as clear as the "see-through" dresses and as revealing as the micro-mini skirts. Adam's rib simply isn't the sedate sanctum that it once was. Eve's pill has changed all that.

Yes, women are now in a new age—although I'm not so sure I would call it a Golden Age. For women are now in an age of unprecedented power in which they are more openly, more candidly, and more honestly pursuing rather than pretending to be pursued—in which they are more openly, candidly, and honestly pursuing whether it be for economic security, personal achievement, or men.

They are doing it with twin authoritative powers of economic security and biological security. My caution to those of my own sex is that with such authority goes serious responsibility and that such power should be very carefully exercised lest it ultimately be the self-destruction of woman and her rightful and responsible place in civilization rather than "man-kind."

The speech was received with chilly silence, a chill that persisted throughout the reception. Whether liked or not, Margaret Chase Smith was still making the fight for the dignity of women that she had started twenty-one years ago in getting them Regular status in the Armed Services. And now she was warning that the dignity of women was in jeopardy unless women continued to earn it, and unless they exercised their earned—and their unearned—power with great care and responsibility.

Answer to a Smear

MAY 21, 1948

Perhaps the most crucial political speech I have given was to the Somerset County Republican Women's Club in my home town on May 21, 1948. This was one month prior to the Republican Senatorial primary. It was the first time I ran for the Senate. My three opponents were (1) the sitting Governor, Horace Hildreth, (2) his immediate predecessor as governor, Sumner Sewall, and (3) a man named Albion Beverage. Hildreth and Sewall were undefeated top vote-getters. What Governor Hildreth didn't have in support from the regular Republican organization ex-Governor Sewall did. This left not very much for me. Mr. Beverage's claim to fame was that he had worked for Nebraska Senator Kenneth Wherry and Indiana Senator William Jenner, each of whom he gave credit for reciting his speeches on the Senate Floor under their own names.

About two months before the June primary, I received a copy of an anonymous printed sheet purporting to present a factual analysis of my voting record. The import was that I was pro-Communist, a traitor to the Republican Party, a tool of the CIO, and a political companion of Representative Vito Marcantonio. A member of the American Labor Party of New York, Marcantonio was considered to be a radical liberal and was charged by some as being pro-Communist. According to the sheet (see Appendix), an analysis of my vote on 242 measures revealed that 29.3 percent of my votes were in opposition to my own party and 44.2 percent of them with Representative Marcantonio.

The identity of the forces behind the sheet was never clearly established. The Chicago *Daily Tribune* of June 22, 1948, stated: "Governor Hildreth assailed her record as a New Dealer masquerading on the Republican ticket and said her voting record in the House was parallel in some respects to that of the Communist spokesman, Rep. Vito Marcantonio." The political editor-writer of the Portland (Maine) *Sunday Telegram* described the sheet as "presumably sent out from Hildreth's campaign headquarters."

In fairness to Governor Hildreth it should be pointed out that in private conversations he disclaimed any knowledge of the source of the sheet. There were those who wondered, however, why he did not issue a press release about it as he had done months earlier about a Drew Pearson column—or why he did not publicly denounce such tactics.

When I first read the sheet, I was disturbed because it purported to be a factual analysis. Such an image might have an appearance of authenticity, even though anonymous. I called Bill Lewis, former General Counsel of the House Naval Affairs Committee and my de facto campaign manager.

"Bill, this is very serious," I said. "People can be fooled about this. I want to refute and answer it as soon as possible before it can do too much damage. I'm not completely surprised by a smear but I am surprised that it would come so early in the campaign. This is much earlier than I had expected!"

Bill was less surprised. He had got wind of some indiscreet bragging by a pro-Hildreth and anti-Smith newspaper editor: Margaret Smith's record would be "exposed" with great publicity two weeks before election day. By the time that the thorough exposure was completed I was to be eliminated from any chance of winning the nomination and Hildreth would have the election cinched.

Bill said that he would have to study and analyze the sheet before preparing an answer. The next morning he carefully checked the Congressional Record for the debate and vote in the specific instances in which the smear charged that I had voted the Marcantonio line.

That afternoon he said, "Don't worry. A complete refutation can be done effectively." But I was impatient and said, "Let's get it out now so that I can stop this smear at the outset!"

Lewis demurred. "That's not the way to handle this. If you answer it now, the smear artists will simply jump to some other form. Let this simmer a little. Wait and see if these sheets are distributed in other places. In fact, the more they're distributed throughout the state, the better. I hope they *saturate* the state. Hold back and let them misinterpret your silence as confirmation that you can't, and dare not, try to answer their charges. Then let them get bolder, way out on the limb. Then saw it off at a time of your own choosing and place and manner."

"But that's very risky," I protested.

"Margaret, nothing is more effective than the truth. But timing is even more important in a political campaign. In this instance, you've got the truth and the facts—but you won't make the most of them if you do not select the best time to use them."

The days and weeks that followed seemed irritatingly long to me. I wanted to answer. Lewis had a large map of Maine mounted. Every time a new batch of sheets surfaced, he plotted the location. A color-topped pin went into the map every time a supporter of mine reported the sheet in an area.

In a relatively short time the map was thoroughly covered. I began to see that the counter strategy of silence might work. The people behind the sheet had taken the bait and the hook.

In fact, the degree of the confidence of the forces against me must have grown as others accepted the sheet as factual. The political writer of the Bangor *Daily News,* Lorin Arnold, for example, quoted the first page of the three-page anti-Smith sheet. Some people felt that it was unusual for a newspaper to quote from an anonymous statement. But this was what he wrote:

Looking again at Mrs. Smith's voting record in the seven sessions of the 76th, 77th, 78th, 79th and 80th Congresses, one observes that in the record vote on 242 measures she cast 71 votes, or 29.3 per cent, in opposition to the majority of her own Republican Party.

And now I quote from a printed statement based on the voting record of Mrs. Smith:

"Analysis of all votes cast indicates that Representative Smith gave her support, in opposition to her own party, to many important measures sponsored by the Democratic Administration, bearing on government operation and economy, consistently opposed machinery for Congressional investigation of un-Americanism . . ."

Lorin Arnold concluded his column by writing:

> There appears to be no good reason why Maine voters
> should not be reminded of the voting records of Mrs. Smith,
> Hale and Fellows, in view of the fact that all are candidates
> for national offices at the June 21 primary election.
> So there it is, folks!

Yes, there it was. Or wasn't. There were those who advised
me not to honor the smear sheet with the dignity of a reply.
They reasoned that by doing so I would only give greater
publicity to the accusations. They reasoned that a reply would
be falsely interpreted by the public as an admission of the
charges. (This was the same type of caution given to me
later, in 1952, before a libel action I initiated.)

The Lorin Arnold sally of "So there it is, folks!" was perhaps
an indication that my opponents felt I couldn't reply—that at
last they had me where they wanted me. Or they felt that
I wouldn't reply because in the past I had shown little disposition for unpleasant, petty bickering. Maybe they interpreted
this as lack of courage. It was such feelings that made them
sure that first, I would never announce for the Senate, or second,
that I would withdraw from the race before the filing deadline.
They should have known better.

On the other side, Bill Lewis, continuing the research in
minute detail, became convinced that my voting record was
even more Republican than he had at first believed. He concluded that the smear sheet couldn't have been more "tailor
made" for a devastating refutation. He urged me to reply but
to withhold a reply until I "saw the whites of their eyes."

I decided to make the first wholly political speech of my
campaign on May 21 at the anniversary meeting of the Somerset County Women's Republican Club, the only women's group
in the state that worked for me in addition to the Maine
Federation of Business and Professional Women.

The clincher on the decision to use this occasion for the refutation of the charges was a bit of fortunate intelligence from a friend inside the Bangor *Daily News*. This came before the Lorin Arnold adoption of the smear sheet appeared in the paper. We learned when it was to run. This was the final indication that the full impact of the sheet would be reached at that time.

I was somewhat troubled with the length of my reply as drafted. I felt it was too long to be able to sustain the interest of my audience. No converts are made after twenty minutes of speaking.

But Bill contended that any reply should be complete—so total that it would discredit the smears one hundred percent and leave no possible answer. He further stressed that while my reply was lengthy, it had plenty of punch to sustain audience interest. "After all," he argued, "it contains exactly what the listeners will enjoy. A home county audience will love to hear their daughter defend herself and rip into the smearers."

Further, he said, it would give impressive evidence that I was a fighter who could hold my own with the men—and indicate my ability to do the same thing in the Senate—and to fight cleanly and fairly. I decided to make the full reply.

"I was in business before I entered Congress," was the way I began. "And as a business woman, I respected the principle that real success cannot be gained by running down your competition. I have respected this principle in politics—and particularly in this campaign."

I refused to attack my opponents, I said, because I was campaigning on my record—not on any mistakes they might have made. But since my opponents had resorted to the distribution of anonymous printed lie sheets, I had decided to answer them lest silence on my part might be misinterpreted.

First I took up the one-page sheet. I have been told, I said, that a relative of one of the candidates is using this sheet to try to charge that I am a puppet of the CIO. This is easy to answer. I voted for the Taft-Hartley Bill and the CIO has called upon its members to make an all-out effort to defeat every

Congressman or Congresswoman who voted for the Taft-Hartley Bill. In addition to this, the CIO specially endorsed my opponent in 1944. What the distributors of the sheet failed to tell, I added, was that the latest CIO scoresheet on Congressional voting revealed I had voted against the CIO ten out of twelve times in 1947.

Then I took up the three-page smear-Smith paper and, charge by charge, vote by vote, showed how inaccurate and misrepresentative it was.* On the matter of the House Un-American Activities Committee, for example, I showed that out of twenty votes concerning the committee in my eight years in Congress, I voted to support, uphold, and continue the committee sixteen times. On each of those occasions Mr. Marcantonio, whom the smear writer charged I voted with nearly 50 percent of the time, voted the opposite way from me.

As for his summary, I wondered how he could select only 242 record votes when there had been more than 1500 such votes during the time I had been in Congress. But taking his 71 handpicked votes—"which I think we can assume is the maximum number of black marks that he has against me in view of the character of his attack on me"—taking those 71 would show that by his own standards, I failed to vote with my party only 4.7 percent of the time. I voted with my party 95.3 percent of the time. The 107 times he claimed I voted the same as Marcantonio would be only 7 percent of the time—and according to the votes picked by the smear writer even the Republican leaders occasionally voted the same as Mr. Marcantonio.

The smear sheet clearly attempted to portray me as a traitor to the Republican Party in more than a dozen votes which it identified by issue and date. It was very easy for me to answer this clumsy and stupid attempt by the simple technique of pointing out that one or more of the then Republican Leaders voted the same way that I did in each of these instances— Republican Leaders like Clare Boothe Luce, John Taber (Chairman of the House Appropriations Committee), Charles Eaton

* The speech appears in full in the Appendix.

(Chairman of the House Foreign Affairs Committee), W. G. Andrews (Chairman of the House Armed Services Committee), Richard J. Welch (top Republican on the House Labor Committee), the other Republican members of the Maine Congressional Delegation including the retiring Wallace White, Jr., the Senate Republican Majority Leader (for whose seat I was running), Joseph W. Martin, Jr. (Republican Speaker of the House of Representatives)—and best of all, B. Carroll Reece, then Chairman of the Republican National Committee.

If he had tried any harder, I concluded, this smear writer could not have picked better instances to show how the Republican Leaders voted the same way I did. It is no wonder that he was too ashamed and afraid to put his name on the smear sheet.

EDITOR'S NOTE:
Margaret Smith never regretted that she made her long and terrific response. Her opponents did. Just as they were about to catch up with her, "that woman" had pulled the unexpected and thrown them completely off balance. Her stinging reply actually was the equivalent of a battle cry for a crusade against professional politics. She emerged as the Joan of Arc leader.

People who up to that time had shown little interest in the campaign and who, in disgust, wanted no part of politics, rallied to the banners of this fighting woman. That smear and Margaret's reply had accomplished a feat unparalleled in Maine's political annals. Margaret had won the primary election a month before the actual voting. Her reply was so devastating that few, if any, Maine voters would have believed any subsequent anti-Smith charges.

"Margaret Smith's Answer" was a part of the organizational kit that went to the local, city, town, and plantation Smith-for-Senate committees the very next day on May 22. The distribution was keyed to her organized campaign effort and her reply to the smear was the battle cry of the crusade of her supporters for her and for clean politics.

Her campaign effort was timed and organized for two weeks of organizing after the May 21 speech and then after that for two weeks of a stretch drive to get the vote out for Margaret Smith and clean politics. As the Portland *Sunday Telegram* political writer subsequently said, small fires of organized support for Smith started lighting up all over the state from Fort Kent in the north on the Canadian border to Kittery in the south on the New Hampshire border.

And when the final vote had been cast on June 21, the totals were:

Smith	63,786
Hildreth	30,949
Sewall	21,768
Beverage	6,399

It is of political interest to note the "Marcantonio line" tactic of attack was first used against Margaret Chase Smith in the 1948 Republican Maine Primary and that there were indications that the so-called research was done by some person or persons on the staff of the Republican National Committee. When Margaret Smith learned that the same "Marcantonio line" tactic—the guilt-by-voting-association—was being used against Representative Estes Kefauver in his campaign for Democratic nomination for United States Senator from Tennessee, she sent him a copy of her refutation. When they were sworn into the Senate together on January 3, 1949, Kefauver went up to her and said, "God bless you, Margaret! I took your answer to the smear and fitted it to my own situation and it was one of the most effective things I did in getting elected."

Two years later, in getting him elected to the Senate from California, Murray Chotiner, the campaign manager for Richard M. Nixon, had him use the "Marcantonio line voting" against another Congresswoman, Helen Gahagan Douglas.

While Margaret Smith's hard-hitting answer to the smear broke the back of the opposition, the campaign story would not be complete without inclusion of her soft-spoken election eve radio speech. The emotion that it conveyed on that Sunday evening before the Monday election is evident even now:

Good Evening:

I look back on the 80th Congress just adjourned this morning at 6:45 with a great deal of satisfaction for during the past two years I have been able to introduce and cause the enactment of several important bills. I could not have done this without the six years of service in Congress prior to the last two years. Those years gave me the know-how and the contacts and the seniority advantages without which I would not have been able to get my measures through.

I shall never forget my service in the House of Representatives. I can sincerely say that it has been a real pleasure to serve the people of the second district—and I shall not forget my friends in the House who made it possible for me to accomplish what I have in the way of legislation because of their personal faith in me and what I proposed—I only hope that I shall be able to expand my service to the people and that my eight years of accumulated know-how, contact, and position in Washington may be continued to the future benefit of the entire State of Maine as your next United States Senator—with the help of divine guidance.

This is the eleventh hour in one of the liveliest and most interesting campaigns that Maine has ever had. You have been subjected to a last-minute barrage of campaign literature, newspaper advertising, and radio appeals.

But in my final address in the campaign I am going to report to the thousands of friends and supporters who have given so much of their time and effort for me. Friends and supporters that money can't buy.

I believe that the people of Maine have made up their minds as to how they are going to vote tomorrow and that last-minute appeals and charges cannot have any material effect upon them.

The only effect that these last-minute efforts can have is to spur the people on a little more to go to the polls to vote for whomever they have decided that they will support.

For instance, I have had several calls today from my supporters throughout the State reporting that desperate last-minute smear sheets have been intensely distributed against me today. This has not given me any concern because these smear sheets merely repeat the misrepresentations which I refuted in detail claim-by-claim weeks ago.

As a matter of fact, the sudden reappearance of these sheets at the last minute has given me even greater confidence that tomorrow will bring victory. I believe they will mean hundreds of more votes for me because, as they have incensed the fair-minded people of Maine before, they will rally many fair-minded people to go to the polls and register their repudiation of such methods by voting for me.

These sheets are actually inspiring my thousands of supporters to do even more than they already have—if that is humanly possible.

I can never express adequately my appreciation for the many, many fine things that you have done for me in this campaign. In fact, I shall probably never know what so many of you have done. This is the only regret that I have in the campaign—that I can't know how much all of you have done individually—and that I can't personally thank each and every one of you.

The only comfort I have in the physical impossibility of thanking each of you personally for what you have done for me personally is in the fact that the issue of the campaign for the Republican nomination for United States Senator has transcended personalities. The fundamental issue of this particular campaign has grown much larger than myself or my opponents— for the people of Maine have come to feel that there is much more at stake in this campaign than the individual candidates themselves.

The candidates for United States Senator are important only for what they symbolize. Each of us symbolizes something to the Maine voters. My supporters say that I am a symbol of a "grass roots" protest against political machines, money politics, and smears. They say that the issue is simple and clear—that the choice is one way or the other. And with respectful humility, I must say that they are right.

I would never attempt to deny ambition, for constructive ambition is something of which each and all of us can be proud.

But from the bottom of my heart, I say to you that I want to win tomorrow more for the sake of those things which people say that I symbolize—and for the sake of those who have put so much faith in me and who have worked so hard for me. Because the victory will not be a personal one for me— it will be a victory for them and their ideals. It will be a victory for the rank-and-file of the people of Maine. It will be a "grass roots" victory that springs from the people themselves rather than from professional politicians.

I want to win for that eighteen-year-old girl in Portland who sent me a one-dollar contribution and wrote, "I regret only two things: that this must be merely a token contribution to your senatorial campaign, and that I am not yet old enough to vote."

I want to win for that Worumbo Mill worker of Lisbon Falls who, in contributing two dollars to my campaign, reported that her job at the mill had been placed in jeopardy because she had the courage to openly support me.

I want to win for that Spanish War veteran of Norway who has contributed some of his life's earnings to my campaign and who has assured old people throughout the State that I am their real friend.

I want to win for that housewife of Bath whose integrity was openly challenged by a committeeman of one of my opponents merely because she was actively supporting my candidacy.

I want to win for that granger of York County whose position in the grange was threatened by higher grange officials merely because he was openly campaigning for me.

I want to win for that World War Two veteran of Bangor who refused the money of one of my opponents to switch to his side—and who fought to keep my banners up when professional politicians were trying to tear them down.

I want to win for that insuranceman in Hancock County who defied great pressure and continued to campaign for me.

I want to win for that Aroostook County woman farmer who courageously called the hand of those distributing the anonymous smear sheets.

I want to win for those State employees in Kennebec County who had the courage to support me despite the risk that it would cause to their jobs.

I want to win for those Court House workers in Knox County who had the courage to support me in defiance of the Sheriff's machine.

I want to win for those people in Washington County who have complete confidence that as Senator I will continue to fight for Quoddy—regardless of the obstacles that others might create.

I want to win for those loyal supporters of mine in Madison who refused the money of my opposition.

I want to win for that editor in Lincoln County who denounced the smear tactics of my opponent.

I want to win for that longshoreman in Waldo County who refused to submit to an order to fight my candidacy because I voted for the Taft-Hartley Act.

I want to win for that teacher in Franklin County who refused to withdraw her support of me even though her job was threatened.

I want to win for that small businessman in Piscataquis County who refused to let one of his large customers tell him how to vote.

Yes, I want to win for these typical independent Republicans and hundreds of other rank-and-file Republicans who have refused to sell their votes, who have courageously resisted political intimidation, who have denounced and fought smears— and who have put their hearts and souls into my campaign because they were convinced that I was their symbol of protest against such things.

Our campaign has been cleanly and fairly waged. We have much to be proud of for we have given the people of Maine the opportunity to show the rest of the nation that while we like lively campaigns, we prefer that they be fair and clean.

And that is one of the principal reasons why we are going to win tomorrow. I have received reports all day from all over the State that the people are rallying to our cause—that great numbers of the former opposition are shifting over to our side and jumping on our apparently victorious bandwagon.

The only thing that we have to fear now is overconfidence—that too many of our people may feel that we have won the campaign and that their vote is not needed. We must guard against this for we cannot underestimate the highly organized and highly paid professional machines of our highly financed opponents.

The issue tomorrow is clear. It is the rank-and-file against the paid professionals. What the voters of Maine do tomorrow will do much to either stop or perpetuate machine and money politics in Maine.

That is why it is so important to get out and vote.

Tomorrow is V-Day—it is Voting Day—it is Volunteer Day—and it will be Victory Day for us if the Smith-for-Senate Volunteer nonpaid workers outwork the paid professionals of the opposition and get the vote out—for the bigger the total vote the bigger our margin of victory.

I have been in campaigns for many years, but never have I seen the sincerity, loyalty, and enthusiasm that you my supporters have given in this campaign. So I know that you will understand and forgive me if I choke up a little when I say thank you from the bottom of my heart—believe me. I appreciate the magnificent job that you have done. But we must carry through on that magnificent job and not let up a bit until tomorrow night. God willing, we will win because we have given the people of Maine an inspiring cause to fight for.

Perhaps the best indication of the effectiveness of the election-eve speech came from Mrs. Mary Allen of Ellsworth, Maine. Mary, though a friend of Margaret Smith's, was an active campaign supporter and worker for Sumner Sewall. She later told the Senator, "As I listened to you over WGUY, I could just hear the ballots dropping in the ballot box for you. I knew it was all over—that you had won—and we had lost." Ever since that time Mary has been all-out for Senator Smith.

After the live broadcast, Mrs. Smith made a transcription of the speech so that it could be used early the next morning

on election day to reach rural areas. The "tomorrow" words of
the speech were changed to "today." Her delivery in the transcription was not nearly as good as her 10:49 P.M. live broadcast. But the transcription got some votes. Later on she was
told that one farmer, listening to the transcription, said that if
Margaret Smith wanted to be United States Senator badly
enough to get up as early as farmers did and give a speech that
early on election morning, then he sure would vote for her.
What he didn't know was that the transcription he heard was
being played while Margaret Smith was sound asleep.

An Article for Eisenhower

OCTOBER 1952

"... *nothing I shall say in this campaign will knowingly violate the sense of the 'generalizations' on which you have quoted me.*"

—General Dwight D. Eisenhower
August 25, 1952

Though my relations with Dwight D. Eisenhower were never warm, I repeatedly went to his defense and I granted every request he personally made of me including my vote for the Dixon-Yates contract, the only vote I ever cast that I later regretted.

I first saw him when I was a member of the House Armed Services Committee and he appeared before that committee as Chairman of the Joint Chiefs of Staff. Apparently I made no impression on him because every time we met thereafter, until he ran for President, he had to be introduced.

During the period of 1949–52 I praised Eisenhower in my syndicated column as a good prospect for President. Though I was to say more in his behalf, I never did commit myself to any candidacy prior to the nominations. On September 16, 1951, I made a statewide broadcast in Maine denouncing a scurrilous sheet against General Eisenhower. Put out by the Partisan Republicans of California and distributed through the mails by Maine's Republican State Chairman Ralph Masterman, a vigorous pro-Taft supporter, the smear sheet called Eisenhower pro-Communist and charged that there was a "New Deal-Communist" plot headed up by Senators Margaret Chase Smith, James Duff, and Wayne Morse to get Eisenhower the 1952 Republican Presidential nomination.

Senator Robert A. Taft also disavowed the smear pamphlet a month later when he announced his Presidential candidacy. Sometime thereafter he sought to get my endorsement but I refused because Taft had gone into Wisconsin and praised McCarthy and all of McCarthy's actions. In addition, the woman in charge of the Taft campaign in Maine was talking against me, calling for my defeat three years hence.

On the eve of the voting for delegates at the Maine Republican State Convention I gave a speech in Orono, Maine, in which I stated that there seemed to be a trend setting in for General Eisenhower and pointed out that Senator Taft had aligned himself with Senator Joseph McCarthy. Though I did not consider the speech a personal commitment, it was interpreted by many as a plea for delegates to support Eisenhower and I was blamed by the Taft forces in Washington for swinging Maine's convention away from Taft to Eisenhower.

I did not attend the national convention because my mother was near death and I stayed with her at the hospital in Waterville, Maine. My absence from the convention did not keep my name out of it, however. Earlier in the year the National Federation of Business and Professional Women had started a drive for Sarah Hughes (later a Federal Judge) for the Democratic Vice Presidential nomination and for me for the Republican Vice Presidential nomination. By the time of our convention the BPW drive for delegates pledged to me had snowballed to a total of 250.

The convention had barely nominated Eisenhower when Bill Lewis got a phone call from Isabella Jones of the Pennsylvania delegation. The BPW women had been notified, she said, that General Eisenhower and Governor Dewey had sent word to the delegates that under no circumstances should my name be placed in nomination for Vice President. The word was that they feared I had enough votes to prevent Senator Nixon— Eisenhower's choice—from getting the nomination on the first ballot. If Nixon didn't get it, there would be a free-for-all and the party simply could not stand another nomination fight.

Next we heard that the Taft forces were so disappointed and bitter over their defeat they were going to support me for Vice President and, with the women, could swing the convention to me. It was also reported that Harold Stassen had threatened to have his name put in if mine was. The end result was that my name was not only not put in nomination but the convention was told—quite erroneously—that my name was withheld at my request.

The Nixon-Smith rivalry was to surface again after the convention during the crisis created by the revelation of the Nixon "slush fund." It was reported in the press that Ike had gone into secluded conference with his campaign advisers to decide whether to drop Nixon from the ticket. For some days his decision was withheld. Reports and rumors that Ike had selected me to replace Nixon on the ticket were so widespread that the press sent queries. My answer was that if the reports were true their veracity was being kept secret from me. The credibility of the reports became academic after Nixon's politically effective "Checkers" telecast and Ike's warm acceptance of it. Nixon, he said, was as "clean as a hound's tooth."

As the campaign began to take shape, an impression grew that Eisenhower had turned his back on the more moderate and liberal elements of the Republican Party who had delivered the nomination to him. It was claimed that he had chosen Nixon as his running mate because of his similarity in views to Senator Joseph McCarthy and that Eisenhower had politically embraced McCarthy and Indiana's militant anti-Communist Senator Jenner in the campaign.

On August 6, 1952, Sherman Adams called and said I was needed out at the Headquarters in Denver in the worst way. The general impression was being created, he said, that General Eisenhower was associating himself with the wrong crowd and that the Old Guard had taken over.

I agreed to make an appearance at the Denver Headquarters but stated that it would be rather difficult for me to come so far right then because of my mother's condition. She was in a coma and could die at any time. I also expressed some hesitancy because of Eisenhower's own actions on McCarthy and because the new Executive Director of the Republican National Committee was a strong McCarthyite from Wisconsin.

Adams' reply was that I was the top elected woman in the country and General Eisenhower wanted to give his headquarters more of my flavor and to be associated in the public's mind with my kind. He said that the General wanted to sit down and talk issues and strategy. I asked when they were coming east and he said around August 24. I said I hoped to see them at that time.

A week later, on August 13, 1952, a telegram arrived from William Peters, Articles Editor of the *Woman's Home Com-*

panion, asking me to write fifteen hundred words on "Why Vote for Eisenhower" and to state where General Eisenhower stood on fourteen spelled-out issues. My article was to run in the November issue, which reached readers on October 24 just eleven days before the election, along with a similar article entitled "Why Vote for Stevenson." He needed the answer right away and had to have the article by August 25 at the latest. I wired back immediately that I could not possibly comply in time for his deadline.

On the same day I also received a telegram from Eisenhower inviting me to a luncheon in Denver, Colorado, on August 19. I regretted because of the condition of my mother.

The next day, August 14, General Eisenhower telephoned. He asked me to reconsider my decision on the *Woman's Home Companion* article. I said that I felt I did not know enough of exactly how he stood on the issues on which the article was to be based.

He assured me that he had taken a definite stand on most of them and promised that if I would reconsider and agree to write the article, he would see to it that I received full material and information on his stand on the issues. Shortly thereafter, Arthur Vandenburg, Jr., called from Colorado to say that he would have the material sent. It soon arrived.

I wrote the article and sent it to William Peters at the *Woman's Home Companion* two days before the deadline. In my letter of transmittal I said:

Frankly, I am not too happy with it because in studying the quotes of General Eisenhower that were submitted to me, I find a surprising lack of definitiveness in the General's expression on vital issues . . . What disturbs me most about the article is that while the generalities of the Eisenhower statements are understandable at this stage of the campaign, in the coming weeks I am sure that General Eisenhower will make his position on the issues more definitive. In that process, it is altogether possible that he may take positions that are in con-

tradiction with the interpretations that I make of his quoted
statements in the article.

Thus, there is a very definite risk in writing this article
from the standpoint of timing and the standpoint of the generalities of the Eisenhower quotes. It is to be borne in mind
that the article is written more than two months in advance
of its scheduled publication and, more important, the two months
of campaigning in which General Eisenhower will make many,
many speeches—speeches that will be far more definite in expression than his statements thus far and the statements with
which I had to work. That, in itself, is going to antiquate, if
not make inaccurate and inconsistent, the article.

I closed saying that I was sending a copy of the letter to
General Eisenhower as well as a copy of the article which I
had written as a personal effort to help his candidacy for the
Presidency.

On August 25, 1952, General Eisenhower wrote saying that
he had trouble finding reasons for my doubts and hesitancies.
"At least I can promise you," he said, "that nothing I shall
say in this campaign will knowingly violate the sense of the
'generalizations' on which you have quoted me." He called the
article "splendid" and said he was "deeply grateful." "I hope,"
he added, "you and the magazine will give us permission to
have reprints made for very wide circulation throughout the
country during the campaign."

Because there turned out to be a vast difference between
what finally appeared in the November issue of *Woman's Home
Companion* and what I submitted, my text is given here in its
entirety:

Why Women Want Eisenhower

If it is not the most important of all elections in our history,
the 1952 presidential election is certainly one of the most
important to women. In this election American women are

literally at the political crossroads of the destiny of our country. They are standing at the crossroads to decide whether to continue what they have had in Government for twenty years or to make a change. What they decide will control the final result at the polls. For never before have women possessed such potential political power in an election. They hold in their hands the power of a clear-cut majority of the electorate.

I am a Republican but I am an American first. And it is as an American that I earnestly hope the women vote for Dwight D. Eisenhower for President. He is a Republican but he is an American first and he will bring to our people that which the women are demanding—a clean house in Government, kept clean by objective Americanism instead of being soiled by partisan politics and political expediency.

I think the women of America should be—and overwhelmingly are—for Dwight D. Eisenhower because more than any other living American he possesses the ability to bring real peace to our nation and to our homes. He is our best hope to bring our men—our sons, our husbands, our brothers, our sweethearts—back home from foreign battlefields. No other living American has the confidence and respect of the other nations of the world as does Dwight D. Eisenhower. No other living American can lead not only our nation but the other nations of the world as well to permanent peace like Dwight D. Eisenhower.

There, in essence, is the whole story of why the women of America should choose Eisenhower for our next President—to bring peace back to our homes and families and to clean up "the mess" in Washington.

Authority for the fact that there is a "mess" in Washington comes from no less than Adlai E. Stevenson, the Democratic nominee for President. Noted for his meticulous selection and use of words, Governor Stevenson has shown admirable accuracy in the adoption of the words "the mess" in the characterization of conditions in Washington that he made in a letter to an Oregon publisher. While differences of opinion do exist between Governor Stevenson, General Eisenhower, and myself on some issues, we are all very much in agreement on the need to clean up "the mess" in Washington. Back on June 30, 1951, I addressed the Young Republicans National Convention in Boston and said, "To win, the Republican Party must have an issue that will stand up and not fall with time and events. There is such an issue. That issue is the moral decay, corruption, and tragic mediocrity of the Democratic Administration. It can be summed up in two words, 'THE MESS.'"

Governor Stevenson says that he can clean up "the mess." I don't think he can and I am sure that the great majority of thinking women realize that he can't. I think they realize this because as housewives they know that they would rather have a completely new broom to sweep clean than merely to have a new handle to the old broom. Governor Stevenson would be nothing more than a new handle to the old Truman broom and he would inherit the dirt swept under the carpet by the present Democratic Administration and the Democrats who swept that dirt under the carpet. In contrast, General Eisenhower would be a completely new broom that would really sweep clean and make the thorough housecleaning in Washington that the women of America want and are entitled to for their sake, for the sake of the children and their families.

You have come to expect frankness from me and I would not be honest with you if I gave the impression that I agree with General Eisenhower on every single issue. I don't suppose that any of us agree 100 percent of the time on all matters with anyone—even our husbands, sons, daughters, fathers, mothers, sweethearts, friends, bosses. But from what I know of Dwight D. Eisenhower's expressed views and his record of getting things done, there are many issues we agree on and very few we disagree on. With deep conviction, I feel that the Eisenhower views are the views that women will approve. Here are some excerpts.

Taxes

". . . long continued taxes that are only a little below the confiscatory level will destroy free government . . . our entire arms program must be under constant scrutiny that not one dollar be spent without full value received. Armament, of its

nature, is sterile; heedless expense is investment in bankruptcy."
[Speech, June 4, 1952, Abilene, Kansas]

My agreement with him on this point of taxes and economy
is shown in my voting record for which the Council of State
Chambers of Commerce has designated me a Champion of
Economy in the Senate. General Eisenhower unhesitatingly recognizes the abnormally high expenditures that defense against
communism makes inevitable. But he says that very condition
makes it all the more imperative that we should get the most
out of every defense dollar spent.

Price and Rent Controls

"I would be in favor of eliminating every single artificial
control unless there is such an obvious necessity that you might
say an overwhelming mass of our population would say, 'Yes,
we need that . . . [I have] much more faith in the interplay
of economic factors than in bureaucratic controls." [Remarks
to Louisiana Republican Delegation, June 24, 1952]

Necessity for controls must be proved before their adoption.
I have supported rent and price control legislation as their
necessity has been proved to my satisfaction. I believe that
housewives working on close household budgets overwhelmingly
support these economic controls during the emergency and will
gladly approve their termination with the end of the emergency.
They have said very clearly, "Yes, we need that." They said
it back in the summer of 1950 after Korea sent prices spiraling.
Congress heard them and heeded their call. But President Truman turned a deaf ear to them. Dwight Eisenhower would
not be deaf to their call.

Taft-Hartley Act

". . . When you say 'Taft-Hartley Act' you are talking about
an omnibus bill with many things. I honestly believe, and all of
us know, that we cannot take legislation that can compel people
to work. That is regimentation. We have got to find a way, a
means, of respecting the advances that labor has made, that
union labor has made." [Press Conference, Abilene, Kansas,
June 5, 1952]

"More benefit for America is to be found in an ounce of real leadership and honest speech than a ton of law that fails to reflect the considered will of the vast majority." [Speech, Abilene, Kansas, June 24, 1952]

These statements show to me that General Eisenhower is fundamentally interested in avoiding the "cornering" of inordinate power by any special group, whether it be management or labor, to the detriment of the public—and that he will oppose attempts to force involuntary labor. I agree with him and that is why I voted for the Taft-Hartley bill and why I have supported certain proposed revisions of the Taft-Hartley Act.

Civil Rights

"I do not believe that we can cure all of the evils in men's hearts by law. When you get to compulsory action in certain specific phases of this thing, I really believe we can do more by leadership and getting states to do it than to make it a federal, compulsory thing . . . so far as my own personal influence can extend in this country, I shall never cease to fight for it . . ." [Press Conference, Abilene, Kansas, June 5, 1952]

"There are other parts, more delicate parts, of this great problem that are going to be solved only through increased education . . . we must be careful . . . never to use a coercive law when we might aggravate instead of help to advance the program of pure equality of opportunity in this country." [Speech, Detroit, Michigan, June 14, 1952]

Thus, General Eisenhower has stated that he favors compulsory FEPC as far as Federal employment is concerned but that he is opposed to forcing a compulsory FEPC upon the states. He feels that as far as the states are concerned there should be a voluntary FEPC and that the problem must be approached through the process of education and voluntary acceptance and not through coercive laws imposed upon the states by the Federal Government.

I am in full agreement with General Eisenhower on this issue as I favor a voluntary FEPC and I believe that the change must come by orderly and gradual evolution rather than by abortive revolution.

Health Legislation

General Eisenhower and I have more than one thing in common on this issue. Both he and I have erroneously been accused of being for socialized medicine when we both have stated our opposition to socialized medicine clearly, vigorously, and repeatedly.

". . . I do believe that every American has a right to decent medical care . . . I helped to organize and supported an organization of private citizens insisting that we must, in these private universities, support medical education by private means, because if we didn't, I believe it is the first step toward the socialization of medicine and I am against socialization!" [Press Conference, Abilene, Kansas, June 5, 1952]

Korea

". . . if we had been less trusting, if we had been less soft and weak there might easily have been no war in Korea." [Speech, Denver, Colorado, June 26, 1952] "If we hadn't allowed ourselves to grow so weak, in my opinion there would never have been a Korean War, with American lads dying." [Remarks, Chicago, Illinois, July 8, 1952]

"We went in there [Korea], as I see it, to support a principle . . . we have got to stand firm and to take every possible step we can to reduce our losses and to stand right there and try to get a decent armistice out of them." [Press Conference, Abilene, Kansas, June 5, 1952]

General Eisenhower makes three points on Korea. The first is that by our acts of weakness we literally invited the invasion of South Korea by the Communists. The second is that our defense of South Korea after it had been invaded is wise and justified opposition to the spread of communism. The third is that our position is not strong enough in Korea to risk expanding that localized war into a third world war by an all-out attack on the Red Chinese.

I agree with him on all of these points. The only possible point of disagreement is that I favor bombing the Manchurian

military installations and supply lines from which troops and
munitions pour into Korea to kill our own boys.

Foreign Policy

"The Communist threat against the free world creates a need
for political and military arrangements that will preserve the
safety of all and assure the continuance of vital commerce . . .
Those who assert that America can retire within its own borders;
those who seem to think we have little or no stake in the
rest of the world and what happens to it, those who act as
though we had no need for friends to share in the defense
of freedom—such persons are ignorant or irresponsible or they
are taking an unjustified gamble with peace. They are no
friends of America's security. They are living in years long
past. Theirs is not the counsel of enlightened self-interest. It
is the counsel of eventual self-destruction. And the American
people have shown time and again that they will not support
this stupid and myopic doctrine." [Speech, Denver, Colorado,
June 23, 1952]

That is clear and direct language. It expresses my own
views and the reasons why I voted for the United Nations,
the Marshall Plan, the North Atlantic Treaty and its implementation.

Communism at Home and Abroad

". . . I am not going to indulge in any kind of personalities
. . . no one could be more determined than I that any kind
of communistic, subversive, or pinkish influence be uprooted
from responsible places in our government. Make no mistake
about it! On the other hand, I believe that can be done with
the use, under competent leadership, of the kind of facilities
and agencies we have now, and I believe it can be done
without besmirching the reputations of any innocent man, or
condemning by loose association or anything else." [Press Conference, Abilene, Kansas, June 5, 1952]

I said the same thing in my Declaration of Conscience speech
in the United States Senate on June 1, 1950, in which I

condemned the Democratic Administration for its complacency to the threat of communism here at home and the leak of vital secrets to Russia through key officials of the Democratic Administration—and in which I condemned tactics of smear and character assassination. Like General Eisenhower, I dealt in principles and not in personalities.

United Nations

"The United Nations in my opinion has not been as effective as I should like, but has been a great agency for the exchange of ideas . . . I cannot tell you how much I would want to support and make stronger and win people to a greater belief in the United Nations in the practice of principles it lays down." [Press Conference, Dallas, Texas, June 22, 1952]

". . . there must be no wavering in our support for the United Nations. Some regard the United Nations exclusively in terms of its shortcomings; others would reduce our support for it to a reluctant minimum. True, the United Nations, in seven years of life, has fallen short of its peace objectives. But the whole world has fallen short—and for reasons which are plain to all of us. Should we, then, surrender our objective? Of course not. Peace is our objective. The United Nations is an instrument of peace. Our aim must be to make it continually more vital and effective." [Radio Address, Colorado, June 23, 1952]

We see eye-to-eye on the United Nations, which I have consistently supported, in which I have found some disappointment, but which I believe to still be our best hope for permanent peace.

Foreign Aid

". . . At a time of such heavy costs as the United States is incurring it is more essential than ever that each dollar be made to count to the maximum. It is my understanding that our Mutual Security Program was adopted because of a conviction that there is no acceptable alternative. The development of collective security through cooperation is obviously more efficient 'and less costly than for any one country to attempt to achieve it alone.' " [Letter to Chairman, Senate Foreign Relations Committee, May 8, 1952]

I agree with these two points of General Eisenhower on foreign aid—(1) that its basis is the strength of collective security and (2) that each foreign aid dollar must be scrutinized very carefully. That's why I have consistently voted for foreign aid but have supported economy amendments that I felt would avoid waste in foreign aid and sheer "handouts" instead of businesslike aid.

Defense

". . . we must be strong! I look forward to the day when, from a position of unassailable decency, we will be able to present to the masters of the Kremlin a just and practical plan for freeing the world from the burden of armaments. If we are strong, they will probably see in such a proposal their own self-interest and will feel obliged to accept, even if grudgingly and slowly, a plan for peace and disarmament. We can speed that day only if we are strong. The language of strength is the only language which the men in the Kremlin understand. We must have unshakable spiritual strength. Let us constantly proclaim to all peoples our belief in God and our devotion to the ideals and causes that spring from such belief . . . That community of belief, of aspiration, and of striving is, I deeply believe, our strongest bulwark and our best defense." [Radio Address, Denver, Colorado, June 23, 1952]

By acts, as distinguished from words, General Eisenhower has made his position on defense crystal clear. By voting for every defense measure presented to Congress during my twelve years in the House and Senate, I have made my position the same as General Eisenhower's position.

But the more important thing to me—and I think to women generally—is the emphasis that General Eisenhower puts on spiritual strength. It places it before military strength in importance on defense—just as I have constantly stated it should be placed.

Women in Government

"... I have had only one criterion: Where is the ability? Where can I get the brains and hearts and devotion to this job? If I find it, under the circumstances you have described, in a woman, she will have the job right now . . ." [Commodore Press Conference, June 7, 1952]

This is a wise and truthful answer. I am not impressed by campaign statements of candidates that they will put at least one or two women in the Cabinet if elected. Neither men nor women have any specific claim to any certain number of posts in the Cabinet. As I have always said, appointments should be made on the basis of ability and qualifications and not sex.

EDITOR'S NOTE:

Although Senator Smith had stated very clearly to the Articles Editor that she understood the final edition of the article would not be published until she saw and approved it, the Articles Editor refused to extend that privilege once she had submitted the text. Not until the day the magazine appeared on the newsstands did she know that her entire paragraph on the subject of communism—including the reference to her Declaration of Conscience speech—had been deleted.

On that same day Democratic Presidential nominee Adlai Stevenson said in a speech at the Cleveland Arena:

In 1950 a group of Republican Senators, headed by Senator Margaret Chase Smith of Maine, issued a Declaration of Conscience denouncing the tactics of smear and slander. The General might have endorsed that Declaration of Conscience. He might have made it the testament of a real crusade. He might have surrounded himself with those who issued this statement or others of his party like them—and there are many

Republicans who have a high regard for the ethics and the function of the two-party system. Instead, by ignorance or choice, he has turned not to them but to the Republican Senator who called Senator Smith a thief and defender of Communists.

The prolonged illness of her mother kept Senator Smith tied down in Maine and unable to lend her liberal Republican image to the Eisenhower candidacy. But even if Mrs. Chase had not been gravely ill and Margaret thus free to campaign throughout the Nation, she still would have been reluctant to do so. This was simply because Joe McCarthy stood between her and Eisenhower, and the people running the Eisenhower campaign showed no disposition to tangle with McCarthy. The nearest they came to doing so was on October 27, 1952. In the afternoon Sherman Adams left word at the Senator's office that he was in Pittsburgh where General Eisenhower would speak that evening, and that he wanted to get certain excerpts from the Declaration of Conscience before the speech and would call me in the early evening at my residence.

The Eisenhower campaign managers were nervous about a nationwide telecast that Joe McCarthy was scheduled to make that night from Chicago. At 7:25 P.M., Adams called me stating that while they had been informed that McCarthy would not deliver the earlier predicted tirade in his TV speech he would nevertheless be making a series of accusations based on hearsay.

He then asked me to read what I considered to be the pertinent excerpts of the Declaration of Conscience. I read eleven paragraphs to Adams' secretary who took them down. Adams said that General Eisenhower wanted to have them in case he found it necessary for him to repudiate McCarthy; he thought the best way he could do so would be to quote the Declaration of Conscience and say that he stood foursquare behind it. This call undoubtedly was prompted by reports that Eisenhower was losing support of liberals and women because of his expressed support for McCarthy.

The Eisenhower forces wanted Margaret badly in those clos-ing days and hours of the campaign. On November 2 at 6:30 P.M., Fred Seaton called from New York asking her to meet General Eisenhower and his party in Boston on the following Monday and to appear on a national telecast from 10 to 10:30 P.M.

Seaton said they would like to have her ask questions and that she could ask about General Eisenhower's position with respect to her Declaration of Conscience, at which time he would say that he agreed with it. Seaton said that they were taking motion picture actress Irene Dunne off the panel be-cause she was considered too theatrical. (We heard other reports that she was so strongly pro-McCarthy they thought it better not to have her on the panel.)

Margaret replied that she would think it over and would call back that evening. She did, at ten o'clock, and agreed to go to Boston as suggested. It was stipulated that she would ask Eisenhower his position on the views she had set forth in her Declaration of Conscience and he would answer that he agreed with the Declaration of Conscience.

The next afternoon at two o'clock, Margaret called Seaton and told him that her mother was in her last hours and that the doctor had advised her to stay in Skowhegan. Seaton ex-pressed his sympathy and later General Eisenhower wired Sena-tor Smith: "I shall miss you this evening very much. I am sincerely sorry that we could not have been more neighborly, but perhaps we shall soon find an opportunity to talk things over. Mamie joins me in sending our sympathy."

Mrs. Chase died at eight forty-five that evening, an hour and a quarter before the ten o'clock telecast. General Eisenhower paid quite a tribute to Senator Smith on the telecast. It looked then as though the Joe McCarthy barrier between Dwight David Eisenhower and Margaret Chase Smith had been removed.

A month later, on December 8, 1952, in going to bat for Senator Taft, Senator Smith criticized President-elect Eisenhower in her nationally syndicated column. Eisenhower had announced his selection of Democrat Martin P. Durkin, who had supported Adlai Stevenson against Eisenhower, to be Secretary of Labor. Taft protested and Margaret Smith publicly supported Taft. She wrote:

> The strength of Robert A. Taft in the Senate does not bear defiance by Ike. It was generally understood within Republican circles that Ike would leave labor policies pretty much to Taft— at least that Ike would not flaunt him by such acts as the appointment of a man who had advocated repeal of the Taft-Hartley Act. Durkin himself did not help the situation by his announcement immediately after his selection that he would arrange a meeting between Senator Taft and labor leaders. He failed to consult Senator Taft before the statement about whether he would be available for such a meeting.

A very significant fact about this appointment was that Taft was the top-ranking Republican of the Senate Labor Committee before whom Durkin's appointment would come for confirmation or rejection action.

When Senator Taft called to thank Senator Smith he learned that she was in Florida visiting Representative Frances P. Bolton at her Palm Beach home. He asked me to come to his office. When I got there he warmly shook my hand. He said he would never forget what Margaret Smith had done for him. "She stood by me when others forsook me like rats leaving a sinking ship."

Senator Taft said that prior to her column there was an incipient, and apparently growing, move to drop him and elect an Eisenhower Senator as the Senate Majority Leader. He said that he had had her column photocopied and sent a copy to every Republican Senator and Senator-elect to bolster his standing. "She picked me up at my lowest point and gave courage to those who were too timid to come forward and support me. After she came forward, the forces began to rally around. I also appreciate what you have done, Bill, because I know it would not have been possible without you."

Shortly before his death in the following year and not long after he and Margaret Smith had teamed together on the Senate Floor to ensure the passage of the Reorganization Bill that Eisenhower had requested (Taft's last legislative activity), Taft wrote Margaret Smith: "I want you to know how much pleasure our association has given me during this session and that I look forward with great pleasure to serving with you for many years, I hope."

Although the old McCarthy barrier between the President and the Senator seemed to have disappeared, certain members of the White House staff were not to let it go. In 1954 Joe McCarthy personally selected Robert L. Jones to run against the Senator in the Republican Primary and arranged for Jones to receive Texas oil financing.

Shortly before the 1954 primary in June, Presidential Assistant Earle Chesney dropped by Senator Smith's office to ask how the campaign was going. I said that it was going well and Chesney said that they wanted to do everything they could at the White House to help.

That was rather difficult to believe, I observed, in view of an item in that morning's newspaper which had clearly revealed the White House attitude and policy on Margaret Chase Smith. The item had reported that the newly appointed Nebraska Senator, Eva Bowring, had been a White House dinner guest the previous evening. Mrs. Bowring had been appointed to the Senate only a few weeks before and though, as I pointed out, Senator Smith had granted every wish that Eisenhower had personally asked of her, she had never yet been invited to dine with President Eisenhower. Even President Truman had invited Senator Smith to dinner at the White House.

Chesney expressed regret and said I had more or less pushed his back to the wall; he had to make an admission which he hated to make. He said that he had pointed this very thing out to people in the White House but that those who were favorable

to Senator McCarthy—a group he identified as being led by
Jerry Persons, Gerry Morgan, and Jack Martin—seemed to be
in control and they had advised the President to avoid any
association with Margaret Chase Smith for fear it might offend
Joe McCarthy.

At the polls on June 21, 1954, Margaret defeated the
McCarthy-sponsored candidate by a better than 5 to 1 margin
and set a new record for a total primary vote. Now one could
ask: if a mere woman could beat Joe by 5 to 1 who need
fear Joe's purging anyone from the Senate? The Senator
received this letter on the next day from President Eisenhower:

> It is with deep gratification I read in the papers this morn-
> ing of your overwhelming victory in the Primary in Maine
> yesterday. As I think you know, I have long admired your
> conscientious approach to public service, your outstanding and
> effective record in the Congress, and your high standards of
> integrity and fair play. It is no surprise that the Republicans
> in Maine are so strongly in support of these qualifications. I
> join with them in saluting the able and charming Senior Senator
> from the State of Maine.

The grip of fear on the Senate had not only loosened, but
the White House silence had been lifted.

Just a month after that primary, Senator Smith, on July 21,
1954, cast the only vote in her entire Congressional service
that she later regretted and would change if given another
chance. It was on the Dixon-Yates contract with the Atomic
Energy Commission and was related to the Tennessee Valley
Authority.

The protagonists on this issue were Senator Clinton Anderson of New Mexico, later Chairman in 1955 of the Joint
Committee on Atomic Energy, and Admiral Lewis Strauss,
Chairman of the Atomic Energy Commission. Six years later
they were again to be principal protagonists when Eisenhower

nominated Strauss to be Secretary of Commerce—and Senator Smith was to play a decisive role with her vote.

Anderson contended that the Dixon-Yates contract was not to supply the power needs of the Atomic Energy Commission at Paducah, Kentucky, and Oak Ridge, Tennessee, but rather to replace the TVA from which the Atomic Energy Commission was then buying power. The Dixon-Yates contract proposal was a favorite of Admiral Strauss and boiled down to a fight between public and private power.

Senator Smith has never been wedded completely to either public power or private power. She has favored whichever could provide the best and lowest service to the public in each individual instance. In this instance, her heart and head—and her woman's intuition—were against the Dixon-Yates contract.

But President Eisenhower called her from Camp David and asked her as a personal favor to him to vote for it and against the Anderson Amendment that proposed to kill it. Against her better judgment, she voted with Eisenhower and Strauss. Only two Republicans voted for the Anderson Amendment and contrary to the wishes of Eisenhower and Strauss. They were Kentucky Senator John Cooper and North Dakota Senator William Langer.

Neither Eisenhower nor Strauss seemed to resent Cooper's and Langer's voting against them. Yet they were furious six years later when Langer and Margaret Smith were the only two Republicans to vote against Eisenhower's nomination of Strauss for Secretary of Commerce. This time the President did not call her, nor did anyone else at the White House. Except for Strauss and Anderson, who actively sought her vote, the only other person who ever mentioned the nominaton was Massachusetts Senator Leverett Saltonstall. In passing by her on the Senate Floor one day, he said briefly, "You're all right on the Strauss nomination, aren't you?" She replied just as briefly, "It depends upon what one considers to be 'all right.'"

The final irony of the pro-Dixon-Yates vote that Margaret Smith wishes she had never cast occurred less than a year later. By then the Dixon-Yates contract had fallen into such disrepute that on July 11, 1955, President Eisenhower canceled it. Five years later, on January 9, 1961, the Supreme Court repudiated the contract.

In the years that followed, the Eisenhower-Smith relations varied from warm to cool, from his 1955 visit to her home in Skowhegan for a combination steak-cookout and lobster-clambake and her defense of him the Sunday prior to the 1956 election in TV debate with Mrs. Roosevelt to his resentment over her vote against the confirmation of Lewis Strauss for Secretary of Commerce and her success in getting the Senate to override his veto of her Kittery Navy Yard Pay Equalization Bill—the first time that either the Senate or House overrode an Eisenhower veto.

In 1956, according to a *Christian Science Monitor* article by Joseph Harsh, Eisenhower informed Republican National Chairman Len Hall that Margaret Smith was one of five candidates acceptable to him as a Vice Presidential running mate. But by 1960 the weather had changed. It is routine and customary for Presidents to have their pictures taken with Congressmen and Senators of their own political party for use in re-election campaigns. Margaret Smith has never had pictures taken for such purposes and has avoided endorsements by people outside of Maine. In the late spring of 1960, Senator Everett Dirksen went to Senator Smith on the Senate Floor one day and told her that he had talked with President Eisenhower about arrangements for Republican Senators to have their pictures taken with the President. He said, "Margaret, I hate to tell you this but Ike said that he would be happy to have his picture taken with every Republican Senator but that Smith woman!"

Margaret replied, "Don't worry, Ev. I'm not offended and I don't blame him for being mad at me on the Strauss vote nor for the first override of his veto. As you know, I have never asked that my picture be taken with him."

Shortly before the photographic eclipse, Senator Smith had defended President Eisenhower against an attack by Senator

Muskie. On May 23, 1960, Senator Muskie rose in the Senate to offer what he called "documentation from the Maine grass roots" and read into the Congressional Record excerpts of three letters from Maine. These letters charged that President Eisenhower "disgraced the United States," urged Americans to "start electing Presidents who are young enough to keep their wits until they finish their terms," and questioned whether "the President, with his apparent distaste for work, has left too much control to undesirable underlings."

Senator Smith took the Senate Floor to disassociate herself from what she considered slurs against President Eisenhower and stated that the letters quoted by Senator Muskie were not representative "grass roots" thinking of the people of Maine. Senator Muskie had not only represented these expressions as "Maine grass roots" thinking, but had implied that they were from restrained people not inclined to write inflammatory letters.

Margaret knew these letters were not from either typical Maine citizens or typically restrained Maine people. She knew because the first two of the three letters Senator Muskie placed in the Record were identical with two she had received. One was from a man who lived in Maine only during the summer months and spent most of each year in France. Over the years he had written many highly emotional, anti-Republican letters to Senator Smith.

The second was from a woman who at the time of her letter had lived in Maine only a very short time, having moved there from South America where she had lived for years. Subsequent inquiry made in the town where this woman lived disclosed that not long after she wrote the derogatory letter, less than two years from the time of her arrival, she left Maine. Long-time residents and natives of the town described her as a highly emotional, unorthodox person—anything but a typically restrained Maine person.

If President Eisenhower was ever aware that Margaret Smith had defended him against such a range of adversaries, from Edmund Muskie to Eleanor Roosevelt to the Republican State Chairman of Maine, he never gave any indication of it. The

Eisenhower-Smith relationship nevertheless ended on friendly terms. In the fall of 1968, General Eisenhower and Senator Smith were fellow patients in the V.I.P. ward of the Walter Reed Army Hospital in Washington. She was recovering from her first hip surgery, performed a month before at Columbia-Presbyterian Hospital in New York. He was in the midst of heart weakness that led to his death there.

The nurses relayed messages between their two prominent patients. Mrs. Eisenhower, who was staying in the ward, frequently visited in the evening with Senator Smith, and Margaret found those visits delightful. Presidential Candidate Richard Nixon paid an hour's visit after one of his sessions with General Eisenhower. Vice Presidential Candidate Agnew did not stop at all when he visited General Eisenhower just two days before going to Maine to speak in the campaign.

When one of the nurses informed Senator Smith that there was going to be a small celebration in the Eisenhower suite on his seventy-eighth birthday on October 14, she told me to get some golf balls, and to get the very best. She sent him three of the new-type solid rubber balls. She selected the golf balls for the psychological effect she thought they might have. It was her expression of confidence that he would recover enough to play golf again.

In what she considered to be a very personal touch on his part, General Eisenhower sent in return two dozen of his yellow birthday roses, a piece of his birthday cake, and his very best wishes.

The mutual, personal touch of this exchange raised the Eisenhower-Smith relationship to its warmest friendly degree—and at a time shortly before his passing.

"Are You Proud?"

". . . as sure as there is a God in Heaven, your evil ways will not prevail."

—Professor Paul A. Fullam
September 13, 1954

A pro-McCarthy campaign against me in the 1954 Maine Republican Senatorial primary was not unexpected. Nor was it difficult to cope with, even if most unpleasant. The charges made by the opposition were unbelievable to me—and fortunately to most of the people in Maine.

But the charges made by the Democratic opposition in the general election campaign were unexpected. They came from one who had been regarded as a friend and enjoyed a credibility that my Republican primary opponent didn't.

Republican primary talk against me was twofold—(1) I was a fuzzy-minded, internationalist left-winger and (2) I was in such poor health that I wouldn't seek re-election. Both assertions were made openly. The charge never made openly, but rather in the form of a whispering campaign, was that I was dying of cancer. The open talk was easily answered: I did file for renomination and re-election and I presented myself in person throughout the State of Maine in the campaign and yet didn't miss one roll call vote in the Senate that year. That should have refuted the ill health charge. But there was no way of meeting the underground whispering campaign. How do you prove that you aren't dying of cancer?

In the general election, the ideological attack shifted from one extreme to the other. Attacked in the primary as a left-winger, I was attacked in the general election as a reactionary conservative. And the physiological attack continued but with a new twist. The theme of the whispering campaign became that I should be defeated because I was running only to save the Senate seat for the Republicans, specifically for Governor Burton Cross—that because I was dying of cancer ("as her mother did two years ago") I would resign shortly after being sworn in so that Burt Cross could then step down as Governor and be appointed to my vacancy by the Republican President of the Maine State Senate—who was himself next in line to the Governor.

In my years as a Congresswoman and in the early years as a Senator, a cordial relationship existed between people at Colby

College (in Waterville, eighteen miles south of my home town) and me. Much of that cordiality stemmed from the Professor of Public Speaking, Herbert C. Libby; the Dean of the Faculty, Doctor Ernest C. Marriner; a Trustee, Carleton D. Brown; and Alumni Secretary Ellsworth W. (Bill) Millett. They were staunch supporters and key leaders in the Waterville area— and remained so even through the 1954 campaign, when the first break came.

My friendship with Bill Millett went back to the days when my husband invited the Colby baseball team to breakfast at our house in Washington. I prepared breakfast for the team. Bill Millett always accompanied the team.

It was through Bill that I met history Professor Paul Fullam. Subsequently, Fullam was to be my guest at lunch in the Senate restaurant and we began a friendly correspondence. On December 16, 1950, he wrote:

Dear Mrs. Smith:

I could not go off to bed tonight without getting through congratulations on your courageous stand in refusing to go along with this abominable pressure to oust Acheson. Because of my contacts with Europe, I fully realize what a staggering set-back our Foreign Policy would encounter if such a move were successful. It is perfectly obvious that with Acheson out of the way, that Truman isolated, becomes the Administration, and as such would be completely vulnerable. But the mentality which would press such a situation in which the stakes are our very survival as opposed to a political victory, is beyond the power of a rational man to comprehend.

I made several attempts to reach you by telephone before you returned to Washington, but couldn't seem to make connections. I still hold the hope that I can talk with you at some length, in the not too distant future.

With our best wishes for a merry Christmas,

Paul Fullam

On April 3, 1951, Millett, Fullam, and Doctor J. S. Bixler (then President of Colby) were my guests at lunch. Not long thereafter, I invited Professor Fullam's daughter to have lunch with me. On October 11, 1951, at the invitation of Professor Fullam, I addressed his Colby history class and he introduced me warmly. On May 2, 1953, I received a warm letter from Fullam in which he expressed at length his views on the Tidelands Oil Bill. In March 1954, Fullam was associated with the circulation of a petition among Colby students concurring with my Declaration of Conscience.

Sometime in January 1954, prior to January 27, Fullam joined in a primary move in my behalf. Shortly before he announced his candidacy (April 16, 1954) for the Democratic nomination for United States Senator, Fullam called by telephone from Princeton to ask what I would think if he ran against me. I told him I didn't think he was serious; he was a Republican. Subsequently, my personal secretary, Mrs. Blanche Hudon, called it to my attention that Fullam had to be a Republican to have participated in the primary movement in my behalf.

As the campaign grew older, and as the Democrats began to smell blood in the evident unpopularity of incumbent Republican Governor Burton Cross, the Fullam race produced attacks that grew bolder and more vigorous. A few samplings of the press reports show that trend. On July 12, 1954, Fullam said that I was riding the coattails of General Eisenhower. One on July 21, 1954, quoted Fullam: "What is that record? I haven't received one single answer to that question from those to whom I have asked it . . . My opponent has millions of blind followers and it is my duty to make these followers see."

The newspapers of July 30, 1954, reported that Fullam had assailed me for saying that Indo-China was the most critical area of our foreign policy. He planned to show Maine voters the difference between historians and politicians with his "A politician looks to the next election, a historian looks to the next generation."

August 5, 1954: Fullam said he entered the race because "he feared Mrs. Smith's thinking regarding the Communist menace."*

A Lewiston (Maine) *Sun* editorial of August 6, 1954, said that Fullam had "told a hushed and thoughtful throng why he thought Margaret Smith was unfitted to play the role a Senator must play in preserving us from the horrible spectre of atomic mass destruction."

August 13, 1954: Fullam said I had just about killed any hope for the $3,000,000 Passamaquoddy Tidal Survey Bill and had made enemies of twenty-nine Senators. (Yet, this was my own bill. In 1953 I had gotten the Senate to pass the bill for the $3,000,000 overall survey without a dissenting vote. The House killed it by not acting on it. Then again, on June 14, 1955, I got the Senate to pass it, again without a dissenting vote, and in 1956 the House finally passed the Smith Bill. By 1958 we had all the money needed for the survey and it was later completed.)

August 20, 1954: Fullam criticized my votes on the Tidelands Oil legislation. "This is like voting the income of a sum of money to a charity, and then throwing the money into a furnace." August 23, 1954: "Senator Margaret Chase Smith's record shows not only a lack of understanding, but an inconsistency the results of which reap no benefits for the people of this state." August 29, 1954: Fullam said on television, "After listening to the Republican candidate . . . a snow job."

Although the snow was falling, and my personal disillusionment with Fullam was increasing, I was inclined to absolve him from blame. These did not really seem to be his true attitudes, but rather those of his speech writers and the professional

---

* EDITOR'S NOTE: This was interesting in at least three respects—(1) on April 16, 1954, when he announced his candidacy, he gave his reasons for running. He did not give this as one of his reasons. According to the press he didn't even mention Senator Smith; (2) the pro-McCarthy primary opponent of Senator Smith also stated that he had decided to oppose her because of her thinking regarding the Communist menace; and (3) after the election she received letters from some Republicans saying they voted for Fullam because of her opposition to McCarthy on the Communist issue.

politicians who had gotten him to run. So I continued to turn my cheek. In August I said:

My own political opponent on the Democratic ticket is an honorable and capable man. He's not a man to stoop to pettiness and meanness. Let us remember that it is only natural for the Democrats to attack, and let us take that attack in good spirit. Let us expect in all fairness to fight on the basis of issues, not personalities.

Then came the straw that broke this camel's back. It was Fullam's speech at Rumford, Maine, of September 1, 1954. There he asked several questions of me (I was not present, of course):

Are you proud of your state . . . with its rising unemployment rate? Proud of your vote against the Kennedy Amendment? Proud that you voted against 75 percent parity for dairy farmers but for 90 percent parity for cotton and peanut oil?

Are you proud that you voted for the twenty-million-dollar cut for TB control? For the cut in the school lunch program? To recommit the Taft-Hartley Act? Proud of the foreign aid cut?

I don't think this constitutes a record of which to be proud, but a record to hide behind generalizations.

When I saw the newspaper account, I was so shocked that I had to read it three times to be sure that I was reading correctly. I had a very clear recollection that in a majority of instances, my votes had been the opposite of what he charged. I asked Bill Lewis what his recollection was. It was the same as mine.

"Bill," I said, "please call the Washington office and have my votes on these issues researched." Jacqueline Phillips took the questions over to the Senate Republican Majority Policy

Committee. Lloyd W. Jones, Staff Director, assigned the project to Mrs. Alice Thompson. Two days later I received a memorandum answer that confirmed our recollection.

I made the first response to Fullam's attacks. But I limited them to simply observing that he was getting "more and more personal." His response was a denial. He claimed that he was only factually exposing my true record and that he had drawn a distinction between me as a person and as a Senator, "between Mrs. Smith and Senator Smith."

He persisted in his pattern of attack on me and my voting record.

For example, he sought to characterize me as undermining the national security of the United States and weakening the United States Air Force when he said on television that I had helped the administration

> put through a five-billion-dollar cut in the appropriation for the Air Force a year ago at a time when Russia was pressing its aircraft developments to the utmost . . .
>
> If we continue to deal with the Soviets on the basis of what we can afford, we shall be selling our birthright for a mess of pottage.

To suggest that I was pinching pennies over the national security and the Air Force was ludicrous if it were not so serious. (After all, I was a Lieutenant Colonel in the Air Force Reserve.) I had tangled with Defense Secretary Charles Wilson on this very five-billion-dollar cut in the Air Force appropriation. My disagreement with Secretary Wilson was so sharp and dramatic that it was given wide press coverage. It even rated a Herblock cartoon in the Washington *Post* showing me sitting on the opposite side of the Secretary's desk facing Wilson who was holding a large placard stating "Less Airpower Is Really More—or—You Never Had So Much." The caption of the cartoon was "You Explain It to Me, Mr. Secretary."

I was convinced all the more that someone was writing his speeches and he was not checking the facts before delivering them. I suspected the Democratic National Committee.

It was this silly charge on the Air Force cut that convinced me to expose his serious misrepresentations. The only remaining question was when to do it. At first I was strongly inclined to do it *after* the election when it could not possibly have any effect on the voters. But ultimately I decided against this. Some would ask what purpose was served to do this after I had won. If I did, I would not be a graceful winner—and if I lost, it would seem sour grapes.

I concluded that I would answer all his charges (or as many as time would permit) in the last television appearance of the campaign, which was to be on Sunday, September 12, 1954, at 11:05 P.M.:

Throughout this campaign I have refrained from attacking my opponent. Instead I have called him honorable, capable, likable—and not a man to stoop to pettiness and meanness.

I have said that I respected him—and that I believed the campaign should be waged on issues, not personalities—and that the basic issue was the Republican record.

To my surprise and disappointment, my opponent has become increasingly personal and erroneous in his attacks on me. When I said so the other day, he accused me of trying to keep my public record private and secret—and of not revealing and discussing my record with the people.

At the end of this address I shall give you the biggest political surprise of this campaign—so keep tuned in.

Nothing could be further from the truth. I have constantly discussed my record and votes with the people—and not just at campaign election time. Every year—not just election year—I spend a month traveling throughout the State discussing my record and my votes with the people—last year I made one hundred speeches and traveled sixty-five hundred miles through all sixteen counties.

And for practically all of the time I have been a Senator I have given the people of Maine a daily report on my record, my actions, and my votes in the form of the daily column I wrote and which was carried by all major daily papers in Maine. In addition to that I have made a Monthly Report to the people in all of the Maine weekly newspapers.

And I call the attention of my opponent to the little primary campaign pamphlet that I distributed which gives my record explicitly and in detail.

I ask my opponent, "Who can match this in reporting and discussing one's record?"

Now as to his denial that he has made personal attacks on me—let's look at his record. On August 4 in Portland, according to the Lewiston *Sun,* my opponent said I was unfit to be Senator. He has accused me of "monstrous injustice." On television he accused me of lacking in conscience. At Waterville on August 15 he accused me of "half-truths."

On television on August 27 he accused me of serving the interests of the Communists—of playing right into their hands. In Lubec on August 10 he accused me of insincerity on Quoddy. In Biddeford on August 22 he accused me of lacking understanding and being inconsistent. On September 5 in Portland he accused me of playing politics with national defense and being trivial. On August 29 in Portland he called my record "a sorry one" in a telecast with Massachusetts Senator Kennedy.

In Portland on a telecast later that night he said derisively that I had done "a snow job." In Washington County he accused me of neglect.

Perhaps he reached the peak of his personal attack on me at Rumford on September 1 with a set of questions designed to shame me publicly. He challenged me to answer a series of "Are you proud?" questions. Here are my answers.

In these questions he literally pointed a finger of shame at me and made grave misrepresentations. First he asked challengingly, "Are you proud of your State with its rising unemployment rate?" To use a harsh word, that is a lie. The unemployment rate in Maine *is not* rising—the truth is that it is falling. For the last four months it has decreased each month from 9.2 percent in May to 5.1 percent in August—in other words, it decreased 4.1 percent. If that trend of decrease continues it would drop to 1 percent by the end of 1954.

These are *authentic statistics* from the Bureau of Employment Security of the U. S. Labor Department.

Another "finger of shame" question my opponent challenged me to answer was "Are you proud that you voted to recommit the Taft-Hartley Act Amendments?" Again this is a lie. I did *not* vote to recommit. I voted *against* recommitting—the opposite of the way my opponent charges I did—check page 5859 of the Congressional Record of May 7, 1954. Ironically enough, by your question, Professor Fullam, you actually condemn all forty-eight Democratic Senators for all of them were for to recommit.

Another "finger of shame" question my opponent challenged me to answer was "Are you proud that you voted for Foreign Aid cuts?" Well, my answer is this, Professor Fullam—look at pages 12495, 12496, and 13802 of the Congressional Record of August 3 and 14, 1954, where the Foreign Aid votes are recorded, and you will find that I did *not* vote to cut Foreign Aid but instead that I voted all three times *against* cutting Foreign Aid.

You are entitled to disagree with my votes but you have no right to misrepresent my record when I voted *against* the one-billion-dollar cut proposed by Democratic Senator Long, *against* the 500-million-dollar cut proposed by Democratic Senator Long, and *against* the 200-million-dollar cut proposed by Democratic Senator Maybank.

Another "finger of shame" question my opponent challenged me to answer was "Are you proud that you voted for the 20-million cut for TB control?" Again this is a lie. I did *not* vote for any such cut. The truth is that such a cut has never been proposed or voted on since the TB control program started in 1944. The truth is that Congress this year voted two and a half million dollars more for TB control than the Budget requested. I voted for more and not less.

Another "finger of shame" question my opponent challenged me to answer was "Are you proud that you voted for the cut in the school lunch program?" Again the truth is that I did *not* vote for such a cut. There was no proposal to cut the school lunch program. Your shame question literally implies that I voted to take food from the mouths of our school children. Nothing could be further from the truth. In this Congress I voted for measures totaling 283 million dollars for food for children in the lunch program.

Another "finger of shame" question my opponent challenged me to answer was "Are you proud that you voted against 75 percent parity for dairy farmers and for 90 percent parity for cotton and peanut oil?" Again, Professor Fullam, you are not being truthful with such a question. There was *no* vote taken on the question of "75 percent parity for dairy farmers." And I did *not* vote "for 90 percent of parity for cotton and peanut oil."

The only other "finger of shame" question my opponent was reported by the papers to have asked me at Rumford was "Are you proud of your vote against the Kennedy Amendment?" This is the only one of your questions in which you accurately stated my vote, Professor Fullam. I voted on the Kennedy Amendment just like the Senate leaders of the Democratic Party on which ticket you are running—I voted the same way that the Senate Democratic Leader and the Senate Democratic Assistant Leader voted—against the Kennedy Amendment.

Yes, I voted the same way the overwhelming majority of the Senate Finance Committee—the expert group in the Senate on this subject matter—voted—14 to 1 against the Kennedy Amendment. You point a finger of shame with this question not only at me but at the Democratic Leadership and the acknowledged experts, both Democrats and Republicans alike, on this Senate vote. We voted the way we did to uphold the principle set originally by a Democratic Senate that the Federal Government should not invade States' rights on this matter.

He talks sarcastically of what he calls "glamour by association." Yet, he himself has sought political advantage by association with respected people by bringing on his television program to support him a Massachusetts Senator and a most respected retired President of one of our great colleges. The interesting thing is that these two telecast associates of his do not share his shame of me.

For within a week after he had the Massachusetts Senator on his telecast that very Massachusetts Senator publicly commended my actions and acts in behalf of the best interest of Maine and New England. And the greatly respected retired college President has many times praised my record and even handed me an honorary Doctor of Laws degree from his institution two years ago.

And on this point of "glamour by association" in which you attempt to ridicule me, Professor Fullam, I note that on your campaign posters you brag of your membership in the American Political Science Association. Now you may be ashamed of me—but the members of that group of which you are so proud of your association—the members of that group disagree with your shame of me—because they once took a poll in rating Senators and they rated me the Sixth Best of all of the ninety-six members of the United States Senate.

My opponent accused me of insincerity on Quoddy—he accused me of having killed Quoddy. He says that he has done more on Quoddy than I have—that he has done more by merely reading a report on Quoddy. And interestingly enough, he brings the late President Roosevelt into this campaign in talking about action for the forgotten man.

But he doesn't tell you that I have accomplished more on Quoddy legislation than President Roosevelt ever did. Even at the height of his power with his rubber-stamp Congress, President Roosevelt could not get the Senate to pass Quoddy legislation. In sharp contrast, this year I got Quoddy legislation passed unanimously by the Senate—not one vote against it. And not long ago at my request the Senate okayed and appropriated funds for a preliminary survey of Quoddy.

My opponent derides me for voting for the Maybank Amendment which proposed banning the letting of Government contracts to people who do not submit the lowest bid—thus for saving the money of the people, the taxpayers. Well, I hope you good people in Bath listen to this. The Maybank Amendment was designed to prevent such things as the loss last February by Bath of those three destroyers to Quincy, Massachusetts, even though the Quincy bid was 6.5 million dollars higher.

Is my opponent interested in Maine and Bath or in Massachusetts and Quincy? Has the Massachusetts Senator he had on his telecast completely captivated him to the cause of Massachusetts? Would my opponent be more interested in representing Massachusetts than in representing Maine?

My opponent has accused me of playing politics with national security and in effect of being an enemy of air power because last year I ultimately accepted the word of President Eisenhower whose military genius led us to victory in World War II—the word of the Secretary of Defense—the word of the Secretary of the Air Force—and the word of the Chief of Staff, the ranking General of the Air Force—on the safe size of our Air Force for National Defense.

He would have a hard time convincing members of the Air Force who watched me back in 1949 as one of a small band of nine Senators who fought for a seventy-group Air Force when the then Democratic President cut the Air Force down to forty-eight groups over the vigorous protest of the then Secretary of the Air Force. He would have a hard time convincing Secretary of Defense Wilson who thinks I am too prejudiced for the Air Force by the sharp and pointed questions I have asked him.

For your information, Professor Fullam, I am not an enemy of Air Power. Instead I have been acknowledged by such organizations as the Air Reserve Association and the Air Force Association to be a Champion for Air Power. For your information, Sir, I am a Lieutenant Colonel in the Air Force Reserve.

My opponent charges that I have played right into the hands of the Communists—in effect, that I have served the cause of the Communists. He says that I did so by introducing legislation proposing consideration of a ban on imports of the then outrageously high-priced coffee from the then Communist-controlled government of Guatemala.

Well, here in very short time, history proved the History Professor to be wrong—for the stern stand of America on the Communist-controlled government of Guatemala, as exemplified by my legislation, led to the downfall and overthrow of the Communists in Guatemala. And more than that, the price of coffee has now dropped sharply.

Thus history is against the contention made by History Professor Fullam as was the word of the specialist on the subject—the word of our top official in Guatemala—our Ambassador to Guatemala—a North Carolina Democrat—who came to me and told me that I could not possibly know how much my legislation had done to arouse the feeling of the good people of Guatemala against the Communist-controlled government and how it stirred them on to finally overthrow that Government and kick the Communists out.

My opponent would have you believe that Maine has not gotten any appreciable Federal business during my service in Congress. Well, what does he call all of the tremendous volume of shipbuilding work at Bath and Kittery—the three-destroyer contract in June to Bath, the atomic submarine to Kittery—the establishment of multimillion-dollar air bases at Limestone, Presque Isle, Bangor, and Brunswick—millions of dollars for Maine potato growers?

My opponent would have you believe that I have turned my back on education and teachers. He tries to make out such a case by my votes on Tideland legislation. In the first place, I ask him to check with Democratic Senator Lister Hill, the author of the Bill "Oil for the Lamps of Learning" Amendment, who will tell him that every time that amendment has come up for a vote I have voted for it.

When the amendment has lost in spite of my vote for it, I have voted for the bill because I wanted to preserve and protect for the State of Maine all of the natural resources of its more than two-thousand-mile coast—if such could not be given to the schools—rather than turning it over to the Federal Government.

It is not entirely impossible that some day oil may be discovered off the coast of Maine as it has been in Texas, Louisiana, and California—and in such event surely we would want the millions of dollars of that oil income to be given to Maine schools and for use by Maine people rather than turned over to the Federal Government.

My opponent not only should but actually does know better than to accuse me of turning my back on schools. He knows of my unbroken support of Federal Aid to Education as I stood together with Senator Taft on this. He knows of my constant support of legislation for school construction, school lunches, and other educational measures. He knows that I am a former school teacher myself.

More than that—he has personal knowledge of how I have worked in Washington for the very school where he has so long taught—Colby College. He also knows of how I have made fund-raising speeches for his Colby College. In spite of this personal, firsthand knowledge, he would have you believe that I have not extended a helping hand to the schools of Maine.

In derogation he has asked me if I am proud of my record and indicated that I should be ashamed of it and that the people of Maine should be ashamed of it. Well, the colleges of Maine are not ashamed of me—they are proud enough that his own great Colby College gave me an honorary degree of Master of Arts, Honoris Causa, in commendation of my congressional record citing me for statesmanship and devotion to duty.

Bowdoin College—the great institution once headed by a great man who appeared on one of your telecasts—was proud enough of me to award an honorary degree of Doctor of Laws, Honoris Causa, to me in 1952 citing my common sense and good judgment and expressing specifically its high regard for me—yes, and your telecast guest, who has often praised my record, handed that degree to me.

The University of Maine of which all Maine is so proud also disagrees with your shame of me, Professor Fullam—for it has expressed its pride in my record by awarding me an honorary Doctor of Laws degree with the citation calling me a conscientious leader true to my heritage.

No, Professor Fullam, you may be ashamed of my Senatorial record—but your own college is proud of my record—your own associates in your American Political Science Association are proud of my record—your own former newspaper of which you are so proud of your association with, the New York Times, has commended my record repeatedly—even the Massachusetts Senator you had on your telecast publicly commended my record within a week after that telecast—even the greatly respected retired college President that you had on a telecast has commended my record.

And now we come to you, yourself—Professor Fullam—what do you think about my record if you brush aside all the political campaign talk you have been making? Do you really believe that I am unfit to be Senator as the Lewiston *Sun* reported you as saying?

I can't bring myself to really believe that you mean those things you have said about my record and me. I can't believe that you really think I am unfit to be Senator—when I look at this notarized and sworn-to document I hold in my hand—sworn to on January 27, 1954. It is one of my primary nomination papers.

You signed that primary paper representing that you were a member of the Republican Party and that you were proposing my nomination for United States Senator and the nomination of no one else but Margaret Chase Smith. Yours is signature No. 32—which I point to—your own handwriting—Paul Fullam, Sidney, Maine.

Now you either misrepresented yourself as being a Republican when you signed one of my primary nomination papers—or you were a Republican at that time and because of that you couldn't even vote in the Democratic Primary this past June for yourself.

You have not revealed this to the people of Maine whose vote you seek—in your campaigning throughout the State you have not revealed this to the Democratic voters or the Independent voters or the Republican voters. Yet, you have accused me of hidng my record behind generalities.

If you feel that I am unfit to be Senator then why did you sign my primary paper? If you feel that my votes—most of which predate your signing that paper—were so reprehensible then why did you propose my nomination for United States Senator? Why did you wait until after the Democratic nomination had been offered to you to attack such votes of mine and take issue with them?

You talk of the need for a strong two-party system in Maine. Is this the way to build such a strong two-party system—by representing yourself to be a Republican and proposing the nomination of a person and then three months later becoming the Democratic opponent of the very person you proposed for nomination?

In closing, I ask you voters of Maine, especially you Democrats: Who has been honest with you about records, both voting and party affiliation? My opponent in his "finger of shame" attacks on my votes has actually attacked your Democratic leaders in the Senate for they voted the same way I did on so many of the votes my opponent criticizes.

You know what you are voting for when you vote for me. But do you know what you are voting for if you vote for my opponent?

I appeal to all voters—Republicans, Democrats, and Independents alike—to go to the polls tomorrow—to get your friends to the polls tomorrow—to show what you think of unfair misrepresentations and to roll up a victory for Margaret Chase Smith for United States Senator.

Perhaps the most dramatic point of my televised answer to the Fullam charges came when I reached that point of my statement saying:

I can't bring myself to really believe that you mean those things you have said about my record and me. I can't believe that you really think that I am unfit to be Senator—when I look at this notarized and sworn-to document I hold in my hand—sworn to on January 27, 1954. It is one of my primary nomination papers.

You signed that primary paper representing that you were a member of the Republican Party and that you were proposing my nomination for United States Senator and the nomination of no one else but Margaret Chase Smith. Yours is signature No. 32—which I point to—your own handwriting—Paul Fullam, Sidney, Maine.

Bill Lewis had instructed the television cameraman to zoom the camera focus close on the signature so that it could be clearly seen by the televiewers and so there would be no doubt about the veracity of my statement.

EDITOR'S NOTE:
At 7:30 P.M. the next day (election day), the chief United Press correspondent in Maine called Senator Smith and said that after her telecast Fullam had sent a telegram to the press in which he characterized her speech as a vicious attack, as McCarthyism, stating: "I repeat what Mr. Welch said to Senator McCarthy, as sure as there is a God in Heaven your evil ways will not prevail."

After the Democratic State Chairman had demanded and received from Senator Smith the full text of her telecast, Fullam made a post-election televised reply on September 17, 1954. His reply, as reported by the Portland (Maine) *Press Herald* was more restrained than his reported election day statement.

Fullam's statement that he had signed the nomination paper because he preferred her to Robert L. Jones, her primary opponent, was debatable from a standpoint of chronology. The Smith nomination paper that he signed was completed and notarized on January 27, 1954, or almost a month before Jones announced his candidacy (February 22, 1954). In addition, the January 26, 1954, newspapers carried Jones's statement of January 25, 1954 (two days before the notarization of the Smith nomination paper signed by Fullam):

So that my position may be clearly established with respect to seeking public office in Maine, I wish to say that I have not been and shall not be a candidate for any political office in 1954.

I hope that this will add further clarification to my previous denials that I am a candidate for the House or Senate.

Senator Smith never saw fit to make a point of this inconsistency.

She was interested in Fullam's revelation that he based his speeches on figures compiled by the Democratic National Committee and it was no surprise to her. She had strongly suspected it and in her suspicion she had been willing to absolve him and place the responsibility on the committee's researchers and writers—that is, up until the time of the September 1 Rumford "finger of shame" speech Fullam made against her. It was obvious that such "research" had done him a real disservice. Yet she had expected him, as a history professor, to be more careful about checking the accuracy of material he received before using it. Nor did she find it particularly admirable that he shunned responsibility and blamed the Democratic National Committee after the fact.

[The Democratic pro-Fullam, anti-Smith version of the campaign was later echoed in a book on women by Peggy Lamson, Massachusetts Democrat, in which Mrs. Lamson credited Senator Edmund Muskie and others with kindness and generosity "in sharing their insights with" her and in which she characterized Senator Smith as "ordinary to the point of banality." In October 1971 Mrs. Lamson became a member of Senator Muskie's Women Advisory Council.]

Fullam's suggestion that the Senator must have gotten the impression of his inaccuracy from "secondhand information . . . probably relayed to her incorrectly" was hardly credible. All the information she had received was from the press, not from gossip, and frequently from his press handouts. There were no reports of his challenging, publicly or privately, any misquotation of his remarks about her.

Fullam's charges did not stop with the post-election telecast. He was still at it in February 1955. In a letter on the sixteenth he lashed out with the accusation that the Senator had accepted $3000 from organized labor, that is, Labor's League for Political Education. In March and April, the Director of the League, and other union and state officials, wrote flatly that no such campaign contribution had been accepted. By letter of April 5, 1955, the President and Secretary-Treasurer of the Maine State Federation of Labor wrote Senator Smith:

> We were as much astounded as you by the statement made . . . by Professor Fullam that you accepted $3,000 toward your campaign for re-election on the 29th of June, 1954.
>
> To our knowledge this statement is completely false . . . Possibly the statement made by Professor Fullam was to embarrass you at some future time. If that is the intent, we will most certainly publicly refute any statement of that sort.

But by then it was too late, as it had once been too much and too little. Mrs. Smith led all candidates on both sides of the ticket in 1954 as she had in 1948.

Medical Research

"She's dying of cancer!"

—Anonymous
February–September 1954

When the House Armed Services Committee was first established in 1947, I became Chairman of the Medical Subcommittee. I gained not only considerable information about medicine and medical programs but also an interest that was never to leave me.

My interest was no doubt rooted in several experiences with disease and death earlier in my life. My mother's third child,* Roland, died from pneumonia at one and a half years of age. Her fourth child, my brother Lawrence, died of dysentery at the age of two years and ten months. And my father died of a heart attack on June 9, 1946.

Death struck at two very strategic times in my public and political career, as I have related. The first time was in April 1940 when our family physician, Dr. Paul Dickens, Sr., a Georgia Democrat retired naval medical officer, recommended that I should become the candidate to succeed my husband in the United States House of Representatives.

When Clyde became sick from what seemed to be indigestion, I summoned Dr. Dickens whose subsequent examination determined that Clyde had had a serious heart attack. After maintaining a close watch over him for several days, Dr. Dickens and his consultant determined that he could not stand a campaign, at least for some time to come.

But the deadline—April 15, 1940—for filing nomination papers was fast approaching. Though Dr. Dickens had suggested that I become the candidate, it would be necessary to obtain thousands of signatures for me to do so. Time was of the essence. An immediate decision was called for. Dickens maintained that if I announced my candidacy other aspirants might be discouraged. If Clyde recovered it would be possible for him to become a write-in candidate at which time I could announce that I had entered the campaign only as a protection to the people of Maine's Second Congressional District; that I would ask the voters to support Clyde.

Clyde and I decided to accept Dr. Dickens' proposal. Clyde issued a public statement from his bed asking his constituents

* I was the first of her six children.

to select me in his place. His statement was released to the press and within a few hours after that he died of a coronary thrombosis. The newspapers and radios in Maine carried simultaneously the news of his announcement and of his death. One cannot help wondering if subsequent medical discoveries had been made early enough to be applied to Clyde whether he might not have recovered and run again for Congress. The second time that a serious failure of health of someone close to me affected my career was when my mother succumbed to cancer. Surgery was performed in late June 1952 and after a post-surgery period of about a week Mother had a relapse. At that time the Republicans were holding their National Convention in Chicago where a titanic struggle was being waged by Taft and Eisenhower forces for the Presidential nomination. The National Federation of Business and Professional Women was conducting a strenuous campaign for me for the Vice Presidential nomination, as they were to do for Sarah Hughes at the Democratic convention.

I stayed in my mother's hospital room throughout the time of the convention.* She lingered between life and death for four months. After two months in the hospital she stayed at the home of my sister, Mrs. Evelyn St. Ledger, and she spent the latter stages of her illness at my Skowhegan home.

Because of her illness I was unable to hit the campaign trail for Ike. But when the election eve national telecast was set for Boston, I agreed to be a member of the panel.

Special air transportation was arranged so that I could fly to Boston at the last minute and fly back to Maine as soon as the telecast was finished. But in the mid-afternoon of that Monday the doctors warned me that my mother's condition was rapidly getting worse and I was compelled to cancel the plans. Mother died that evening at eight forty-five, an hour

---

* EDITOR'S NOTE: The Senator's women enemies at the convention sabotaged the BPW drive for her and maneuvered to prevent her name from being placed in nomination. Her fervent supporters felt that had she been at the convention the sabotage could have been prevented and the Senator might have become the Vice Presidential nominee instead of Richard M. Nixon.

and a quarter prior to the ten o'clock telecast. It was years earlier, in 1947, when I was in Cairo on a Europe-Middle East tour of the House Appropriations-Armed Services group that I came face-to-face with death in wide epidemic form. An epidemic of cholera hit Cairo with such widespread contagion that the Egyptian Government was running out of serum vaccine. I was so shocked by what I saw that I sent a personal appeal to the American Government. The almost immediate arrival of serum vaccine rapidly slowed the epidemic to controllable limits.

Though I had witnessed death and suffering of others, I myself had enjoyed almost phenomenally excellent health. It was ironic that my health should become the subject of a whispering campaign against me when I first ran for re-election to the Senate in 1954. In the Republican primary that year, the overt theme used against me by the McCarthyites was that I was a "fuzzy-minded, left-wing internationalist soft on communism." The covert theme was that I was dying of cancer like my mother two years before.

For quite a while I remained unaware of the whispers about my health. On the weekends I returned to Maine to campaign, I began to notice sadness in the face of some of my constituents. Finally I asked a friend to explain. "Dear Margaret," she said, "don't you know that your cancerous condition is well known even if no one speaks of it openly?"

After I won the primary by a 5 to 1 margin the opposition's attack shifted. Whereas I had been characterized during the primary campaign as a left-winger, I now was being called a truly reactionary conservative.

The whispering campaign that I was dying of cancer continued—but with an interesting variation. It was claimed that a vote for me was wasted because I was running only so that Governor Burt Cross could arrange to have himself appointed to succeed me. The theory was that if both of us were re-elected we would take our oaths of office and a few days later I would announce that because I had cancer I was resigning. Governor Cross would then resign and be appointed to fill the Senate vacancy by the new Governor—the President of the Senate who would become Governor as provided by law.

How was I to handle the vicious rumor? Though I could strike back at the left-winger and the reactionary conservative charges by citing chapter and verse of my voting record, I could not shout from a stage, "I am not dying of cancer!" The more I would shout the more people would become convinced I really was dying. So I had to take it quietly, limiting the truthful answers to the rare few questions that were asked about my health.

The rumor reached the point where the political reporter for the Gannett newspapers called my personal physician to inquire if I had cancer. And a reporter of the Boston *Post* called Bill's father long distance at three-thirty one morning to get a denial or confirmation of my coming death. Not long after my return to the Senate (and the confirmation of my continued good health), a young summer resident of Maine, Hank Bloomgarden, a New York public relations man with the women's apparel company, Lerner's, started bombarding me with letters asking me to make a Declaration of Conscience for medical research and to take the leadership in expanding the Federal medical research program. He was not to be denied and finally on December 19, 1955, I issued a public statement that in the coming session of Congress I would make a drive for a five-year, billion-dollar ($200 million annually) program for expansion of medical research. An important factor in my decision was the editorial position of the highly conservative Bangor *Daily News* in July 1955 calling for a billion dollars for medical research. I publicly credited the Bangor *News* with greatly influencing my decision.

In December I issued a press release announcing my forthcoming bill and on January 12, 1956, I introduced S. 2925 on which I got thirty Senators to cosponsor. The salient provisions of the bill and my arguments for it were outlined in the speech I made that day to the Senate:

Mr. President, I have today introduced a bill designed to initiate a bold new program of medical research in this great Nation of ours.

Before outlining the details of my proposal, I wish to make it clear that I am following in the footsteps of some of the most distinguished Members of this body—such leaders and experts as the Senator from Alabama [Mr. Hill]—in proposing an expanded program of medical research. During the first session of the 84th Congress, the Senator from Alabama, together with the Senator from New Hampshire [Mr. Bridges] sponsored a bill for research laboratory construction, and the Senator from Alabama, and an additional eleven Senators from both parties, sponsored a bill to aid medical education. I heartily commend these efforts and I am deeply and humbly aware of the inspiring leadership of these distinguished Senators.

I believe that my proposal is unique in one very important respect. It is an attempt to blueprint a long-range plan for medical research. It is an omnibus proposal, inasmuch as it covers all the elements which we must combine to create a total offensive against disease.

Mr. President, I propose that the Federal Government spend an additional $1 billion over the next five years for three major purposes:

First. A doubling of the present research and training expenditures of the National Institutes of Health, the research arm of our National Government. During the current year the Institutes have been allocated approximately $100 million for their research, training, and related activities. I propose that, starting with fiscal 1957, this be raised to $200 million a year.

Second. A desperately needed program for the construction of laboratories and other medical research facilities. These construction funds shall be made available at the rate of $30 million a year for the next five years, and they shall be matched in equal part by the institutions receiving them.

Third. A long-range plan of aid to our medical schools, the keystone of medical research in this country. I propose that $70 million a year be allocated over the next five years for the construction of medical-school teaching facilities, and that these sums be matched by the medical schools receiving them.

I have been concerned with the question of medical research for a long time. However, an editorial in a great Maine newspaper—the Bangor *Daily News*—last July set me to thinking about ways in which I, as a legislator, could further medical research and save thousands of precious American lives. The editorial, entitled "How About $1 Billion for Health?" got to the heart of the problem in these simple but eloquent words:

There are occasions when we feel Congress is too generous about spending the taxpayers' money. But today we'd like to point out an instance in which we think the Federal legislators are being downright niggardly. We refer to funds for medical research on major killing diseases . . . Why not $1 billion? This may sound startling, at first. Yet what better investment could be made for the welfare of the Nation? Let us suppose the sum found the answer to dreaded cancer, for instance. Suppose it gave us new information on heart ailments and their treatment . . . It occurs to us that we Americans may have lost our perspective as to the relative importance of things. A Federal highway program running into many billions undoubtedly will be put on the books within a short time. We are spending billions upon billions for national defense. Other billions have been poured overseas in the form of foreign aid. Yet we discuss medical research in terms of only millions . . . We startled and frightened the world with the atomic bomb. Would we not win the gratitude of the world if, by a billion-dollar research program, we were able to give the human race the answers to the diseases that kill and cripple?

On November 19 of last year, in a follow-up editorial, the Bangor *Daily News* urged immediate action in this editorial statement:

The important thing is to set our sights higher and get busy. We know that a single billion dollar appropriation isn't going to win the war against disease, any more than a single billion can win a modern war between humans. But it would be a starting point. It would put the problem in proper perspective. There's something wrong in our thinking when Americans spend more on lipstick than on cancer research, more on ball-point pens than on heart studies.

For some time I have studied the facts underlying this problem and last winter I began the drafting of the proposal which I submit to the Senate today.

My first line of study was to determine the dimensions of the problem of disease in this country. Were the proponents of expanded medical research exaggerating the size and extent of the problem?

In my study of this subject I leaned heavily upon the volumes of hearings issued by the House Interstate and Foreign Commerce Committee following more than six months of intensive investigation during 1953 and 1954. Under the brilliant guidance of its chairman, Representative Charles A. Wolverton, the House committee conducted the most thorough study to date of the impact of illness upon our economy.

In a statement on January 28, 1954, Representative Wolverton summed up the highlights of the committee findings in these words:

We were told that heart disease is the leading cause of death in the United States, causing more than one out of every two deaths each year. It is the leading cause of death among children, and exacts a toll from every age group.

At the rate at which we are acquiring cancer, fifty million of the present population of the United States probably will acquire cancer, and about twenty-five million will die from that disease.

The number of mentally ill patients in the United States exceeds the number of patients suffering from any other type of disease. Furthermore, approximately one half of the 1,425,000 hospital beds in the United States are needed and used for the various mental illnesses.

Arthritis, with a total of ten million victims today, and with one million people permanently disabled, afflicts more people, cripples and disables more people, and brings more pain to more people than any other chronic disease.

Last year more than 250,000 Americans of working age were unable to work because of active tuberculosis.

In the committee report summing up the massive evidence gathered from more than a hundred physicians and scientists and from countless agencies, there is this statement which should give pause to every single one of us in this great country.

Four major diseases alone—heart, cancer, tuberculosis, and

arthritis—have resulted in an annual loss of 370 million man-days of productivity. This accounts for over half of the total man-days lost annually due to chronic diseases.

During the course of our hearings we received startling testimony that the annual cost to the Nation from illness is roughly equivalent to the total income tax revenue, or $30 billion annually.

I do not think I need present any further evidence of the staggering size of the problem. But what have we done in the way of mounting an offensive against these diseases which bring heartbreak to millions of American families?

In 1953 the President's Commission on the Health Needs of the Nation summed up our national medical research effort in these words:

Last year's (1952) total expenditure of $180 million amounted to only three tenths of 1 percent of the Nation's defense budget. It was less than the amount spent on monuments and tombstones . . . Last year, one industrial company spent more on business and product research than our entire Nation spent on research into heart and circulatory diseases . . . The Federal Government itself spends over two hundred times as much on military research as on research in heart disease.

A year later, the National Science Foundation released a set of figures which dramatically illustrated how little of all research moneys was going into medical research. It listed total governmental and nongovernmental research of all types as exceeding $4 billion annually. Industry spends more than a billion dollars annually searching for new products and improving existing ones. The chemical industry alone spends $300 million annually and this expenditure has made possible a fourfold increase in chemical sales from 1939 to 1954. Furthermore, American industry will spend $300 million in the next four years on atomic-energy research.

In 1954 the Federal Government spent approximately $2 billion on research of all kinds. Of this sum more than 85 percent, about $1700 million, was allocated to military-weapons research. Medical research expenditures were near the bottom of the list.

The major criticisms of the inadequate level of Federal support for medical research have come most recently from the distinguished reports of the Hoover Commission. In both task force and full Commission reports, the Commission has criticized both the inadequate sums expended for medical research and the lack of any long-range plans. In these reports there is a recurrent plea for a five-year program, and I am frank to state that the arguments of the Commission have had a great influence upon me in proposing an overall five-year plan. I would like to quote just a few of the more telling points made in these Hoover Commission reports released during 1955:

A. Task Force on Federal Medical Services of the Hoover Commission. In its report, released in February 1955, the task force gave powerful support to the whole idea of a five-year plan. Criticizing short-term annual research grants as uneconomic and lacking in stability, the report stated:

Where the Federal Government has made its grants for research in the form of five-year block grants to institutions or agencies instead of short-term awards to individuals, persons conducting the research have been able to plan their studies without fear of an abrupt end of financial support; and also the Federal administrative authority has had help from the institutions in the difficult task of appraising individual requests for research grants . . .

The task force recommends that the present system of project grants for research pertinent to health be modified and that it be gradually replaced by a system of five-year block grants to institutions or agencies which would be in accordance with an approved overall plan for health research submitted by each.

The task force also attacked what it referred to as a 35 percent cut between 1952 and 1954 in Federal health grants for preventive campaigns against the major diseases. As an example, it singled out the inadequate sums being spent against mental illness. It proposed a $5 million additional annual Federal appropriation in the mental-health field, with most of the money earmarked for increases research grants to universities and other research centers for investigation of mental health and disease and for continued and expanded grants for advanced training for psychiatrists and workers in allied fields.

B. The full Hoover Commission Report on Research and

Development in the Government, released in May 1955, included a sharp criticism of the Department of Health, Education, and Welfare for requesting inadequate sums for medical research, and for neglecting basic research. The report noted:

Of all the special research and development activities inside and outside the Federal Government, the most beneficent to mankind has been in medical and health research. Basic research in these fields covers such subjects as anatomy, physiology, biochemistry, bacteria, viruses, their contagions and their control . . . The actual Federal expenditure applicable to basic research in the medical field is only about $18 million, or less than 1 percent of the total Government research and development expenditures. The report of this Commission on Federal medical services, together with our task-force report, have outlined constructive steps toward better organization and support in this field.

It should be noted that, although Congress has treated appropriations requests for medical research and development generously, there are still many approved projects which have not been undertaken because of the lack of funds. These projects, primarily in the field of basic research, have been approved by several important research agencies.

An instance is the so-called backlog of 723 projects totaling about $7,400,000 which the National Institutes of Health predict will not be undertaken by them in fiscal year 1956 because funds have not been requested by the Department of Health, Education, and Welfare or the Bureau of the Budget. Of this amount, about $1,900,000 is for basic medical research. We are concerned over the apparent failure of the executive branch to indicate these backlog projects to the Congress. That such amounts have not been recommended to the Congress or supported by the Congress may indicate a tendency to de-emphasize basic and medical research. Possibly, this results from the belief that the Congress will be more receptive to requests for funds devoted to projects likely to produce startling and dramatic results. But it should be noted that there are also the dramatic accomplishments of basic and medical research.

. . . We must make sure of general support to this field

which daily demonstrates such potential benefits for mankind. We urge also that this is a problem for the Nation as a whole. We therefore recommend that greater Federal support be given to basic and medical research.

I was additionally influenced in making my proposals by some remarkable figures recently released by the National Health Education Committee. Startling as they are, they deserve the sober attention of all of us.

With ten million American men and women victims of heart disease, we are spending only about $1.60 per person afflicted to find cures and better methods of treatment for this most vicious of killers.

With the American Cancer Society estimating that twenty-five million Americans now alive will die from cancer unless new treatments, cures, or preventive measures are found, we are spending only $1 on research for each of these potential victims.

With mental illness costing this country approximately $2.5 billion a year, we are spending far less than 1 percent of this sum for psychiatric research.

In May of last year Dr. Paul Dudley White, the distinguished cardiologist who is now attending our great President, appeared before a Senate appropriations subcommittee to testify about medical research on heart disease. Dr. White, in his quiet methodical way, startled the committee with some of the evidence he presented. He pointed out that each year heart disease was growing in its power to destroy precious American lives. In 1935 heart disease claimed 450,000 victims; in 1945, 600,-000 victims, and in 1954 more than 800,000 victims.

Dr. White also presented figures on the ravages of heart disease during World War II. During the four years of our participation in that conflict, two million people die in this country of diseases of the heart and circulation—nearly eight times as many people as were killed in action in the Armed Forces. More than 300,000 men in the prime of their life were refused induction into the Armed Forces because of heart disease. In addition, 97,500 men were given disability discharges from military service or died in military service from heart disease during the years 1942–45. This manpower loss from heart disease, a total of 397,500 men, would have been sufficient to man twenty-seven army infantry divisions.

During the Korean conflict, the ravages of heart disease increased far beyond the World War II figures. Out of 245,000 registrants for military service examined between July 1950 and June 1951, 16 percent, or close to 40,000, were rejected for heart disease.

Dr. White also pointed out that heart disease causes tremendous productive and economic losses on the mobilization front. According to the United States Department of Commerce, heart disease causes a $2 billion annual loss to our economy. In a period when we are trying to stretch every dollar to increase our military procurement, this $2 billion could purchase 1500 to 2000 of our latest combat fighter planes, or it could outfit twenty-nine infantry or airborne divisions at a per division cost of $69 million. In addition to all this we must remember that compensation and pension payments to veterans with heart disease are costing us another $200 million a year.

Dr. White also stressed the fact that contrary to popular impression, heart disease is far from confined to the elderly. For example, among children under fifteen more than twice as many die of heart disease as of polio. More significant is the fact that heart disease cuts down one out of every three Americans in the prime of life in the years from forty to sixty-five. Only in recent years has American industry begun to face one of the most serious challenges in our productive economy—that many of its young executives, after years of training for top posts, fall victim of coronary heart disease and hypertension just as they begin to realize their full potential.

If heart disease continues to exact its present annual toll, eighty-three million Americans now alive will eventually fall victim to it.

Appealing for greatly increased funds for heart research, Dr. White, in forthright fashion, laid the facts on the table in these memorable words:

It happens that the United States is one of the most unhealthy countries in the world today, in large part because of this serious threat of coronary heart disease. I have traveled widely and have found that any citizens of any country in the world who live the way we do are subject to this disease. In most countries, however, only a relatively small percentage of the population can afford to live the way we do and in that sense can afford to be sick in the same serious way. While everyone knows about the very bad health conditions in south Asia and Africa due to infections and undernutrition, not so many have realized that at the opposite extreme, in countries like the United States which boast of their sanitary conditions, the health of the professional and business leaders is constantly threatened and apparently more and more so every year. This problem, therefore, is just as vital as that of the starving multitudes in countries far away.

Despite the fact that there are many researches going on in this country on animals and to a certain extent on man, we have not the answer yet . . . If I had had time, I would have shown you today a man in the thirties crippled by angina pectoris at this early age because we don't know how to prevent the disease as yet or even how to delay its onset. There are many thousands of patients of his age and a little older but still relatively young men who are similarly affected. This problem seems to have been increasing greatly within the last decade or two. Why this is so and what we can do about it remains the $64 question. Fortunately, researches in this field have been increasing steadily but many more are being contemplated, more than we can afford to pay for now.

These are the considered words of a great scientist who today is treating our President and who has treated members of this body. And this man, in 1955, had to spend money out of his own pocket because Government funds were not available for the vital research he was pursuing.

In the light of all the foregoing evidence, I think that it is beyond dispute that this country must spend vastly increased sums to reduce the toll exacted by disease and premature death. I, therefore, regard my proposal for an additional $100 million a year over the next five years as a modest one, limited in scope only by the availability of the research scientists and facilities needed to carry on this additional research. During the past few years congressional committees of both Houses have received documented evidence from the Nation's most eminent scientists that inadequate financial support is the great bottleneck to a major expansion of medical research.

However, there are always those who argue that expansion cannot go much further because the men and the laboratories are not immediately available. In answer to them, I cite the example of the magnificent clinical center of the National Institutes of Health. It cost $60 million to construct and it is regarded today as the finest research plant in the entire world. Yet when appropriations for it were under consideration before Congress a few years ago, there were some who argued that it would never be possible to staff so enormous a research enterprise. How wrong they have been proved. On the site of what was once a sleepy Maryland farm, there are now more than four thousand medical researchers and auxiliary personnel engaged in a magnificent offensive against the killers of our time. And all this has happened within the past decade.

As the various Hoover Commission reports noted, and as prominent scientists have pointed out in congressional testimony, there are thousands of research ideas in all parts of this land which need only financial backing to come to fruition. Furthermore, many of our most talented young research workers leave the field because they see no real evidence of a long-range plan with some guaranty of continued financial support. We must plan, and plan boldly, if we are to win the total war against disease.

Mr. President, I should now like to address myself to a very important question. If we double our present research expenditures over the next five years, what kind of return can we expect on our investment? In other words, apart from humanitarian considerations, is it good business sense to invest additional moneys in medical research?

The history of medical research over the past few years offers an eloquent answer. Over the past decade alone, medical research has added five full years to the life expectancy of the average American. This increase which encompasses a reduction in deaths from all causes of about 10 percent, occurred between 1944 and 1952. We all know something of the wonders of penicillin, streptomycin, isoniazid, cortisone, and a host of other battlers against disease. These miraculous products of medical research, along with new surgical techniques and blood plasma,

have brought about these percentage reductions in the death
rates of some of the major killers and cripplers:

	Percent
Influenza	77
Appendicitis	69
Acute Rheumatic Fever	66
Syphilis	56
Tuberculosis	50
Pneumonia	50
Kidney Diseases	43

Now let us translate this into terms which a hardheaded businessman can appreciate. During those eight years, a total of
845,000 American lives were saved. These 845,000 people,
who would have died if research knowledge had remained
constant, earned and added approximately $1,500,000,000 to
the national income in 1952 alone. And from these earnings in
1952, the Federal Treasury received approximately $234 mil-
lion additional in income and excise tax receipts. Please note
that this increase in tax receipts was more than seven times
the $33 million spent on research in 1952 by all the major
institutes of the United States Public Health Service. Putting it
very simply, medical research has returned seven dollars in
Federal taxes for every dollar spent by the United States Public
Health Service.

Medical research has even made for better and cheaper
agricultural crops and fatter and healthier cows, pigs, and
chickens. The antibiotics provided by medical research have
initiated a revolution in both the quality and quantity of livestock
and poultry production.

Mr. President, I could cite scores of examples of the savings
resulting from medical research. All of us in this body know
that tuberculosis, once one of the most terrible scourges visited
upon man, is now coming increasingly under control due to
the new drugs supplied by medical research. In the past seven
or eight years the tuberculosis death rate has dropped a gratifying 66 percent. Tuberculosis hospitals all over the country are
closing their doors. Last year, New York City saved $46 million

in hospital and construction costs because of the new advances in tuberculosis therapy.

We all know of the wonders of the Salk vaccine, and we have high hopes that poliomyelitis will soon fade into insignificance.

Mr. President, let me give one small example of what a single Federal research grant did in one area of disease. It was a grant of only $41,000, but it resulted in the discovery of the cause of a condition which was producing blindness in prematurely born children.

Over the past decade eight thousand children had been blinded by this disease. Their special care and training through their average life span will cost $100,000 each, or a total of $800 million, according to Dr. Cornelius Traeger, one of the Nation's leading neurologists.

As Dr. Traeger pointed out before a Senate committee, had that $41,000 worth of research been undertaken ten years earlier we would have saved that $800 million. But the grant was finally made, the research was successful, and for the small investment of $41,000 we will, through each future decade, save the precious sight of eight thousand children and save ourselves hundreds of millions of dollars.

Granted, then, that medical research is a blue-chip investment paying fantastic dividends, can this Nation afford additional expenditures for it? One of the most eloquent answers to this question is contained in a volume of the 1953 report of the President's Commission on the Health Needs of the Nation, devoted to how we can finance a broader health and medical-research program for America.

The testimony of some of the Nation's economists recorded in that volume reflects deep puzzlement and concern as to why this Nation is not spending more for medical research and health services. Economists, aware of the fact that in an expanding economy we must provide millions of new jobs to achieve a growing rate of national productivity, do not understand why we are not making plans now to shift many of our workers into medical research and health services.

Viewed in the cold perspective of an economist, our national research and medical plant is woefully underfinanced, handicapped by obsolescent physical facilities, and hamstrung by severe shortages of manpower and inadequate salaries. These deficiences reap an inevitable harvest.

Those areas of the country where medical research and health services are at the lowest point are the very same areas where industrial productivity is low, and consequently, Federal and State tax revenues are low.

In pointing out that this Nation could not much longer afford a $30 billion annual drain upon its productivity, the 1953 report argued that medical research must become big business if it is to succeed. It recommended that the Federal Government spend an additional billion dollars a year for medical research and related health activities. It put the problem this way:

Medical research must learn from American industry the cardinal fact that it cannot expand properly until it recruits and holds more of this country's top brains. It cannot do this on a skimpy financial base. If medical research is to compete with industrial research for skilled investigators, it must build up its physical plant and it must offer these workers good salaries and reasonable security.

I submit, Mr. President, that human life is the most precious commodity we have in this democracy of ours. However, our Federal budget seems to belie this. During the current fiscal year, about $60 million will be spent by the National Institutes of Health on research activities designed to save human lives.

Compare this with more than $90 million appropriated by the last session of Congress for the research activities of the Department of Agriculture. And add to this $90 million for the Department of Agriculture the sum of $250 million which is paid out to farmers for soil conservation practices.

I do not want to imply that I am not heartily in favor of greatly expanded agricultural research. I have always supported these research activities, but I think it is about time this country brought research on human lives up to the level of research on animals and plants.

I have proposed a medical-research expenditure of $200 million a year with full knowledge of comparable expenditures by the American people. In 1955 the people of this Nation spent approximately $10 billion on alcoholic beverages and more than $5 billion on tobacco products. Our annual expenditure for chewing gum, $264 million, is $64 million more than I am asking for research to save human lives.

Mr. President, the second part of my proposal would provide $150 million over a five-year period in matching grants for the construction of research laboratory facilities. For the most part, these grants would go to hard-pressed medical schools, hospitals, and private foundations in all parts of the country.

This proposal is a most conservative one. In 1953 the Senator from Minnesota [Mr. Thye], then Chairman of the Senate Appropriations Subcommittee on Health, Education, and Welfare, sent out a questionnaire to all research installations in the country, asking them for a detailed analysis of what additional laboratory facilities were needed to expand medical research in this country. He received replies indicating that these installations needed in excess of $150 million in matching grants to expand their very vital work.

I commend the two volumes of the Thye report to every Member of this body. It presents a picture of the shocking physical conditions under which medical research is carried on in many parts of this land. I think millions of Americans would be ashamed to learn that much medical research today is being carried on in firetraps, reconverted barns, and abandoned tombstone factories.

After a careful study of the Thye report, the members of the Senate Committee on Labor and Public Welfare voted unanimously in 1955 to hold a series of hearings on this critical situation in medical research. In that same year the Senator from Alabama [Mr. Hill], and the Senator from New Hampshire [Mr. Bridges], introduced a bill providing $90 million over the next three years in matching laboratory construction grants. In three days of hearings, the Senate committee received irrefutable documentation to the effect that this country's rundown medical-research plant was holding back hundreds of vitally important research projects.

In the report unanimously adopted by the full Senate Labor and Public Welfare Committee, the research laboratory crisis is stated in these words:

Actual experience in the making of research grants through the National Institutes of Health has disclosed a serious deficiency which is not only holding up already planned and much-needed research projects but which threatens the future of medical research insofar as it is serving to block the entry of young scientists into this field. Experience has shown that often the most potentially gifted men in the field of research, men who could and would devote their lives and their talents to the attempt to conquer diseases, men who had been chosen by the advisory councils of our National Institutes of Health as admirably qualified to carry on essential research projects, are unable to make their services available to the people of America simply because they do not have the laboratories, facilities, and equipment with which to do the work the Nation and the Congress very much want to have done.

We have, of course, provided excellent facilities and equipment, chiefly at the National Institutes of Health, where men of science employed by our Government have been and are carrying on promising research projects. But we neither can nor should we try to concentrate all medical research in Federal laboratories. Hundreds of established leaders in medical research and thousands of young scientists eager to work with them if it were possible are identified with non-Federal hospitals, universities, and other nonprofit research institutions scattered throughout the Nation. If we are to enlist their services in our behalf, we must help build the laboratories and other essential facilities where they and their patients are.

In the course of the hearings, many of the Nation's most distinguished scientists not only urged passage of the bill, but pointed out that research construction grants made by the Congress prior to the Korean conflict had meant an enormous saving of human lives. The report has this to say of the testimony of Dr. Cornelius Rhoads, generally regarded as America's greatest cancer researcher:

Dr. Cornelius Rhoads, scientific director of the oldest cancer hospital in the United States, the Memorial Center for Cancer and Allied Diseases in New York, and director of the Sloan-Kettering Institute for Cancer Research, gave us three succinctly stated reasons for his enthusiastic endorsement of this bill. He said:

"1. It is the best possible investment in terms of the economic as well as the social welfare of this country.

"2. It is an absolute necessity that these facilities be made available if hundreds of thousands of lives are not to be needlessly lost.

"And, thirdly, if they are made available, this wastage of life can be prevented, from all the indications presently before us."

Dr. Rhoads went on to tell us that cancer is costing us from three to ten billion dollars a year directly and indirectly and explained how a $250,000 laboratory has saved nearly a thousand lives over the last five years in his institution alone. Two hundred and fifty dollars for a human life.

Dr. Sidney Farber, director of research at the Children's Cancer Research Foundation in Boston, told the Senators of how a construction grant to his institution speeded up the miraculous development of the Salk vaccine. I quote the committee report on Dr. Farber's testimony:

He told of a $300,000 grant made to the Children's Cancer Research Foundation by the National Institutes of Health some years ago. With that seed money to go on, the trustees of the foundation went out and raised $1,600,000 more.

It was in the building thus created that Dr. John Enders conducted that epochal research which resulted in the discovery of a method of growing the poliomyelitis virus in tissue culture and won for Dr. Enders the Nobel Prize. It was this discovery which made possible first the mass testing and now the mass-immunization program with Salk vaccine. As Dr. Farber told us, because of the construction of this one building, as the result of a Federal grant, it is conservative to say that Dr. Enders' work was brought to fruition some two to three years ahead of the time it would have taken in his former antiquated and totally inadequate quarters.

In the light of this impressive testimony, the Senate unanimously passed the Hill-Bridges research construction bill in July of last year. I hope that the House will take immediate action on this problem and that it will vote the full $150 million provided in my proposal. I am confident that the Senate will accept the higher figure in conference.

The final section of my bill would provide $70 million a

year over the next five years in matching grants for the construction of medical-school teaching facilities.

The medical school is the backbone of our medical-research effort in this country. Our Nation's eighty-one accredited medical schools not only do the bulk of medical research but they train practically all our research scientists. However, with the decrease in private endowments and the rise in the cost of modern medical education, our Nation's medical schools have run increasingly into the red.

The full Hoover Commission report on Research and Development in the Government expressed itself in the strongest possible terms on the manner in which the financial plight of the medical schools was causing an alarming restriction of medical research and a desperate shortage of doctors and research technicians. I quote from that report, as follows:

We are greatly concerned over the inadequate public and State support of our medical schools where our research technicians are trained and an important part of basic medical research is carried forward. No greater instance of university research need be cited than the dramatic accomplishment at the University of Pittsburgh by Dr. Jonas Salk in basic research which produced the polio vaccine. The universities have contributed much to understanding and alleviation of mental diseases, cancer, and many other fields. The National Fund for Medical Education, which raises about $2 million annually to support the medical schools, has repeatedly stated that these institutions in the United States are carrying an aggregate annual deficit of $15 million which in the instances of university medical schools must be made up by diversions from other branches of education. One consequence is that the medical schools are compelled to restrict the amount of their research, and the number of their students. The Nation is today short of both technicians and doctors. And there are today a large number of youths who have completed their premedical education and cannot find admission to medical schools.

We cannot afford stagnation of our medical research in our medical schools or the training of our technicians.

The task force on Federal medical services of the Hoover Commission also pounded away at the need for greater Federal support for medical education. It singled out the schools of public health as an illustration of how inadequate financing was jeopardizing the Nation's health. I read the following statement prepared by the task force:

The United States needs additional trained public-health personnel—physicians, dentists, engineers, nurses, health educators, laboratory scientists, and other types of professional people, the report noted. "Many positions in public health agencies now are unfilled because of the lack of qualified applicants. A tenth of all budgeted positions for public health personnel in official health agencies—Federal, State, and local —were unfilled in 1951 (the latest study) with the budgeted positions representing only a fraction of the real need. More than half of the over 35,000 persons now employed in public-health work have received inadequate training. It has been estimated that to meet its needs, the Nation's schools of public health should, in the next five years, provide postgraduate education for some 20,000 people. Yet, as of 1952–53, these schools were granting postgraduate degrees to only about 600 persons each year.

Obviously, the Nation's ten accredited schools of public health cannot, as they now operate, educate enough students to meet the Nation's needs for additional trained public-health personnel. Already the schools have serious financial problems; increased enrollment based on present financing methods would only compound existing difficulties . . . The average cost to the schools of educating 1 student in 1952–53 was $4100, only 14 percent of which was met by tuition and fees . . .

We believe that these schools should have Federal financial assistance . . . The majority of the task force concluded that the Federal Government, without interfering with the internal affairs of the schools, should make grants to accredited schools for training at the graduate level, and provide funds on a matching basis for capital outlays at the schools.

The National Fund for Medical Education, of which former President Herbert Hoover is honorary president, has estimated that the Nation's medical schools need from $250 million to $300 million in construction funds, and an additional $15 million a year to overcome operating deficits.

Early this year the Senator from Alabama [Mr. Hill], and other Senators from both parties, introduced S. 1323, a bill which would provide $250 million in matching construction grants to the medical schools over a five-year period. At Senate hearings in May 1955, the Committee on Labor and Public Welfare was informed that 96 percent of the medical school deans endorsed the bill. It has also been strongly endorsed by the American Medical Association.

It is important to realize that research knowledge is of no use unless there are enough doctors to apply it to sick people. In testifying for S. 1323, Dr. Howard A. Rusk, Chairman of the Health Resources Advisory Committee, warned the Senate committee that the doctor shortage in this Nation had reached a critical point. Dr. Rusk quoted the following from an official report which his committee, made up of some of the Nation's leading physicians, had transmitted to the Office of Defense Mobilization in February of last year:

There are unmet demands today in medical education, public health, mental and tuberculosis hospitals, industry, and rehabilitation, to name only a few areas. Many rural areas and small towns are in need of practicing physicians . . . If the threat of attack on the cities of this country were to materialize in any of the presently predicted forms, the combined effect of civilian casualties and casualties in the health professions would place a considerably heavier burden on the population than did the last war, when the civilian population suffered neither military attack nor such an occurrence as the influenza pandemic of the First World War. A civilian disaster of the magnitude possible today could put an incredible load on the civilian health personnel.

The sum of $350 million is recommended for the medical schools as an absolute minimum. S. 1323 provides for construction only. However, there is need for at least $20 million a year for the next five years to bolster the operations of the medical schools.

There is no argument about this. The Rusk Report pointed out that only twenty-one of the seventy-two four-year medical schools meet present faculty standards set by the American Medical Association. There are close to three hundred unfilled full-time positions on medical-school staffs, due to the desperate shortage of doctors. Eighty percent of the medical-school faculties are composed of part-time men.

I view this Federal grant program as complementary to the many commendable private efforts being made to bolster the financial condition of our medical schools. I was heartened, as I know all of us were, by the recent announcement that the Ford Foundation would grant $90,000,000 in endowment income to the Nation's forty-two private medical schools.

In a comprehensive article analyzing the impact of the Ford grants upon the medical schools, Earl Ubell, the distinguished science editor of the New York *Herald Tribune,* pointed out that the Ford grant will merely enable the medical schools to keep up with the ever-rising cost of medical education. Here is what Mr. Ubell wrote:

Because the needs have run so far ahead of income, the Ford grant, even though it will increase by 10 percent the medical schools' annual funds for instruction, can do no more than hope to preserve the status quo. The total additional money which will become available annually out of interest from endowment will be between $3,500,000 and $4 million. Even $10 million a year—if it could be raised—would not keep up with medical school budgets growing at a rate of $11 million a year.

Furthermore, it is important to realize that the Ford grant provides no money for construction or equipment. In my proposal, a minimum of $250 million, and possibly $300 million, would go for construction.

Mr. President, I want to emphasize very strongly that my overall proposal has absolutely nothing to do with any aspect of socialized medicine. I am unalterably opposed to socialized medicine. This program would have no aspects of socialized medicine, since it is in keeping with recommendations and endorsements made by the Hoover Commission, the American Medical Association, the Administration's Health Resources Advisory Committee, the Nation's medical-school deans, and the country's leading research scientists.

Mr. President, I believe there is nothing closer to the heart of Americans than medical research. Surely it is not a matter on which to practice false economy. Surely it is a matter for imperative, immediate, and sustained expansion. Surely it is a

wise investment that American taxpayers will gladly and un-
stintingly make and give.

The promise of medical research is a really fabulous one.
It is now merely on the threshold of its greatest advances
against disease and premature death. Our young children growing up today will live longer and be more productive and
useful citizens because in the past 15 years we have begun to
support medical research. On November 7, 1955, Dr. Leonard
A. Scheele, the distinguished Surgeon General of the United
States Public Health Service, expressed this magnificent potential of medical research in words far more eloquent than any
I can summon. I quote Dr. Scheele:

It would seem then that in another generation—two or
three decades hence—the population of the United States
could be as free of venereal disease, tuberculosis, paralytic
poliomyelitis, rheumatic fever and rheumatic heart disease,
and the complications of streptococcal infections as it is today
from smallpox, typhoid fever, yellow fever, and malaria.

This healthier population would present the Nation with a
military potential virtually free of such former causes of rejection as dental decay, ear defects due to streptococcal infections, chronic nephritis, tuberculosis, disabling rheumatic
heart disease, and crippling due to poliomyelitis . . .

As the scientific, medical, and public-health professions
have overcome difficult problems in the past, we may expect
to solve many of the remaining problems through full cooperation of our scientific, medical, and health services potential. Healthier in its freedom from many diseases now
prevalent, the population of tomorrow will expect, and will
enjoy, higher levels of physical and mental health.

EDITOR'S NOTE:
Senator Smith's entry into this field of medical research legislation was not exactly welcomed. Despite the fact that she
was the former Chairman of the House Armed Services Med-

ical Subcommittee, she was considered by many in the Senate a Margaret-come-lately on this subject. Some friends of Alabama Senator Lister Hill, long-time Chairman of the Senate Labor and Public Welfare Committee and the Appropriations Subcommittee on Health, Education, Welfare and Labor, and the acknowledged Senate leader on medical research legislation, viewed her thrust as an attempted usurpation of his leadership. In fact, aides of some Senators told me that they had been called by a top majority staff member on the Senate Labor and Public Welfare Committee and urged to get their Senators to boycott sponsorship of the Smith Medical Research bill.

But if Senator Lister Hill resented Senator Smith's thrust, he never so indicated. Instead he worked very courteously and cooperatively with her and Senator Warren Magnuson on medical research appropriations. The leaders on the House side were John Fogarty of Rhode Island and Melvin Laird of Wisconsin, both members of the House Appropriations Committee. Invariably the principal leaders in the House-Senate conferences on medical research appropriations were Fogarty, Laird, Hill, Smith, and Magnuson.

Senator Smith's S. 2925 was referred to Lister Hill's Senate Labor and Public Welfare Committee—and it never saw the light of day. Nor did the Democratic-controlled Senate (1955 to date) ever pass legislation bearing the principal sponsorship of a Republican in this field. Senator Smith may not have been welcomed in this field and a specific bearing her name may not have been passed, but that does not mean that she was not effective in her drive.

To the contrary, at the time she started her drive, Congress was appropriating only $81 million a year for medical research for the National Institutes of Health and it had been appropriating at that approximate level for several years. Only after Senator Smith started her drive for greater appropriations did Congress significantly increase them.

In fact, that rate of increase was dramatic and breathtaking. From an annual rate of $81 million for fiscal year 1955, it rose to $98.5 million in 1956, ultimately to $1307 million by

1967. In other words, after she started her crusade for more funds the annual level increased more than sixteen times.

The rate of increase was, in fact, too great after a point for the simple reason that there weren't enough trained personnel and skilled technicians to administer and apply all of the funds appropriated for medical research. Perhaps she had overdone it.

A measurement of her effectiveness was revealed on September 16, 1960, when a Testimonial Dinner was held for her at the Mayflower Hotel in Washington by four medical groups —American Association of Medical Colleges, American Cancer Society, National Association for. Mental Health, and Research to Prevent Blindness, Inc. At this dinner, multiple awards for medical research support leadership were presented to Senator Smith. She was very moved by the testimonials and spoke only briefly in response, observing that:

> In all the twenty years in which I have served in Congress, this is the one and only testimonial dinner ever given to honor only me. I shall never forget it.

The honor came at a time of special meaning. In Maine, her Democratic opponent, Lucia Cormier, was campaigning for the Senate on the theme that Miss Cormier was the Senatorial candidate who "cared," implying that incumbent Senator Smith either didn't care or didn't care enough. The partisan attack by her local opposition contrasted ludicrously with the national nonpartisan recognition of her concern for the health of all people. The recognition from such Democratic leaders as Lister Hill, John Fogarty, and Mary Lasker, a hostess and patroness for the dinner, was a thunderous answer to the false "not caring" attacks back home.

The impetus for this testimonial dinner came from Colonel Luke Quinn, an Air Force Reservist, who was the Washington representative of the American Cancer Society. Luke believed in Margaret Smith ever since those crucial hours in Cairo in

1947 when, as Air Force liaison officer on that trip, he saw how quickly and effectively Representative Smith moved to get that serum vaccine from Washington to help stop the cholera epidemic.

One of Margaret Smith's favorite sayings is "Give to the world the best you have and the best will come back to you." It applies no more poignantly to any part of the Senator's life than to her contribution to medical research. Up until 1967, she had enjoyed phenomenally excellent health. Then she began to have sharp pains in her left leg, sometimes centering in her ankle. Later it turned out that the pain in her ankle was what was called "referred" pain and that the pain actually came from her left hip.

Initial diagnosis was that of a calcium spot in her left hip and the treatment was to try to dissolve that calcium. It proved ineffectual. Then the diagnosis was that she had an arthritic left hip which was well on its way to freezing at the femur junction. Should this freezing take place, she would be a cripple for the rest of her life. She had five different medical institutions take X-rays, examine and diagnose. Each independently diagnosed the trouble as osteoarthritis. Four recommended surgery within a year. One Washington orthopedic doctor recommended against surgery and said that Senator Smith would just have to learn to live with the pain for the rest of her life.

Senator Smith decided to have surgery. It was an arthroplasty performed by Dr. Frank E. Stinchfield of the Columbia-Presbyterian Hospital, Harkness Pavilion, in New York City. Another doctor had estimated that the operation would put Senator Smith on crutches for two years. In contrast, Dr. Stinchfield told the Senator that surgery was only one tenth of the recovery and that the remaining nine tenths depended on the patient's determination to exercise.

When surgery was performed on August 6, 1968, Dr. Stinchfield discovered to his surprise that the trouble arose from a congenital dislocated hip. Apparently at birth Margaret's left hip was slightly dislocated and her swift walking for so many years, and especially with steel spike heels in the later years, had produced a steady trauma on the femur joint so as to wear away the cushion cartilage in that section and start the bones grinding on each other and developing spurs.

Dr. Stinchfield is considered the best orthopedic hip surgeon in the world by many authorities. Margaret is sure of it. She says that she never knew a doctor who had as much empathy, outside of the Smith's family physician, Dr. Dickens. But Dr. Stinchfield says Margaret is the best patient in the world. She went a long way to prove that he was right. For she shed her crutches in less than six months, much less than two years. Although the surgery was a tremendous success, it entailed a serious personal loss to Margaret. The surgery was performed while the Senate was recessing for a month for the 1968 Republican and Democratic National Conventions. Margaret was hoping against hope that her rate of recovery would be such that she could return to the Senate on September 6, 1968, and not miss any record roll call votes. At that time, she had set the all-time Senate record of 2941 roll call votes without a miss.

I talked Dr. Stinchfield into letting her leave the hospital a week earlier than scheduled. I learned from the Air Force that a medical aeroevac plane would be landing at Floyd Bennett Field at eight in the morning of September 6, 1968, to discharge one litter patient and two ambulatory patients after a flight from McGuire Air Force Base in New Jersey. It was arranged to have the Senator placed in a stretcher on the plane to replace the discharged litter patient and to have the ambulance deliver her to Floyd Bennett Field fifteen minutes ahead of the plane landing.

Previously Senate Majority Leader Everett Dirksen and Senate Majority Leader Mike Mansfield assured me that the Senate would not vote until one-thirty or two in the afternoon. So that when the ambulance carrying Senator Smith, medical attendants, and myself rolled up to the edge of the runway at Floyd Bennett Field fifteen minutes ahead of the Air Force aeroevac medical plane, the Senator felt that luck was going her way. The flight to Andrews Air Force Base at Washington would take only an hour and fifteen minutes thus getting her into Washington at least four hours before the scheduled roll call vote. She could keep her record unbroken.

But the best laid plans of mice and men and machines are often interrupted. Foggy weather set in, and though commercial airlines were flying, the Air Force aeroevac medical plane would not take off because of the danger of turbulence to its passenger patients. The plane sat on the runway for more than three hours waiting for the weather to clear.

Finally, at ten minutes after eleven, it took off. This still left us a fighting chance to get to the Senate Floor before the roll call as arrangements had been made to take her onto the Senate Floor in a wheel chair. Under reasonable conditions she could be on the Senate Floor by twelve forty-five, somewhere around an hour ahead of the time of the vote.

The Air Force plane landed at Andrews Air Force base at about twelve-twenty. Before the ambulance departed, I went into the operations building, telephoned the Senate and talked with J. Mark Trice, the Secretary of the Minority, at twelve-thirty, to check on the status of the session. Then the roof fell in. Trice told me that the Senate had already voted at twelve-fifteen instead of waiting until one-thirty or two as understood. The reason he gave was that some Senators wanted to speed up the session in order to get away earlier that afternoon.

The Senator's cherished roll call voting attendance record had come to an abrupt halt. So close—and yet so far. I went back to the ambulance and instructed the driver to proceed to Walter Reed Hospital. Then I told the Senator the bad news, "Your record string has come to a halt.* There will be two more roll call votes this afternoon, but you have been thinking more about your voting than yourself. Now that you missed one, it's time to start thinking about yourself and forget about these other votes."

She agreed.

Less than two years later, trouble developed in the Senator's right hip. Neither she nor Dr. Stinchfield hesitated this time. On July 8, 1970, she had the Charnley type "total hip replace-

* Her first miss since June 1, 1955.

ment and low friction arthroplasty," a vast improvement over the method of the first surgery in 1968. One week later she took her first step. Sixteen days after the operation she left the hospital—and nineteen days after the operation she was back in her office at work—and she has had no pain whatsoever since the operation. Again, on August 25, 1971, Dr. Stinchfield performed the Charnley hip replacement surgery on her left hip. Three weeks later on September 15, 1971, she stood on the Senate Floor making a major address.

Yes, "Give the world the best you have and the best will come back to you." Senator Smith gave the best she had in support of medical research, and medical research returned the best to her. For it was through research that these miraculous forms of surgery were developed. They removed the intense pain she had suffered and no doubt saved her life. It had been this kind of arthritic hip debilitation that ultimately killed Secretary of State Christian Herter. She was boundlessly grateful.

But her greatest satisfaction came not from her recovery, but more from what it had done for others. The extensive news coverage on her hip surgery prompted a flood of inquiring mail from persons throughout the Nation suffering from hip ailments. Many of them learned of the new operative procedure* as a result of the news coverage of the Senator's surgery and gained courage to undergo the same surgery themselves. Senator Smith felt that indirectly she might have been the cause of relief from pain and suffering to many people throughout the Nation—and this was the greatest benefit that came to her out of her own physical adversity.

* See Appendix for detailed summary of hip operations.

A Debate With Eleanor Roosevelt

"Face the Nation" Telecast
November 4, 1956

From my earliest time in Congress, Eleanor Roosevelt was a good friend. Our friendship, which crossed party lines, was based, I think, upon mutual respect. Certainly I respected and admired Mrs. Roosevelt for her intelligence and active leadership and also because, in whatever circumstances, she was a lady. This First Lady achieved great dignity in her very active role as the wife of the President—and in other roles as well.

Eleanor Roosevelt was an unusual First Lady at that point in history. In addition to the grace she gave to the White House as the President's wife, she was not content to serve only as his hostess. Instead, she dedicated herself to causes, and not just to causes but to their leadership. Although not content to be a shy, retiring White House wife, and becoming instead a world traveler to promote the welfare of people, she did not neglect her duties as hostess.

Despite her drive, Mrs. Roosevelt attained something that not all aggressive women do—she avoided being officious or offensive. She was a good example of a woman who did not lose her femininity, even though a public figure. Mrs. Roosevelt managed to be respected by the men of government and to be liked by their wives as well.

I was often at the White House because of the kindness of Mrs. Roosevelt—a guest on her radio program on the Mutual Broadcasting System, and later on her television program.

And I became a "stablemate" with Mrs. Roosevelt in the United Features Syndicate family that distributed her "My Day" column to many papers throughout the Nation. For in early 1949, Larry Rutman, General Manager and Executive Vice President of United Features, convinced me that I should write a daily column too.

It was my impression that perhaps Mr. Rutman's motivation was that Mrs. Roosevelt was discontinuing her column. This had been rumored. Following the announcement that I had signed a contract, it was reported that Mrs. Roosevelt had changed her mind and decided to continue with "My Day."

In early October 1956, the women's division of the Republican National Committee asked me to debate Mrs. Roosevelt on television. CBS had requested the Republican National Committee to provide a Republican woman to speak in support of President Eisenhower. The Democratic National Committee had agreed to supply Mrs. Roosevelt to speak in support of Presidential nominee Adlai Stevenson. The debate was to be held on CBS's "Face the Nation" panel-forum program on November 4, the Sunday before the election.

I was hesitant and so declined, suggesting other Republican women who were more effective and sharper debaters. Several days later the National Committee came back, saying that all the other Republican women they had invited had declined. The committee official also said that President Eisenhower had personally expressed a strong desire for me to be the Republican debater.

Still reluctant, I instructed Bill Lewis to ask about the planned conditions of the debate. He was told that there would be a panel of three or four reporters who would direct questions at Mrs. Roosevelt and me. They would alternate in asking the questions—and alternate in soliciting the initial answers between Mrs. Roosevelt and me. We would each have the opportunity to comment on the other's answers.

Lewis suggested some revision of the format. Both Mrs. Roosevelt and I should be afforded two-minute opening statements and two-minute closing summaries, the order to be decided by a flip of a coin. I said, "All right, tell them that under that arrangement, I'll do it."

The next day the committee office called Bill Lewis and said that CBS had balked at the suggestion of the opening and closing statements. They would take too much time out of the program—eight minutes out of a net of twenty-seven minutes left after time taken by commercials. Lewis said, "Then Senator Smith will not go on."

The next day, CBS offered a compromise—no opening statements but okay to close with summaries. I agreed. The time was set.

Such was the first part of planning for the debate. Bill and I planned the details of my performance as well. I felt that I was far from a match for Mrs. Roosevelt in debating and in the breadth and depth of knowledge of issues. The first order of business was to try to anticipate the questions and the issues and to do detailed and meticulous homework.

In all the planning, there was one predominant consideration—how and what would Mrs. Roosevelt do in each aspect. Because of her great confidence, her long experience in innumerable radio and television discussions, her depth and breadth of knowledge on vital issues, and her heavy personal schedule, Mrs. Roosevelt might not take much time to prepare for the debate. She was very busy and there was no need for her to so do.

The next consideration was my appearance. This was staged like a scene. What would I wear? How would my hair be styled? These weren't just *my* questions—they seemed to be of consummate interest to Bill too. Again there was guessing: what would Mrs. Roosevelt wear—what would her hair style be?

The reason for this type of analysis and anticipation was to achieve a favorably sharp contrast between Mrs. Roosevelt and me. I felt that this would be as important, if not more important, than whatever we said in the debate.

In order to seek a contrast, the comparison had to start with Mrs. Roosevelt. She was a much larger and taller woman. But her towering height over my five foot three inches would show only if we were standing. The usual format had the reporters sitting on one side and the guests sitting opposite them at separate tables. Thus, my minor size would have to be dealt with from the tabletop level up. There was not much to be done about that except to wear clothes of a color and style that effected slimness.

This accentuated the importance of hair styling. What was Mrs. Roosevelt's hairdo apt to be? I remembered that she usually had a full-bodied hair style, rather loosely rolled and pinned back. Bill Lewis asked if there was not a good chance that she would wear a hat. November 4 meant cool weather. If so, such a hair style plus a hat would tend to give her a top-heavy appearance.

This was our guess. So it was decided that for maximum contrast, I would not wear a hat and I would wear my white hair in the usual soft waves, at medium length. No special change there.

The next part of our guessing game was clothing. Again, we considered the likely temperature and weather of November 4. My memory of Mrs. Roosevelt's clothes led us to think that with her crowded schedule and personal temperament, she probably would not dress especially for the program.

Chances were that she would come directly to the studio from some other activity. On a cool or cold day, that would ordinarily mean heavier clothes than usual. I guessed that she would wear a tweed suit.

A natural contrast for this (on black-and-white television) would be a dark dress—black or navy blue—very plain and simple with full or three-quarter sleeves. Jewelry and accessories? My decision was to limit such to a short strand of pearls and my trademark, a red rose. This would not only effect a contrast of trimness, perhaps, but of simplicity.

So much for attempted contrast in physical appearance. Next was demeanor or conduct—air or style some might say—not only toward the interrogating reporters of the panel but to Mrs. Roosevelt herself.

As I had no intention of being anything but courteous and polite, the only question was how best to project that courtesy and politeness. Again the question was on contrast—how would Mrs. Roosevelt, a courteous woman herself, act?

Our guess was that Mrs. Roosevelt would principally project great self-confidence—which was natural and genuine. She would be courteous to me but probably not particularly warm in anticipation of the debate. Her attitude was apt to be detached and really objective with respect to the reporters and me but subjective in her championing of Adlai Stevenson.

The best contrast for this, and my only "choice," really, was to be myself.

I did plan to show respect and deference to Mrs. Roosevelt

and to her seniority as a national leader—and under no circumstances would I try to match her forcefulness. Further, on any
preference for seating or other arrangements—with the sole
exception of the flip of the coin on sequence on the summary
statements—I would defer to Mrs. Roosevelt.

This brought the guessing and planning to the final consideration. How would I handle the questions?

Knowing what we did about Mrs. Roosevelt, we decided that
she could be expected to speak with conviction and an impressive tone of authority, fluently and at length—and in a decidedly
partisan manner. Now I could not hope to exceed her knowledge, depth, breadth, or fluidity. To attempt to do so would be
unnatural and could be disastrous. I am anyhow (except in
this book) a woman of few words. I speak rarely in public—
and then briefly. If a question can be answered with "Yes" or
"No," that's the way I answer.

Again, we figured that the best contrast would be the natural
contrast. I would answer the questions as briefly as possible,
slowly, deliberately, in a low, even-pitched tone. This, of course,
entailed a risk: as a good debater, Mrs. Roosevelt might dominate the debate and I could look weak in contrast. But I preferred this risk to laboring answers or observations and over-
extending myself to the point of vulnerability.

I was confident that in a summary statement, I could offset
any appearance of weakness that might result from brevity and
restraint. Hence from the time of the commitment to the debate
itself we drilled on the issues and on that summary statement.

Bill Lewis and I arrived at the CBS studio at station WTOP-
TV in Washington well in advance of broadcast time. It was a
little after 4 P.M. Shortly after meeting with those in charge of
the broadcast, Bill was informed that there would be no closing
summary statements because of the time they would take.

Bill said: "Then Senator Smith will not go on. You have
broken your commitment on closing statements. You've done it
at this last minute and without prior notice."

CBS officials insisted on the change. Bill consulted me and I

said, "I will not go on under such a change." He then informed CBS officials. After some discussion, they agreed to keep
summary statements in the format. (Some weeks later one of the
reporters on the panel told Lewis that the reporters had threatened not to go on unless the summary statements were cut out.)

Mrs. Roosevelt came in late, as the TV makeup girl was
finishing a few touches on me. She said a sort of perfunctory
hello, and then centered her attention on the incoming news
accounts of Eisenhower's stand against the Israeli-French-Brit-
ish invasion attack on the Suez Canal and Egypt. I noted that
she was wearing a loose-fitting beige shantung suit, a hat—and
an Adlai Stevenson button.

Very shortly she joined the reporters and me in the studio.
There was a table for the reporters—and facing that table a few
feet away was a table for Mrs. Roosevelt and me. We were asked
for our preferences in seating. I deferred to Mrs. Roosevelt.
Mrs. Roosevelt chose to sit at the right.

A flip of the coin was made. I won the flip and elected to make
a closing statement after Mrs. Roosevelt had made hers.

After the usual opening, the show quickly got into the questions and answers. Mrs. Roosevelt was extremely articulate and
fluent. I stuck to brief answers. My deference to Mrs. Roosevelt
was seemingly to avoid controversy and that disturbed the director of the program who naturally was hoping for an exciting,
unrestricted verbal exchange. Standing in the sealed-off control
booth with him, Bill Lewis was amused to hear him moan in
frustration. "Talk *more*, Senator Smith," he cheered me on,
"Eleanor is monopolizing the discussion."

Meanwhile, in front of the cameras, it was evident that Mrs.
Roosevelt was caught by surprise as I refrained from tangling
with her. The more that I spoke softly and smiled faintly, and
the less I said in reply, the more Mrs. Roosevelt seemed to be
put off balance. And this made her talk more to try to regain her
composure and emotional balance. (A transcript later showed
that Mrs. Roosevelt had talked twice as much as I did.)

For the whole debate, on points of argument, Eleanor Roosevelt was winning hands down. Only her apparent uneasiness at our strategy of brevity and restraint caused her to talk even more than she intended. This began to come through to the viewers, I was told, to the point of diluting the effectiveness of her excellent arguments and blunting the edge she deserved.

That is the way it went until our summary statements. As she went first, there was nothing new in Mrs. Roosevelt's summary. She did the orthodox and logical thing and simply summarized the arguments she had made.

My statement for the most part was not a summary of what I had argued. Instead, I tried to make it a series of unanswerable arguments. I had saved them for the finale. I said:

Yes, I think we all want the H-bomb tests dropped, but not until we have the [mutual inspection] guarantees that are demanded by President Eisenhower.

The domestic policy record of the Eisenhower Administration is told in the nonpolitical finding made by McGraw-Hill that "the American economy is more prosperous than ever before, by almost any measure"—a fact proved by statistics, not a mere political claim.

The foreign policy record of the Eisenhower Administration is one of moral principle for peace and against aggression, whether by friends or foes. [On this I was answering Mrs. Roosevelt's heavy denunciation of Eisenhower's pressure as he tried to get Israel, France, and Britain to withdraw from their Suez Canal invasion.] As one who has publicly condemned irresponsible accusations of treason and pro-Communist against Democratic Presidents and leaders, I condemn the current politically motivated charges that President Eisenhower is pro-Communist and a supporter of dictators Perón, Nasser, and the evil men in the Kremlin.

Americans, regardless of political party, resent such accusations against President Eisenhower because Americans believe in fair play.

That our moral leadership in world affairs and world respect and confidence for our nation is the highest ever, is proved by the record-breaking 65 to 5 support given in the United Na-

tions to our stand against aggression in the Middle East—
and by Britain, France, and Israel standing with us on opposition to Russian aggression in Hungary.

This part of my summary was orthodox in that it did answer
Mrs. Roosevelt's criticisms. What was surprising about it, perhaps, was my abrupt change in delivery. It was not the soft,
restrained, measured delivery in deferential tones—nor was it
said with a smile. Instead it was a biting staccato.

I suppose to her the most annoying part of my summary was
yet to come:

Democratic Presidents, together with leaders of our Allies,
chose Dwight D. Eisenhower to lead our nation to victory in
World War II and to head up NATO to stop the spread of
communism. In fact, he was so good the last Democratic President asked him to be the candidate for President on the
Democratic ticket. It is strange to see and hear Democratic
leaders now accusing him of not being a leader. Why the
difference? It is clearly the difference between principles and
politics. They chose him on a nonpolitical basis of principle—
they now attack him just because he is not a partisan Democrat.

Tuesday, Americans—whether Democratic, Republican, or
Independent—will again choose principle instead of politics and
re-elect Dwight D. Eisenhower.

EDITOR'S NOTE:
Who is to say who won the debate—Mrs. Roosevelt or Margaret
Smith? Yet, it was clear who was happy at the conclusion of
the debate and who was not.

The game plan which had called for a useful contrast between the two women had worked well. Shantung was not

tweed but on the black-and-white television of that era, there wasn't much difference. Even without the added advantage of the planned contrast, Senator Smith's grooming and general appearance were nicely telegenic anyhow.

When Senator Smith reached over to shake hands with Mrs. Roosevelt, the First Lady pulled away, turned her back, and said to her companions as she walked away, "Did you hear what she said!" Mrs. Roosevelt's anger was certainly understandable. It was her husband, President Franklin D. Roosevelt, who, with Winston Churchill, had selected Dwight D. Eisenhower to be Commander-in-Chief of our Allied Forces in Europe and to lead our nations to victory in World War II—and it was Roosevelt's chosen successor, his Democratic Vice President Harry S. Truman, who as President not only had picked Eisenhower to command NATO but had asked him to be the Democratic candidate for President in 1952.

Any sense of satisfaction the Senator might have felt at the end of the debate was tempered by Mrs. Roosevelt's refusal to shake hands. Mrs. Smith did not feel that her reference to the Democrat's preference for Eisenhower—until he revealed himself as a Republican—was unethical because it was that party which had raised rough questions about his leadership ability.

Whether this debate, almost on the eve of election, had much effect on the electorate one can only guess. It did not appear to decrease the vote for President Eisenhower. His winning margin was 50 percent larger than his previous plurality in 1952.

Generals in Retreat

Little did I anticipate when Jimmy Stewart, the movie star, kissed me on April 19, 1955—right in front of the news cameras—that I was to become a villainess to many of his loyal admirers. I have always admired Jimmy Stewart and was enjoying this chance to be with him. The occasion was the Sixteenth Annual Awards Dinner of the Overseas Press Club of America in New York, and I was the principal speaker.

Within two years, on February 25, 1957, when Air Force nominations for three Reserve Major Generals and eight Reserve Brigadier Generals were sent to the United States Senate for confirmation, the list included the name of Jimmy Stewart. The nominations were made public around noon of that day, but I did not learn about them until the protest calls began pouring in. The first was from Air Force Reserve Colonel Roger Zeller, National President of the Reserve Officers Association, asking me to make a full investigation of all the nominations. He took greatest exception to Stewart's nomination on the grounds that Stewart's activity in the Reserve since the end of World War II had been minimal at best, and his selection was a blow to the morale of thousands of far more active Air Force Reservists. Air Force Reserve Colonel Thomas H. King, who had been President of the Reserve Officers Association in 1954 and 1955 when the Reserve Officers Personnel Act (Reserve promotion bill) had been passed in the Senate under my guidance, echoed Zeller's objections.

There were yet other protests—not from Reservists and not against Stewart. These were from several Regular Air Force Generals against another nominee, John B. Montgomery. A former Regular Air Force Major General, Montgomery had resigned from the Air Force after twenty-two years of service to become Vice President of American Airlines and after his resignation had been commissioned at the highest possible rank for a Reserve direct commission of Colonel. The protesting Generals were contemporaries of Montgomery and resented the fact that he had left the Air Force for the much higher salaried job in industry; by resigning from the Regular status and transferring to the Reserve [under a loophole in the Reserve law], in eight years after his resignation he would be able to secure his right to as much retirement pay as a Regular Major General.

At our customary end-of-the-day conference I told Bill about the calls and he told me of the many he had received. I said to him, "You know, Bill, if I do investigate, you must realize you will be accused of getting me to do it. You will take a lot of abuse." [He was a Colonel in the Air Force Reserve.]

Bill replied, "So will you. [I was a Lieutenant Colonel in the Air Force Reserve.] But I can't ask you to refuse to investigate. I couldn't look my father* in the face—or his colleagues—or my Reserve contemporaries."

"Then it is settled," I said. "You'd better examine the profile sheets on each nomination and draft a letter to the Secretary of the Air Force." Three days later the analysis and the letter were finished. The final form of the letter was delivered on February 28. It read:

February 28, 1957

Honorable Donald A. Quarles
The Secretary of the Air Force
Department of the Air Force
Washington, D.C.

My dear Mr. Secretary:

As you know, for many years I have been very active on Reserve legislation and intensely interested in the Reserve programs of our Armed Forces. My activity and interest has been prompted by my deep belief that the only way in which our country could maintain the necessary national defense strength in a world constantly threatened with war without bankrupting itself was through the formula of a Regular Establishment backed up by the largest possible and best trained Reserve. Otherwise in striving for military security we would run the risk of losing economic security and thus the economic struggle to those who would subvert our country.

* His father, Brigadier General William C. Lewis, Sr., had been the driving spirit of the Air Reserve Association.

My efforts and activity in this regard on the Reserve are not of mere recent vintage and not limited to only a few years—as is the case of at least one of the individuals recently nominated for a Brigadier General Air Force Reserve appointment—for it goes back more than fourteen years to 1943 instead of merely to June 1955. In the past fourteen years I have probably introduced more Reserve bills and resolutions than any member of either the House or the Senate. More specifically, in connection with the matter about which I express myself in this letter to you, I have been the principal congressional sponsor of ROPA legislation—so much so that it has been extensively referred to as Smith Acts.

It is in that connection that I so express my deep concern to you. Specifically, I am shocked at some of the names nominated for Brigadier General in the Air Force Reserve. I cannot believe that you are fully familiar with the Reserve record of all of the nominees or would condone what appears to me to be action that constitutes debasement of the Air Force Reserve. It creates a considerable cloud as to the integrity of the United States Air Force and the Department of the Air Force. And it certainly violates what I, as the chief sponsor of ROPA legislation, consider to be the spirit and the objectives of the Reserve Officers Personnel Act.

At this time I am not in possession of complete facts with respect to each of the individuals nominated for Brigadier General officer rank in the Air Force Reserve. This situation was called to my attention by complaints registered by members of the Reserve Officers Association on February 25, 1957, and I have been supplied with enough information since that time to shock me at what has been done. The more that I look into this matter and the more information that I receive on individual nominees the more disturbing the situation gets.

I shall notify the Chairman of the Armed Services Committee of my reservations as to one or more of the nominees and request that the appointments be held up until such time as the Committee has received full and pertinent information on all of the nominees. The information that I shall request will be for the purpose of determining to what extent and for how long each nominee has been a practicing Reservist. I shall request that the selection folders on each nominee be made available for inspection by the Committee with particular reference to AF Form 712 and AF Form 1085. I shall request a full inquiry as to the operation of the Selection Board, what instructions they were given by you, how many recommendations you requested from the Board, how many recommendations they submitted to you, and if the list of nominees as submitted to the Senate includes all recommended by the Board originally or any not originally recommended by the Board.

Because of my confidence in you and believing that you would not knowingly be a party to the situation as indicated by the following information which has been submitted to me, I am showing you the courtesy of notifying you of my intended action prior to the time of taking it up with the Chairman of the Committee. Let me make it abundantly clear that I do not do so with any idea of action on your part as a result of this letter, but rather so that you will not be taken by surprise and unprepared in the matter. I now call to your attention very disturbing facts in the following individual cases.

Colonel John Beverly Montgomery

I personally know this nominee and admire him. He has an excellent record as a Regular officer. That is not to be challenged. But it is not a sufficient basis upon which to justify the action taken in using and abusing the Air Force Reserve for his personal prestige and financial gain.

On June 13, 1955, this nominee resigned and was honorably discharged from his position as a Regular Major General in the United States Air Force. It is reported to me that he had applied for retirement as a Regular Major General but that his application had been turned down. I am further informed that he then resigned in order to accept *a more remunerative* position in civilian life as a Vice President of American Airlines. Thus, the value of twenty-two years of service and experience of this capable forty-three-year-old Regular officer with a *potential of nineteen more years of service* to the United States Air Force was lost by the Air Force and the United States Government because of his resignation to better himself financially.

It would appear at first glance that he had made a great

personal sacrifice and given up the twenty-two years of retirement pay by his resignation. But upon closer examination it will be seen that he actually made *no such sacrifice* but instead made a *very significant financial gain.*

For on the *very next day* after his resignation from the United States Air Force he was given a commission of full Colonel in the Air Force Reserve—the *highest* direct Reserve commission permitted under law. Thus, he not only avoided missing a single day of service credit for retirement purposes—but through such maneuvering and manipulation he gained *more* than he had had —he gained more than that which the Air Force had refused to give him when he applied for retirement from the Regular Air Force.

For under Title II of Public Law 810, upon being commissioned in the Air Force Reserve, he could apply *at any time* and upon approval of the Secretary of the Air Force be retired with pay at any time. And he would get not only two and a half percent of the annual base pay of a Major General for every one of his twenty-two years as a Regular but also for every additional year as a Reservist even if he put in *as few as* thirty-five training periods in a Reserve status year—or *approximately seven times* as much retirement pay and credit in each Reserve status year as the vast majority of Reservists could get. Thus, he can accumulate up to seventy-five percent retirement pay.

The statement could be made that the Secretary could always refuse to accept the retirement application of an officer under the above circumstances. When the Air Force would accept applications from other Regular officers whose total service equals that of this officer's combined Regular and Reserve service, the Secretary would have difficulty in refusing to accept the application.

This situation arises because of the language of Title II and it *dramatizes* a need for Congress to give serious consideration of *revision* of the law in that respect for greater parity with the provisions of Title III.

Now let us consider this nominee's record as a practicing Reservist. As stated before, his record as a Regular is admirable and without question. But that is not a criterion for record as a Reservist.

He was appointed a Colonel in the Air Force Reserve on June 14, 1955. The record of service on him up to date as of February 1957 as furnished to the Senate Armed Services Committee shows that during that time his Reserve service was limited to one fifteen-day period from October 1, 1956, to October 15, 1956. In other words, on the standard or criterion of his evidenced interest and participation in the Air Force Reserve and as to whether he was a practicing Reservist actively participating in the Air Force Reserve program, the record shows in the absence of any non-active duty training periods:

(1) That in a period of nineteen and one half months, he participated actively in the Reserve *only* fifteen days;

(2) That in the first fiscal year following his appointment as a Colonel in the Air Force Reserve (FY ending June 30, 1956) he had *absolutely no active duty in the Air Force Reserve* (hardly an indication of real interest and participation in the Air Force Reserve)—and there is no indication that he earned any non-active duty training points in that period;

(3) That he did not take *any* active duty training for *more than fifteen and a half months* after he was commissioned in the Reserve—and significantly enough such indicated interest, activity and participation only came suddenly and very shortly before the convening of the Selection Board for promotion of Reserve Colonels to Reserve Brigadier Generals; and

(4) That under the cut-off date set by the Secretary of the Air Force (December 31, 1955) for consideration of Reserve Colonels for promotion (no Reservist thus being eligible for consideration unless he became a full Colonel on or before December 31, 1955), this nominee got *under the rank deadline* by only a few months—on which there could be some suspicion as to whether the deadline was almost *tailor-made* for him.

This is *hardly* the record of a practicing Reservist. It is hardly the record of one *truly* interested in the Air Force Reserve program. It is hardly a record of *active* participation in the Air Force Reserve.

From practically *every* standpoint to be considered, it is a record of *cutting* corners and of *tailoring* to the *tremendous* accommodation of this nominee. His selection by a Selection Board seems hardly justified—and it raises considerable doubt as to the *independence* of the Selection Board. It gives rise to considerable suspicion that in his case, the Selection Board met *only to go through the motions of complying* with the provisions of ROPA, with the circumstantial evidence strongly indicating that the decision to promote him to Brigadier General in the Air Force Reserve at the first selection time being made at the time of the acceptance of *his resignation* from the Regular Air Force and his commissioning in the Air Force Reserve, regardless of *how little* he participated in the Reserve program.

Perhaps an *overall insight* into this case comes from information reported to me—that the principal recommendation for making this nominee a Brigadier General in the Air Force Reserve came from a Regular officer who is reported to have said to the Chairman of the House Armed Services Subcommittee on Reserve Forces that in his opinion *there was no need or justification for an Air Force Reserve.* If that report is true, then this recommending Regular officer apparently did *ultimately* find *some* use or *excuse* for the Air Force Reserve as it became a *vehicle* for personal *gain,* both financial and prestige, for his *former fellow Regular.*

Colonel James Maitland Stewart

I personally know this nominee and admire him, both his war record and his motion picture accomplishments. But his record as a practicing Reservist is *deficient* in my opinion.

After World War II, his service records show only *two* tours of active duty. The first of these tours was an eight-day tour from August 24, 1952, to September 1, 1952. The second was a fifteen-day tour from July 10, 1956, to July 24, 1956.

In other words, this nominee did not have *any* active duty in the fiscal years of 1954, 1955, and 1956—a total of three years in which he was deficient on active duty training requirements.

Further, this nominee did not get in any required fifteen-day active duty after World War II until July 10, 1956, to July 24, 1956—so that with the exception of the current fiscal year, he has been *deficient* on the active duty training requirement.

I base this on my understanding that retention in the Active Reserve, the Ready Reserve, requires an annual fifteen-day active duty tour and that the only exception is that one waiver can be given in one out of every three years.

This raises a serious question as to whether this nominee is *qualified for the Ready Reserve,* much less a question about meeting either the letter or the spirit of the regulations with respect to required participation in the Reserve.

Like Colonel Montgomery, this nominee did not get in *one* fifteen-day active duty training tour until within *a few months* of the meeting of the Selection Board. The circumstances create suspicion.

As fine a person as Colonel Stewart is—as popular as he is—as much as he has done from a public relations standpoint for the Air Force, his is not the record of a real practicing Reservist. He has a record of interest in the Air Force—but it is *not* a record of *sustained* interest and *active* participation in the Air Force *Reserve.*

It is my understanding that the principal recommendation for this nominee came from the *same Regular officer* reported to have stated there was no need or justification for an Air Force Reserve.

Colonel Daniel De Brier

While this nominee has several short periods attending meetings, he did not perform a fifteen-day active duty training period in the years of 1953, 1954, and 1955—*no fifteen-day active duty period from 1952 to 1956.*

Again as in the case of Colonels Montgomery and Stewart, his fifteen-day active duty tours came late in 1956 and *just shortly before* the Selection Board convened.

The question existing with respect to this nominee is his deficiency on the requirement of fifteen-day active duty tours.

Colonel John Richardson Alison

This nominee admittedly has a most admirable war record and the distinction of being a past President of the Air Force

Association. But again such is not a criterion of active participation in the Air Force *Reserve*.

For *nine* years from August 11, 1946, to August 7, 1955, this nominee had *no activity in the Air Force Reserve*. Suddenly he became active in 1955 after a nine-year lapse. So that his record of active interest in the Air Force Reserve is relatively most recent.

The record of this nominee is not that of a practicing Reservist for a long and sustained period earning promotion.

Colonel Ramsay Douglas Potts

This nominee admittedly has an admirable war record. But again that is not a criterion of active participation in the Air Force Reserve.

His record shows that he did not have a fifteen-day active duty tour in 1951, and 1954. He was on extended active duty in 1949 and 1950 and 1952—but he had no fifteen-day active duty tour in those years.

In other words, since 1949 he has had only three years—1953, 1955, and 1956—when he had fifteen-day active duty periods.

Obviously, he is by far more of a practicing Reservist than the others I have thus far analyzed. But obviously there are *many well-qualified* Reserve Colonels who have a *better* practicing record.

Colonel Jess Larson

This nominee is a good friend of mine. I think that since he joined the Air Force Reserve he has a good record as a practicing member of the Air Force Reserve. But his case is not exactly one to *inspire the morale* of thousands of loyal practicing Reservists in the Air Force Reserve. It is not—because he did not enter the Air Force Reserve until August 4, 1952—transferring from the Army Reserve. In other words, he was brought in from the outside over other loyal Air Force Reservists. Ultimately this resulted in the ridiculous situation of his Deputy in the Reserve outranking him with the rank of Brigadier General for two years.

Thus, of the eight Reserve Colonels nominated for Brigadier General, I have reservations that range from a deeply serious degree to relative deficiency on six nominees. When I can find deficiencies in *three fourths* of the nominees, I cannot help but be *skeptical* of the manner in which the nominees were selected. This much is sure—that as a whole they *do not qualify* as a group of *real practicing Reservists* who have been active in the Air Force Reserve for a *respectable* length of time. To the contrary, a majority of them would fall more into the category of *"Johnny-Come-Latelies"* in active membership in the Air Force Reserve.

These facts are extremely disturbing. They raise serious doubts as to the *sincerity* of the Air Force with respect to the Air Force Reserve and the *use* that is made of the Reserve—more properly put, the *abuse* of the Reserve—as a *vehicle* for benefits that *former Regulars* cannot get otherwise or as a means of giving prestige to Reservists who are *not* practicing Reservists and who clearly have not *earned* such recognition or prestige. The potential blow to the morale of the members of the Air Force Reserve is obvious.

Mr. Secretary, in making these observations, I do not speak to you *only* as a member of the Senate Armed Services Committee. I speak to you as the *congressional sponsor of the ROPA* laws under which these nominations have been made and by which, I feel, at least the spirit and intent of ROPA laws have been subverted by clever manipulation and hardly ethical or confidence-inspiring action.

I speak to you not only *as a Senator* with the solemn responsibility of voting to confirm or reject these nominations, but *as an Air Force Reservist* myself. I speak to you as an *employer* of a real practicing Reservist whose activity in the Air Force Reserve has been at considerable sacrifice to my office.

Thus, (1) as a *Senator* acting on confirmation of these nominations, (2) as a member of the Senate *Armed Services Committee,* (3) as a member of the Senate *Appropriations Subcommittee on the Defense Department,* (4) as the chief congressional sponsor of ROPA under which these nominations are made, (5) as the member of Congress who has been the *chief proponent* of Reserve legislation, (6) as an Air Force

Reservist *myself,* and (7) as the *employer* of a practicing Air Force Reservist, I am in a most *unique* position to judge this matter—and I consider it to be *shocking.*

Sincerely yours,
Margaret Chase Smith, U.S.S.

A few days later, the Air Force Director of Legislative Liaison called on me and stated that the Secretary of the Air Force was going to be abroad for two or three weeks and would like to talk with me at my convenience upon his return. Shortly after his return, I went to his office and conferred with him and the Air Force Chief of Staff. I told the Secretary I had no desire to wash the Air Force's dirty linen in public but that such was inevitable in the public hearing that would be required. The Secretary and the Chief of Staff refused to budge. The only concession the Secretary made was that he did feel that the Selection Board could have selected a stronger list. In our frank discussion the opinion was expressed that on the basis of his lead role in the movie *Strategic Air Command* Jimmy Stewart rated being made a Brigadier General. I observed that surely Jimmy Stewart suffered no sacrifice or loss in making the picture and that undoubtedly he was paid several hundred thousand dollars for making the picture and that surely such could not be considered Reserve duty and participation.

"You do not really seriously believe Jimmy Stewart rates a Brigadier Generalship for playing in a movie?" I asked incredulously. "Yes," came the vigorous, decidedly positive response. "Then why don't you make June Allyson a Brigadier General for playing the female lead in *Strategic Air Command!*" I was the only one who grinned.

The inquiry into the nominations began with formal letters to the Air Force listing detailed questions about the records of the nominees and Air Force regulations and policy. I notified Chairman Russell that when the Air Force had provided written answers to the questions, I wanted a hearing held on the nominations.

Six weeks later the hearing was held on May 2, 1957. Word came to me that the Air Force witness, Lieutenant General Emmett O'Donnell, Jr., Deputy Chief of Staff for Personnel, had refused to be briefed by the Air Force Legislative Liaison or the Air Staff. The report was that he said angrily that no "skirt" was going to tell the Air Force whom it could or could not promote.

The hearing started with Chairman Russell asking General O'Donnell if he had any statement he desired to make. He answered, "I do not." Chairman Russell then turned to me and I made my opening statement, the highlights of which were:

The most important premise of this legislation [Reserve Officer Personnel Act of 1954], in providing for an Active or Ready Reserve, is that members are trained in order to perform a specific assignment when called into an active service. The Active or Ready Reserve by definition is that segment of the Reserve which is trained and ready for immediate call.

The best measure we have for knowing whether an officer is trained is his participation in training duty. If there are officers who do not complete the required training or need not do so, then by definition there is no requirement for them in the Active Reserve. They should be either discharged or placed on the inactive status list, which is the place to which persons who need no training may be assigned. If discharged, they could always be reappointed in the proper grade in the event of mobilization, if they are still available.

. . . While civilian positions of business prominence, and even glamour, may have considerable value to the Air Force in a variety of ways, they should have no relevance in the consideration of promotion to general officer. These various positions do not create a stronger Air Force Reserve.

After all, Regular Air Force officers are elected for general-officer rank on the basis of their record of active service, which indicates whether they possess the potential for broader responsibilities.

Likewise, I believe that the Reserve service record of Reserve officers should be the basis for selection to Reserve general rank. There should not be a double standard.

I then started questioning General O'Donnell. His attitude was openly derogatory. His answers implied that I was either making misrepresentations or did not know what I was talking about. Except for a few questions by Senator Symington, former Secretary of the Air Force, in a heavy tone of defense of the nominees and General O'Donnell, the hearing amounted to a verbal dual between the General and me. Senate committees extend a courtesy to witnesses to let them edit their testimony before the hearings are printed. That courtesy is limited to improving the grammar or expanding their answers so long as they do not change the sense of the answers they gave at the hearing. When this courtesy was extended to General O'Donnell, he completely reversed his answers in several instances. For example, on page fifty-four of the transcript, I asked General O'Donnell in reference to Colonel Stewart being rated as only a pilot instead of Command Pilot or Senior Pilot although his mobilization assignment was Deputy Director of Operations of the Strategic Air Command, "Is it not a fact that the overwhelming number of rated Reserve General officers are either Command Pilots or Senior Pilots?" To this General O'Donnell answered with a vigorous and unequivocal denial saying, "Oh, no. Definitely not." This was a double denial. Yet in his penciled changes he struck out that answer and substituted for it a complete reversal with the answer of "Yes."

He made changes on sixty-two of his eighty-three pages of testimony. I wrote a letter* to Chairman Russell about his "wholesale rewriting of one's testimony," and Russell notified the Air Force that such rewriting would not be permitted by the committee.

In reading the transcript of the hearing, I found three or four instances in which my grammar could be improved. When I

---

* See Appendix for complete letter.

talked to Bill about changing them, he cautioned me that O'Donnell supporters would seize upon even such few and meaningless changes as evidence that I was seeking to do for myself what I opposed O'Donnell's doing. "You give them something to put their hat on, Senator, and they'll end up putting a whole wardrobe on."

So I made not one change in the transcript of the hearing. Bill's caution proved to be somewhat prophetic. For subsequently the committee staff director revealed that a member of the staff of a Senator had gone to the committee to ask to see what changes Senator Smith had made in the transcript. It must have been disappointing to his Senator, a supporter of O'Donnell, to learn that I hadn't made a single one.

The committee did not finally act on the nominations for four months—time for a full barrage of the anticipated press attacks. Basically the charges were that I was blocking Jimmy Stewart because I myself had not been promoted to full Colonel in the Air Force Reserve and that my assistant Bill Lewis had not been promoted to Brigadier General.* The tactics of the Stewart-Montgomery-O'Donnell forces were such that I wasn't at all surprised when a Senator approached me privately and said, "Miss Margaret, I am authorized by the Air Force to warn you that if you don't remove your objections, your name will be blackened from coast to coast along with that of Bill Lewis. I will deny that I ever said this to you."

* EDITOR'S NOTE: The charge against her was false on its face for she was the coauthor of the bill that gave women a permanent place in the armed services and the bill provided that only one woman could be a Colonel in the Air Force and that had to be the head of the WAFs on extended active duty. She would not have left the Senate to head the WAFs even if she could have. In short, she had co-written a law that barred her from being promoted.

As for promotion for her assistant, she and I know that her opposition to the nominations would certainly prevent that. A Maine man who was the public relations strategist for General O'Donnell in this controversy bragged to the United States Attorney of Maine that Lewis would never get promoted as a result of what Senator Smith had done.

About seven weeks after the May 2 hearing, I accidentally learned that my mobilization assignment had been downgraded by order of a Headquarters Operations Instruction issued by General O'Donnell's Personnel command. I was not so notified by the office of my Reserve assignment. Shortly thereafter the Air Force formally acknowledged that this was the only instance of downgrading that year.

"Will be?" I replied. "Why, they have already done it." About a month later, this same Senator came to me and said, "Miss Margaret, if you will relent and let these nominations be approved, I promise you I will do everything I can to get Bill Lewis made a General." All I could say to this was, "Senator, obviously you don't know either Bill Lewis or me very well. I have no intention of withdrawing my opposition." During this four-month waiting period, the Air Force deliberately sent Jimmy Stewart across the country to my state to do part of his Reserve training at Loring Air Force Base in Limestone, Maine. They were so confident that Stewart would be confirmed that five days before the vote, Jim Lucas, the Scripps-Howard military correspondent, [acting on information which he later told us came from a Senator] forecast disaster for me. He wrote:

> The Senate is set to authorize a general's star for Hollywood actor Jimmy Stewart over the opposition of its only lady member . . . Some of Mrs. Smith's colleagues are ungallant enough to suggest she's balking because her own administrative assistant, William Lewis, a reserve Air Force colonel, wasn't on the promotion list . . .

The morning of Thursday, August 22, 1957, found considerable tension in my office. This was the day of the showdown meeting. About five minutes before the scheduled ten-thirty meeting time, I walked into the committee room with my nine-page, double-spaced statement in hand. The committee went into closed, executive session. Chairman Russell called on me, and I read it, slowly and deliberately. When I finished no one spoke up for Stewart, not even the Senator who had so vigorously supported his nomination. The Stewart nomination was rejected unanimously, 13 to 0. One Senator made a very personal plea for Montgomery; but when the vote was taken on Montgomery, that nomination was rejected by an 11 to 2 vote, the second vote coming from a proxy left with the Montgomery pleader who cast it with his own. I then informed the committee that I did not oppose any of the other nominations and they were approved. I was content to terminate the controversy at that point, having no desire to gloat over the victory. It had been a very unpleasant experience for all concerned.

But the Senator who had relayed the Air Force threat to me, who had attempted to soften me up with promised support for Bill Lewis, and who also had been the one who misinformed Jim Lucas, did not consider the issue closed. He challenged me to stand publicly on what I had said in the closed, executive committee session that rejected the Stewart and Montgomery nominations. I accepted his challenge and placed in the Congressional Record on August 23, 1957, my statement against the nominations. [See Appendix B.]

This then evoked a statement on August 26, 1957, from General O'Donnell, obviously embarrassed as a result of the insistence of his Senate champion that I make my statement public. The tone of the O'Donnell statement was not just a denial that he had made false statements to the committee but strongly implied that he had been taken advantage of and not permitted to be adequately prepared. "I had no prepared statement for the committee," he said, "because I could not anticipate the scope of the hearings."

It is to be remembered that the hearing was not held until May 2, 1957. More than two months prior to that time, in response to my questions, the Air Force sent much of the basic material on the nominees to the committee. On March 20, 1957, I requested further information and the Air Force provided that information a month prior to the hearing. In addition, the Air Force was given thirty-one written questions relating to the entire gamut of Air Force Reserve matters, including details on the nominees and written answers were prepared by the Air Force and submitted many days prior to the hearing.

There was no attempt to take General O'Donnell by surprise. His inadequate performance tended to confirm the earlier reports that he had angrily refused to have the normal briefing by Air Force Legislative Liaison and the Air Staff prior to testifying before the Armed Services Committee. Whether that report was accurate or not, it was abundantly clear that General O'Donnell simply didn't do his homework in preparation for the hearing.*

EDITOR'S NOTE:

An immediate result of the Air Force controversy was that Chairman Russell introduced a bill to close up the loophole in the Reserve Retirement law which would have permitted Montgomery to draw full retirement pay in his Reserve status regardless of how little he had participated. Russell asked Senator Smith to cosponsor the bill. She did and the bill was quickly enacted and the Montgomery loophole closed up.

That was not to end the Stewart-O'Donnell-Montgomery controversy, however. Both Stewart and Montgomery were renominated again two years later. Again the Air Force put out stories to the press. A United Press International article appearing on February 13, 1959, stated that an Air Force "spokesman said Stewart is a qualified B-52 pilot." Later in answer to written questions from Senator Smith, the Air Force admitted that this was untrue and that Stewart couldn't be a qualified B-52 pilot with his low training category "D."

When Senator Smith had first opposed the Stewart nomination, she said that two basic changes would have to be made before she would withdraw her opposition to his promotion to Brigadier General. The first was that he would have to comply with training requirements just like any other Reservist seeking promotion. The second was that he would have to be shifted away from the assignment of Deputy Director of Operations of the Strategic Air Command to something more realistic, like an assignment in Information.

* Senator Smith's full reply to General O'Donnell is on pages 16708–19 of the Congressional Record of August 30, 1957.

Yet, when the Air Force resubmitted his name in February 1959, nothing much had changed. And so the committee simply sat on his nomination for five months.

Not until very shortly before resubmission of his nomination had the Air Force acted to change his assignment from Deputy Director of Operations of the Strategic Air Command. Even then the Air Force did not make the change to a more realistic one in Information. Instead he was put into another unrealistic slot in the Strategic Air Command as Chief of Staff of the Fifteenth Air Force. Another Air Force Reserve officer was expelled from the position and Stewart moved into the vacancy. Ironically, the displaced Reservist was later promoted to Major General. Stewart himself had beefed up his participation record, but the Air Force remained adamant about keeping him in the unrealistic Strategic Air Command mobilization assignment.

When the committee met on July 16, 1959, to vote on the list of nominees, Senator Smith stated that she would not oppose Stewart, since he had improved on his training participation, if his mobilization assignment were changed. Chairman Russell then sent a message to Air Force Secretary Douglas stating that the committee would not clear the Stewart nomination until two conditions were met: (1) the committee would have to receive a certified copy of Air Force orders changing Stewart's mobilization assignment from Chief of Staff of the Fifteenth Air Force to Information and (2) the Air Force would have to issue a press release stating that Stewart had been assigned to Information.

The Air Force finally transferred Stewart and on July 18, 1959, issued the release:

FOR THE PRESS:

James M. Stewart, nominated for the rank of Brigadier General in the U. S. Air Force Reserve, has been assigned a mobilization position as Deputy Director of Information Services, Office of the Secretary of the Air Force.

END

The question of Senator Smith's own retirement from the Air Force Reserve had come up quite coincidentally at the time the Stewart and Montgomery promotions were first proposed. Yet on his June 22 broadcast carried by radio stations throughout the nation Drew Pearson charged that Senator Smith was seeking special treatment as an Air Force Reservist and that General O'Donnell was refusing to give her special treatment with respect to her retirement.

The truth was just the opposite. Lieutenant Colonel Paul Newman of the office of the Assistant Chief of Staff for Reserve Forces had come to me to explain that under an Air Force Directive implementing the Reserve Officer Personnel Act of 1954 (which Senator Smith was instrumental in getting enacted) she would have to resign that year on December 14, when she reached the age of sixty, or else be kicked out by being involuntarily discharged. She could not become a retired Reservist because she had only eight years in the Air Force Reserve rather than the required twenty.

Newman said that because of all that Senator Smith had done for the Air Force,* they would be very unhappy to have her forced out because of the regulations and inquired if it would be agreeable with her if they made an exception in her case. I replied that under no circumstances would Senator Smith agree to being given special treatment. Senator Smith wanted to be treated like everybody else. I did observe that it seemed shortsighted and unfair to force a Reservist to resign or be kicked out simply because he had less than twenty years status, particularly since he was ineligible for retirement pay. The restrictive directive was subsequently canceled on December 20, 1957, and since that time the Air Force has not been kicking

---

* The question has often been asked as to why the Air Force offered Senator Smith a commission in the Air Force Reserve. George S. Robinson, a Maine man, was the instigator. He was the Legal Adviser and Special Assistant to the Director of Air Force Legislative Liaison. He says that he proposed that she be given an Air Force Reserve commission for what she had done for the Air Force and because at the time there was some speculation that the Navy wanted to add her to its stable of Reserve officers that included Senators Lyndon B. Johnson and Warren Magnuson and Representative Sterling Cole. He proposed that the Air Force get her before the Navy.

out any sixty-year-old Reservist with less than twenty years service. Because the business manager of Drew Pearson's syndicated radio program was Ed Hart, a good friend of ours, I complained to him about the unfairness of Pearson's June 22 broadcast. Pearson told Hart that the original piece had been written by his assistant, Jack Anderson, and was far more severe than what Pearson ultimately used. He promised to give Hart a photocopy of the original Anderson piece to give to me so I could see how Pearson had softened the Anderson piece. He never did.

Senator Smith received several rumors that O'Donnell was spreading derogatory stories against her. One Air Force Legislative Liaison officer had told me that O'Donnell had purposely planned to fight Senator Smith through a public relations campaign. Consequently, when O'Donnell's own nomination for his fourth star came before the Senate Armed Services Committee for confirmation (he was being shifted from Deputy Chief of Staff for Personnel to Commander of Pacific Air Forces), Senator Smith disqualified herself from voting on the nomination because of her personal resentment with the reported actions of O'Donnell. O'Donnell testified twice in closed session with the committee before it acted on his nomination. In the June 19, 1959, issue of the New York *Herald Tribune,* David Wise reported that O'Donnell had denied to the committee feeding the material to Drew Pearson against Senator Smith. Wise also wrote:

> However, Mr. Pearson declared: "Following the broadcast I found I had been given erroneous facts regarding Sen. Smith and wrote a full column setting the facts straight." The column dated August 29, 1957, accused "Air Force propagandists" of spreading the stories which formed the basis for the broadcast . . .

After he denied feeding information to Pearson for the broadcast, the committee voted 12 to 1 to confirm O'Donnell. Only

Senator Harry F. Byrd, Sr., of Virginia voted against him. Two and a half years later on January 29, 1962, Pearson called me and asked if I would see his assistant Jack Anderson. He said that Anderson wanted to establish friendly relations with Senator Smith and me, that Anderson realized that he had been unfair and erroneous in the past, wanted to so acknowledge and make amends. I told Pearson that I would see Anderson.

An hour and a half later, Anderson entered Senator Smith's offices and came into my room. He told me that he realized that he had been unfair to Senator Smith on past occasions and had written erroneously about her, that he had been misled by some people, that he wanted to express his regrets and hoped that he could resume friendly relations.

I observed that neither Senator Smith nor I desired unfriendly relations with Anderson but that it was only natural to resent the unfair and false things he had written for Pearson about Senator Smith, specifically the June 22, 1957, broadcast material. Anderson then acknowledged that he had been misled in that instance at the instigation of General "Rosie" O'Donnell and expressed his resentment at being misled.

Two days later Pearson called me to inquire if Anderson had properly and adequately made his peace. I said yes and added that Anderson had identified General "Rosie" O'Donnell as the instigator of Pearson's broadcast attacking Senator Smith. Pearson replied that while it was his policy not to identify his informers that in this instance he would have to say that Anderson had spoken truthfully and that O'Donnell was the instigator.

Thus, four and a half years after the Pearson broadcast and two and a half years after the committee vote on the O'Donnell nomination came the admission.

The rejection of the Stewart and Montgomery nominations created in its wake an unusual assignment for the Senator. Air Force Secretary James Douglas asked her to perform a two-month-active-duty mission for him. "Critical-skill" enlisted men and junior officers were leaving the Air Force at such a rate that the Air Force was alarmed. The Air Force wanted

Senator Smith to find out why their men were not staying in.

Secretary Douglas said that though he trusted his Air Force commanders in the field, he did not believe that an airman or lieutenant would talk unreservedly across the desk to a commanding officer Colonel or General. He was confident, however, that they would "level" with Senator (Reserve Lieutenant Colonel) Smith for two basic reasons.

The first was that the vast majority of such Air Force personnel were Reservists—and no one possessed the confidence of Reservists to the extent that Margaret Chase Smith did. The second was that these personnel would feel that they weren't wasting their time and breath talking to a blank wall but would feel that something would be done about their gripes because Margaret Chase Smith was a member of the Senate Armed Services Committee, the Senate Appropriations Committee on Defense, and the Senate Preparedness Investigating Subcommittee. No one else possessed these two unique qualities, Douglas said, and that was why he was asking her to accept the mission—a mission he described as of top priority to the national security.

The Senator told Douglas she would think it over. The arguments he made to her were not easy to answer. Frankly, she could not deny them. And although the Senate was out of session for the rest of the year and performing the mission would not cause her absence from any Senate session, she felt reluctant to say yes. She suspected that the Air Force may have been buttering her up after the recent nominations controversy.

During the few days she was weighing her decision she received a report from inside the Air Force that General O'Donnell, with extreme vigor, was protesting against her being given the mission. He was claiming that it would be a serious reflection on his personnel policies and his personnel administration. That did it. She notified Douglas that she would accept the assignment but for one month only rather than two. This was agreed to—also her stipulation that she would not be in uniform when conducting the conferences with the airmen and junior officers.

In the one-month mission, she held interview-conferences with more than three hundred Air Force personnel, ranging from airmen to four-star generals, and filed a 101-page report of findings, statistics, analyses, and recommendations. Her assignment had come at the time of the release of the Cordiner Report, which had found that the need for higher pay was the prime reason for the high drop-out rate. With the Cordiner Report the military were pushing Congress for a pay raise, and Senator Smith had suspected that this may have been another reason the Air Force had asked her to conduct an inquiry.

But she decided to set that suspicion aside until after she had made her study. It was well that she did because her study disclosed that "Job Dissatisfaction" was the primary reason for leaving the Air Force. It led the list of reasons with 44 percent. "Pay" was a poor second with only 21 percent; followed by "Promotion and Recognition," 12 percent; "Living Conditions," 12 percent; "Lack of Security," 7 percent; and "Discipline," 3 percent.* Before filing her final report, Senator Smith asked to be informed of the total amount of expense she had incurred in performing the mission. She was informed that it was $690.01. She then wrote her personal check in the amount of $690.01 to the Treasurer of the United States.

Her final assertion of independence came when she was told that she had been recommended for the Legion of Merit decoration for the performance of the mission and her report. She wrote Douglas: "This is to request that the recommendation be denied." Douglas replied that he would "respect the request," thanking her for "an outstanding service to the Air Force and the Nation."

A prediction made by an Air Force General during the height of her controversy with the Air Force eventually came true. "Margaret Chase Smith will be a United States Senator," he said, "long after Rosie O'Donnell has retired." Rosie O'Donnell did retire several years ago. He had gotten his fourth star, but no Distinguished Service Medal or any other decoration for

* Fourteen years later the Air Training Command was using the Smith Report as a personnel guide and reference.

his performance during the controversy or his six years as Deputy Chief of Staff of Personnel. On retirement, he did receive the Distinguished Service Medal for his subsequent performance as Pacific Air Forces Commander. Jimmy Stewart got his first star but was never selected by the Air Force for another, and he got the Distinguished Service Medal upon his retirement from his Information assignment a few years ago.

One day, fourteen years after the nominations put-down, the Air Force Chief of Staff, General John D. Ryan, made a visit to Senator Smith in her office. His purpose was to get her clearance on the selection of General Lewis to be the Chief of Air Force Reserve. This was Major General Homer Lewis, and no relation to me. The Senator gave her assent. After General Ryan left, I looked at her and smiled. "Senator, you've come a long way since the days of Rosie O'Donnell!"

NOTE: An item in the *Navy Times* of October 20, 1971, stated:

Gen. John D. Ryan, Air Force Chief of Staff, has sent a blistering letter to Air Force Reserve and Air National Guard general officers advising them to be more discriminating in the selection of star rank.

The general made it clear that he is fed up at Capitol Hill legislators turning up evidence of unfitness of Reserve force star nominees after general officer nomination lists have been sent to the Capitol for confirmation.

Woman Versus Woman

TV-RADIO DEBATE WITH LUCIA CORMIER

NOVEMBER 6, 1960

"On none of these have I attacked Mrs. Smith. I have criticized her party for its stand on those issues."

—Lucia M. Cormier
November 7, 1960

My campaign for re-election in 1960—for my third term in the Senate—marked the only time in American political history when the nominees of both the major political parties for a major office were women. I was so successful in the 1948 and 1954 elections in overcoming the campaign argument that "the Senate is no place for a woman," that I must have overdone it. For the Maine Democratic leaders concluded that their best chance to beat me was with a woman of their own—Lucia Cormier.

She was a political gem as the likable, dynamic Democratic Floor Leader in the Maine State Legislature. She was an educator with brilliant ability to articulate, and a top-notch debater. We had been good friends as fellow members of the Business and Professional Women's Clubs of Maine. In the 1952 Presidential campaign when India Edwards, top woman on the Democratic National Committee, wanted my support for Adlai Stevenson against Dwight Eisenhower she sent Lucia to ask me. In my early years in the Senate, Lucia had once returned from a Washington visit and given a glowing report to her home town paper in Rumford, Maine (where Senator Edmund Muskie was born), praising me and reporting that I was popular in Washington.

It was not easy to campaign against a friend and the difficulty was intensified by the fact that we were running woman-against-woman. Both of us recognized that we had to guard against actions or developments that might reflect on women generally—on women in public office, women in politics. We wanted to avoid the slightest appearance of a clawing, scratching "cat" fight.

National news media, sensing that a cat fight would make more sensational and interesting reading, continually maneuvered and pressured for open controversy between the two of us.

Their basic tactic was to try to get each of us to make a statement about the other. My repeated refusal brought on me the label of the "silent candidate." Repeatedly, I was told that if I didn't make a statement for television or radio I couldn't demand equal time with Lucia. I resisted this throughout the campaign because I recognized that once I gave in I would have surrendered control of my campaign to the national news media. Not only that, but each time I engaged in such a desired exchange, it would give Lucia a gain of increased political exposure and would tend to narrow the public recognition gap between the incumbent defender and the challenger.

Another unpleasantly new factor in this campaign was that for the first time a Senate colleague was actively seeking my defeat—the junior Senator from Maine, Edmund S. Muskie. The only other time another Senator had gone into Maine to urge my defeat was in 1954 when John F. Kennedy made one television appearance with my Democratic opponent.

This time was different, far more than a single shot appearance in Maine. Senator Muskie handpicked Lucia to run against me. He helped launch her campaign with two luncheons at the Capitol in early February 1960. He held a press conference for her at which he stated that he had had her go on the Senate Floor to sit in one of the Senate seats so that she could begin to warm up a seat he said she would take the next year as the new Junior Senator from Maine when he would become the Senior Senator.

It was rather gratifying when several Democratic Senators came to me to disassociate themselves from these tactics. Many eyebrows were raised in the Senate Club; for it was one thing to have partisan campaigning against a colleague back in the home state but it was not an accepted practice to bring such tactics right onto the Senate Floor in such a direct way as to embarrass a colleague from one's own state.

With respect to the first luncheon, Senator Muskie announced in advance that he had invited Lyndon Johnson. But Lyndon refused to attend and called to tell me he would boycott any opposition to me even if it was Democratic opposition. Those who did attend—Carl Hayden of Arizona, Tom Hennings and Stuart Symington of Missouri, and Muskie —posed with Lucia in a post-luncheon picture of clasped hands of "all for one, one for all." Later Tom Hennings came to me and apologized, saying he had not realized what he was getting into and would not knowingly do anything to oppose my re-election. And Carl Hayden came two years later in 1962 to ask me to pose with him in a picture to be used in his re-election campaign bid.

The second luncheon was with the freshmen Democratic Senators of Senator Muskie's 1958 class. Subsequent to this luncheon, Sam Shafer of *Newsweek* called Bill Lewis and told him that Senator Muskie and Miss Cormier were confident of defeating me by getting a solid French-Catholic vote for French-Catholic Lucia. He said this had been reported by Senator Eugene McCarthy to the press in an informal chat. Bill responded with incredulity. No one controlled voters in Maine on a religious basis, he said. Three of the four most senior members of my staff were all Catholic (two French-Catholic, one Irish-Catholic) and he couldn't conceive of their voting against me and for Lucia Cormier.

The demand for a Smith-Cormier debate came early. Lucia announced that she was willing to debate with me, but she did not challenge me. Don Larrabee, the Bangor *News*'s man in Washington, wrote a piece suggesting the possibility of a national debate between the two women candidates. Though my office stated that I would have no objections, I certainly had no desire for such a debate.

In the first place, I just don't believe that political TV debates are either constructive or informative. I consider them a form of political bloodletting responsive more to desires for sadistic entertainment than constructive enlightenment.

In the second place, it is a well-established political truth that almost invariably the out-of-office challenger gains and the in-office incumbent defender loses in a public debate. This is because the incumbent inescapably is on the defense of his record. Such an exchange pulls the incumbent down and the challenger up—gives the challenger publicity and public exposure he couldn't get otherwise and lessens the initial advantage of the incumbent.

In the third place, I felt that Lucia would win easily in the debate because she is a trained and skilled debater, with master's and doctor's degrees, and a more aggressive nature. There was no reason for me to be anxious to have a debate I thought I would lose.

In the fourth place, I felt that such debating could give credence to the cat fight image of the Maine Senatorial race so assiduously promoted by the national press. While such characterization made for good and interesting copy, I was determined to avoid it at all costs even if it resulted in the quietest campaign possible. Not only did I not seek "free" radio and TV coverage in newscasts and guest appearances, I went to the extreme of turning down requests made by the various news media for interviews and guest appearances. By doing so I prevented their giving equal time and coverage to Miss Cormier.

A case in point was when NBC engaged an independent reporter-cameraman, Phil Coolidge of Boston, to get a filmed interview at a Republican campaign meeting in late October in Augusta, Maine. Apparently the objective was to get me to make statements on certain issues and next to go to Miss Cormier and get her statements taking issue with Senator Smith's already filmed statements, then to cut, splice, and paste the two films together in a composite job that would effect a debate between the two of us.

Bill conveyed my declination to Coolidge. He said that the meeting at Augusta was to be a pleasant social gathering of Republicans in the closing days of the campaign and that no speeches were to be made and that I would be there for pleasure only and would not make a speech and would not issue campaign statements. Although Coolidge pressed Bill, he did so in a very courteous manner and finally realized that the declination was firm and that I would not relent.

When Coolidge reported back to NBC in New York, he was told that they would send someone up from New York who could get the job done. While the other networks made similar requests and received the same declination for the same reason, they did not press the issue. Not at any rate until the night of the Republican social gathering in Augusta. The networks were there in force with blood in their eyes. They were not willing to admit that any politician could turn them down. Harry Reasoner, then of CBS, seemed to be their leader and spokesman. He first approached Bill with a soft and friendly request that I make a statement. Bill said that I had no statement to make as the meeting was purely social. He then asked that I submit to questions from the network representatives. Bill said that I was not going to make political statements of any nature at this social gathering.

This would be to my disadvantage, Reasoner contended, as Miss Cormier had already been interviewed and their presentations would be one-sided if I did not respond. Bill replied that such was a political disadvantage I was willing to accept.

Then Reasoner complained that the network representatives had come all the way from New York to get statements from me at this meeting and that it was unfair in view of the time and expense entailed for them to be refused. Bill then reminded Reasoner that the networks' specific prior requests with respect to this meeting had been clearly declined in advance and for the same reason; despite that, and with full knowledge, they had still chosen to make the trip and such was their own responsibility and not mine.

During the Reasoner-Lewis exchange, Bill saw Coolidge standing by with a rather satisfied smile on his face. Finally Reasoner became convinced that I really meant "no." He turned around to his colleagues and told them to pack up their gear and head back south. As the last one straggled out, Coolidge walked up. "God bless you, Bill. You made an honest man out of me. Those so-and-sos in New York didn't believe me. They thought I was just a local hick too light to get the job done!"

Because of my refusal to be drawn into the "equal time" trap, I won no popularity accolades from the news media. Yet, I was willing to pay that price as I was determined that they would not run my campaign to my disadvantage. I meant to control the situation—and I did.

One time the news media did pierce my wall of resistance was when Miss Cormier made the cover of *Time* magazine's September 5, 1960, issue and I was given "equal" space on the cover with her. Bill Lewis wryly observes that the only time I ever made the cover of *Time* magazine was "piggyback" style on Lucia Cormier.

Perhaps what got my back up most in dealing with the press was an extremely unpleasant experience with a Washington gossip reporter. This woman reporter made a long distance call to me one morning at 2 A.M. She wanted to do a campaign profile story on me and wanted to come up and live at my house and drive around with me in my car for three or four days. She said she expected me to provide her with lodging, food, and transportation while she was in Maine.

I was so dumbfounded by this brazen demand made at such a time in the morning that I thought I must be having a nightmare. I told her that I could not provide lodging, food, and transportation and could not let her live with me for three or four days. I pointed out that to do that for her, I would have to do it for many other women reporters who wanted to follow me in the campaign—and that I had neither the money nor the facilities to comply with all requests. She could follow me around, I said, but she would have to arrange for her own food, lodging, and transportation.

The gossip reporter came up shortly and hired a car and followed me around for a couple of days. I let her ride in my car for a considerable time during that period. The reporter left two major impressions with me and Bill Lewis. The first was her penchant for standing close to me eavesdropping on some of my most personal conversations. The second was her saccharine praise of me. "Brace yourself," Bill warned. "That spoken sugar is going to turn to vinegar in print."

It did. The gossip columnist wrote a scathing hatchet piece that was extremely careless with the facts. Three weeks prior to the appearance of the column, I had accepted an invitation from radio-television station WCSH-TV, Portland, to do a thirty-minute TV debate with Miss Cormier on November 6, 1960. Yet, the gossip columnist falsely reported that I had refused to debate with Miss Cormier.

Her sources for adverse comment included "one college professor," who called me a political "duenna." Frankly, I didn't know what a "duenna" was until I went to the dictionary and found out it was "an elderly woman who watches over a young woman" and a "governess" for children. I recognized the unnamed college professor as a disgruntled former supporter from Bowdoin College who the year before had guided one of his young Republican students in writing a thesis that predicted my overwhelming defeat in 1960.

Until the final six weeks of the campaign, Miss Cormier had been content to talk on issues and to refrain from direct attacks on me. Then, however, just as the Democrats had done in the previous campaign, she started firing salvos at me, and from that time on was relentless.

The theme of her attacks was that she "cared" and I did not. She accused me of having a calloused attitude toward the aged, of being cold and arrogant and unsympathetic to the problems of working men and women. She claimed I had not spelled out my views on vital issues and was "insulting the intelligence of Maine voters," that I was for high interest rates, that I was opposed to natural resources power development, as well as to the REA program and the TVA.

EDITOR'S NOTE:
As for the charge of being calloused toward the aged and not caring for them, the Townsend publication of September 22, 1960, stated about Senator Smith that "She has a wonderful record and has been most friendly to the Townsend organization . . . I certainly hope you will see fit to vote for her

November 8." As for the charge of not caring about the problems of working men and women, the October 22, 1960, issue of the publication *Labor* reported that nineteen railway unions had endorsed Senator Smith for re-election "because of her fine voting record and her staunch defense of the public interest" and textile union leaders had stated that "the members of our union surely know that you have done everything in your power to assist them in their struggle to maintain their jobs, families, and communities."

As for the charge of not spelling out her views on vital issues, Senator Smith's speeches during the campaign had covered practically all of the issues, and her views had been clearly recorded on 2022 roll call votes in twelve years in the Senate. As for "high" interest rates, only two years before, when he was running for the Senate against Frederick Payne, Miss Cormier's mentor and sponsor, Edmund Muskie, had on September 3, 1958, stated: "Senator Margaret Chase Smith has consistently voted against higher interest rates."

As for the charge that Senator Smith was opposed to natural resources power development, Senator Smith had voted for the TVA in the southeastern region, the Southwestern Power Administration and the Colorado Storage projects in the southwestern region, the Niagara Power project in the northeastern region and the Bonneville Power project and the Hells Canyon project in the northwestern region. As for the charge of being against the REA, the General Manager of the National Rural Electric Cooperative Association had made a signed commendatory statement to Senator Smith of "Congratulations from the millions of farmers and rural electric consumers to whom this project could mean so much." The President and Executive Director of the Citizens for TVA similarly had made a signed statement commending Senator Smith for supporting TVA legislation.

In a pamphlet put out by the Cormier-for-Senate Committee, Senator Smith was further charged with being against (1) Tidelands Oil for schools, (2) ceiling on housing loans,

(3) social security for those under sixty-five, (4) tax cut for lower income families, (5) improving unemployment compensation, (6) surplus food for the needy, and (7) old age medical aid under social security. All of these charges were misrepresentations and false. Senator Smith had documentary evidence to prove that she had voted for each of these proposals and could cite chapter and verse on her actual votes.

The Cormier-for-Senate pamphlet also implied that Senator Smith was against (1) the Passamaquoddy Tidal Power project, (2) aid to depressed areas, (3) improved unemployment compensation, (4) improved minimum wage, (5) Federal Aid to Education, and (6) medical care for the aged. The truth was that Senator Smith had (1) done more for Quoddy legislatively than any other person; (2) cosponsored the original Aid to Depressed Areas Bill with Democratic Senator Paul Douglas, and served as the first witness to testify in support of such legislation, and had supported such legislation year after year; (3) not only voted for improved unemployment compensation, but was the only Republican to vote for the McNamara-Kennedy Unemployment Compensation Bill on March 25, 1959; (4) been a Senate leader for improved minimum wage, having introduced such legislation and repeatedly voted for such legislation; (5) been one of the foremost advocates of Federal Aid to Education, so much so that the February 4, 1960, Bulletin of the Maine Teachers Association stated: "In all her career, as a Senator, Margaret Smith has never failed us when the chips were down"; and (6) voted for medical aid for the aged, having voted for H.R. 12580 just as did Senator Kennedy, Senator Muskie, and Congressman Coffin of the anti-Smith pamphlet team.

Miss Cormier, in making broad and general attacks on Republicans, picked some issues on which Senator Smith had gone against the Republican majority. But in her broad attack on Republicans on these issues, Miss Cormier did not acknowledge that Senator Smith had voted against the position taken by the Republican majority. Some of Senator Smith's votes were accurately cited, but on all of these, Senator Smith had voted the same way as the Democratic Majority Leader of the Senate and cognizant Democratic Committee Chairmen.

I chose not to answer charge by charge, for to do that would permit Miss Cormier to maintain the lead and the momentum of the campaign. I would be playing disastrously into her hands as she could keep me spending the time talking negatively on the defensive. So I deliberately chose not to respond until the closing period of the campaign. Instead I stressed such positive facts as my champion roll call voting attendance record. It was hardly assailable, though Miss Cormier made an ineffective effort to ridicule it.

About a month before the end of the campaign radio-television station WCSH-TV in Portland invited Miss Cormier and me to debate each other on Sunday, November 6, 1960, from 5 to 5:30 P.M., two days before the election. [It was four years prior that I had debated Mrs. Roosevelt at 5 to 5:30 P.M. on the Sunday before the November 1956 election day on the CBS "Face the Nation" telecast.] The format was to be patterned after the Nixon-Kennedy debates with two-minute opening and closing statements by each of us and answers to questions from four newsmen panelists and comments on each other's answers. We both accepted. This was one invitation I was not reluctant to accept because I considered the timing to be right.

Despite my silence during the campaign, I had not been unmindful of Miss Cormier's attacks and taunts. On the contrary, each attack and taunt had been immediately recorded, analyzed, and evaluated—and the legislative records were checked and refuting answers were prepared. If this was a "powder puff" contest as some called it, then I was keeping my political gunpowder dry until the proper time for its use.

Bill put all of the ammunition into a three-hole looseleaf notebook. It contained my opening and closing statements and the documented analyses and answers to some thirty of the charges made against me. He indexed and tabbed the charges and answers so carefully that I could cite any of my pertinent votes and statements of specific individuals, including Maine Democratic leaders, about my record. Studying these notes gave me so much confidence that I began to look forward to the debate. I was actually delighted about it by the time we headed for the studio.

This was an ideal forum, one in which I could answer all of Miss Cormier's attacks to a statewide audience at the most favorable time on the Sunday evening before the election. And there would be little time left for Miss Cormier to launch new attacks.

As I had for the debate with Mrs. Roosevelt, I paid special attention to my clothes and grooming. This time there was little contrast between appearances of the debaters. Both of us wore dark dresses and necklaces and our hair was similarly groomed. The chief difference was in our adornment. I had my single rose in a lapel vase while Miss Cormier wore earrings and glasses.

Miss Cormier's second was Milton P. Semer, an attorney on the staff of Senator Muskie's Housing Subcommittee of the Senate Banking and Currency Committee. He had come from Washington to Maine (where he was a legal resident) to help on her campaign and had accompanied her to the studio for the debate. Upon the flipping of the coin I won and elected to go last on the closing statements. Miss Cormier then had the choice on the opening statements. When she chose to go first, Bill was so surprised that he blurted out, "Do I understand that you want to go first?" Miss Cormier replied, "Yes." I later told Bill that perhaps Miss Cormier felt that by going first she could take the initiative with such impetus that I could never catch up with her.

We stood at separate lecterns facing a table of four newsmen and a moderator. After her opening statement, I began mine:

At the outset of this discussion, I want to state my attitude and feeling toward my opponent. Although she has repeatedly characterized me throughout this campaign as being cold and arrogant, not caring about the older persons and the working people, of insulting the intelligence of Maine voters, ridiculing my voting record, implying that I was afraid to debate, chiding me for my independence of thought, and making other attacks on me—I have never made an attack on her or voiced criticism of her.

Instead I have expressed respect and praise for my opponent saying that she was the finest Senatorial candidate the Democrats could have selected. I said it at the outset of the campaign and I repeat it today. So that there may not be the slightest doubt about this, I say to you that she is one of the finest persons in the State of Maine.

I want to set the record straight on some of her charges against me. On her charge that I do not care about the working people of Maine, there are some very important working people who disagree with her.

For example nineteen railway unions two weeks ago called for my re-election because of what they describe as a fine voting record and staunch defense of the public interest.

For example, on July 26, 1959, the Lewiston Joint Board of the Textile Workers Union of America unanimously adopted a resolution commending me on my effective efforts in getting Senate passage of legislation for the protection of jobs of textile workers.

For example, on August 23, 1957, Mr. Denis A. Blais, Manager of the Lewiston Joint Board of the Textile Workers Union of America, wrote me stating: *"the members of our union will surely know that you have done everything in your power to assist them in their struggle to maintain their jobs, families, and communities."*

For example, on April 13, 1959, Michael Schoonjans, the

Biddeford-Saco Union Leader, issued a public statement to the press commending my effective efforts on getting Government work for workers there and he stated specifically: *"The Biddeford-Saco Joint Board, TWUA, AFL-CIO, is indeed grateful and proud of our Senior Senator Margaret Chase Smith for her untiring efforts in securing this Government contract for our area."*

For example, another union leader, Mr. Bert Demers, on July 31, 1957, wrote me stating: "You have once again demonstrated your keen interest in protecting Maine people . . . and *you have shown a willingness to serve the many textile workers who depend on you."*

Then the questioning began. To my delight I found that for the greater part I didn't have to refer to those carefully prepared notes for I had worked so hard on them I remembered them well. In the very few instances in which I did cite them I found that they gave me confidence and composure.

The questioning and answers and counter-comments went fast and smoothly and relatively quietly and most ladylike. To my surprise Miss Cormier was not an aggressive debater and she had no comments on my replies to her charges. The brilliant oratory from the extremely skilled debater just didn't come off.

I took up one by one Miss Cormier's charges on Federal Aid to Education, Depressed Areas legislation, REA, TVA, natural resources power development, unemployment compensation, high interest rates—and set the record straight. Finally, I said:

My opponent has charged that she would be more effective and cooperative than I—yet the late Democratic Governor Clinton Clauson publicly in Bangor in 1959 praised the manner in which I had cooperated with him—and on January 13, 1959, Democratic Senator Muskie made a public statement saying he knew that Maine people recognize the value of Senator Smith's prestige, experience, and seniority to the state—

and on the same day Democratic Congressman Oliver said to the press about Senator Smith: "I feel there can be much good work done by supporting her experienced leadership in the best interest of the state."

EDITOR'S NOTE:

The moment the program went off the air, Mr. Semer, Miss Cormier's second at the verbal duel, dashed up to the panel and charged that the questioning had been rigged to the disadvantage of Miss Cormier. The newsmen were stunned—Phil Johnson, Ross Hammond, Henry Magnuson, and Fred Gage. And the moderator, Larry Geraghty, was visibly shaken. There was a dead silence. Semer turned his back abruptly, strode to Miss Cormier's side and immediately escorted her out of the studio. Senator Smith and I remained for a few minutes to chat. Once we were outside and alone I told Senator Smith I was almost ecstatic over her performance. Less prejudiced persons may not be so quick to say who won the debate, I confessed, but it was evident there wasn't any doubt in Semer's mind who had lost!

Later that evening the Democratic candidates and leaders gathered at Lewiston where Kennedy was scheduled to speak. In her speech Miss Cormier denied that she had attacked Senator Smith on such issues as Federal Aid to Education, Depressed Areas, and REA, claiming that her attacks in these instances were on Republicans generally, and that while Democratic Senator Muskie and Democratic Representative Oliver had said some nice things about Senator Smith they still were supporting Miss Cormier. Senator Smith for her part made no post-mortems, extension of remarks, or rebuttals.

Who won the debate? Who is to say? Mr. Semer said plenty. And so did the voters of Maine two days later. They gave Senator Smith the biggest vote in the history of Maine and the highest winning percentage of all Republican Senatorial candidates. Though Nixon lost nationally, he and the entire Maine Republican ticket were swept in behind Senator Smith's record vote.

And although she lost by a crushing margin, in the end Miss Cormier didn't do too badly. She was generously rewarded by Senator Muskie and President Kennedy with a Federal appointment to the position of Collector of Customs for Maine.

Nuclear Credibility

SEPTEMBER 21, 1961
SEPTEMBER 21, 1962

". . . *the devil in a disguise of a woman* . . . *has decided to beat all records of savagery.*"

—Nikita Khrushchev
October 13, 1961

"*Threats are made to destroy our homes, to kill our husbands, to take the lives of our children . . . just one American name—Margaret Smith.*"

—Mrs. Nikita Khrushchev
November 15, 1961

A cornerstone of the foreign policy of President Dwight D. Eisenhower, as expressed by his Secretary of State John Foster Dulles, was that of "massive retaliation," specifically the capability of nuclear power to defend the United States. It was the Eisenhower-Dulles modus operandi for deterrence of any Russian attack on the United States.

Dulles was castigated by many for what was characterized as his indulgence in "brinksmanship," walking the edge (or going to the brink) of war in the search for peace. Yet, the quick and decisive action of Eisenhower in the Lebanon crisis and the Straits of Formosa crisis almost instantly quenched the incipient fires of international war. Nothing since has been as effective and as minor in cost as the unhesitating show of American determination and will and the strategic application of American military power to effect peace and stop war before it started.

At the initial urging of General Maxwell Taylor—and the subsequent implementation by Secretary of Defense Robert McNamara—President John F. Kennedy early in the first year of his administration repudiated "massive retaliation" as a policy of deterrence. He replaced it with a policy of controlled response, of selection of options for graduated response, and of the downgrading of nuclear capability and the upgrading of conventional capability.

Many close observers were disturbed with this change. The Eisenhower-Dulles "massive retaliation" policy based upon nuclear capability entailed grave risks. Yet, it had proved successful during the Eisenhower tenure and produced the greatest and longest period of peace for the United States since the days of pre-World War II.

Specifically, they were disturbed with the actions accompanying the Kennedy policy. For they saw McNamara espousing a rationale that we should downgrade our military strength to no more than that of a parity with Russia in order to convince the Kremlin leaders that we wanted peace.

This was, some said, in essence a theory of "peace through weakness" or "peace through less strength"—quite contrary to the "peace through strength" policy that Winston Churchill had stressed to me when we conferred at 10 Downing Street in November 1954. Whether one called it "parity for peace" or "weakness," I thought the theory was fallacious. I remembered the quick dismantling of our armed forces after World War II —and the vacuum this dismantling had created. I recalled how Russia had moved into that vacuum to take over Eastern Europe and was well on the way to a takeover of Western Europe until the United States awakened and set up the Marshall Plan and NATO.

John Kennedy was impressive to me, and millions of Americans, when, in his March 23, 1961, televised press conference, he pointed to a map and eloquently explained why we had to stand firm on Laos—and in which he issued an ultimatum to Khrushchev to get Communist forces out of Laos. But when Khrushchev called Kennedy's bluff and defied the ultimatum and Communist aggression increased in Laos, I was disillusioned. Kennedy had failed to back up his strong words.

Some months later I made a request of the Air Force intelligence briefing officer (who gave the weekly briefings to the Congressional 9999th Air Reserve Squadron) asking him to provide two maps of Laos—one showing the Communist occupied areas of Laos at the time of Kennedy's televised ultimatum to Khrushchev and the other showing the Communist occupied areas several months after that defied ultimatum. Contrasting maps would show the Communist gains in Laos after the Kennedy ultimatum. So it was no surprise that such maps, although promised, were never supplied.

In the months that followed the dramatic Kennedy television show, the Communists increasingly overran more and more of Laos and Kennedy did nothing about it. This, together with several other incidents, strongly indicated a lack of will on the part of the President. Kennedy's unwillingness to use the power of the United States had led to the dangerous result of the Berlin crisis. I decided that the time had come to speak out on the matter. Among those sharing my concern was Brigadier General Jerry D. Page, one of the young bright thinkers in the Air Force. Bill Lewis talked with Jerry Page and asked him for some thoughts and Page responded with a memorandum by Colonel Royal Roussel of his staff. That memorandum became our major working paper.

On September 21, 1961, I stood on the Senate Floor and said:

Mr. President:

What I am about to say is addressed not only to the members of the United States Senate but to all Americans—and most specifically to the President of the United States.

Many times during the last decade or more we have been able to draw comfort from knowing we had strength and will that could command the world's respect and deter the Communists. But recent history is not reassuring. Ominous signs plague us.

Everywhere the Communists press forward stronger. Khrushchev, vowing to take over the world for communism, and acting with all the confidence of a winner, threatens to put an end to civilized survival for the world if we do not let him have his way.

In an effort to generate global enthusiasm for submission he has stained the sky and polluted the air with nuclear bursts.

At the dividing line in Berlin he has dared to make a frontal attack on Freedom.

In speaking of the future he has embraced the risks of dire threats and ultimatums.

It is a grim spectacle such as we have never seen.

My purpose in asking your attention today is not to emphasize that this is a time of corroding fears and tensions.

—You know this as well as I do.

It is not to suggest that I have some special talent which permits me to see clearly the way out of the never-never land between high hope and deep despair, into which we have wandered.

—That would be presumptuous of me;

—But although we do not yet know a way out, I am sure the

time has come to *find a way out,* and to go once again to the high ground we enjoyed just a short time ago.

My purpose is not to recite our List of Losses in the great conflict with World Communism.

—Being a long list, it is painfully evident, not only to us but to the rest of the world; and its implications are frightening.

My purpose is not to recite facts that all of us know well enough, but to pose a vital question, the answers for which *none of* us yet knows well enough.

—Not a question that I have composed, but which suggests itself.

—Not a question of selfish or parochial origin.

—But one far more important.

—A question of national interest.

The question for which I urge your attention is spawned from the ugly union of communism's unswerving ambition and its unscrupulous methods.

The implications of this question have put a chill into the hearts of millions who yearn for peace, yet it is spoken by few of us.

It now demands our attention.

While we still have time we must examine it to its deepest foundations, its remotest associations.

We must do this now.

If we fail to do it now, we may not be free to do it later on.

It is a question that challenges us to merciless objectivity and realism.

It is a challenge that is addressed not only to us who are here today. It is addressed to every American; in fact, to every free man and woman . . . and to every person who yearns to know what freedom is, or to regain a freedom wrested from him by force, or lost to him by inaction or bad advice.

What we learn from our examination, what we do about it— or *fail* to do—may be the difference for us between peace or war, win or lose, fear or freedom, and perhaps even life or death.

We must look at it against the backdrop of Khrushchev's reckless confidence, against the foul clouds of his nuclear blackmail blasts; then we can see the question I am about to pose to you as the most crucial the American people have faced since the Declaration of Independence launched us as the United States into the world of nations . . . not the strongest, not the largest; but nevertheless confident, firm, and fearing no one.

The question which is posed to all of us, the question for which we *must* find the right answers across the board—realistically and urgently—is this:

—*What has happened that permits Khrushchev to act as he does?*

Let me repeat:

—*WHAT* HAS HAPPENED that lets him do it?

Understand me, please. Not what is he *doing*. We know that only too well. Our national honor bears the scars and stains of what he is doing now and has done in the past. And he has warned us, arrogantly, of what he intends to do in the future, which is even worse.

These things we know.

—But today—now—why does he feel free to do as he does? . . . WHY?

This also we must know. And if we do not know, we are likely to lose all control over shaping our future. Worse, we may lose our future itself.

We have been exhorted to have the moral courage to live with continuing conflict. No true American will argue otherwise, nor doubt that we are equal to the rigors of our moment in history. But let us also make sure we have the courage to go straight to the reasons *why* the conflict so often runs against us and burdens us so heavily . . . why Khrushchev so often has the initiative and we are satisfied only to *react*.

I sense a tendency, strange to the American character in world affairs, to retreat from circumstances rather than to face up to them realistically and master them. I am greatly disturbed by it. I am sure we can assume that Khrushchev is greatly pleased by it.

So let us here and now make a start on our examination of the question I have posed, by asking a related question:

—Is Khrushchev free to act as he does because the Soviets have *suddenly* gained the over-all military advantage?

I say no.

The primary determinant for over-all military advantage today is the capacity for total nuclear war.

No matter how fervently Khrushchev, we, the nonaligneds, or anyone else would like to make it different, this is an inescapable fact and we must face it firmly and deal with it realistically.

No matter what the immediate objectives may be, no matter in what circumstances a critical conflict situation might develop, it is the capacity which both of us—the United States and the USSR—must put into the scales first. And until the day comes when there is much more faith and good will in the world than there is today, it will invariably be the weight which tips the scales one way or the other . . . for us or against us—

—Toward winning or losing;

—Toward resoulteness or retreat;

—Toward firmness or passivity;

—Toward strength or submission.

It is generally agreed that as of today the over-all military advantage rests with us and our allies. We may be sure the Soviets also recognize this fact. When they undertake to assess their risks in any venture that they contemplate—Berlin, Laos, Africa, the Middle East, Cuba—they must begin at the top, with that for which their fears are greatest and their chances smallest. It is as true for them as it is for us that they cannot hide from realism.

All of us rightly fear that the conflict may go to the ultimate level of total nuclear war. No one can say whether or not this is the destiny of our generation. God grant that it is not. None can doubt that we are in grave danger, but this I feel strongly:

—We are, as the President has said, engaged in a contest of will and purpose as well as force and violence.

—If today, and in the days immediately ahead, we *fail* to meet the Soviets at the ultimate levels of *will and purpose*, the danger will be greatly widened that we will have no choice later on but to meet them at the ultimate levels of *force and violence;* either that or submit to their will. How much farther do you think Khrushchev would go today, how much faster would he move, if he was confident the over-all military advantage was on his side and not ours? . . . if he did not have to worry

about the risk of acting dangerously without having the over-
all military advantage?

Let me say it again:

—*The over-all military advantage is on our side.* But the day
we lose sight of this fact, we are in danger of frightening
ourselves . . . of being mesmerized by Khrushchev's confidence
and *deterring ourselves* instead of deterring the Soviets. While
we are concerned with all that might happen to us, we must
never forget that *Khrushchev also has reason to be afraid; and
the main reason is plain:*

—There is a grim prospect indeed for a postwar USSR stripped
of its strength and reduced to a third- or fourth-rate nation, even
though in the process of losing it he has wrought great damage on
us. This is the *choice he* must face.

To say that the Kremlin's risks are great does not make our
own risks less. But it does encourage perspective and this is
important.

The risks run both ways. This is not enough to eliminate the
conflict; I believe the Communists will always go as far and as
fast as we indicate we will permit them to go. But it does create
an environment in which our deterrence can be effective, if we
are firm enough, if our will and purpose are equal to the test.

I am disturbed that there are some who say, in effect, we can
do *more* in deterring the Soviets by preparing to do *less* against
them if they should provoke armed hostilities. I refer specifically
to the highly articulate and persuasive zealots who argue
that increasing conventional forces is the best way to create
more effective deterrence. They believe that flexibility in the
application of military force can come only from conventional
forces.

—I know of nothing in political or military history which
supports a thesis that it is safer to be weak than strong.

—Until the Soviets change their ways and join the society of
respectable nations, I see no hope of deterring them by making
the risks they must face *less fearful* for them.

—I know of no reason why we should be driven to a
concept which—no matter how it is phrased—means that in
order to prove our determination we would risk sacrificing the
lives of men in the battle line rather than risk holding the enemy
against the prospect that is most fearful to him.

That is a weak choice of risks for the strongest people in the world.

What is the origin of this fear of risks? It is not part of our heritage.

The greatness of this country was not won by people who were afraid of risks. It was won for us by men and women with little physical power at their command who nevertheless were willing to submit to risks. Could it not be lost for us by people with great physical power at their command but nevertheless willing to risk submitting? I believe it could.

So may I plead once more for perspective. Nothing has happened which suddenly has transferred the power of the overall military advantage from us to the Soviets. *We can defeat the USSR at any intensity of armed conflict unless we have degraded our fighting capacity greatly by self-imposed restrictions, such as restrictions on the use of tactical nuclear weapons.*

Our words concerning early use of tactical nuclear weapons if required can be invalidated quickly if our actions demonstrate that our major efforts and investments in time of great peril, such as now, are directed mainly towards increases in conventional forces.

Mr. President, brave words are fine—but action speaks louder than words and deters Khrushchev much more.

We have the military basis for clearly demonstrating our will and purpose . . . for making deterrence work. But we will never deter the Soviets by backing away, or by offering to fight *on their terms* because we are fearful of provoking them by indicating beyond all doubt that we will fight, if fight we must, on *our terms.*

I would be the first to urge great caution; but I would also be the first to urge great firmness, and the last to cease opposing the submission of the unlimited interests of 180 million Americans to the stupidity of limited deterrence. There are other countries, once free, that have learned too late that the ultimate cost of partial security can be total defeat, or subjugation.

I repeat that it is not military strength *suddenly* acquired by the Soviets which permits Khrushchev to act as he does.

Is it then that our own military strength has suddenly deteriorated?

—Have we been *suddenly* weakened?

Again I say no.

Every military authority presently responsible for our military posture will attest that our forces are stronger, not weaker; more alerted and ready, not *less* prepared.

—We cannot conclude that *this* gives Khrushchev cause for his reckless confidence . . . He has not *won* the military advantage from us, and it has not *accrued* to him through our own military deficiencies.

So we must go further and ask yet another question:

—*Is it conceivable that Khrushchev could assess that the will of the American people has collapsed?*

—That we are ready to submit?

—That he can win with blackmail?

—That Americans, as the saying goes, would rather be RED than dead?

How do you respond to a question as impossible as this?

And yet it must be asked, for, as I have said, we must examine the fundamental question I have posed to its deepest foundations.

—*What has happened that permits Khrushchev to act as he does?*

—What gives Khrushchev his ticket to such great confidence?

—What does he assess about us that makes him so sure?

—What have we indicated to him that causes him to be so arrogant . . . to take such *wide risks,* in our view, in going so far?

If we hold the military advantage, why, you may well ask, is our deterrence not more effective? What's the reason it is not?

The reason is that deterrence is not a matter of forces and firepower alone. The restraints and influence are projected from the capacity to accomplish a purpose; *not just from what we have but from what we will do.*

—Deterrence cannot be regarded as an assured fact. It is a sensitive condition, always subject to proof.

Nevertheless there are influential advocates of the so-called stable deterrence.

I believe such proposals to be, at worst, demonstrably false and, at best, highly questionable.

We are dealing with military power on both sides that is infinitely complicated, composed of many critical elements. This power itself floats on a sea of uncertainty, constantly subject to the restless tides of progress and the tidal waves of great change. *To say that we can count on achieving and maintaining a balance or stability in these conditions—even if we had the Soviet's cooperation, much less their opposition—is nothing short of wishful thinking . . . a form of "nuclear escapism" to dodge the hard, cold facts.*

I am frightened by inferences that we can get rid of the nuclear peril by this device of sweeping it under the rug. I fear it would trip us and catch us off balance sooner or later.

We must examine yet another facet of this critical situation, namely, what is it that Khrushchev most likely assesses from what our spokesmen say, in the context of what we do and fail to do?

—What are the measures that we have taken to convince him, and the rest of the world, of our will and purpose?

—What kind of raw material have we provided for Khrushchev to analyze, study, assess, and use as a basis for his conclusions and actions?

I recall some of the inspiring words of the President's inaugural address, as our nation turned with high hope toward this year 1961.

Specifically:

". . . to those nations which would make themselves our adversary, we offer not a pledge but a request; that both sides begin anew the quest for peace, before the dark powers of destruction unleashed by science engulf all humanity in planned or accidental self-destruction.

"We dare not tempt them with weakness. For only when our arms are sufficient beyond doubt can we be certain beyond doubt that they will never be employed."

As I see the dark clouds that now hang low over the new frontiers of hope toward which the attention of Americans and the rest of the world was directed on that day, I wonder what it is that has tempted Castro to stoke the fires of hatred still higher in his communized Cuba and to challenge United States strength and influence throughout Latin America.

—I do not *know* what Castro thinks;

—But I doubt that he has been *tempted* by a *high* assessment of our *will and purpose.*

Like millions of Americans, I was deeply impressed with the President, when, in his televised press conference, he pointed to a map and eloquently explained why we had to stand firm on Laos.

The words were brave and inspiring—but only to be followed by no brave action to back up those words.

As I see the perils that press in on us, I wonder what it is that impelled Khrushchev to choose the moment of his return from his Vienna meeting with the President to fling into the face of the American people his ultimatum on a treaty with East Germany and thereafter to bring on the Berlin crisis.

—I do not *know* what Khrushchev thinks;

—But I cannot believe that he has been *tempted* in his Berlin gamble by a *high* assessment of our *will and purpose.*

Neither can we know how many others wonder about the course of events in much the same way as I do. But that there *are* others we do know, and I quote one now: Mr. Chalmers Roberts, in the Washington *Post* recently:

"Power and willingness to use it are fundamental to great nations. That the United States has the power is not doubted in Moscow, by every sign available here. But Khrushchev's latest actions indicate that he doubts the President's willingness to use it.

"And so it now appears that Khrushchev has decided to take the world to the brink for a test of will on the outcome of which may depend the future not only of West Berlin but the freedom of mankind."

We have a decided nuclear capability advantage over Khrushchev—and he knows it. Otherwise he wouldn't have resumed nuclear tests and would not have been deterred in the past in the slightest.

But he is confident we won't use it for he sees us turning to emphasis on conventional weapons—and ironically he has an obviously great superiority in conventional weapons and manpower over us.

We have in effect played into his hands—for the kind of

warfare in which he knows he can beat us. We have restricted ourselves on the freedom of choice to use the nuclear tactical weapons which he knows would defeat him if he started war.

In short, we have the nuclear capability—and he knows and fears it. But we have practically told him we do not have the will to use that one power with which we can stop him.

In short, we have the nuclear capability—but not the nuclear credibility.

I recall some of the ringing words by the President in his address to the Nation last July.

Specifically:

"We cannot and will not permit the Communists to drive us out of Berlin, either gradually or by force."

I cannot know what Khrushchev thinks, what it is that influences him, what he looks for when he makes his judgments:

—But I fervently hope that he would not make his final assessment as to our will and purpose in Berlin on the basis of what he has seen and deduced from, for example, Laos and Cuba.

God forbid that the pattern of brave words on Laos and Cuba followed by no brave action be repeated on Berlin.

As fervently as I hope Khrushchev *would not* be influenced unduly by what he might assess from the record in Laos and Cuba, I hope with even greater fervency that he *would* recall other times and other places, where American strength and American will have prevailed in American purpose.

For example:

—Lebanon, in 1958, where we acted promptly and unequivocally to prevent the threatened overthrow of a government friendly to us.

Admittedly, no one can know what might have happened if our forces had not been sent promptly to the scene. *But everyone knows what did happen after they were sent there . . . The threatened trouble dissolved.*

—Or the Berlin airlift of 1948–49, through which the Soviets' first major effort to force us out of Berlin was defeated . . . admittedly under circumstances different from those we face today, but nevertheless by firm and prompt action under the same principles to which we are dedicated today.

—Or the offshore islands in the Straits of Formosa, where long ago our firmness was proved to the Communists beyond doubt.

I am thankful that we have such examples of will and purpose to balance the record in some degree at this vital time—

—When we can be sure that every indication of our determination or lack of it is submitted to the most critical of examinations in Moscow;

—When a miscalculation in this respect by Moscow could bring on the greatest calamity since the first day of the recorded history of mankind.

Last April, when the American Society of Newspaper Editors met in Washington, the President beautifully phrased his address to them. Referring to events associated with Castro's Cuba, he said he wanted the record to show that "our restraint is not inexhaustible."

I not only agree wholeheartedly with the President in this reflection of our feelings, but I urge that we apply the same thought most seriously in other vital considerations, because—

—Neither is our deterrent capacity inexhaustible. It must be revitalized appropriately with actions as well as with words and military forces.

—Neither can we afford to assume that the confidence of the American people is inexhaustible. We cannot expect the national will to overcome forever the enervating effects of repeated losses without its being revitalized by the new strength of meaningful victories.

I am confident that we *can* do better.

I believe with all my heart that we *can* win our objectives.

These are the reasons why I speak as I do today in appealing to all Americans—and especially to the President of the United States on the eve of his address to a United Nations that is threatened with collapse for lack of will and determination.

These are the reasons why I could not take myself away from the Senate Chamber and go back to the people whose trust I hold without making my concern known, without asking—

—How much longer can we afford to lose? When will we start to win?

—*Where* will we draw the line?

—If we fail to stand firm in Berlin . . . if we fail to stand there with *the best we have,* where in the world will we draw the line?

In the name of the courage, determination, and sacrifices of our forebears, *let us not be afraid to be right* at this critical time.

General de Gaulle made a statement in his press conference on September 6, 1961, which the leaders of the West could well consider because it exemplifies the realism and the determination that is so desperately needed. I place it in the Record at this point of my remarks and I invite your study of it. [See Appendix.]

I urge the President of the United States to consider these thoughts I have expressed before he makes his address to the United Nations assembly. While I agree with him that we should not negotiate from fear or fear to negotiate—I say we should not fear to refuse to negotiate on any matter that is not negotiable.

In these perilous hours, I fear that the American people are ahead of their leaders in realism and courage—but behind them in knowledge of the facts because the facts have not been given to them.

I would hope that every American would read what I have said today and would express themselves by direct correspondence to the President.

A defense of President Kennedy was made by Senator Stuart Symington, who contended that the United States would use its nuclear tactical power if necessary and not limit itself to conventional weapons.

My response was:

I am delighted with the statement of the Senior Senator from Missouri, who apparently spoke in the capacity of spokesman for the President in answering my remarks—and whose statement is apparently a clear and unequivocal message to Khrushchev that the United States will not limit itself to conventional weapons but will use nuclear tactical weapons whenever and wherever it is deemed necessary to defend the peace of the world and the security of our country.

If my address accomplished nothing else, it has produced such a strong assurance from the distinguished spokesman for the Kennedy Administration on our national defense policy. It is a glimmer of hope for the beginning of a nuclear credibility, which has too long been tragically absent.

A few days after that, President Kennedy addressed the United Nations General Assembly in New York and forcefully stated that the United States would not hesitate to use its nuclear capability if necessary for its defense and in the interests of defense of peace. There were the same strong and brave words as in the televised Kennedy ultimatum on Laos. I hoped that the tragic pattern of brave words without action would not be repeated this time.

While President Kennedy's reaction to my speech was clear, he never referred to me publicly. In a subsequent article in *Look* magazine, Fletcher Knebel wrote that Kennedy was greatly angered and characterized me as "ignorant."*

There was swift reaction from Moscow. On September 23, 1961, radio commentator I. Orlov in Moscow accused me of having "another attack of cannibal instinct" and the next day the Russian radio complimented me as "that bloodthirsty little woman." Attacks from the Russian news media were nothing new. The Russian press had called me "a poison pen artist" in 1954 and "an Amazon warmonger hiding behind a rose" in 1955. Some Amazon. I'm five foot three.

Shortly thereafter it was reported that Khrushchev and the Kremlin had sent word to American Communists to start a

---

* EDITOR'S NOTE: In contrast, columnist James Reston wrote: ". . . his past words and actions on Cuba and Laos have not jibed. He has talked like Churchill and acted like Chamberlain. This is why even so wise and moderate a woman as Sen. Margaret Chase Smith of Maine rose in the Senate last week and, in a remarkable speech, asked whether we had lost our national will to risk everything for our beliefs."

letter-writing campaign against me and had issued the call for the attack through the *Daily Worker.*

Sometimes the effectiveness of a statement can be measured by the severity of the attacks on the statement and the identity of the attacker. Apparently my speech cut deeply, in view of the severity of the Communist denunciation of me. Apparently my message got through to Khrushchev clear and loud.

That it got through seemed evident for he sent a letter to fifty-nine Labor Party members of the British House of Commons denouncing me as "the devil in a disguise of a woman," beating "all records of savagery." When the press asked me for comment, I laughed it off. "Khrushchev isn't really mad at me. I'm not that important. He is angry because American officials have grown more firm since my speech."

The Khrushchev attack took on team proportions when a month later Mrs. Khrushchev joined her husband's attack. She did it in a letter to a leader of the Women's Strike for Peace in which she accused me of being a warmonger. My response was that if Mrs. Khrushchev really wanted peace and sane survival then she should have a heart-to-heart talk with her husband and tell him to start acting for peace by doing two specific things—stopping the evil, open-air nuclear explosions completely and tearing down the wall that divides Berlin.

But, new official firmness or not, in the year that was to follow I became more and more convinced that President Kennedy's bold words were not to be supported with any action. His policy continued to undermine the nuclear credibility of the United States to the detriment of our Nation, and to the advantage and the increasing boldness of Khrushchev.

There were disturbing reports coming out of Cuba. Senator Kenneth Keating of New York was reporting grave news from refugees out of Cuba about missile bases in Cuba. Angry denials were issued by the White House.

I consulted several people whose judgment and frankness I greatly respected. Again, among those were Jerry Page, who had become a Major General. He was to aid me again when, after much thought, study, and deliberation, I made an anniversary speech on September 21, 1962. This was it:

One year ago on this day—impelled by concern over the fact that everywhere the Communists were pressing forward stronger —I stood in this Chamber and posed to my colleagues, to the American people, and particularly to the President of the United States, several questions which I considered to be of the utmost importance.

I asked:

How much longer can we afford to lose?

I asked:

What have *we* done (or failed to do) that permits Khrushchev to act as he does?

And:

Why is it that the Communists so often have the initiative and we are satisfied to *re*act?

And:

When will *we* start winning?

In the year that separates us from the occasion of those remarks the course of events has been, to say the least, an unpromising one for us. The Communists, far from exploring new frontiers of friendship and cooperation, have continued the pressures of their attacks against liberty.

Not only that, but more.

Indeed, they have *increased* their efforts. And there is little in their attitude toward any problem anywhere to indicate that they intend to change for the better.

—Not in the U.N.
—Not in Berlin
—Not at Geneva
—Not in Cuba
—Not in Southeast Asia
—Not anywhere

And why should they change? Why should they, as long as they are making progress toward their goals?

The NATO Alliance, protecting an area of the non-Communist world which is of great and immediate importance to the United States, is plagued by troubles, doubts, criticisms, and uncertainties.

—More and more there is danger that Khrushchev, casting an acquisitive eye toward the Western doorstep of the Soviet Empire, will be tempted toward new challenges by military vulnerabilities that he believes exist there, or by his assessment that the Free World's will is so low as to negate its power.

A prominent, highly respected American—and very good friend of President Kennedy—recently talked at length with Khrushchev and what he reported on Khrushchev's assessment of our will made headlines on the front pages of our newspapers, on television and radio throughout the country. He reported that Khrushchev had stated that he believes that the United States will not fight to protect itself.

Certainly one of the realities that faces us today is in the form of a challenge to adopt policies and take actions which will build the confidence of NATO Europe.

—Could we possibly hope to build this confidence by demanding acceptance of U.S. policies that are not palatable to them? Would not this course be more likely to destroy their confidence than to build it?

Let us not forget that for twelve years NATO was a solid and cohesive force against Communism. In the last one and one-half years difficulty has piled upon difficulty. De Gaulle was President of France prior to this troubled period. Macmillan spoke for Great Britain, Adenauer for West Germany.

—*What has changed?*

In Laos our objective of a truly neutral and independent country is stalled by the refusal of the pro-Communist elements to comply with the peace agreement that was signed only a short time ago at Geneva.

—It makes one wonder if we based our own agreement on a concept that the Communists are becoming more friendly and cooperative.

—Do we really believe that such agreements with the Soviets will accrue to the benefit of anyone but themselves?

And do we have a basis for our actions which *does* assume an accommodation with the Soviets?

In Cuba the Bloc countries and Castro blatantly defy the principles of the Monroe Doctrine and proceed with the Communization of that island—and in recent weeks an acceleration of transforming Cuba into a Communist arsenal.

—I ask you: Are we better off here than we were a year ago?

In Vietnam we are committing ourselves, bit by bit, to a more involved war, as the result of fashioning our responses to the patterns chosen by the enemy.

And in the realm of space the Soviets' new achievements cast the shadow of a tremendous new military potential across the whole Free World.

—Our spokesmen, calm almost to the point of placid satisfaction, enjoin us not to worry . . . "We are far behind. But we will catch up. And meanwhile, there's no great military significance in the Soviets' feat. And Cuba really presents no threat."

Words and more words.

About the only tangible action we get is the call-up of the Reserves in which Khrushchev, in his alternating policy of first blowing hot and then blowing cold, psychologically dangles our Reservists on the end of an "on-again-off-again" line in a war of nerves—in which we react as he anticipates our reaction.

But who is really so blind as not to see that under the pressures of the last year the outlook for us has deteriorated steadily? And now it has reached such a disturbingly low level that its effects surely must be to banish the last vestige of complacency from our national attitude and to require each of us—whatever his position, whatever his responsibilities, and whatever his affiliations—to face the truth.

It is inconceivable that any amount of polished phrases— no matter how expertly put together and how adroitly presented —could longer conceal the hard facts from the American people.

—We are simply not breathing the air of success.

—In more ways than ever before within the memory of most of us our beloved country is rapidly becoming a second-rater.

No amount of contrived double-talk can longer divert the impacts of reality.

—In the eyes of the world our flag does not fly high and proudly as it once did.

And so today—impelled by the same concern that caused me to address the subject of our security and welfare a year ago—I ask again:

—*When will we start winning?*

—How much longer can we *risk* waiting?

—What can we do to turn the tide more surely in our direction?

Mr. President, it would be unwise as well as incorrect to imply that there is a short route back to the position of eminence, influence, and well-being that our country enjoyed in better days. But I have no hesitancy in asserting that there *is* a route back and that we had best get our feet on it, and follow it, before we lose the chance to do so.

I would not be so presumptuous as to say that I am able to see every straightaway and turning of this route all the way to its ultimate destination (which, I hope, would be a secure and peaceful community of nations) but, once again, I have no hesitancy in asserting that I *can* see where our *starting point* should be.

—We must start, and fashion our future progress toward an improved position, on a basis of military advantage . . . Of this I am certain.

—Not a fancied or limited advantage in a single technique, or in a particular locale, or to react to one specific situation . . . but a realistic over-all military advantage reposing in a capability to win our objectives at any level of conflict, from the lowest to the highest.

If we are determined to have and hold the benefits of this advantage, it would be the height of folly not to take new warning from the Soviets' recent two-man orbit.

—It was a remarkable accomplishment.

—We would have been proud to claim it.

—It is unfortunate for the Free World that we could not claim it.

I deem it unfortunate because it portends physical power of indescribably greater dimensions . . . and I know of nothing in the long record of aggression under the Communists to indicate that they *do not intend* to exploit, either overtly or by blackmail, any elements of physical power within their reach, if given sufficient opportunity to do so.

—Knowing how Khrushchev, Malinovsky, and others boasted

of their new power after the recent space flights, who can close his eyes so tightly against the light of reality as to believe the Soviets *do not intend* to develop military power in space as fast as they are able?

Or looking toward NATO Europe:

—Knowing that the Soviets have nuclear-armed forces available, who can stray so far from the path of reality as to believe that they *do not intend* to exploit these forces if they should consider it to their advantage to do so?

—And I also ask, Mr. President:

. . . Are we trying to increase our conventional forces in NATO *at the expense* of our tactical nuclear forces?

. . . Are we trying to convince the people that we are conjuring up a less dangerous kind of war for them to fight?

Or looking toward the jungle areas and underdeveloped regions:

—Knowing that Khrushchev has espoused "wars of liberation," who can cite valid evidence that the Communists *do not intend* to exploit the physical power and emotions of human beings in insurgency operations and other disruptive activities, whenever it suits their purpose to do so and they have sufficient opportunity?

My thesis—my reason for addressing you today—is, I feel sure, clearly evident by now; but let us accord it the emphasis that will come from additional discussion.

The President and some of his principal policy and strategy advisers have been deeply occupied with the subject of risks.

—We have been cautioned on more than one occasion that we cannot do thus-and-so because it would risk provoking the Communists;

—that, for example, we must urge NATO Europe to be satisfied with trying to defend itself by conventional means because of the stated conviction that even the highly selective use of tactical nuclear capabilities against military targets would escalate the conflict toward general war proportions.

The whole country has heard about the inhibiting effects that these risks, and other similar ones, impose upon our national policy and strategy.

It is well to be aware of these circumstances and to evaluate them carefully. But I regret to say that from the same sources

I have heard comparatively little about the risks of adopting wishful thinking as a substitute for hardheaded realism in overcoming the Communists' drive for power and keeping the balance on our side.

—Can we risk the survival of our country on anyone's "opinions" as to what the Communists' *intentions* are?

I say no. It is unthinkable.

—Surely there is something better for us than gambling on a guess that the Communists *do not intend* to use every part of the military capabilities that they now have or may develop later on, if and when it suits their interests to do so.

—Or to put it another way, could we possibly risk gambling on the dangerous assumption that *their intentions will be good?* . . . Of course not.

—Therefore, we must clearly see and clearly understand what is required of us to hold the military advantage.

What we must be prepared to do is counter the *military capabilities* that constitute a threat to us.

—We must protect ourselves against that which we *know the Communists are capable of doing.*

As you know, the concept of being prepared to counter the *military capabilities* of the Communists is generally referred to as *counterforce.*

The World being what it is today, you would think that no one in this country would even remotely consider taking issue with this concept.

—Who could possibly quarrel with the purpose of winning our objectives in defense of our country?

But it has become increasingly clear that there are some who, obviously failing to understand the concept, take sharp issue with it. For example, when the Secretary of Defense referred to it in a speech at Ann Arbor, Michigan, on June 16, there followed a flood of negative reaction that is still running . . . and there has even been a deep silence from the Secretary's colleagues.

I have waited for just one of them to speak out directly in support of the views he expressed. But none has—and to break his lonely position I speak out today in support of his Ann Arbor speech and say that it was the most encouraging expression to come from the Kennedy Administration since the time of my speech a year ago.

Typical of the opposition was a three-column "anti-counter-force" advertisement that ran in the New York *Times* of August 21. The signers are 175 most highly respected and patriotic faculty members of a dozen universities and colleges of recognized standing. They urged abandonment of our counter-force posture.

—Why? Because, in their view, it is provocative to the Communists;

—and it tends to promote an arms race;

—and it increases the likelihood of war.

The solution which they, in all sincerity and seriousness, recommend is to reduce our arms (even disproportionately, if necessary) for the purpose of seeking a closer approach to equality with the USSR.

With this example in mind, let us see clearly and understand fully what the most vocal and influential of the well-intentioned critics are saying. Reduced to simple terms, it is this:

—*We* are largely to blame for the Soviets' continued intransigence.

—Because we maintain the strength to counter their military capability, we give the Soviets reason to fear that we are preparing to attack them.

—They are driven to excessive secrecy and distrust by their apprehension of our strength.

In substance, these critics contend that the Soviets are bad because *we* make them bad. Hence, if we reduce *our* military strength, their attitude will improve, and they will become more tractable.

—Do these good and sincere people who are so critical really believe that we would be better off *without* a margin of military advantage across the board?

—Are they really willing to risk the survival of our country on their opinion of the Soviets' intentions?

—Is it conceivable that, in the present atmosphere, we would deliberately plan *not* to have more than the Soviets have?

—Is there any worthwhile evidence to cause us to see *that* way as the path toward more effective deterrence and greater security?

There are some who seem to think that deterrence is, in a manner of speaking, old-fashioned;

—that it has been overtaken by events in the forward rush of technology;

—that deterrence, as we know it today, has no future.

I disagree.

We have had effective deterrence for the majority of time over the last fifteen years. We have effective deterrence now. And I believe we can continue to have effective deterrence in the future.

—And in the future, as in the past, there is no doubt that effective deterrence will stem fundamentally from our counter-force capability;

—from our capability to win over the enemy's military forces.

With those who favor placating the Soviets at the terrible cost of deliberately downgrading our own military advantage and settling for parity or near parity, it is unpopular to say that we can win.

—With dangerous positiveness and shallow reasoning they say that in nuclear war there could be no winner.

With all the emphasis at my command, I disagree.

—We *can* win.

I do not mean to imply that we could win cheaply. But neither do we have to manipulate ourselves into a position where we would be absolutely dead. It would not *have* to be a Pyrrhic victory. Winning and losing are not fundamentally questions of the intrinsic costs of damage suffered in a war. We *could lose by eroded resolve* and ultimate capitulation without suffering any physical damage at all from the enemy who defeated us. But if we are attacked, I hold with the concept that our "second-strike" force must be stronger than the force remaining to the enemy after his initial strike. If we retained this advantage we would be in a winning position.

And what kind of reasoning, may I ask, is behind the accusation that by keeping ourselves strong in the face of a determined and capable nation, whose leaders are our avowed enemies, we are promoting an arms race?

—Let us not surrender to this kind of self-incrimination any longer but instead set the facts straight.

—We are *not* promoting an arms race; *not* through counterforce or *any other* means.

The forces that we have and expect to have are not just someone's "idea." We do not get them like numbers pulled out of a hat. Far from that, our requirements are based on the most careful and complete information regarding the Communists' capabilities that it is possible for us to have.

—And that is the way we must continue to do it, no matter what the prophets of fear and doom say.

—For I repeat, it would be folly for us, in the present climate of relations with the USSR, *not to be able* to counter those capabilities.

So if we are engaged in anything that resembles an arms race, let there be no mistake about who is at the bottom of the trouble: the Communists are to blame, not our concepts and strategy.

And while we are at it, let us get rid of the fiction that our military posture indicates an intention on our part to initiate war against the Soviets by striking first.

—If this *were* our intention, would we not be stupid indeed to burden ourselves with the expense of an *aerospace defense system,* our ballistic missile *early warning* facilities, the Strategic Air Command *alert,* and other precautions of that sort? If we *intended* to strike *first,* could we not *forego* these things and put *all* of our effort and resources into *offensive* means?

Our policy leaders stress repeatedly that we must have flexibility, a choice among alternatives. *I agree.* Certainly we want to have *several* alternatives available if we are attacked. Counterforce response against military targets is *only one* of them; but a very *desirable one.*

—Don't we want to do everything within reason to avoid needless destruction?

. . . Of course we do.

—Don't we want to provide the enemy with every possible incentive *not to attack our cities?*

. . . Of course we do.

—Do we want to subscribe to or be limited to a policy of indiscriminate devastation, which would provide an enemy with a strong incentive to attack our own cities?

. . . Of course we do not.

I do not comprehend the reasoning of those who cry for the abandonment of our counterforce posture.

—I do not understand how they believe that we can find greater safety in greater weakness.

But I am sure of this: if we *do* believe that counterforce is essential—if we *do* want to preserve it—the time has arrived for all of us . . .

—those of us here today;

—the American people everywhere;

—the President of the United States;

—not just a lonely Secretary of Defense;

—indeed, *all of us,* to do *more* to make the concept of countering the enemy's capabilities better understood and more widely accepted;

—to protect it from even those well-intentioned patriots, who through fear of imagined or real risks, or through ignorance of the facts, would destroy it and cast us adrift on the stormy seas of far greater uncertainty.

I do not intend to imply that counterforce is the answer to *everything. It is not.* But even in the very worst context that can be contrived without going to impossible extremes, we are still vastly better off *with* it than we could possibly be *without* it.

No one claims that it is a panacea. *No one* could say for certain that because we have a counterforce capability the future will be *easier.* But *there is* every reason to believe that if we *resolutely maintain* a counterforce capability the future will be *less difficult* than it might be otherwise. And that is a goal which, although not spectacular, we must not ignore.

———————

EDITOR'S NOTE:

This time there was no recorded reaction from either the White House or the Kremlin. Neither Kennedy nor Khrushchev blew his top. However, the Senate defender of the Kennedy Administration the year before, Senator Stuart Symington, praised Senator Smith's later speech, calling it "one of the most thought-provoking addresses on our military posture it has been my privilege to listen to in the Senate. I hope every American will have an opportunity to read and consider her thoughts."

Senator Kenneth Keating, who was reporting the grave news from Cuba, called her speech a "remarkable analysis" and took a crack at Defense Secretary McNamara by saying that Margaret Smith had "devastated" the argument of those who believe that the best way to deal with the Russians is to reduce our military might to their level.

It took only one month to prove the validity of the thesis of her September 21, 1962, speech. The statement had turned out to be rather prophetic. For on the evening of October 22, 1962, when Senator Smith was speaking at Thomaston, Maine, on the need for greater and firmer leadership, President Kennedy, in a grave television-radio broadcast, revealed to the American people that there was a Soviet offensive build-up in Cuba and that he was ordering a naval and air quarantine on shipment of offensive military equipment to the island.

Finally, President Kennedy had faced up to the kind of danger that Senator Smith had warned about in two speeches in the past year—and had taken the firm position that she advocated. But he had done it so late as to have the world on the brink of World War III. She was particularly proud of Kennedy's condition for "on site" inspection to make certain that the missiles had been removed.

Firm as he was, at long last, he was later to renege on that supposedly firm "on site" inspection requirement to the lifting of the quarantine.

Perhaps the final note to this "nuclear-capability-nuclear-credibility" issue between Margaret Chase Smith and John F. Kennedy came later with the revelation that the real reason why Kennedy could stand eyeball-to-eyeball with Khrushchev and demand and get removal of the missiles from Cuba was the nuclear superiority that we had over Russia—a nuclear superiority that Eisenhower had built up and which Kennedy and McNamara had proposed to downgrade to parity with that of Russia.

Conventional capability, which Kennedy, Taylor, and McNamara had stressed so much and started building up while denigrating nuclear capability, was of no more than secondary significance at best in this crisis and in the ability to force Khrushchev to back down. Fortunately, the downgrading of nuclear capability to the Kennedy-McNamara goal of parity with Russia had not progressed enough to remove the crucial superiority that forced Khrushchev to back down.

It was the "counterforce posture" that had saved the day—and the United States—and the world. The same counterforce posture that some had been urging we abandon—the same counterforce posture that Margaret Chase Smith, on September 21, 1962, pled be maintained and not abandoned.

The Kennedy Twist

"Nepotism is dangerous to the public interest and to our national morality."

—John F. Kennedy
October 18, 1960

On June 18, 1953, James D. Ewing, then copublisher of the Bangor (Maine) *Daily Commercial* and son of Oscar Ewing (former Director of the Federal Security Administration), wrote to Senator John F. Kennedy:

Hon. John F. Kennedy
United States Senate
Washington, D.C.

Dear Jack:

I followed up on your thought that perhaps Margaret Smith would feel able to assume leadership in the formation of an organization of the New England delegation.

As I suspected, she is keenly interested in the idea and recognizes the need for such a step. But, as I feared, she does not feel she can take on such a task at this time. She has a campaign coming up next year, as well as heavy committee assignments.

I still think your idea is very sound and I hope you will be able to develop it. We need a hard-hitting New England team.

With best regards,
Sincerely,
James D. Ewing

Some time earlier, Jim Ewing had sounded me out on Jack Kennedy's idea for a New England Senatorial Conference. I was flattered to be asked to lead it but I felt it would be going behind the back of the Senior Senator from Massachusetts, Leverett Saltonstall, a fellow Republican. If the Democratic Junior Senator from Massachusetts was going to team up with a Senator of the opposite political party it made more sense for him to team up with the Senior Senator from his own state.

And that is what Jack Kennedy did. Subsequently Leverett

Saltonstall and Jack Kennedy set up the New England Senatorial Conference and made Ted Sorensen, a member of Kennedy's staff, the Secretary.

Perhaps this declination was a political mistake in view of Jack Kennedy's subsequent rise to the Presidency. But I would take the same position again—even though Jack Kennedy went on to the Presidency and even though he sought my defeat the next year in 1954. In that year Jack Kennedy refused to support the Massachusetts Senatorial Democratic nominee against Leverett Saltonstall and gave as his excuse that he was too ill to campaign. He nevertheless came into Maine to campaign against me and urge my defeat.

Not only was it significant that his health was good enough for him to go to another state to campaign against the Senator he had sought to team up with in the previous year but it was doubly significant that no other Democratic Senator would agree to campaign against me. It was an interesting political twist, a foreshadow of what was to come.

In the two years that Jack Kennedy and I served in the House together, 1947 and 1948, we had very little contact with one another, much less any political rapport. We did have considerable contact in the Senate on the Reorganization Subcommittee of the Senate Government Operations Committee. When Joe McCarthy, in violation of all Senate custom and tradition, kicked me off that subcommittee and replaced me with Richard M. Nixon, Joe piously claimed that he was not taking retaliatory action against me but that he was promoting me to the top Republican position on the Reorganization Subcommittee.

When the Republicans won control of the Senate two years later in 1953, I became Chairman of the Reorganization Subcommittee and Jack Kennedy became one of the Democratic members. One of the principal pieces of legislation to come before us was on retirement pay for legislative employees. The bill was fathered and pushed by Walter Reynolds, Chief of Staff of the Senate Government Operations Committee.

I gave the bill my full and enthusiastic support and Jack Kennedy fought it. He was so bitterly opposed that one day he pushed Walter Reynolds against the wall and physically threatened him.

In his fight to lower the benefits, Kennedy had allies not only in Mike Monroney of Oklahoma and Albert Gore of Tennessee but as well in Ted Sorensen, who had been a staff assistant to the Joint Committtee on Railroad Retirement Legislation and who tried to have the legislation amended downward to the scale of railroad retirement. These persons did succeed on the Senate Floor in whittling the bill down drastically. But this did not concern Walter Reynolds and me too much because we knew that when the bill went to the House, the House would beef it back up with amendments.

The House did just that—and when it returned the beefed-up bill to the Senate, there were reports that Jack Kennedy had stated that he would get the bill emasculated again by the Senate. When these reports reached me, I said, "We'll take care of the angry young man from Massachusetts. Instead of asking the Senate to act on the House version of the bill, I'll request a conference and between Everett Dirksen, myself, and the House conferees, we'll handle him."

We did—on February 4, 9, and 11, 1954. The end result was that the Senate and House conferees sent a bill to the Senate and the House that differed insignificantly from the strong House version and the threatened vigorous Senate opposition to the Conference Report faded away.

When the Democrats regained control of the Senate, Jack Kennedy became Chairman of this same Reorganization Subcommittee and I became the ranking minority member. During these years, Jack Kennedy was running hard for the Presidency and consequently was not around enough to have a very active subcommittee. But if he was not an active Chairman, Jack Kennedy was nonetheless jealous of the jurisdiction of his subcommittee. In January 1957 a move was started with the introduction of Senate Resolution 74 to establish a Senate

Select Committee to Investigate Improper Activities in Labor-Management Relations.

Kennedy called me on the telephone and said, "Mrs. Smith, I think we should fight against this Select Committee because lobbying by labor leaders really comes under the jurisdiction of our subcommittee. I'm having a press conference later today to announce my opposition to it. I hope you will help oppose it, and I would like to say so at the press conference."

I replied, "I have no particular feeling about this. But I'll be happy to support you in opposing it if that is what you desire—and you may say so." That was at nine o'clock in the morning.

Two hours later, Kennedy called again. "Mrs. Smith, I have thought this Select Committee proposal matter over and have decided not to oppose it and I have called off my press conference." It was evident that subsequent to his earlier call Kennedy had been promised a place on the proposed Select Committee and that this accounted for his sudden change of heart. Yet he gave no indication that he was to become a member of the Select Committee. I suspected that he had used my promise to oppose the Select Committee as the lever to open a place for himself on the Select Committee if he did not oppose it.

I didn't put it this bluntly to him. What I said was: "I understand, Senator. I hope you will enjoy serving on the Select Committee." When the Select Committee was appointed, not only was Jack Kennedy made second in line to Chairman John L. McClellan but his brother Bobby was made Chief Counsel to the Committee.

It was another personal experience with a sudden turnabout—a sort of twist—by Jack Kennedy.

Having some personal knowledge of Jack Kennedy's ability to reverse his field and having observed him in the office of the Presidency for more than a year, I could speak with some authority about him when I was asked to address the National Republican Women's Conference Banquet on April 16, 1962.

At that time the dance craze was "The Twist" and it was especially in vogue at the White House and with the Kennedy set. It surprised no one that my speech became known as "The Kennedy Twist." This was it:

I shall begin tonight with a prologue—a prologue which you will not find in your printed copy of my speech. A prologue directed at the actions of last week.

As a Republican, I applaud the results of President Kennedy's use of the high office of the Presidency with all its enormous prestige and power to mold and marshal public opinion against a resented steel price rise. In United States Steel he couldn't have had a better political "patsy."

But I do not applaud *other* tactics that he resorted to in this matter—tactics such as the threatening of criminal prosecution and the use of police state methods such as the FBI routing a reporter out of bed in the middle of the night.

Nor do I believe that price control should be effected by Presidential action solely on one industry. If price control *is* needed then the proper course is the enactment of legislation covering all the industries and business and covering wages.

For those who applaud the tactics of threat of criminal prosecution and the use of the FBI in police state methods, I would say—to the consumer housewife that if the President alone can set the price of steel, then he can set the wage that her husband receives—to the corner grocery store man or the corner drugstore man that if the President alone can set the price of steel, then he can tell them how much they can charge for a loaf of bread or a tube of toothpaste—to the members of the press that if the President or the Attorney General can order the FBI to rout a reporter out of bed in the middle of the night on a news story, then it can be done to you sometime on some news story you have written.

Strength, the American way, is not manifested by threats of criminal prosecution or police state methods.

Leadership is not manifested by coercion, even against the resented.

Greatness is not manifested by unlimited pragmatism, which places such a high premium on the end justifying *any* means and *any* methods.

We are here tonight as a partisan group at a partisan meeting for a partisan purpose. There are those who decry partisanship. It does deserve condemnation if it is selfish and uninformed. But partisanship deserves praise and active support when it champions the advocacy of truth. For then it serves a real purpose in American life—and it provides the best kind of politics and the most effective politics.

We of the Republican Party are in the minority. Because a Democrat occupies the White House, of necessity the Republican national record must be, for the greater part, written in Congress.

But even there we are the Minority Party by almost a ratio of two to one. Since a Democratic-controlled Congress will not let Republican-sponsored bills out of committee to be voted upon by the House or the Senate, our only chance to write a Republican record—a Republican story—in Congress is by offering amendments and by challenging the actions of the Democratic President and the Democratic Majority when we disagree with their actions and proposals.

On those issues on which we stand solidly, we do write a Republican record. We Republicans don't always agree among ourselves because we simply have honest differences of opinions. I am thankful that there is nothing monolithic about us—and that we do not permit one man to tell us how to vote—that we reject political blackmail as we rejected it on the brazen attempt of the Democratic President to paint us as racial bigots on the issue of his proposed Urban Affairs Department.

But while we do have our internal differences of opinion, we are not as hopelessly split as is the Democratic Party—the Southern Conservatives pitted against the Northern Liberals— the Democratic Speaker against the Democratic President—the Secretary of Defense against the Democratic Chairman of the House Armed Services Committee.

Last year it was my privilege to lead a fight against a Democratic move in the Senate—a fight on which the Senate Republicans stood solidly together and voted solidly together. It was the fight against the Democratic Party's playing politics with National Defense on the West Virginia Political General Nomination.

We lost that fight by a vote of 45 to 37. But the manner in which the Democratic Party so brazenly and crassly played politics with National Defense on this issue was so repugnant that eight Democrats could not swallow it and defied Democratic Party orders and voted against the confirmation.

Many Democratic Senators came to me before and after the vote and stated that the nomination was disgraceful but that their hands were tied as Party instructions had gone out that they had to uphold the political honor of the Democratic Governor of West Virginia and that they held their noses and looked the other way and voted for the nomination.

Yes, here was an instance on which the Republicans in the Senate wrote a legislative record loud and clear—a record of unanimous Republican rejection of playing politics with National Defense—a record of very clear opposition to that of the Democratic Party in its 45 to 8 record of putting the prestige of the Democratic Party—the Democratic Governor of West Virginia—ahead of the National Security interests of our country.

There are many other instances in which Republicans in Congress have been writing a legislative record of shining contrast to the record of Democrats in Congress. You know them and I need not review them with you.

The basic way in which any minority party writes a record is in the traditional role of the loyal opposition. It is the hard way because it automatically brings down upon us the charge of obstructionism.

In that role we have the responsibility to be honest and reasonable. But we have just as much responsibility to scrutinize, carefully and independently, the proposals, the actions, and the record of the Democratic President—just as much as to maintain loyalty to the President in our loyalty to our country—for we have a loyalty responsibility to the people.

Yes, we even have the responsibility to remind the President of what he has or what he has not done on his promises and representations to the people when he was seeking their votes and on which promises and representations he got their votes. We have the responsibility to compare candidate promises with Presidential performance.

In his castigation of the Eisenhower Administration, Candidate John F. Kennedy uttered very, very strong words—and made unqualified statements. With those strong words and unqualified statements he won the Presidency. Having gained the authority he sought, he must now accept the responsibility for those words and statements by which he gained that authority.

Let us look at but a few of those strong words and un-qualified statements of Candidate Kennedy and compare them with the actions of President Kennedy. First let us take the B-70—or RS-70—plane issue over which President Kennedy and his Democratic Chairman of the House Armed Services Committee were warring last month.

When seeking votes of B-70 aircraft workers, Candidate Kennedy said to them in San Diego on November 2, 1960, "I endorse wholeheartedly the B-70 manned aircraft." You will note two very important things about this statement. It was unqualified—and it was a vote-seeking attack on the Eisen-hower Administration's rejection of the proposed B-70 program.

But when he became President, John F. Kennedy reversed his position for in his press conference of March 7, 1962, President Kennedy said he felt that B-70 production would be "not the most judicious action"—and he clearly indicated that he was willing to battle Congress to the end on this issue.

While as Candidate Kennedy he attacked Eisenhower's posi-tion on the B-70—when he became President Kennedy he adopted the very Eisenhower position he had opposed as Candidate Kennedy. He talked one way as a Candidate but acted the opposite as President.

Perhaps it would be appropriate to call this the "Kennedy Twist"—a rhythm in reverse action.

Next let us take the issue of Presidential impounding of Defense funds voted by Congress. As Candidate Kennedy seeking votes before the National Convention of the Veterans of Foreign Wars, he made a scathing attack on the Eisenhower Administration on the Presidential impounding of Defense funds voted by Congress with the unqualified statement that "these funds must be unfrozen and spent."

Yet, just as soon as he got into office—as soon as he became President Kennedy—he did the very thing he had criticized as he impounded and froze Defense funds voted by Congress and refused to spend them. He did not practice what he preached. He did just the opposite. Again it was the "Kennedy Twist"—a rhythm in reverse action.

Next let us take the issue that he made as a Candidate about

Federal Judge Appointments. In my home state of Maine at Bangor on September 2, 1960, Candidate Kennedy in an obvious appeal to Republican voters stated: "I must say that if I am elected President of the United States, I am not going to attempt to select men for positions of high leadership who happen to have the word Democrat after their names . . ."

More specifically on Judicial Appointments he wrote the President of the American Bar Association decrying the fact that, in the past, appointment of Federal Judges had been made according to their political party and stated specifically, "I would hope that the paramount consideration in the appointment of a Judge would not be his political party but his qualifications for the office."

What is the record of President Kennedy on the promise of Candidate Kennedy not to appoint Federal Judges according to the political party—not to appoint just Democrats? It is a record that was condemned by the Federal Judiciary Committee of the American Bar Association, the very organization to whom he made his specific pledge—by a report on February 19, 1962, that condemned the Kennedy process and the lack of qualifications of Kennedy judicial appointees.

As of March 12, 1962, President Kennedy had made one hundred and eleven *new* lifetime Federal Judge appointments and of this number the score was 111 to 0—one hundred and eleven to zero—against the Republicans with not a single Republican in this group of Kennedy appointments. Since that time he has made three or four Republican appointments.

President Kennedy did the very opposite of what he promised as Candidate Kennedy and so appointed Federal Judges on the basis of Democratic politics that his record has been condemned by the Federal Judiciary Committee of the American Bar Association.

And significantly enough, it is a condemnation that President Kennedy must share with his 1960 Campaign Manager, brother Robert Kennedy, who became Attorney General and second only to President Kennedy on control of the Federal Judge selections and appointments.

Again it is the "Kennedy Twist"—with the additional terpsichorean movement to the "Kennedy Twist" being that this time it is a duet of the Kennedy brothers.

Next let us take the issue made by Candidate Kennedy on Presidential appointees staying on the job for the duration. Repeatedly Candidate Kennedy criticized Eisenhower appointees for leaving the positions to which they had been appointed.

In Springfield, Ohio, on October 17, 1960, Candidate Kennedy emphasized and underscored his point with the statement of "Preference in appointments will be given to those willing to commit themselves to stay on the job long enough to apply what they learn. The goal is a full-time effort for the full tenure of the Presidential term . . ."

Yet, what happened to the first Kennedy Secretary of the Navy? Did he remain enlisted for the duration? Did he "stay on the job long enough to apply what" he had learned? Did he give "full-time effort for the full tenure of the Presidential term"? Did President Kennedy insist that he stay on the job as Secretary of the Navy?

Did the Kennedy performance and requirement as President match up with Candidate Kennedy's promise? The answer to all of these questions is "No!" For the first Secretary of the Navy left the job in less than a year—and with the full blessing of President Kennedy—and quit to run for what the two of them agreed was a higher duty than that of service to the United States on our National Defense—to run for Governor of Texas.

Yes, and now he is engaged with that other pre-eminent Democrat, Major General Edwin A. Walker, who left the National Defense effort to run for Governor of Texas. They are now engaged in mortal political combat to see who is to be the Democratic leader of Texas.

Yes, again it is the "Kennedy Twist"—this time done to the tune of "Deep in the Heart of Texas."

Now let us take the issue that Candidate Kennedy made on interest rates. On September 7, 1960, in Salem, Oregon, Candidate Kennedy made the flat and unqualified statement of ". . . we will reverse the disastrous high interest rate-tight money policies of the Republican Party."

Compare that with the New York *Times* issue of March 17, 1962, reporting a statement of Democratic Senator Albert Gore the day before with "Senator Albert Gore, Democrat of Tennessee, said today that to his 'disappointment and regret' the

Treasury under the Kennedy Administration was continuing high interest rate policies of the Eisenhower Regime."

Yes, again it is the "Kennedy Twist" with President Kennedy adopting the very interest rate policies that he had attacked as Candidate Kennedy—but this time the "Kennedy Twist" was not compatible with the square dance tempo of that noted Tennessee fiddler Albert Gore.

Next, let us turn to the subject of nepotism. With the Kennedy Administration's record on this I could talk all night. But first let me say that I do not condemn nepotism, provided the relatives really work.

After all, I am a product of nepotism—a living symbol of nepotism—for I wouldn't be in the Senate today had I not been a $3000-a-year secretary to my late husband when he was in the House—and I have a relative by marriage on my staff. We both have earned our pay.

But Candidate Kennedy condemned nepotism in strong and unqualified language on October 18, 1960, to the Washington News, which was waging an exposé crusade against nepotism, as he said, "Nepotism is dangerous to the public interest and to our national morality."

Keep your perspective on this. As a candidate he condemned nepotism unqualifiedly. But as President he acted the opposite —and it isn't necessary to run through the long list with you. Suffice it to say that it is a little more exclusive than the so-called social "400."

Yes, again it is the "Kennedy Twist"—this time instead of being just a duet of the two senior Kennedy brothers, a regular conga line has been formed that at times stretches clear around the world.

Now let us turn to the Kennedy-pressed issue of secrecy in government. Candidate Kennedy repeatedly castigated the Eisenhower Administration on what he alleged to be inexcusable secrecy in government. At Mount Clemens, Michigan, on October 26, 1960, he said, "I believe that the American people in 1960 are entitled to the truth, the truth with the bark off, the facts of the matter."

Yet on April 19, 1961, the newspaper editors of our country condemned President Kennedy for violating promises of an open-door information policy with the statement that John

F. Kennedy "was on record in writing as believing in freedom of information and in his duty to see that the people are informed. To date, neither he nor his Administration has lived up to his promise."

Less than two weeks later on the April 30, 1961, "Meet the Press" television and radio program, the Democratic Chairman of the Senate Foreign Relations Committee was similarly critical of President Kennedy on his failure to live up to the promises of Candidate Kennedy.

Senator Fulbright said on that occasion, "I would hope that the President will give special attention to informing us over the television . . . to inform all of us the nature of the conditions that we confront and what we ought to do about it . . . my principal criticism of the new Administration . . . is the failure to go through with this thought of outlining more clearly what our situation is, where we are, and then what we ought to do and where we ought to go, and I think this is very necessary."

In other words, both the American newspaper editors and his own Senate Foreign Relations Chairman took President Kennedy to task for failing to give the American people "the truth with the bark off" as he had promised as Candidate Kennedy. He was indicted of being guilty of the very thing he had alleged against President Eisenhower—of lacking in leadership on information.

Again, it was the "Kennedy Twist"—but without accompaniment by the Arkansas Traveler.

Now let us turn to the issue of prestige and prestige polls that Candidate Kennedy made in 1960. What happened when he became President? Well, with the Cuban fiasco dropping our international prestige to an all-time low under President Kennedy, his Administration ordered the prestige polls abolished as contrasted to his demands as Candidate Kennedy that they be published. This time the "Kennedy Twist" had a Cuban beat!

And of course, everyone—but everyone—recalls how Candidate Kennedy pounded away at what he called the "missile gap." Yet, less than three weeks after he became President, his Secretary of Defense revealed that there was no "missile gap." Since everyone also knows that even Jack Kennedy couldn't possibly close the alleged "missile gap" in so short a period as three weeks, it was evident that his campaign-claimed "missile gap" was only a politically expedient myth—now dumped in the boneyard of the "fall guy" CIA.

Again it was the "Kennedy Twist"—and this time the rhythm in reverse action was first put into reverse by the person whom Society Columnist Betty Beale has revealed is the champion "Twister" at the White House parties, Defense Secretary McNamara. Betty says he is "terrific" on the Twist. I've never seen him do it—but I must say that he was "terrific" when he revealed that there was no missile gap.

And you remember well how Candidate Kennedy denounced personal diplomacy and summitry—but shortly after becoming President how he engaged extensively in personal diplomacy and summitry in trips abroad.

He went to the summit with Khrushchev in Vienna where Khrushchev delivered a tough ultimatum to him that he did not reveal to the American people until after Khrushchev had announced the ultimatum himself.

Again—the "Kennedy Twist"—this time to the tune of a Viennese waltz.

And to those of us in New England where the baked bean is a regional tradition and "must," we shall not forget how Candidate Kennedy downgraded the bean in the campaign, particularly in the TV-Radio debate on October 7, 1960, when he said, ". . . you can't tell me anyone who uses beans instead of meat . . . is well fed or adequately fed . . ."

This from the man from the "Region of the Bean and the Cod!"

Yet, when he became President he regained his taste for beans as his Administration proudly announced on February 27 and April 27, 1961, that it was making the pea bean a "part of the effort to expand and improve the quality of food for needy persons."

Again, the "Kennedy Twist"—and even against the beans that made Boston famous even if they were Eisenhower Program beans when Candidate Kennedy denounced them. It seems that since becoming President he now knows his beans as Eisenhower did.

Next let us turn to the growth rate issue that Candidate

Kennedy raised in 1960 when he repeatedly attacked the Eisenhower Administration on what he characterized as the threat of Russia overtaking us economically. At Valley Forge on October 29, 1960, Candidate Kennedy said, "That requires a rate of growth no less than 5 percent a year, and we are not growing at that rate today. Our average for the past eight years was 2.5 percent."

Richard Nixon answered this gloom and scare talk of Candidate Kennedy repeatedly with the same answer he had given to Khrushchev: "They are not going to catch us in seven or seventy years, if we remain true to the principles that have made America the richest and the best country in the world today." Dick Nixon also pointed out that the Soviet rate of growth was on a lower base.

When John F. Kennedy became President, he adopted the Nixon line on this—that Russia would not overtake us and that Russia started from a lower base—as President Kennedy stated at his June 28, 1961, press conference: "Soviet output will not reach two thirds of ours by 1970 and our rate will be easier to sustain or improve than the Soviet rate, which starts from a lower figure."

Again it is the "Kennedy Twist"—with Kennedy as President adopting the arguments of the man he argued against when he was Candidate Kennedy—in fact, I think maybe Dick Nixon could sue him for plagiarism on this point.

You may recall how Candidate Kennedy taunted President Eisenhower on the charge of failing to be a leader—of how in New York City on November 5, 1960, Candidate Kennedy said:

"I want to be a President who acts as well as reacts—who is the Chief Executive in every sense of the word—who responds to a problem not by hoping his subordinates will act, but by directing them to act—a President who is willing to take the responsibility for getting things done, and take the blame if they are not done right . . . In short, I believe in a President who will formulate and fight for his legislative policies, and not be a casual observer of the legislative process.

"A President who will not back down under pressure, or let down his spokesmen in the Congress—a President who does not speak from the rear of the battle but who places himself in the thick of the fight."

How does President Kennedy measure up to these words of Candidate Kennedy? Well, the pro-Kennedy Washington *Post* made a measurement in its lead editorial of February 27, 1962, in which it gave just what I have quoted and then said of President Kennedy:

"Maybe it would be more apposite to wonder what sort of leadership Congress is getting from the White House . . . The simple sending of an eloquent message to Congress can hardly be said to fill the bill. President Eisenhower sent eloquent messages to Congress . . . and Candidate Kennedy taunted him pretty roughly about his failure to do any more . . . unless a President . . . arouses the people to cross a new frontier . . . New frontiers never get crossed . . . without leaders who really lead . . . Without such leadership, there can be no new frontier."

In other words, the Washington *Post* condemned President Kennedy for lack of leadership—and accused him of a leadership gap!

Again it is the "Kennedy Twist"—with the pro-Kennedy Washington *Post* condemning his failure to be a leader on domestic issues and legislation—and saying in substance that the tune of "New Frontiers" had changed to that of "Lost Frontiers."

Everyone—but everyone—knows what an issue Candidate Kennedy made on Cuba against the Eisenhower Administration —of how Candidate Kennedy said, "We must attempt to strengthen the non-Batista Democratic anti-Castro forces in exile, and in Cuba itself, who offer eventual hope of over-throwing Castro. Thus far these fighters for freedom have had virtually no support from our Government."

Well, what did Jack Kennedy do, when he became President, about giving the anti-Castro forces real support—when he had a chance to back up his strong talk with action? The world knows the very tragic story of how he called off the support they needed most—the air support when they made the in-vasion attempt at the Bay of Pigs and how they were defeated so disastrously because of the lack of that desperately needed air support.

If anyone has the slightest doubt about this, let him or her read the Charles Murphy article "Cuba: The Record Set Straight" in the September 1961 issue of *Fortune* Magazine—or the Stewart Alsop article "The Lessons of the Cuban Disaster" in the June 24, 1961, issue of the *Saturday Evening Post.*

Why the best that Jack Kennedy, as President, could offer for that which he criticized, as Candidate Kennedy, was the pitiful and degrading "Tractors for Freedom" deal that fell through.

Again it was the "Kennedy Twist"—done in agony to a Cuban beat.

The Kennedy record on Laos is nearly as tragic. Repeatedly Candidate Kennedy called for a strong stand on Laos. Even after he became President he threatened a strong stand in his map-talk at his nationally televised press conference on March 23, 1961. He issued an ultimatum to Khrushchev to stay out of Laos and strongly indicated that we were ready to go to war if Khrushchev didn't heed the ultimatum.

Yet a year later what is the score? Khrushchev called the bluff and Kennedy did nothing. And the Communists have taken over more and more of Laos.

On May 24, 1961, Washington *News* Columnist Richard Starnes summed up the record this way:

"The President's ringing declaration on March 23 that Laos was worth a war . . . is now revealed as an empty statement by a man who either didn't know what he was talking about, or who was foolishly trying to run a bluff on the master bluffer of them all."

And today it is even worse than it was at the time of the Starnes column a year ago.

Again it is the "Kennedy Twist"—of talking one way and acting another way or not even acting at all—of brave, strong, and eloquent words but not to be matched by any real action.

These truths I do acknowledge—that as an American I must support the President of the United States regardless of the difference between his political party and mine—that criticism is easy to make by the person who does not have the authority and responsibility to act—just as easy for me today as it was easy for John F. Kennedy when he was a candidate in 1960—

that one should be careful and fair in indulging in that luxury of criticism—and that changing one's mind or opinion is not always a betrayal of weakness but rather often is a hallmark of courage.

While these truths may, to some extent, mitigate the instances of Kennedy reversals that I have cited to you, by no means do they excuse them or place a taboo upon discussion of them and bringing them to the attention of the American people.

It is more important for the American people to have a strong President than for either political party to win a Presidential election. It is in that spirit that I speak tonight.

I do not necessarily take exception to the stand that John F. Kennedy has taken on every issue—I do not mean for my remarks about him to be personal or to reflect any unfriendly spirit toward him. And while I can surely be charged as speaking as a partisan, I have only cited the factual record to you as the American people are entitled to know it.

Inescapable is the fact that the image that John F. Kennedy deliberately and successfully created of himself in the 1960 campaign is far different from the actual John F. Kennedy as revealed thus far by his record as President.

The record as I have outlined it to you tonight reveals two very basic and fundamental things—first, that the record of President Kennedy is a record of repeated reversals of the campaign pledges of Candidate Kennedy—and second, that he has not been the strong President that he promised—for what strength he has displayed has been in words—eloquent, brave, and inspiring words only to be followed by no action or by timid action at best.

In the words of that distinguished New York *Times* Columnist and Washington Bureau Chief, Scotty Reston:

"He has talked like Churchill and acted like Chamberlain."

And I repeat:

"He has talked like Churchill and acted like Chamberlain."

Candidate Kennedy's campaign theme was "This is a Time for Greatness"—Candidate Kennedy's campaign promise was "Leadership in the Sixties"—thus far, President Kennedy has given neither greatness nor leadership—neither greatness nor leadership.

No—leadership is not manifested by coercion and police state methods.

No—greatness is not manifested by unlimited pragmatism.

EDITOR'S NOTE:

That this speech was not to enhance relations between the two of them was evident. But neither publicly evidenced at first what could be interpreted as ill feeling. To the contrary, on July 23, 1962, Senator Smith wrote a letter extending to President and Mrs. Kennedy an invitation to use her home at West Cundy Point, Cundys Harbor, Maine, which was in the area where it had been announced that he would be sailing. The Senator had been particularly appreciative of Mrs. Kennedy's thoughtfulness when inviting her to social affairs at the White House. Mrs. Kennedy extended the courtesy of including an escort of the Senator's own choosing—something that had never been done before at the White House.

When a President makes a visit to a state, it is routine political courtesy for him to invite the two United States Senators of that state and the Congressman from the district that he visits to accompany him on his plane—then *Air Force One,* now known as the *Spirit of Seventy-Six.* This routine political courtesy is extended even to Senators and Congressmen of the opposing political party.

For three weeks after the Senator had invited the President and Mrs. Kennedy to use her home there was no response from the White House. Finally on the morning of the President's scheduled departure for Maine, a reply to her letter declining her invitation was received from a member of the President's staff.

Meantime no invitation for Senator Smith to join the President on his flight to Maine was forthcoming either, though Senator Muskie was scheduled to be on the flight. An invitation did come from the Commanding Officer of the Brunswick (Maine) Naval Air Station asking Senator Smith to attend that station's Charity Festival and draw the tickets for the prizes to be awarded on Sunday, August 12. That was two days after President Kennedy was scheduled to land there on Friday. She accepted and the Navy offered to send a plane to pick her up Friday so that she could spend the weekend and then return her on Sunday after the ceremonies at the Charity Festival.

Early Friday morning the Brunswick Naval Air Station Commander called Senator Smith's office to inquire if she still wanted the Navy to fly her to the Festival or if she would be accompanying the President, who was scheduled to arrive at Brunswick late that afternoon. It was embarrassing to answer that President Kennedy had not invited Senator Smith to ride with him. The Navy called twice later but the response was the same—no invitation had come from the President.

Finally it became clear that the Navy would have to provide the transportation, and early enough so that the Navy plane could arrive in time for Senator Smith to join in welcoming the President. As soon as she answered the last roll call vote about two that afternoon, Senator Smith was driven to the waiting Navy plane—an R4D, not a jet like *Air Force One.*

Shortly before casting her vote, she made a short speech in the Senate:

> It was my hope and my plan to be at Brunswick this afternoon to greet President Kennedy upon his arrival in Maine in the Naval Air Station there at 6:15 P.M. I wanted to join in on giving him the warmest and most gracious welcome and reception . . .
>
> But it is doubtful that I can get to Maine in time to be present to welcome the President because this last roll call vote, on which I voted at one twenty-seven, leaves me practically no time, as the field will be closed down at five-thirty and no other planes are allowed to land there after that time.
>
> The Navy Department was kind enough to arrange to fly me to Maine to join in the welcome to the President but the

R4D plane that it made available is not jet aircraft—and informed me that I would have to be at Andrews Air Force Base in time to depart not later than one-thirty this afternoon. Consequently, time closed in on me and I sincerely regret it.

But I am sure that the President and everyone will understand fully that my official Senate duty to answer roll call votes and to remain here to do what I was elected to do—to legislate and vote—takes priority over even the pleasant activity of greeting and welcoming the President of the United States to the State of Maine.

I wish him a most pleasant, enjoyable, and relaxing weekend in Maine—and that he will enjoy it so much that he will return many times to Maine.

Later it was reported that Senate Majority Leader Mike Mansfield was shocked to learn from the speech that she had not been extended the routine political courtesy of being invited along on *Air Force One*. He expressed his incredulity to Mike Manatos, the White House Senate Liaison officer.

Though the R4D left Washington at least an hour and a half ahead of the President's plane, it became a tortoise-hare race between the propeller-drawn R4D and the jet *Air Force One*. Commander Olsen, our pilot, revved the motors so much it felt as though the plane would come apart. Not only was he getting maximum speed out of the plane but he was getting permission from flight control towers to cut corners in the normal flight patterns and flying distance.

This had to be done because the Brunswick Naval Air Station was to be secured at least ten minutes before the scheduled arrival of *Air Force One*. No planes would be permitted to land or even be in the air over the station. Thus, if the R4D didn't get in at least ten minutes before *Air Force One*, the R4D would have to land some other place. Meanwhile, back in Washington, White House Senate liaison Mike Manatos had called the Senator's office to issue a belated invitation from President Kennedy for her to ride with him on *Air Force One*. The receptionist replied, "Sorry, but Senator

Smith had to leave an hour ago," wondering as she said it whether we would ever make it. We did. The R4D landed in a pouring rain with exactly five minutes to spare. Margaret sped directly to the stand where President Kennedy was to go through a receiving line. Ten minutes later when he and Senator Muskie reached the stand, Margaret quipped to Senator Muskie, "Hi, Ed! What took you so long?"

Both Jack Kennedy and Margaret Smith were political realists. A year later, on August 2, 1963, the Senate was to hear Margaret Smith refute partisan attacks on President Kennedy and his brother Senator Edward Kennedy for the choice of Boston for an Electronics Research Center. It was claimed that the Space Agency (NASA) had selected Boston on the basis of pork-barrel politics dictated by the President and his brother. Senator Kennedy expressed gratitude to Senator Smith for coming to his defense.

The next time *Air Force One* flew into Maine the President invited Senator Smith along well ahead of time. He was to receive an honorary Doctor of Laws degree from the University of Maine at a convocation on October 19, 1963. Not only did he invite Senator Smith to accompany him on *Air Force One* but he also invited her to attend the convocation with him even though the University had not invited her. Not until a very long time after President Kennedy had invited her did the University of Maine President Lloyd Elliot finally send her an invitation.

It was on this trip that Jack Kennedy and Margaret Smith came to know each other best. In extended talks they had flying up and back, they discussed national problems and issues. On the way up President Kennedy excused himself about fifteen minutes before the plane landed. He explained that since he did not wear a topcoat he had to go change into his thermal underwear—a change he was to regret when the temperature rose. Later he whispered to the Senator, "Wasn't it hot? I never was more uncomfortable!"

When he started to get off the plane, President Kennedy stepped aside for Senator Smith to go first. "No, Mr. President," she said, "you should go first for the President comes ahead of women even." Frowning and in a pleading tone he replied, "Please, Mrs. Smith—you don't know the number of letters I get bitterly criticizing me for walking ahead of Jackie! Please spare me from getting this criticism!" They compromised by walking side-by-side in leaving the plane.

The next day, in telling me about her serious conversations with the President, she said, "Jack Kennedy has matured greatly as President. I think he's learned a lot. I don't think he's going to make the mistakes that he has in the past."

And the last known comment of John F. Kennedy on Margaret Chase Smith came at a Presidential press conference very shortly before his assassination a month later. When asked what he thought of Margaret Chase Smith as a potential Presidential candidate, he stated that he had great respect for her and that she would make a "formidable candidate."

The day after the assassination Margaret Smith walked to the desk that John F. Kennedy had last occupied in the Senate and placed a single rose on it. Later, in response to appreciation from the Kennedy staff, she said that the credit should really go to Senate Majority Leader Mike Mansfield, who had suggested the idea, but that she had been deeply pleased to do it.

Nuclear Test Ban Treaty

"They wish only that she had not let political ambition stand in the way of conscience on the test ban treaty."

—Drew Pearson
September 28, 1963

Ever since its establishment, the United States Senate has been plagued by two questions: (1) Should a United States Senator vote in the selfish best interests of the state that elects him or should he vote on the basis of the national interest? and (2) Should he vote the wishes and will of his constituency or should he vote according to his own conviction and conscience?

Most Senators claim that they vote according to national interest and, yet, in the same breath say that they will not turn their backs on the wishes of their constituents and best interests of their states. The truth is that a Senator usually votes the parochial interests of his state and constituents because he wants to get re-elected and survive politically. Before you can become a statesman you first have to get elected, and to get elected you have to be a politician pledging support for what the voters want.

Yet, there comes a time when a Senator's own conviction runs counter to the indicated will of the majority of his constituents. Often this is because he has more information on the issue than his constituents, sometimes inside information not available to the public for security reasons.

The Nuclear Test Ban Treaty ratification Senate vote on September 24, 1963, was such an instance. The Senate Preparedness Investigating Subcommittee, of which I was a member, held very extensive hearings, both public and closed. As the hearings wore on, the mail ran very heavy. It was overwhelmingly against the treaty from writers outside of my state, but Maine writers were substantially for the treaty.

In the closed hearings, military leaders vigorously opposed the treaty, setting forth with grave facts the serious risks of the treaty. They were joined in their opposition by such outstanding scientists as Dr. Edward Teller, one of the fathers of the atomic bomb, and Dr. John S. Foster, Jr. Dr. Foster was later appointed as Director of Defense Research and Engineering, the Number Three man in the Pentagon under Defense Secretary McNamara and Deputy Defense Secretary Nitze (both militant advocates of the treaty).

But their devastating testimony against the treaty was put under lock and key never to be permitted by President Kennedy and Defense Secretary McNamara to be released to the American people. This one-sidedness so disturbed me that I made a Senate speech on August 2, 1963, in which I warned publicly of it.

Most of the discussion which had already taken place over the partial nuclear test ban treaty had, it seemed to me, concentrated only on the advantages to be gained by its ratification. It was said that the treaty as proposed would tend to slow down the nuclear arms race, prevent the spread of nuclear weapons to nations not now possessing them, create a favorable climate for entering into other agreements designed to reduce world tensions, and, of course, prevent any further contamination of the air we breathe.

Conspicuous by their absence thus far in these discussions, I said, were the disadvantages which would accrue to the United States should this treaty be ratified by the Senate. These disadvantages related to the risks which we must be willing to assume by entering into a treaty which was not self-executing all of its provisions and to the evaluation of the need of the United States to conduct further atmospheric tests in the interests of its own national security.

The Preparedness Investigating Subcommittee had heard many witnesses express grave concern over the impact which this treaty would have upon our national security. The difficulty, of course, lay in the fact that the information, apart from being very technical, was so highly sensitive that most of it could not be made public. But in view of the testimony which I had heard thus far, I said, I was constrained to reserve judgment on this treaty until all the evidence was in and we could then take a cold, hard, impassionate appraisal of the treaty and all its consequences. A week later, in an effort to call attention to the serious risks without breaching the imposed security, I put forth the first of two sets of questions I was to ask concerning the treaty. It was on September 9,

1963, when I gave my speech on the Nuclear Test Ban Treaty asking the first set of sixteen questions:

Mr. President, today marks the beginning of formal debate in the Senate over ratification of the limited test ban treaty by the terms of which further nuclear tests in the atmosphere, underwater, and in outer space are to be prohibited for such time as the treaty shall remain in force.

We have already experienced in this Chamber a great deal of comment concerning this proposed treaty most of which, I daresay, stressed the advantages to be gained through its ratification with very few remarks devoted to a consideration of the risks involved and the consequent disadvantages which might accrue to the United States. Certainly, these, too, must be harshly examined and evaluated in order to determine whether all these purported advantages do indeed far outweigh the cumulative risks.

Without presuming to suggest or define the parameters within which the debate should be confined, I will, nevertheless pose certain questions which I feel must be satisfactorily resolved during the course of debate on this treaty. Otherwise, I shall personally feel that I possess insufficient information upon which to exercise an informed judgment when vote is taken.

I am not unmindful of the fact that one of the parties to this agreement is the same country which, in recent years, among other things, ruthlessly repressed the Hungarian uprising; erected a shameful wall of tyranny around Berlin; surreptitiously deployed ballistic missiles in Cuba and, after months of stealthy preparations, shattered a moratorium on nuclear testing which had been in effect for thirty-four months. It has also seen fit to abrogate virtually all the agreements and treaties it has ever entered into with other nations whenever it served its purpose to do so.

My questions, however, do not concern the good faith or trustworthiness of the Nation with which we are here dealing as the questionable reliability of the leaders of the Soviet Union in abiding by the letter and spirit of their obligations is already a disgraceful matter of common knowledge and public record.

I would point out, however, that in August of last year at Geneva, a proposal by the United States, which was very similar to the treaty now under debate, met with adamant intransigence on the part of the Soviet Union and I consider it more than mere passing-strange that suddenly the Soviet Union found this limited agreement to be so vital to her national interests that it was negotiated, initialed, and signed with remarkable expediency and haste. The poor draftsmanship of its provisions, and the utter lack of definition of its terms not only reflects this haste but defeats its very purpose through the varied interpretations to which it is subject.

The 1961–62 series of nuclear tests conducted by the Soviet Union were massive, sophisticated, and impressive. Ours, on the other hand, were too hastily contrived to give us all the data which we might otherwise have acquired had there been time for more orderly preparation. With this knowledge of relative testing in mind, I would then ask:

First. Has the Soviet Union, through its most recent atmospheric test series, now achieved a nuclear advantage over the United States of a military or scientific significance?

Second. Are we reasonably confident and secure in the knowledge that our ballistic-missile retaliatory second strike force will survive and operate in a nuclear environment?

Third. In seeking to slow down the arms race as a purported advantage of this treaty, will we adopt nuclear parity as the basis for deterring thermonuclear war rather than nuclear superiority?

Fourth. Will the treaty, as claimed, prevent the proliferation of nuclear weapons when France and Red China refuse to be bound and when underground testing is sanctioned for all nations whether they sign or not?

Fifth. How is one to define or interpret that which shall constitute an underground test within the meaning of article I, section 1, subsection (a) of the treaty?

Sixth. Do we possess the capability to detect all nuclear detonations occurring in the three environments prohibited by the treaty?

Seventh. Can any significant advances in nuclear technology be achieved by clandestine testing in those three environments at yields which may possibly be below our ability to detect?

Eighth. Will we be able to differentiate between a shallow underground explosion and an atmospheric burst detonated close to the surface of the earth?

Ninth. Can we, in fact, maintain an adequate readiness to test in those prohibited environments in the event the treaty should suddenly be abrogated?

Tenth. Will our scientific laboratories and the interest of our scientists deteriorate under a treaty which permits only underground testing?

Eleventh. Will we be restrained from ever determining feasibility, developing and deploying any defense whatever against ballistic missile attack?

Twelfth. Will this treaty permit the Soviet Union to achieve equality in the low-yield tactical weapons where it is generally acknowledged that we have an advantage and yet preclude us from ever achieving equality in the high-yield weapon where the Soviet Union is unquestionably superior?

Thirteenth. To what extent can we satisfy, through underground testing, the military and scientific requirements which were to have been investigated by atmospheric tests planned for next year?

Fourteeth. What is the human tolerance for radioactivity and what is the truth about the danger of atmospheric contamination, even at previous rates of testing, in causing genetic damage and leukemia to the living and yet unborn?

Fifteenth. What will be the effect of ratification upon our Plowshare program—a project designed to deepen harbors, dig tunnels and canals, or otherwise cause beneficial changes to the topography through controlled and contained nuclear explosions?

Sixteenth. Will the participation of East Germany in this treaty constitute even so much as a tacit, implied, or suggestive recognition of that Communist regime as a sovereign national entity?

These, Mr. President, are the questions which, in my opinion, must be resolved in the course of this debate and I look forward with keen interest to their eventual resolution. Without satisfactory answers to them, it will be virtually impossible for any of us to measure and evaluate the gains versus the risks of entering into this limited test ban treaty.

I am also aware of the consequences which might flow from a failure to ratify this treaty. Some Members of this Chamber who had earlier expressed guarded reservations about it have already been labeled as "atom mongers" by the Russian-controlled press. Similarly, our national image in the world as a country desirous of peace with justice would undoubtedly be attacked and vilified by such propaganda were we to fail to ratify.

However, I shall continue to reserve judgment on this issue until such time as the evidence convinces me that the paramount issue of our national safety and security will not be put in jeopardy by ratification of this treaty.

I wrote both Defense Secretary McNamara and Secretary of State Rusk the following day posing the sixteen questions to them. A week later on September 16, 1963, Senator John Sparkman of Alabama, second senior Majority member of the Senate Foreign Relations Committee, in collaboration with the State Department, responded to the questions. I had the highest respect for John Sparkman* and listened very closely.

Senator Sparkman said that there were no single factual answers available to most of the questions I had posed and admitted that the answers he and the State Department were making were only speculative. He contended that the answers had high probabilities and were based upon interpretation of available facts and that "final resolution of most of" the "questions would come only from data collected after a full-scale nuclear war between the United States and the Soviet Union." He complained that many of the questions involved highly secret data. Again the one-sidedness of the presentation of the issue resulted from the imposition of security on the arguments against the treaty.

* EDITOR'S NOTE: In 1954 Senator Smith had provided Senator Sparkman with documented evidence that Texas oil millionaire H. R. Cullen and his son-in-law Douglas Marshall had helped finance the campaign of Laurie Battle against him.

When Sparkman finished, I replied that although I was not a lawyer and had had no legal training, there were certain ambiguities in the nuclear test ban treaty that raised questions. The wording of the treaty raised these questions, and I hoped that before the debate had been concluded, legal answers would be supplied.

Thereupon I received consent to have my second set of questions read into the Record:

I

Under the wording of the first paragraph of article I of the treaty each of the parties to the treaty undertakes to prohibit, to prevent, and not to carry out any nuclear explosion, "at any place under its jurisdiction or control:

"(a) in the atmosphere; beyond its limits, including outer space; or underwater, including territorial waters or high seas; or."

Questions raised:

1. Could a party to the treaty carry out a nuclear explosion in the atmosphere above an uninhabited island not claimed by it and justify its action upon the ground that the explosion did not occur at a place under its jurisdiction or control?

2. What nuclear explosions in outer space are banned by this paragraph in view of the fact that outer space, and particularly the more remote regions thereof, is not considered to be within the jurisdiction or control of any nation? If Russia explodes a nuclear device in outer space and we claim that such action is prohibited by this paragraph, are we placed in a position where we must simultaneously admit that Russia has jurisdiction over or controls the particular region of outer space in which the explosion occurs?

3. Would a nuclear explosion underwater in the middle of the Pacific Ocean be barred by this paragraph in view of the fact that the high seas are not considered by nations to be within the control or jurisdiction of any particular nation?

4. Does the ban on "any other nuclear explosion" prevent

us from operating atomic energy plants for the production of electricity, the steamship *Savannah,* or any atomic submarine, all of which are operated by means of controlled atomic explosions?

5. Will we be branded as a violator of the treaty if we have an accidental explosion at one of our atomic energy plants?

II

If Section I of article I means what it appears to say, and relates only to nuclear explosions carried out by a party at a place under its jurisdiction or control, it becomes necessary to look elsewhere in the treaty for language prohibiting a party from carrying out explosions at places not under its jurisdiction or control.

Paragraph 2 of article I of the treaty does not contain the limiting language "at any place under its jurisdiction or control" and would therefore have much wider application than paragraph 1 of that article, if it is the intention of the parties that it should apply to direct acts of the parties as distinguished from indirect acts of the parties. The explanation of paragraph 2 contained in the letter to the President from the Acting Secretary of State, dated August 8, 1963, and containing an explanation of the treaty, indicates that paragraph 2 was designed to be applicable to indirect action but does not state flatly that it does not apply to direct acts (see Executive M, 88th Cong., 1st sess., p. 6).

Questions raised:

1. Does paragraph 2 apply to direct acts of the parties or only to indirect acts of the parties? For example, does it apply to a nuclear explosion by Russia in the atmosphere above Russian soil or is it intended to apply only to such a situation as a nuclear explosion by the Communist Chinese regime in the atmosphere above China which is caused, encouraged, or participated in by Russia?

2. If paragraph 2 does apply to direct acts of the parties, how do you resolve the conflict between its provisions, which are not limited by the phrase "at any place under its jurisdiction or control," and the provisions of paragraph 1, which are limited by such phrase?

III

Article IV of the treaty provides that a party desiring to withdraw from the treaty must give notice three months in advance.

Question raised:

If the U.S. decides to withdraw from the treaty because it has irrefutable evidence that Russia has violated it, would we not be compelled to wait three months before resuming nuclear testing unless we were willing to risk being branded as treaty violators?

Two days later on his own initiative Secretary of State Dean Rusk sent me the State Department's answers to my five legal questions and the following day I received letters from both Secretaries Rusk and McNamara in response to my earlier, more general set of questions. All of the answers were read into the Record (see Appendix) along with my observations. I said in essence that the answers were too speculative and without the definitiveness and assurance I had sought.

When the showdown vote came on September 24, 1963, I was the last Senator to declare my position on the treaty. No one had tried to pressure or persuade me to vote either way, for which I was quite appreciative. There was one eleventh-hour exception, however. Leo Goodman, CIO lobbyist and specialist on nuclear politics, unexpectedly dropped by the reception room of my office at 10 A.M. to try to get me to vote for the treaty. The Senate had already convened and he was told I had left for the Senate Floor. (The Senate was having its picture taken that morning—the then sole historical exception to the strict rule prohibiting pictures of the Senate in session.) Goodman then went to the reception room off the Senate Floor where he found Bill Lewis waiting in line to sign the register enabling him to go on the Senate Floor. Goodman told Bill he wanted to talk to me about my vote.

Since this was about ten-fifteen and I was scheduled to make my speech between the picture-taking at ten-fifteen and the roll call vote at ten-thirty, Bill told Goodman he was not only late but also presumptuous.

By this time I had of course decided how I was going to vote. It was one of the most difficult votes I ever cast. In my speech just before the roll call, I told why:

Mr. President, the vote on ratification of the nuclear test ban treaty is one of the most difficult votes that I have ever cast as a United States Senator—or even in my twenty-three years in Congress. The difficulty is not with respect to my single vote having any effect on the outcome of the final vote by the Senate. That outcome was a foregone conclusion from the very start—overwhelmingly for ratification.

During the debate I have raised several questions. I had hoped that the answers to these questions could be definite and clear—at least enough for the resolution of any doubts that I had about the treaty. But they have not been. Admittedly, the answers have been speculative.

This issue is not only dominated by speculation. It is dominated by emotions. Those who support the treaty have been called pro-Communists. They have been charged by some extremists with treason and with selling out to Khrushchev. How ridiculous can one get with these charges? The charges are so ridiculous that no sensible person would take them seriously.

They remind me of those tragic days in the early fifties when articulate courage was almost eliminated by the techniques of "guilt by association" and "trial by accusation." The extremists of the Right did our country a great disservice by those unsubstantiated charges. The damage was irreparable. What it did to our scientists and the way that it shackled our free scientific effort was revealed in the later fifties when Russia's Sputnik revealed how tragically we were lagging behind Russia in science and technology.

I know—because I was a target of the extremists of the Right. They called me "pro-Communist" and a "fellow traveler" because of my Declaration of Conscience.

But many, many of those who, back in the early fifties,

decried the "guilt by association" and "trial by accusation" tactics of the Extreme Right are today guilty of the same abuses and excesses on the Extreme Left of the ideological spectrum.

For too many of the Extreme Left now charge those who oppose the treaty of being "murderers" and of deliberately poisoning the milk for children with lethal doses of Strontium Ninety. At the outset of this debate, the press quoted one Senator as saying that any Senator who voted against ratification of the treaty should have his head examined.

Have we lost all sense of reasonableness? Cannot members of the United States Senate have honest differences of opinions without being charged with mental deficiency or treason or crassly poisoning milk and killing babies or being "pro-Communist" by those who so emotionally disagree with them—both on the Extreme Right and on the Extreme Left?

What does the majority of the American people want? Ratification or rejection of the nuclear test ban treaty? The Gallup Poll and the Harris Poll report that an overwhelming majority of the American people want the treaty to be ratified.

But that is not what my mail shows—and it is the heaviest mail that I have ever received in all of my entire service in Congress. More than that, it is not just organized pressure mail. Instead it is individual mail in personal handwriting—not just printed or mimeographed mail—or printed cards distributed in great volume for persons just to automatically sign without thinking.

This mail is individually composed. It is highly emotional and often inflammatory—but equally so on both sides, whether for or against the treaty. Nevertheless it is clear that the people are expressing themselves with deep feeling—not just merely echoing what someone has told them to write. And the mail is from every section of the nation.

Were I to be guided by what the mail indicates is the wish of the majority of Americans, I would have to vote against the treaty. For by better than an 8 to 1 margin the senders of letters and telegrams and postal cards to me have registered vigorous opposition to the treaty.

Yet, the pattern varies when just the Maine mail is taken— for the Maine mail has favored the treaty by a 2 to 1 vote.

But even with Maine the expression of feeling has changed. Prior to Labor Day and during the summer season, the Maine mail was better than 3 to 1 in favor of the treaty. But after Labor Day the Maine mail has turned in the other direction with a majority registering opposition to the treaty. It would be difficult to conclude with any certainty what a majority of year-round Maine residents feel—since obviously a great deal of the Maine mail prior to Labor Day came from out-of-state summer visitors.

The totals of my mail run heavily in contradiction to the reports of the Gallup Poll and the Harris Poll. The only reconciliation that I can conclude is that if the Gallup Poll and the Harris Poll accurately reflect the position of a majority of Americans, then those who support the treaty apparently aren't sufficiently enthusiastic for it and won't take time or effort to write—or those who are against the treaty have such a higher degree of intensity in the opposition to the treaty that they will take the time to write and express themselves.

One thing is quite clear. Regardless of whether the majority is for or against the treaty, the degree of articulated intensity of those against the treaty is much greater than those who are for the treaty.

Another thing is clear—that the polls and the mail—and the seasonal factor in the Maine mail on this issue—are too contradictory for me to let the mail have any significant influence on my final decision.

In trying to arrive at a conscientious decision, I have considered what would happen if the Senate did reject the treaty. First, it is clear that Khrushchev would spew vitriolic propaganda charging that the United States had thus proved that it did not want peace and that we were "warmongers" intent on poisoning the air with Strontium Ninety. Even though he is guilty himself of having broken the last test ban agreement with the multi-megaton open air test nuclear explosions that Russia set off, his false propaganda would be believed by some and we would lose significant ground in the psychological war.

But Senate rejection of the treaty would not be the act that started the United States to resume open air nuclear testing. It would not for the very simple reason that President Kennedy has taken the position that the United States would refrain from open air testing as long as Russia refrained from open air testing.

Now let us face reality and the truth on this point. The Senate vote on the test ban treaty will neither stop open air testing if the treaty is ratified—nor start it if the treaty is rejected. It will not stop open air testing because it has already been stopped by President Kennedy in agreement with Khrushchev's keeping Russia from open air tests. By the same token, Senate rejection of the treaty will not start open air testing again.

I think Khrushchev feels that it is to the military advantage of Russia to keep us from resuming open air tests in the belief that Russia is significantly ahead of us in the high yield weapons and will stay ahead as long as we do not make the open air tests that are necessary if we are to close the high yield weapons gap that so heavily favors Russia.

And he doesn't need a treaty to do this. All he needs to do is to refrain from conducting such open air tests. He knows that by the simple expedient of restraint, he will stop the United States from open air testing because of the expressions made by President Kennedy. Consequently, I believe it would be most unlikely that Khrushchev would order resumption of open air testing if the Senate were to reject this treaty.

Perhaps my conclusion in this regard can be criticized as being "speculative." But it is no more speculative than the answers given to the questions that I have raised in this debate —answers that even those providing the answers have admitted were "speculative." I believe that my conclusion in this regard is far less speculative.

So that in the final analysis, my decision must rest on whether the political and psychological disadvantages stemming from rejection of the treaty would be greater than the obvious national security disadvantages stemming from ratification of the treaty. Fortunately, the political and psychological disadvantages of treaty rejection have been very ably and fully presented out in the open to the public. And make no mistake about it, they are tremendously impressive arguments—almost compelling arguments.

Unfortunately, the national security disadvantages stemming

from ratification of the treaty have not been as fully presented out in the open to the public. They have not because of the secrecy that has been invoked on key aspects that indicate the grave threat that the treaty can create to our national security. The public cannot be told.

But it can be told enough of the implications—implications so grave that even the enthusiastic proponents of the treaty unreservedly admit that the treaty is a calculated risk.

In the questions that I have asked in this debate, I have tried very hard to find a basis for which I could conscientiously vote for ratification of the treaty. I regret to say that the answers have not supplied such a basis.

On the other hand, it has been argued with sincerity and conviction that one could not conscientiously vote against the treaty because such a vote would be a vote against peace—or at least a first step toward peace. I cannot challenge that argument with complete certainty in my own mind. But in equal degree, I cannot challenge with complete certainty the argument made that the treaty may be a first step toward the undermining of our national security.

There have been several speeches expressing the gravest of misgivings about the treaty—only to be concluded with the announcement by the speakers that they would vote for the treaty.

I conclude my statement by saying that I have very grave misgivings about the harmful effects of rejection of the treaty—but by stating that in my opinion the jeopardy that the treaty imposes on our national security is a more compelling argument against the treaty than the political and psychological disadvantages that would stem from rejection of the treaty.

That is why I shall cast a very troubled vote against the treaty.

EDITOR'S NOTE:

That the treaty would be overwhelmingly approved (80 to 19) was a foregone conclusion. Only these Senators voted with

Senator Smith against the treaty: Richard Russell, Chairman of the Armed Services Committee, John Stennis, Chairman of the Preparedness Investigating Subcommittee, Bennett, Harry Byrd, Robert Byrd, Curtis, Eastland, Goldwater, Len Jordan, Lausche, Russell Long, McClellan, Mechem, Robertson, Simpson, Talmadge, Thurmond, and Tower. Senator Smith was not even in the majority of her own Armed Services Committee. The only majority she was in was that of the Preparedness Investigating Subcommittee; the members of that group voted 4 to 3 against the treaty. We fully anticipated the attacks to come. In fact, as we walked back to her office following the vote, I predicted that Goodman would go to Drew Pearson and that a Pearson column attacking her would appear four days later. I made the four-day prediction because most columnists file their columns four days in advance of publication. The column appeared right on schedule four days later (September 28, 1963). Pearson excoriated the Senator for her vote and accused her of turning her back on Leo Goodman, whom Pearson characterized as her political benefactor. The Senator did not respond, but I did. A month after my letter to Pearson, when Senators Russell and Morse exposed misrepresentations made against them by a Washington paper, Senator Smith commiserated with them and inserted my letter in the Congressional Record. Pearson never answered or referred to it. The letter stated:

U. S. Senate,
Washington, D.C., October 4, 1963.

Mr. Drew Pearson
Washington, D.C.

Dear Drew: Over the years you have frequently praised Senator Smith in your column—and you have frequently condemned her. Your record of reaction to her, I think, is actually an unconscious tribute to her independence. For when you praised her on such matters as the declaration of conscience, her vote against Admiral Strauss, and her vote against CIA Director John McCone, others denounced her and impugned her motives on the very positions which you praised.

Over the years you have frequently made misrepresentations against Senator Smith. Many of those misrepresentations were fed to you by those who wished to reap revenge against Senator Smith and discredit her through your column. On one occasion you made a public statement that you had been in error and had been unfair to Senator Smith on a radio broadcast you had made two years prior.

On the other hand, I know of occasions when some of her enemies have given you information and urged you to write against her on the basis of that information—but before doing so you have checked on such information and finding it to be untrue, you have refused to be a party to misrepresentations against Senator Smith. There have been occasions when you called her office to check on facts before writing a column against her. For example, prior to writing your column of September 17, 1963, in which you were critical of Reserve members of the Preparedness Investigating Subcommittee, you called me and told me that you were writing such a column and wanted to check on whether Senator Smith was in the Air Force Reserve. I confirmed that she was a lieutenant colonel in the Air Force Reserve, retired (incidentally she does not and never will receive retired pay in that status). I think that the opinions that you expressed in that column were not justified but you are entitled to your own opinions.

It is when you are in error on facts and have not made an effort to be sure of your facts that I take issue with you. That is why I take issue with your column of September 28, 1963, which is replete with misrepresentations and on which you did not check with Senator Smith or her office prior to writing that column as you had on the prior column of September 17, 1963, related to the same subject of the test ban treaty.

Instead you accepted the misrepresentations given to you by Leo Goodman, whom you cast in a magnanimous forgiving role and Senator Smith in the role of a political ingrate. You made no effort to check on the accuracy of the charges made by Goodman against Senator Smith. Those charges were (1) the implication that Goodman had singlehandedly elected Mrs.

Smith in her first race for Congress and which you characterized as a struggle for her; (2) the charge that Goodman had "asked for an appointment with" Senator Smith during the week of September 15–21; and (3) the charge that Senator Smith had refused to give Goodman an appointment and that I had "bawled out" Goodman "for trying to influence her vote."

It is evident not only that Goodman supplied your story against Senator Smith from the manner in which you quote him but that he contacted you on Tuesday after the vote that day and gave you the story with the false charges. It was a strange performance of forgiving on Goodman's part. Let me set the record straight on the Goodman charges against Senator Smith.

1. That Goodman went to Lewiston, Maine, and singlehandedly elected Mrs. Smith when she first ran for Congress.

In her first election to Congress, Mrs. Smith won by an 11 to 1 margin over her opposition. That is hardly a narrow margin for which any individual or any group could claim credit for singlehandedly electing Mrs. Smith. As for whether Goodman's going to Lewiston was a decisive factor or not, let the record speak for itself—Lewiston gave Mrs. Smith a tremendous total of 303 votes in that election.

Goodman's labor affiliation is with the CIO, now the combined AFL-CIO. What is the record of the CIO? Is it one for which Senator Smith has any political indebtedness? Hardly, for Goodman's CIO opposed Mrs. Smith in 1944, in 1954, and in 1960.

For example, in 1954 her Democratic opponent officially reported that a majority of all his campaign funds came from the CIO's Political Action Committee. And in 1960, although 1960 COPE voting scorecard rated Senator Smith 80 percent right (higher than its ratings for Senators Estes Kefauver and Clinton Anderson whom COPE vigorously supported for reelection that year), the AFL-CIO's COPE was the largest source of campaign funds for Senator Smith's opposition and COPE made an all-out effort to defeat Senator Smith. If Goodman is the friend to Senator Smith that he contends he is, then it would appear that his influence with his own CIO with respect to Senator Smith is nil.

2. That Goodman had "asked for an appointment with" Senator Smith during the week of September 15–21.

The truth is that Goodman did not ask for an appointment during the week of September 15–21 (the week he apparently represented to you). In fact, he did not ask for an appointment at any time. Instead he suddenly appeared in the reception room of Senator Smith's office at ten o'clock the morning of September 24, 1963, just thirty minutes before the test ban treaty vote at ten-thirty—without any previous request by letter or by telephone call—and asked to see Senator Smith immediately. The receptionist told Goodman that the Senate was convening at that very minute of ten o'clock and that Senator Smith had to be in her seat at ten-fifteen for the only time a picture has ever been taken of the Senate in session (for historical purposes—Senators had been warned the day before to be in their seats at that time—see page 17775 of the Congressional Record of September 23, 1963—and a call had been received by the receptionist at nine-thirty before Goodman arrived, reminding of the necessity of being in the Senate at ten-fifteen) and that she thought that Senator Smith had already left the office for the Senate Floor for the start of the session. The receptionist then buzzed Senator Smith's office and when there was no answer on the telephone, she informed Goodman that there was no answer. He then left the office.

3. That Senator Smith had refused to give Goodman an appointment and that I had "bawled out" Goodman "for trying to influence her vote."

The truth is that Goodman had not sought an appointment as set forth above. As to whether I "bawled out" Goodman is a matter of interpretation. I would not in the slightest deny that I spoke to him very bluntly and that I expressed my resentment that he would be so presumptuous that he would think that he could at the last minute come up and tell Senator Smith how to vote.

The truth is that Goodman came up to me as I was standing in line with other Senatorial staff assistants at the register door to sign for a pass to the Senate Floor and said that he wanted to talk with me about her vote on the test ban treaty. In very blunt words I told Goodman that he had had weeks before to come up and talk with Senator Smith but had made no effort

until at that last minute and that it was highly presumptuous
of him to attempt to influence her vote at that time, which
was around ten-fifteen. I have checked this with another Senatorial staff assistant (of a liberal Democratic Senator who voted
for the test ban treaty) who witnessed the entire exchange
and who later termed Goodman's tactic as "incredible."

Inasmuch as Goodman has apparently misrepresented to you
that he had tried unsuccessfully the week before for an appointment with Senator Smith, it is relevant to point out that the
truth is that the last time that Goodman contacted Senator Smith
or her office was on August 1, 1962, or more than a year
before his sudden appearance on September 24, 1963. On
August 1, 1962, Goodman called on Senator Smith in her
office and requested her to endorse him for appointment as
an Atomic Energy Commissioner. Senator Smith told him that
she would be delighted to do so—but said that as a friend she
wondered if her endorsement would not hurt more than help
since it would be to Democratic President Kennedy, whose
personal dislike of her was evidenced in the fact that he was the
only Democratic Senator who had agreed to go into Maine to
campaign against her. That was in 1954 when Joe McCarthy
attempted to have her defeated, as you well remember—and
when Senator Kennedy refused to support the Massachusetts
Democratic Senatorial nominee against Senator Saltonstall but
did go into Maine to campaign against Senator Smith. Senator
Smith told Goodman to think it over and call her later if he
still felt her endorsement would help—that she would be delighted to do it if he still wanted her to after thinking it over.
She never heard from him that time until his sudden appearance
more than a year later on September 24, 1963, minutes before
the test ban treaty vote.

Thus far, I have dealt with the major misrepresentations
in your column that were apparently given to you by Goodman. In conclusion, I want to comment on your false charge
in that column that Senator Smith voted her political ambitions
instead of her conscience on the test ban treaty. You sought
to indict her with a motivation of a 1964 Goldwater-Smith
ticket because she voted the same as Senator Goldwater in
voting against the treaty.

This is reminiscent of guilt by association and trial by accusation tactics that Senator Smith denounced in her "Declaration of Conscience" on June 1, 1950—tactics which you yourself have repeatedly denounced when criticizing those with whom you disagree. In indicting Senator Smith with this guilt by association tactic on the grounds that she voted the same way that Senator Goldwater did in voting against the treaty, you conveniently omitted the fact that on the only direct vote with respect to Senator Goldwater on the test ban treaty—the Goldwater reservation—she voted against Senator Goldwater by voting against the Goldwater reservation.

Have you forgotten your column in which you alleged that Senator Goldwater said that she would not get a "nickel" from his Republican Senatorial Campaign Committee (of which he was Chairman) because she voted against the confirmation of Admiral Strauss?

You have every right to disagree with Senator Smith's vote on the test ban treaty. You have every right to criticize and attack her on that vote. But you have no right to make misrepresentations against her and impugn her integrity merely because you disagree with her.

> Sincerely,
> William C. Lewis, Jr.
> Executive Assistant
> to Senator Smith

It was reported that when President Kennedy was informed that the Senate had ratified the treaty, he asked, "How did Miz Smith vote?" When told that she had voted against the treaty, he registered bitter disappointment.

As was to be expected, the treaty vote was used against her in her re-election bid in 1966. Her opponent claimed that it proved that she was not a supporter of peace.

But there were some positive aftermaths of her negative vote. The challenging questions that she raised in the debate over the treaty—her Senate statements and speeches—were a powerful force leading to the establishment and appointment of a Subcommittee on Safeguards on the Test Ban Treaty. The safeguards were set up to try to insure compliance with the treaty by Russia and to provide a speedy machinery for the United States to return to testing in the event that Russia should overtly or covertly break the treaty.

Senator Smith was made a member of this "watchdog" subcommittee that was to maintain close surveillance on Russian performance.

Closure of Kittery-Portsmouth Naval Shipyard

No one ever wins a popularity contest by bearing bad news. This is especially true in politics. And it is even worse if the source of the bad news cannot be revealed and the source is the highest authority in the Nation.

That is what happened to me in mid-December 1963. Because the Federal Government had been drastically reducing its support of a merchant marine fleet and withdrawing subsidy support for maritime operations, the private shipbuilding industry was receiving fewer and fewer contracts for ship construction. Defense Secretary McNamara charged to their aid by insisting that the costs of private shipbuilding were so much lower than the costs of government shipbuilding that government shipyards should be closed. Thus government naval shipyards were coming increasingly under attack. Maine had a government shipyard. Although it was called the Portsmouth Naval Shipyard because its post office address had been made "Portsmouth, New Hampshire" many, many years back when it was established, it was physically located in Kittery, Maine. Through the years all attempts to get the name changed to the Kittery Naval Shipyard have been to no avail.

As far as the Kittery-Portsmouth Naval Shipyard was concerned, McNamara had a militant ally in Vice Admiral Hyman Rickover, the Navy expert on nuclear ships, especially nuclear submarines. Kittery-Portsmouth built submarines for years, including nuclear submarines. In a very short time under McNamara, General Dynamics became the foremost builder of nuclear submarines through its subsidiary, Electric Boat Company.

Rickover, and his associates, openly expressed disregard for the Portsmouth Naval Shipyard. A direct attack was made on the Portsmouth Naval Shipyard workers by Navy admirals in an open meeting of the Maine Congressional Delegation on August 6, 1963. Admirals William A. Brockett and Charles A. Curtze, Chief and Deputy Chief of the Bureau of Ships, stated in front of the press covering the meeting that the workers in that shipyard "just don't work."

The angry reaction of the workers was to be expected. They

demanded an investigation by the Senate Permanent Investigations Subcommittee of which Senator Muskie of Maine and
Senator McIntyre of New Hampshire were members. They
contended that the "just don't work" charge of the two admirals
should be proved by the Navy or withdrawn. I supported their
demand.

The shipyard workers never got the investigation they demanded. Muskie's and McIntyre's subcommittee turned them
down, and neither Senator supported their demand. The treatment of our Maine workers was so unfair it made me determined
to do something.

It took me three months and I got no help from anyone in the
Maine and New Hampshire Congressional delegations. But finally, on November 4, 1963, Assistant Secretary of the Navy
Kenneth E. BeLieu wrote me stating that the admirals' charge
was not correct and concluded with commendatory remarks
about the workers.

Previously the head of one of the shipyard's unions had accurately analyzed the attack as a prelude to the Navy's dropping
Kittery-Portsmouth as a construction yard for submarines and
denigrating it to a submarine repair yard. It was not long after
that when the change was made in its mission.

This shipyard seemed always to lose out in its competition
with other government shipyards, especially the one at Boston.
The Boston Naval Shipyard had enjoyed tremendous political
advantage under the Democratic aegis of Speaker John McCormack of Boston and later President John F. Kennedy of
Boston and Hyannisport. For a reason never explained, despite
many Congressional demands for an explanation, Democratic
President Harry S. Truman in 1948 separated the Kittery-
Portsmouth Naval Shipyard from the wage area of Boston and
relegated the wages of the Kittery-Portsmouth shipyard workers
to a level considerably below that of their earlier parity. I tried to
get Eisenhower to rescind the order and when I got no response
from him, I sponsored legislation to return the parity to the
Kittery-Portsmouth workers.

My bill was passed by both the Senate and the House, but
then Eisenhower vetoed it. The Senate turned right around on

August 12, 1958, and overrode his veto 69 to 20—the first time that either the Senate or the House voted to override an Eisenhower veto.* Senate Majority Leader Lyndon B. Johnson proclaimed it the greatest personal tribute a Senator ever received from the Senate.

Johnson had given me active support in overriding the veto. Another Senator who voted against the veto and also for my bill was John F. Kennedy. Two years later in the 1960 campaign Kennedy promised the Kittery-Portsmouth Naval shipyard workers that if he were elected President he would by executive order give them the pay parity that the Smith Bill had proposed. With that campaign promise, Kennedy got a big vote from the shipyard workers that helped give him his razor-edge national margin over Nixon. In the 1960 campaign, Kennedy had not only promised to restore parity to the Kittery-Portsmouth shipyard workers but he had also criticized Eisenhower appointees for having left their positions and stressed that he expected his appointees to stay on the job for the duration of his term. He said specifically, "Preference in appointments will be given to those willing to commit themselves to stay on the job long enough to apply what they learn. The goal is a full-time effort for the full tenure of the Presidential term."

Now what about these campaign promises of Kennedy and what about his first Secretary of the Navy? Well, Kennedy turned his back on the Kittery-Portsmouth shipyard workers and never kept his promise to order restoration of pay parity to them—despite repeated reminders. He rejected the pay parity proposal in an official letter to the Armed Services Committee through his Secretary of the Navy, John Connally. Connally was one of those appointees who was supposed to give "a full-time effort for the full tenure of the Presidential term." Connally resigned with less than a year's service to run for Governor of Texas.

And what about Lyndon B. Johnson, who so effectively sup-

---

* However, the Eisenhower veto prevailed when the House failed to muster a two-thirds majority vote to override. Since it takes a two-thirds majority vote of both the House and Senate to pass a bill over a Presidential veto, the bill finally failed of passage.

ported the overriding of the Eisenhower veto of my pay parity bill for the workers? As President he never moved to implement what he had voted for nor to keep the Kennedy promise. Instead, like Eisenhower and Kennedy, he retained Truman's 1948 discriminatory order against the Kittery-Portsmouth shipyard workers.

After the assassination of President Kennedy on November 22, 1963, it appeared that the favored treatment of the Boston Naval Shipyard was coming to an end. In the early part of December 1963 it was reported in newscasts that Defense Secretary McNamara had decided to close the Boston Naval Shipyard, the Philadelphia Naval Shipyard, and the San Francisco Naval Shipyard. But the next morning, newspapers revealed that the Massachusetts, Pennsylvania, and California Congressional delegations had risen up in arms and that their shipyards would not be closed.

Such was the partial history of Kittery-Portsmouth prior to a friendly and personal telephone call that I was to receive which, despite the personal friendliness of the call, placed me in a very difficult position. The caller rang me at my house on the afternoon of Sunday, December 15, 1963. It was President Johnson.

"Margaret," he said, "I want to belatedly give you my good wishes on your birthday yesterday. I intended to call you yesterday but got so tied up that I didn't get around to it. I called Drew Pearson Friday to wish him well that day as his birthday is the day before yours."

He then reminisced about the years we had served together in the House and the Senate on the same committees.* He spoke of his admiration for me and of the fondness that both he and Lady Bird felt for me. Then he showed how seriously he felt about our friendship. "The other day," he said, "McNamara and Nitze (Navy Secretary) brought in to me the list of the naval shipyards they propose to close and on which they sought my approval. Your Kittery-Portsmouth yard headed the list. I told them that I couldn't do that to my dear friend

---

* No two other members of Congress in its history had ever served jointly on so many of the same committees in both the House and Senate as we had.

Margaret Smith so soon after becoming President,* and to take your shipyard off the list."

He continued, "But Margaret, McNamara has made a strong case against government shipyards and a strong argument that they are not justified economically or securitywise. Your shipyard in Maine is on its way to being closed before too long." President Johnson did not specify the date for the closing but clearly indicated that it was only a matter of time.

I said I felt that McNamara was shortsighted, first, because the nation needed government shipyards for security insurance in the event of strikes in private shipyards during an emergency, and second, because the Nation needed government shipyards as standards of measurement to keep the government from being at the mercy of private shipyard prices.

Johnson's reply to these arguments was that there would always be a government shipyard on each coast—the Boston Naval Shipyard on the Atlantic and the Puget Sound Naval Shipyard at Bremerton, Washington, on the Pacific.

The President did not place any restrictions on what he had said to me. But I have always adhered to the custom that you don't quote the President or reveal publicly what he has said to you until he so authorized or the information is officially announced. I revealed the President's warning to only one person, Bill Lewis.

Now I was in a severe dilemma. If I revealed the warning but declined to identify by name or title the source of the warning, then the credibility of my warning would be subject to challenge. Realistically, there was serious question as to whether the workers would appreciate such frankness anyway. We all share a human tendency to disbelieve bad news and at least to resent it.

On the other hand, I could not justify keeping secret the advent of such economic tragedy for some seven thousand workers and the area they supported. I had an obligation to let people know as far in advance as possible so that they could plan for loss of their jobs and other drastic changes to come.

* He had been President only a little more than two weeks.

Eventually I would be asked how long I had known about it, and I would have no choice but to say truthfully since December 15, 1963. In the long run that would be even more damaging to my personal credibility. This was particularly true in view of the fact that Senator Edward Kennedy had said to me only two or three days before the President's call that there would be no closing of government shipyards until after the 1964 election. My conscience simply would not allow me to remain silent for almost a year and until after the national election.

So I decided to go to the Senate Floor the next day and make a speech. I said I had followed with great interest the developments of the past week on the reported or threatened closing of defense establishments and that I was reminded of what had happened more than two years ago—nearly three years ago—on March 30, 1961, when Defense Secretary McNamara had announced the decision to close many defense establishments throughout the Nation. I remember quite well because my own State of Maine was hard hit. I then quoted what I had said three years earlier:

I regret that in the rapidly changing character of the security and defense of our country—and specifically in the development of the missile program—the long anticipated inactivation and termination of the now outmoded SNARK program and the resulting scheduled closing of the Presque Isle Air Force Base have now become realities, as a result of the decision by President Kennedy.

The far easier course for me to pursue politically would be to vigorously protest this action and, as a Republican Senator, to point out that the decision was one made by a Democratic President, and to make a political attack on the decision of President Kennedy.

The far easier course for me to pursue politically would be to demand the now outmoded SNARK program be continued, so that the Presque Isle Air Force Base be kept operating, to aid the economy of the area and to avoid the impact and dislocation that its closing is bound to have on the economy of this area.

But in all good conscience I cannot do this, for this would

simply be playing politics with our national security, our national defense, and our taxpayer's dollar. It would be submitting to the economic philosophy that our National Defense Establishment and our national security program must be operated primarily for the local economy.

I shall do what I can to help the Presque Isle area absorb the economic impact of this unpleasant decision made by President Kennedy; and while I can understand and appreciate the concern of the people of the area, I am confident that the great majority of the people of the area are not only fair-minded about this long anticipated development, but also are of such admirable self-reliance that they will meet the impact well and successfully.

I said I was prepared to take the same position with respect to future closings of defense establishments in Maine—closings on the basis of no further defense justification for their existence—but that I wanted the justification for any such closing proved beyond the shadow of a doubt.

In the past week certain things have been said to me that are most disturbing. First, a member of the Senate said to me that there would be no closings of government naval shipyards until after the 1964 election. I am disturbed by the political implications of any such delay of closings, if there are to be closings, because such political timing is not fair to the workers at these yards, nor can it be justified with the taxpayers.

I repeated the history of my concern as I have related it here and then got on to the point:

I have outlined this history of my efforts for the Kittery-Portsmouth Naval Shipyard to illustrate my continuing concern and effort for it, for the workers and for the people of the area— and as prelude to the bad news I am about to reveal. I realize that what I am about to say does not make for political popularity. But I must speak my conscience in all fairness to the workers of the Kittery-Portsmouth Naval Shipyard and to the people of that area.

It has been no great secret in Washington that Defense Secretary McNamara has taken the position that the costs of private shipbuilding are so much lower than the costs of government shipbuilding that government shipyards should be closed. Last week his position came to the surface even if only momentarily and to be quickly submerged for cover after the massive congressional counter against him.

Over this weekend, a government official of full authority informed me that the government shipyards were on their way out under Defense Secretary McNamara as being economically and "Defensely" without justification. When I asked about the importance of having the government shipyards in time of emergency, his answer was that we would always have the Boston Naval Shipyard and the Puget Sound Naval Shipyard at Bremerton, Washington. He said that the Kittery-Portsmouth Naval Shipyard was on its way to being closed and that it was merely a matter of time without indicating when that closing might come.

Mr. President, if there should develop a situation in which it is proved beyond a doubt that there is absolutely no justification or Defense need for the Kittery-Portsmouth Naval Shipyard, I shall take the same position as I did on the closing of the Presque Isle Air Force Base. I will not submit to the economic philosophy that our National Defense Establishment and our national security program must be operated primarily for the local economy.

I am confident that the people of Maine feel the same way. And I am confident that the people of the Kittery, Maine; York County, Maine; and Portsmouth, New Hampshire, feel the same way. I think they can emulate the people of Presque Isle who accepted the blow without whimpering but instead set themselves to provide a substitute for a military establishment for their economy.

But I do think that the workers in the Kittery-Portsmouth Naval Shipyard are entitled to have this bad news now so that they can make their own plans for the future—instead of suddenly without warning, or with very little warning at best, being told that their jobs are ending. I think that the leaders, both civic and business, of these communities should have advance warning to start plans and activities designed to absorb the shock of what has been represented to me as the inevitable closing of the Kittery-Portsmouth Naval Shipyard.

It is reported that Defense Secretary McNamara has cost details which reveal the comparative costs of each government naval shipyard—comparative with each other and comparative with private shipyards. I believe that public disclosure should be made of these costs so that it can be more accurately determined if the closings are made on the basis of costs—if the more costly government shipyards are closed first rather than the basis of closing being dominated by politics—and rather than the timing of the closing being determined by elections with delays being made until after the 1964 election.

For example, how do the two government shipyards indicated to me to be spared from closing—how do they compare with those government shipyards slated to be closed?

Mr. President, I propose that that subcommittee which President Lyndon B. Johnson once chairmanned—the Senate Preparedness Investigating Subcommittee—immediately start an investigation and study of this matter with a request for the comparative cost study that Defense Secretary McNamara reportedly has and with a request for the schedule of the closings of the government naval shipyards. I have so written the Chairman* of that subcommittee requesting such an investigation and study.

I think we should get this matter out into the open. That is the least that we can do for those workers and those areas that will have to bear the brunt of the economic loss with the closing of these shipyards. They are entitled to have the truth—and they are entitled to have it now.

EDITOR'S NOTE:
The warning drew instant and angry denials. Senator Thomas McIntyre's [of New Hampshire] was the most vehement. He

* Senator John Stennis of Mississippi, who had a large private shipyard in his state, was the Chairman; I was a member of the subcommittee.

accused Senator Smith of irresponsibility, of "calculating to panic employees," of being politically, selfishly motivated, and of doing a disservice to the entire United States Senate.

Deputy Defense Secretary Gilpatric issued a vigorous and unequivocal denial, and Senator Muskie joined in the chorus. The Portsmouth (New Hampshire) *Herald* editorially excoriated Senator Smith and later its reporter who had covered the news story joined the staff of Senator McIntyre. The Portland (Maine) *Press Herald* reprimanded Senator Smith and expressed its disbelief that an authoritative source had made the warning: "So far as we can discover, no one in 'full authority' has told Sen. Smith that Kittery was in jeopardy." It was the kind of attack on her credibility that the Senator had fully anticipated.

Her response was that she was willing to identify the source by name to Defense Secretary McNamara if he would ask her to do so and that she would then let him decide if he thought the source was reliable and authoritative. McNamara never asked for identity of the source, for he obviously knew. And President Johnson publicly kept his silence.

The sole editorial supporter of Senator Smith's credibility was the Lewiston (Maine) *Daily Sun.*

Senator Saltonstall of Massachusetts joined Senator Smith in her request for an overall investigation of capability and costs of both government and private shipyards. Chairman Stennis agreed to have the subcommittee staff make "a preliminary study" on "shipyard capacity and operations." The staff study was made at a very leisurely pace and it was rather apparent that it was going nowhere and producing nothing of any significance. The staff claimed it could get nowhere because McNamara, the Department of Defense, and the Department of the Navy were not responsive and would provide no meaningful cost information. When it appeared that Chairman Stennis would not insist that such information be provided,* Senator

---

* She was not surprised for earlier after the Senate Permanent Investigations Subcommittee had refused to investigate the admirals' "won't work" charges against the shipyard workers, she had asked Stennis to have the Preparedness Investigating Subcommittee make such an investigation. He never did and later gave as an excuse that he thought such an investigation would not have been good for Maine or for her. Her response was, "Don't you think it is

Smith decided to turn to the Comptroller General and the General Accounting Office.

At her request, the Comptroller General and the GAO made a detailed study of comparative costs of government shipyards. After several weeks, the GAO made its report. It must have been very embarrassing to McNamara in view of his self-proclaimed advocacy of cost effectiveness. The GAO found that the Kittery-Portsmouth Naval Shipyard had the second lowest total hourly cost of all eleven government shipyards and was the lowest cost shipyard on Direct Labor Hourly rate of all eleven shipyards. The Boston Naval Shipyard had the worst record.

In the meantime, the deniers of the Senator's warning about the impending closing of the Kittery-Portsmouth shipyard were having a taste of sweet revenge after the humiliating defeat she suffered in the Portsmouth area in the March 1964 New Hampshire Presidential primary. The Portsmouth shipyard workers turned their backs on her and voted heavily for candidates who had never done anything for the shipyard, proving the political axiom that the way to lose votes is to bear bad news. They made the Senator pay dearly for telling them the truth.

It took a long time for the accuracy of her warning to be revealed. It was December 16, 1963, when she first had warned that it had been decided to close the Kittery-Portsmouth Naval Shipyard and that the announcement would not be made until after the November 1964 Presidential election. Eleven months later, and two weeks after the election, on November 19, 1964, at a ten o'clock morning press conference, Defense Secretary McNamara announced that it had been decided to close the Kittery-Portsmouth Naval Shipyard.

The normal pre-announcement notification courtesy to members of Congress from the affected states and districts had been extended to Senators McIntyre and Muskie. [McIntyre in fact had announced a press conference which turned out to follow

---

better for you to give me the courtesy of letting me decide what is best for myself and my state than for you to presume to make that decision for me? I know much better than you."

immediately after McNamara's press conference.] But the courtesy was not extended to Senator Smith. She got the news over her car radio as she was driving to New York to the Annual Dinner of the National Institute of Social Sciences where she was to receive the Gold Medal award along with Secretary of State Dean Rusk, AT&T Board Chairman Frederick Kappel, and Bob Hope for "distinguished services to humanity."

In his press conference, McNamara asserted that he had notified Senators McIntyre, Muskie, and Smith of his decision to close the shipyard and that in response to their objections to the closing of the shipyard he had agreed to a graduated ten-year phase-out of the closing. Senator Smith was shocked at such direct misrepresentations. Not only had she not been notified at any time by McNamara, but the Defense Department had vigorously denied that the shipyard was to be closed in refuting her warning eleven months before. Neither had she ever been told of a ten-year phase-out. She promptly wrote McNamara making these observations.

He referred her letter to the Assistant to the Secretary of Defense for Legislative Affairs, David McGiffert, who answered in a snide letter that they had tried to reach Senator Smith prior to the announcement but to no avail, thus admitting that McNamara was untruthful in his public claim that he had notified Senator Smith. In effect, they were trying to justify his lie by placing blame on her for their not having actually notified her.

McGiffert went further. He sought to make the distorted interpretation that after-the-fact Senator Smith was actually objecting to the ten-year lease on life that McNamara had given the shipyard in his closure order. He concluded by saying that if Senator Smith so requested they would be glad to announce their error along with announcing that Senator Smith was opposing giving the shipyard a ten-year lease on life. Thus, they had not only admitted that they had lied twice about Senator Smith but they had the audacity to suggest a third lie about her.*

* Later McGiffert was promoted to the post of Undersecretary of the Army. When Nixon took over the reins of the Presidency and asked Stanley Resor to

The day following McNamara's announcement of the closure of the Kittery-Portsmouth shipyard, Senator Smith stated that the unnamed informant in her warning speech of the previous year had been the President of the United States. She felt that the McNamara announcement had not only borne out the truthfulness and accuracy of her warning but as well had released her from any obligation to withhold any longer the identity of her informant. [See Appendix for full text.]

Five days later, on November 25, 1964, she followed up with a letter to President Johnson, the main thrust of which was to give him the details of the Comptroller General's report on the cost effectiveness of the government's shipyards.

The findings showed, she wrote, that

. . . in Fiscal Year 1964 (1) Kittery-Portsmouth had the second lowest Total Hourly Cost of all eleven government naval shipyards; (2) Kittery-Portsmouth had the lowest Direct Labor Hourly Rate of all eleven government naval shipyards; (3) while the condemned-for-closing Kittery-Portsmouth Naval Shipyard had the lowest Direct Labor Hourly Rate, the spared-and-retained Mare Island Naval Shipyard (the other nuclear submarine construction government naval shipyard) had the highest Direct Labor Hourly Rate; and (4) while condemned Kittery-Portsmouth had the second lowest Total Hourly Cost, spared-and-retained Mare Island had the second highest Total Hourly Cost and spared-and-retained Boston had the highest Total Hourly Cost and the highest Overhead Rate.

These findings and conclusions of the Comptroller General's report not only refute the false charge made by Navy management that the Kittery-Portsmouth workers "just won't work," since they actually have the lowest Direct Labor Hourly Rate —and thus meet your own goal of receiving a dollar of value for every dollar spent on defense—but also strongly indicate that any cost problems at the Kittery-Portsmouth Naval Shipyard

---

remain on as Secretary of the Army, Resor later pressed to have McGiffert continue as Undersecretary of the Army. But after the experiences she had had with McGiffert, Senator Smith said McGiffert had to go, and McGiffert went.

stem from the management since the Overhead Rate at Portsmouth is exceeded only by that at Boston and Charleston, both of which have been spared from closing.

There is one saving grace in the decision on Kittery-Portsmouth and that is the ten-year phasing-out. It is a saving grace because it provides an "escape clause" by which the injustice and the error of selecting this government shipyard for closing, when it has a lower Total Hourly Cost than eight government naval shipyards which have been spared from closing—by which, such injustice can be removed and the error corrected by reviewing and revoking that decision to close this shipyard.

I have received reports that a superior Navy management team than that of its predecessor has now been installed in the Kittery-Portsmouth Naval Shipyard. In all sincerity I urge you to give this new management team a full opportunity to bring down the Overhead Rate before irrevocably sealing the doom of the Kittery-Portsmouth Naval Shipyard.

In summary she went over once again the shabby treatment of the workers at Kittery-Portsmouth and urged him to reconsider and revoke the order closing the shipyard.

The plea went unheeded. Johnson did nothing toward rescinding the closure order. The thin hopes for the shipyard were kept alive by Senators Smith, Cotton (N.H.), and McIntyre and Representatives Wyman (N.H.) and Kyros (Me.) who together obtained legislation and money for improvements of the shipyard. Senator Smith remained the key person, being the only member on both the legislative and appropriating committees and having top seniority of each. With McIntyre on the Senate Armed Services Committee, she got the items in the authorization bills approved by that committee. With Cotton on the Senate Appropriations Committee, she got that committee to make the necessary appropriations.

After Nixon took over the Presidency she made repeated appeals to him to rescind the closure order but never got more than a promise that he would seriously consider a rescission of the closure order. A few weeks before the 1970 election, Representative Louis Wyman announced that President Nixon had said that there need be no worry about the future of the shipyard. This announcement was represented as a commitment by the President to rescind the closure order.

Subsequent inquiries to the Defense Department and the Navy Department by the press, by Senator Smith and others gained nothing but denials that any instructions or indications had come from the President to recind the order. Finally the source of the report was established as Murray Chotiner, aide to the President, and manager of his 1950 Senatorial campaign against Helen Gahagan Douglas. Chotiner acknowledged that he had given such a report to Wyman but hedged when asked if a rescission had been ordered or was being prepared. Ron Ziegler, White House Press Secretary, responded in a similar manner to inquiries made to him.

Contradictory to this report were the facts that the President (1) had not included any improvement items in his budget for the shipyard and (2) had given no instructions to the Defense Department or the Navy Department to deviate from plans to close the shipyard in 1974. Representative Louis Wyman of New Hampshire got the House Armed Services Committee to include improvement items for the shipyard in the military construction authorization bill. Senators Smith and McIntyre got the Senate Armed Services Committee to retain those items in the bill when it reached that committee. But no word was sent from the White House to the committees in support of these originally unbudgeted items.

Then Representative Wyman's own House Appropriations Committee refused to appropriate funds for the items and such funds were omitted from the bill when the House passed the Defense Military Construction Appropriations Bill. There was still no White House request for the items to be put in the appropriations. It took Senators Cotton and Smith to get the items back into the appropriations bill in the Senate after the House had rejected them. On the last Saturday in 1970, Senator Smith went to the Kittery-Portsmouth Naval Shipyard and conferred with the shipyard Commandant, Captain Kern. He told her that he could get no confirmation of Representative Wyman's report that the shipyard would not be closed. He felt he had no choice but to proceed on the basis of the unconfirmed reports despite the denials and instructions of his superiors in the Navy Department. This confusion made matters extremely difficult and constituted his greatest single problem in the operation of the shipyard.

Margaret was so disturbed by this revelation that upon her return to Washington she wrote the President urging him to make a clarifying announcement without delay. In her letter to the President she stated:

Earlier this year an ambiguous statement was made by White House staff personnel to the news media that you had stated that there need be no worry about the future of the shipyard. This has been interpreted by many as tantamount to an official announcement that the closure order has been rescinded.

I have made inquiries to both the Department of the Navy and the Department of Defense for corroboration of this oral report. Representatives of both departments have answered that they have nothing to confirm the report and that there has been absolutely no indication or word from the White House, oral or written, to them indicating that the closure order would be rescinded. They profess to be mystified by the White House report to the news media.

I went into this matter with the Commandant of the shipyard and he told me that he had made similar inquiry and that his superiors in the Navy Department told him that they had not received any notice or information to indicate a rescission of the closure order. Despite this, the Commandant of the shipyard feels that he has had no choice but to proceed in future planning on the basis that the unconfirmed oral report of the White House to the news media is the true situation and that you have decided that the shipyard will not be closed.

For several years now, there have been recurring rumors that the Kittery-Portsmouth Naval Shipyard will ultimately be taken over by the Electric Boat subsidiary of General Dynamics. There is some speculation that the ambiguity of the White House statement of "no need for worry about the future of the shipyard" was actually not tantamount to a rescission of the closure order but was possibly an indication that there need be no worry because Electric Boat would purchase and operate the shipyard.

I fervently hope that you have decided to rescind the shipyard closure order. And I hope that if you have so decided that you will remove the existing ambiguity, confusion and speculation by so formally and officially announcing without delay.

I believe it to be in the best interests of the workers and citizens of the affected area. I believe that in basic fairness to everyone concerned—including the shipyard Commandant—that the ambiguity and uncertainty be removed as soon as possible.

I make this request to you not only as a Senator from Maine concerned for the best interests of my constituents—but I make the request as well as the top-ranking member of your own political party on the Armed Services Committee in what I consider to be the best interests of our Nation and our national defense.

The letter was hand delivered to the White House by a Senate Riding Page on the day it was written, December 28. An acknowledgment of it was not received until nine days later, and it merely stated that her letter would be brought to the attention of the President. It was evident that the President would not take the requested prompt action.

A month passed after the December 28, 1970, letter to the President and when no reply had been received from the President, Senator Smith on January 28, 1971, wrote the President pointing out that she had not received an answer and repeated her request.

This time Presidential Assistant Kenneth E. BeLieu, a very good friend of Senator Smith, acknowledged for the President. "The status of this installation has been, and is currently, under active review at the highest levels," he wrote. "I am informed that you may expect a substantive reply in the very near future."

As the next monthly anniversary of her first letter approached, and possibly to ward off an anticipated third letter, officials at the White House and in the Defense Department assured Senator Smith that the matter was receiving the most serious consideration. So she didn't write a third letter.

On March 4, 1971, Secretary of Defense Melvin Laird and New Hampshire Senator Norris Cotton came to Senator Smith's office and conferred with her for an hour on the future of the shipyard. After that meeting Senator Cotton told the press that Laird had promised an early decision and announcement. Senator Smith told the press that Laird had been so nebulous and inconclusive that she had nothing to report and that the press would have to ask Laird himself.

Two weeks later, New Hampshire Senator Thomas McIntyre (who had excoriated Senator Smith more than seven years before for her warning of the coming closure order) stated to a reporter of the *Foster's Daily Democrat* (Dover, New Hampshire) that Laird had told him "there is no decision imminent on the yard." He was so quoted in the March 19, 1971, issue of that paper, which further reported that McIntyre said it was his guess that a decision on the Kittery-Portsmouth Naval Shipyard would not be reached until December 1971.

Senator Cotton called early on March 22, 1971, to tell me about the McIntyre statement and expressed his resentment since Laird had said there would be a decision in the near future. When I relayed this to Senator Smith that afternoon she wrote a third letter to President Nixon and sent it by Senate Riding Page to the White House. In that letter she said:

March 22, 1971

The President
The White House
Washington, D.C.

My dear Mr. President:
  You will recall that on December 28, 1970 I wrote you urging that you make an announcement as soon as possible as to the

future of the Kittery-Portsmouth Naval Shipyard to remove the confusion and speculation created by oral reports emanating from members of your staff.

Mr. Timmons responded in your behalf and stated that my letter would be brought to your early attention.

When a month passed without a response from you, I again wrote you on January 28, 1971 again urging you to take action to remove the confusion and speculation. Mr. BeLieu of your staff responded to my letter and in doing so promised an early response to my request.

On March 4, 1971 at 4:30 p.m., Defense Secretary Laird met with Senator Cotton and me in my office and at that time indicated an early decision and announcement. From past experiences, I declined to make any comment to the press on that meeting. I find that it is better to receive written expressions and commitments rather than to rely on oral statements and commitments.

Senator Cotton this morning informed me that the New Hampshire press has reported over the weekend that Secretary Laird has stated that "there is no decision imminent on the yard."

I have tried to be patient in this matter but my patience is at an end. The pattern in this matter is certainly not one to enhance the credibility of the White House or the Department of Defense.

> Sincerely yours,
> Margaret Chase Smith
> United States Senator

The next afternoon Laird called Senator Smith on the telephone stating that they were still trying to work out the matter and in view of her third letter to the President he wanted to inquire as to just what she wanted. Her reply was, "I don't want an oral statement from you. I want an answer in black-and-white from the President. Nothing less than that will be acceptable to me."

Later that afternoon, Presidential Assistant Ken BeLieu came to her office to discuss the matter. Although he was most co-operative and expressed the opinion that she deserved a clear answer without delay, she repeated her firm statements that she had made to Laird. She said since the unconfirmed rescission rumor had emanated from the White House several months past, and not from the Defense Department, she expected an answer from the President and not from Laird.

The next morning at eleven o'clock BeLieu called Senator Smith out of a Senate Armed Services Committee meeting at which Laird was testifying. When she came out, BeLieu handed her a letter from the President. It read:

THE WHITE HOUSE
WASHINGTON
March 24, 1971

Dear Margaret:
I have delayed answering your questions on the future of the Portsmouth Naval Shipyard until the review I requested was completed.

Now, on the basis of that review and the recommendations made to me, I am pleased to inform you that the McNamara order closing the yard in 1974 will be rescinded and the workload established at a level to be determined by the Secretary of Defense.

The Secretary of Defense will be prepared to answer any other questions you may have.

Warmest regards,

The Honorable Margaret Chase Smith
United States Senate
Washington, D.C.

Senator Smith and BeLieu then went to her office. She called me in and I prepared a press release which stated simply:

March 24, 1971
Senator Margaret Chase Smith
For Immediate Release
  Senator Margaret Chase Smith received the attached letter
from the President this morning.

  The release created a good deal of speculation within the
press because for several days several reporters had been trying to
find out how Senator Smith would vote on the Super Sonic Trans-
port aircraft appropriation amendment. The vote was set for four
o'clock that afternoon, and it was expected to be decided by
the closest of margins. The release on the Nixon rescission of the
McNamara closure order on the shipyard caused many reporters
to jump to the conclusion that this was a last-minute attempt
of the White House to buy Senator Smith's vote. President Nixon
had publicly stated he strongly wanted the SST appropriations
to be passed.
  A member of the press called me and characterized the
White House as being "ham handed." I told the reporter his
interpretation was completely erroneous and unfair to President
Nixon, that neither the President nor anyone else in his administration had attempted to pressure or sway Senator Smith on the
SST vote in any manner. I then recounted for the reporter the
chronological developments outlined herein that led to the letter.
  Senator Smith did not consider in any manner that she had
been put in an embarrassing position. To vote either way was
not easy. Surely it would not be easy to vote against the SST
after this favorable action by the President and to vote for the
SST could bring upon both the President and Senator Smith
the accusation that they had made a deal and trade for her vote.
  Because of the anticipated possibility of a tie vote, in which
case Vice President Agnew could vote to break the tie, the Vice
President was presiding over the Senate. Just before the roll call
started on the vote, he looked up at the public visitors in the
Senate Gallery and announced that no demonstration or audible
expressions from the visitors would be permitted. The visitors

in the Senate Gallery remained quiet and orderly until Senator Smith's name was called. When she said "No," an immediate ripple of approval ran through the Gallery. The SST was defeated by a vote of 51 to 46.

One person's good news all too often in politics is another person's bad news. Senator Smith was sorry to see her party's President lose his vote that day but rejoiced with her constituents at Kittery-Portsmouth. For them the news had finally turned from bad to good.

Presidential Candidacy Announcement

JANUARY 27, 1964

"Margaret Chase Smith . . . as a possible candidate for President . . . is very formidable . . ."

—John F. Kennedy
November 1963

"She is just ornery enough that if she were a man she would make a hell of a good President!"

—Richard B. Russell
January 1964

For a dozen years talk and speculation had persisted about putting my name on the national ticket in the Vice Presidential slot. In the fall of 1963 it started up again. This time my name was linked with that of Arizona Senator Barry Goldwater who publicly stated that he was not opposed to a woman Vice Presidential running mate.

Then unexpectedly the talk moved me up to the Presidential level and I received a significant volume of mail from throughout the Nation urging me to seek the Republican Presidential nomination. That talk reached such proportions that President Kennedy was asked at his last press conference on November 14, 1963, how he would view me as his 1964 opponent. His smiling answer was gentlemanly and graciously respectful:

> I would think that if I were a Republican candidate I would not look forward to campaigning against Margaret Chase Smith, or as a possible candidate for President. I think she is very formidable, if that is the appropriate word to use about a very fine lady. She is very formidable as a political figure.

Members of the Women's National Press Club knew that by this time I was seriously considering whether to become a candidate. They asked me to speak to them on December 5 and to withhold the revelation of my decision until then. I agreed, and I also made commitments to lecture at the Air War College on November 24 and to go on the NBC "Today" program on December 6, the Metromedia network on December 8, the Jack Parr program on December 16, and other programs.

On the afternoon of November 22, I was in the midst of a filming session with an NBC television crew in my office when Bill Lewis stepped in and told us the terrible news about President Kennedy. We stopped the filming session at once and Bill canceled all of my public appearance commitments in deference to the President.

After President Kennedy's assassination, speculation increased as to whether I would enter the New Hampshire Presidential primary in March. There was an interesting aspect to this. Earlier in the year when I had voted against the nuclear test ban treaty, some of the embittered liberal press accused me of voting that way in hopes of getting on the ticket with Goldwater. Now that the death of President Kennedy had completely changed the 1964 campaign outlook, some members of the press suddenly discovered or recalled that I had shown independence from Goldwater on the test ban treaty voting.

On December 1, 1963, the editor of the San Diego *Union* wrote a very complimentary piece speculating on the prospects of my candidacy:

> If Mrs. Smith announces she will enter the New Hampshire primary in March, her presence would have to be taken seriously by Rockefeller, Goldwater or any other male candidate. It is inconceivable that Mrs. Smith would win the primary. But she could gain a delegate or two. And she doubtless would win a respectable vote, possibly enough to make the difference between Goldwater and Rockefeller if they are the other contestants . . . Whether the country or either party is ready for a woman on the presidential ticket remains to be seen. But Mrs. Smith will have her say. And just the possibility that she may run has advanced the cause of women candidates, perhaps more than most of their male opponents realize.

Such were the observations of Editor Herbert G. Klein who, in 1969, was to become President Nixon's Coordinator of Communications.

Up to this time, the only person with whom I had seriously discussed the "to run or not to run" question was Bill Lewis. The principal arguments against running were (1) lack of money and organization, (2) my determination not to miss roll call votes, and (3) the humility of expected crushing defeats. The principal arguments for running were (1) I could offer a choice between Goldwater and Rockefeller and (2) break the barrier and pioneer the way for women. I liked the way that Herb Klein had put it: "just the possibility that she may run has advanced the cause of women candidates, perhaps more than most of their male opponents realize."

Subsequently I weighed the pros and cons at dinner with the Republican Dean of the Senate, Vermont's George Aiken, Lola Pierotti (his administrative assistant and later his wife), and Bill. I outlined several tests that my running provided and discussed the heavy mail from New Hampshire asking for a moderate, middle-of-the-road candidate. Aiken said that I could win if it was limited to a three-way race between Goldwater and Rockefeller and me—and he so stated to the press.

The address to the Women's National Press Club was rescheduled for January 27, 1964. I felt that two months allowed a respectful period of mourning for the President. In December four young Republicans flew from Illinois in their private plane to urge me to let them enter my name in the Illinois April 14 Presidential primary. I declined to make any commitment to them and stated that I would not announce my decision until the press luncheon on January 27.

As the January 27 press luncheon drew closer, the news media pounded at Bill and me trying to get clues to my decision. They displayed an unending variety of tricks and approaches. For example, they observed that they could not give my speech good coverage if they could not write before its delivery. This meant they had to have the text in advance. The television and radio networks said they would not cover the speech if my decision would be not to run—that it would not be newsworthy in the event of a negative decision.

None of the approaches worked. I gave Bill my general ideas on the factors involved in my decision and asked him to draft a speech with two endings, one declining to run, the other announcing my candidacy. When Bill handed me the draft with the two alternative endings, he asked me to refrain from telling him which ending I would use. He said that very frankly he didn't want to know, if for no other reason than that he would be able to say so to the news hounds.

He told the networks they would have to take their chances on my decision and if any of them opted not to cover the speech that was their right and responsibility. When he distributed the text of the speech to the Senate Press, Radio-TV, and Periodical Galleries the morning of January 27, 1964, they found that the only omission was the announcement of my decision. I kept the two endings to myself.

It was one o'clock in the afternoon when I began my speech:

I always enjoy being with the members of the Women's National Press Club—even when you give members of Congress an unmerciful going over. I think that I enjoy being with you not only because of the many good friends that I have among you but also because I was a newspaperwoman myself before becoming a member of the House and Senate.

Many years ago I worked for the weekly newspaper in my home town—*The Independent Reporter*—in a succession of a variety of jobs ranging from general reporter to circulation manager and some of them concurrently performed as can be done only on a weekly paper. My only claim to fame in that effort was that in its class, while I was circulation manager, *The Independent Reporter* reached the seventh highest ABC rating of all weekly newspapers in the entire nation.

But it was when I did five columns a week nationally for United Feature Syndicate for more than five years that I felt a greater professional kinship with you. I learned what a chore it was to produce seven hundred words almost daily.

It has been my privilege to address your club more than once. The first time was when I had been a United States Senator for only six days. Five days before I had surprised, if not shocked, some members of the press when I voted for Robert A. Taft for Chairman of the Senate Republican Policy Committee rather than for Henry Cabot Lodge. Some even denounced me as a traitor to the cause of Republican liberalism.

And it was only a year and a half later that others in the press were calling me a traitor to the cause of conservatism because of my Declaration of Conscience made on June 1, 1950. Some even called me pro-Communist on the basis of the Declaration of Conscience.

I have often thought of those instances in which I have been the target of the extremists on both the left and right. I remember how in the 1948 campaign when I first ran for the Senate an anonymous sheet was put out in the primary charging that I voted "the Marcantonio line." It failed. But the same technique was used successfully two years later against Helen Gahagan Douglas.

I remember how in the 1954 campaign I was accused in the primary of being soft on communism and a dangerous liberal— and then in the general election of being called a reactionary and an all-out effort made by the CIO to defeat me just as COPE did in 1960.

Yes, I have often thought of that January 8, 1949, speech that I made to this club in which I described myself as a Moderate, pointing out that I had previously given myself that label when asked a question on the "Meet the Press" program on December 10, 1948.

I have thought frequently of these things in recent months when reading the editorials and articles expressing the opinion that our nation is more rampant with bigotry and hatred than it has ever been. Many conclude that such was the cause of the assassination of President Kennedy—some even erroneously charging the assassination to racial hatred and bigotry.

In my opinion, any hatred or any bigotry—even the slightest hatred or bigotry—is too much for our nation and is to be deplored. But I cannot agree with those who contend that now there is greater hatred and bigotry than ever existed before in our country. Instead I believe that our country is far freer of bigotry and hatred than it was ten years ago—or at the time of my Declaration of Conscience, when I specifically denounced Fear, Ignorance, Bigotry, and Smear.

Let us examine a few of the contentions that bigotry and hatred are greater now than ever before. First, let us take the first claims and the first news reports on the assassination of President Kennedy. The first headlines were to the effect that President Kennedy had been shot by a Southern extreme racist, by a racial bigot. This was immediately seized upon and exploited by the Russian Communist press for propaganda purposes.

Then after the initial smoke and when heads began to clear and emotions cool, the truth came out—and it was not a Southern anti-negro extremist that shot President Kennedy but instead it was a Marxist, a mentally deranged Communist. Further, it was by accident of geography that this mentally deranged Communist was in Dallas, Texas—when it might have happened in Russia where he lived for some time or in other sections of the United States where he had lived.

No, the assassination of President Kennedy was clearly not what was first represented—the result of Southern anti-negro extremism but rather the act of a mentally deranged Communist.

Next, let us take the case of the John Birch Society and the extreme statements that it has issued against American leaders like former President Dwight D. Eisenhower. You might get the impression that never before was there an organization like the John Birch Society making such attacks.

Well, let me explode that myth by pointing out that in the early fifties there was an organization calling itself the Partisan Republicans of California that put out a smear publication charging that I was a leader of a—and I quote—"New Deal-Communist plot" to get Dwight D. Eisenhower the Republican nomination for President and to get him elected President.

To those who contend that hatred and bigotry is now greater than it ever was, I would urge a review of the conditions of the early fifties. I would recall to their memories those days of guilt-by-association, of character assassination, of trial-by-accusation. I would recall to their memories those days when freedom of speech was so abused by some that it was not exercised by others—when there were too many mental mutes afraid to speak their minds lest they be politically smeared as "Communists" or "Fascists" by their opponents.

I would recall their memories to a United States Senate that was almost paralyzed by fear—when some said that when I made the Declaration of Conscience that I had signed my political death warrant—and when that elder statesman who called one of your members and said that the Declaration of Conscience would have made Margaret Chase Smith the next President if she were a man—when such elder statesman was so clearly in the minority in his political evaluation of my speech.

Perhaps I know and feel this more strongly than some of those who evaluate and editorialize that bigotry and hatred are at their greatest heights now—because I felt the whiplash of the hatred and the bigotry from both the extremists of the Right and the extremists of the Left—when I fought such extremism both on the Floor of the Senate and in the Federal Court—and Thank God, for common decency, when I won not only in the Senate and in the Court—but with the people at the polls.

No, there is less bigotry and hate now than there was ten or fifteen years ago—and we have very impressive proof of this. The late John F. Kennedy helped prove this. After his victory in the 1960 elections, who can confidently claim that there has been more bigotry and hatred in the sixties than there was in the fifties? Who can seriously contend that there was more bigotry in 1960 than in 1928?

And who can deny that the rights of negroes are greater in 1964 than they were in 1954? Who can deny that there has been progress on civil rights in the past decade? Perhaps not as much as there should have been. But who can truthfully say that we have gone backwards and become more bigoted in 1964 on civil rights than we were in 1954?

No, I am proud of the progress that our nation and our people have made in the past decade in significantly, encouragingly—and yes, inspiringly—reducing hatred and bigotry in our nation and among our people. There is much room for improvement. But there is no need to hang our heads in shame—there is no need for us to wallow in a deep and heavy national guilt-complex.

For where in the world is there a nation as free of bigotry and hate as the United States? Where in the world is there a nation that has provided "equality in freedom" in the degree that the United States has for its people? Where in the world is there a nation that has done so much to export this concept of "freedom in equality" as has the United States in the billions of dollars that it has poured into efforts to give "equality in freedom" to the other peoples of the world? What other nation has poured out its resources and its heart to practically every other nation in the world in the past twenty-five years besides the

United States—even to Russia with the multi-billion-dollar aid in World War II?

Is such the record of a nation of hatred and bigotry? Is such the record of a nation torn between radicals and reactionaries— between the Far Right Extremists and the Far Left Extremists?

I think the answers are clear. I think it is abundantly clear that the United States and its people are not hopelessly entwined in bigotry and hatred. To the contrary, I think the record shows that the American people are winning the battle against bigotry and hate—not losing it. I think the record shows that we have made significant progress in the last fifteen years.

I think it is abundantly clear that we are not a nation of extremists. To the contrary, the extremists of both the Left and the Right are very, very small minorities in size and only seem larger than they really are because they make a greater noise than the quieter non-extremists.

No, the vast majority of Americans are not extremists. They have no use for extremists of either the Far Left or the Far Right. If there be any doubter of the relative freedom of Americans from bigotry and hatred as compared to the other peoples of the world, then let him take a good long look at the Statue of Liberty and particularly those words inscribed at its base of:

"Give me your tired, your poor, your huddled masses yearning to breathe free, the wretched refuse of your teeming shore. Send these, the homeless, tempest-tossed, to me . . ."

For more than a year now I have been receiving a steady flow of mail urging me to run for President of the United States. At first my reaction was that of being pleasantly flattered with such expression of confidence in me. I was pleased but did not take the suggestion seriously for speculation prior to the past year has been limited to Vice Presidential possibilities.

And so I answered the letters by saying that I was pleased and flattered but that I was realistic enough not to take the suggestion seriously. I was sure that the trend would be short-lived and would end. But instead of fading away the mail increased and by mid-November of last year reached a new peak.

At that time one of the most persistent writers pressed hard for more than my reply of "I am pleased and flattered but know it could not possibly happen," and in response to his pressing I replied that I would give the suggestion serious consideration and make a decision within a relatively short time. My answer was picked up by the local press and some two weeks later the Associated Press queried my office quoting from the letter and asking if the quote was correct. My office confirmed the quote as being correct and then the mail began to pour in.

The mail came from all of the fifty states and to my surprise I found that the writers were taking a possible Margaret Chase Smith Presidential candidacy more seriously than I had been. Now I try to be serious without taking myself too seriously —but this mail was not what I had seriously expected. Frankly, it had its effect.

With the tragic assassination of President Kennedy came the political moratorium and the cancellation of the original date of this address. Again I anticipated that during the interim period this mail would fall off. And it did for a few days but then it started up again and now has returned to a level above that prior to the moratorium period.

In fairness to everyone, I concluded that I should make my decision before the end of January—and I have done so. It has not been an easy decision—either "yes" or "no" would be difficult. The arguments made to me that I should become a candidate have been gratifying.

First, it has been contended that I should run because I have more national office experience than any of the other announced candidates—or the unannounced candidates—with that experience going back to 1940 and predating any of the others.

Second, it has been contended that regardless of what happened to me, should I become a candidate was not really important—but that what was really important was that through me for the first time the women of the United States had an opportunity to break the barrier against women being seriously considered for the Presidency of the United States—to destroy any political bigotry against women on this score just as the late John F. Kennedy had broken the political barrier on religion and destroyed once and for all such political bigotry.

This argument contends that I would be pioneering the way for a woman in the future—to make her more acceptable—to make the way easier—for her to be elected President of the

United States. Perhaps the point that has impressed me the most on this argument is that women before me pioneered and smoothed the way for me to be the first woman to be elected to both the House and the Senate—and that I should give back in return that which had been given to me.

Third, it has been contended that I should run in order to give the voters a wider range of choice—and specifically a choice other than that of Conservative or Liberal—to give those who considered themselves to be Moderates or Middle-of-the-Road advocates a chance to cast an unqualified vote instead of having to vote Conservative or Liberal. In this contention, it has been argued that this would give the voters a greater opportunity to express their will instead of being so restricted in their choice that many of them would not vote.

Fourth, it has been contended that I should run because I do not have unlimited financial resources or a tremendous political machine or backing from the party bosses—but instead have political independence for not having such resources.

There are other reasons that have been advanced but I will not take your time to discuss them. Instead let me turn to the reasons advanced as to why I should not run.

First, there are those who make the contention that no woman should ever dare to aspire to the White House—that this is a man's world and that it should be kept that way—and that a woman on the national ticket of a political party would be more of a handicap than a strength.

Second, it is contended that the odds are too heavily against me for even the most remote chance of victory—and that I should not run in the face of what most observers see as certain and crushing defeat.

Third, it is contended that as a woman I would not have the physical stamina and strength to run—and that I should not take that much out of me even for what might conceivably be a good cause, even if a losing cause.

Fourth, it is contended that I should not run because obviously I do not have the financial resources to wage the campaign that others have.

Fifth, it is contended that I should not run because I do not have the professional political organization that others have.

Sixth, it is contended that I should not run because to do so would result in necessary absence from Washington while the Senate had roll call votes—and thus that I would bring to an end my consecutive roll call record which is now at 1590.

You know of other reasons advanced as to why I should not run—and so I will not take your time to discuss them.

As gratifying as are the reasons advanced urging me to run, I find the reasons advanced against my running to be far more impelling. For were I to run, it would be under severe limitations with respect to lack of money, lack of organization, and lack of time because of the requirements to be on the job in Washington doing my elected duty instead of abandoning those duties to campaign—plus the very heavy odds against me.

So because of these very impelling reasons against my running, I have decided that I shall enter the New Hampshire Presidential preferential primary and the Illinois primary.* For I accept the reasons advanced against my running as challenges —challenges which I met before in 1948 when I first ran for United States Senator from Maine, when I did not have the money that my opposition did—when I did not have the professional party organization that my opposition did—when it was said that "the Senate is no place for a woman"—when my physical strength was sapped during the campaign with a broken arm—when my conservative opponent and my liberal opponent in Maine were not restricted in campaigning by official duties in Washington such as I had—and when practically no one gave me a chance to win.

My candidacy in the New Hampshire primary will be a test in several ways.

(1) It will be a test of how much support will be given to a candidate without campaign funds and whose expense will be limited to personal and travel expense paid by the candidate.

(2) It will be a test of how much support will be given a candidate without a professional party organization of paid

* EDITOR'S NOTE: When she said that she found the reasons against running to be far more impelling, a groan went up from the mostly female audience. But when she said in the next breath that because of these very impelling reasons against running she *would* run, the audience roared with delight. They were delighted not only with her decision but as well with the suspense that she had kept them in and with the unorthodox reasoning on which she made her decision.

campaign workers but instead composed of nonpaid amateur volunteers.

(3) It will be a test of how much support will be given a candidate who refuses to absent herself from the official duties to which she has been elected and whose campaign time in New Hampshire will be limited to those times when the Senate is *not* in session voting on legislation.

(4) It will be a test of how much support will be given to a candidate who will not purchase political time on television or radio or political advertisements in publications.

(5) It will be a test of how much support will be given a candidate who will campaign on a record rather than on promises.

I welcome the challenges and I look forward to the test.

EDITOR'S NOTE:
Once she had declared herself, the Senator fully expected some defections. They are part of the political game. Two New Hampshirites, former Governor Wesley Powell and former United States Senator Maurice Murphy, were among the first to defect. Back in November they had made a trip to see Senator Smith and offer Powell's support. Powell's only reservation was that in order to be effective, the support would have to be in the form of a direct mail campaign which would cost ten thousand dollars. Senator Smith thanked them and no definite commitments were made. Subsequently the Powell group decided to head up a write-in campaign for Nixon instead of her. She did not mind such lapses in loyalty. What surprised her and hurt her was what two women on her staff did.

Her campaigning in New Hampshire was to be limited to one week when the Senate was in recess (for Lincoln speeches) and one other weekend, and her campaign expenses were to total $250. Her major campaigning was scheduled for the week of

February 9 to 16. Consequently an intensive drive was made in the week before to clean up the entire backlog of hundreds of pro-Presidential letters and to return all the campaign contributions sent her. She wanted to go to New Hampshire caught up on everything.

She is one of the most considerate people on Capitol Hill toward members of her staff. For many years she has maintained a very firm policy that all members (except her Executive Assistant) must complete their work and be out of the office at five o'clock sharp. If they have leftover work, then they have to come in a half hour early the next morning at eight-thirty. In addition, she does not work her staff on Saturdays or Sundays. There had been some rare exceptions caused by last-minute urgencies. But it had been about six years since there had been an instance of the staff working after five o'clock. Starting on Monday, February 10, I called for all members to accelerate their work in order to be able to have it all cleaned up by Friday night so that the Senator could leave for New Hampshire on Saturday morning. Departure from the office at five sharp was maintained. But early Thursday afternoon I estimated that the backlog of work couldn't be completed on schedule and informed the staff that it would be necessary to work that evening. The staff worked until ten o'clock. Senator Smith and I worked until one o'clock in the morning.

The next morning, Friday, one of the most senior (but younger) women on the staff gave notice stating that she was leaving the staff in two weeks because her husband said that he would not stand her having to work such late hours. This was a shock to the Senator for the resigning woman fully realized the importance of the campaign. A few minutes later a call came in from one of the less senior (but older) women on the staff stating that the work the day before had made her so ill that she would not be coming in. This was a second blow to Margaret. Two of her most trusted staff members had let her down when the chips were down.

The only alternative left was to work on Saturday and to delay the departure for New Hampshire to Sunday. Two women and one man outside the staff—Marion Budlong and Carol Wilson and Bill Deachman (of Plymouth, New Hampshire)—volunteered to fill the breach and help meet the crisis of the mail backlog. One of the girls on the regular staff worked that Saturday but only to make up on some leave she had taken. No other girl on the regular staff volunteered to work extra.

The crisis crew of three outside volunteers plus two men and one girl on the regular staff worked at a frantic pace and by nine o'clock Saturday night all work was completed and the backlog completely eliminated. At 4 A.M. Sunday morning we set out for New Hampshire—the Senator, Bill Deachman (Minority Counsel of the Senate Space Committee and an appointee of the late New Hampshire Senator Styles Bridges), and myself at the wheel of her car. For most of the twelve-hour drive the Senator signed letters that had been typed the day before. We arrived in Colebrook, New Hampshire, in a little more than twelve hours.

The Senator hit the campaign trail at six-thirty the next morning going north to Pittsburg near the Canadian border. The first two voters she approached were Alvin Young and Linwood Bressette, two startled loggers loading pulpwood on a truck at the roadside. When she stopped at the general store operated by William Little the temperature was twenty-eight degrees below zero.

Working her way south with Bill Deachman introducing her to his fellow natives, she shook hands in the streets, spoke at service clubs, to women's clubs, to schools, visiting factories, and the press. Cold as the weather was, she was warmly greeted everywhere.

When she reached Washington late Sunday night February 16, she was exhausted but exhilarated. She had one major concern. Her entry into the primary had been on the suggestion that New Hampshire voters wanted a middle-of-the-road choice between conservative Goldwater and liberal Rockefeller. What she found in that week of campaigning convinced her that her appraisal had been accurate. But there was now widespread talk that a highly organized direct mail campaign was under way for a write-in for another middle-of-the-roader, Henry Cabot Lodge, Jr.

If Lodge did not stop the campaign, Margaret sensed that he would pull away most of such vote that she would ordinarily get. He had a prestigious image as our country's Ambassador in Vietnam who was trying to get our boys out of there. People also remembered him as the man who, on a national telecast, had dramatically exposed Russia before the United Nations by holding up the United States Seal (from the Embassy in Moscow) and pointing to where the Russians had placed an electronic spying bug. And coming from Massachusetts, Lodge was as much a neighbor as was Smith from Maine.

Senator Smith returned to New Hampshire the next weekend to campaign in the southern part. The people were warm and most friendly, just as they had been farther north in the state. But the Lodge talk was increasing and that spelled trouble for her. In addition the recent refusal of the Oregon Secretary of State to consider her as a bona fide candidate or to put her on the ballot there, was no help to the prestige of her candidacy.

On election night, when she and her staff gathered in her office to take in the returns, the Senator braced herself for disappointment. Lodge won an overwhelming victory with Goldwater, Rockefeller, and Nixon trailing in poor second, third, and fourth positions and Smith in an even poorer fifth. She did outpoll Scranton, Romney, and Stassen. The people seemed to have given her their hearts but not their votes.

Particularly crushing was the poor vote she received in Portsmouth. She was the only candidate who had done anything for the Kittery-Portsmouth Naval Shipyard and yet the votes went to those who hadn't done anything. She felt that the Portsmouth voters were repudiating her for the unbelievably bad news she had given them in December about the forthcoming announcement of the decision to close their shipyard. They punished her for telling them what seven months later would be revealed as the gospel truth.

Though Senator Smith had proved her point—that most Republicans in New Hampshire wanted a candidate between the right and left of Goldwater and Rockefeller—it was not easy to witness those votes going to Lodge.

She had never had any real hope of winning, but she had not anticipated such deep disappointments as she suffered in that month of the New Hampshire primary. They were enough to discourage her from staying in the race. First there had been the disappointment of the two departing staff women. Then came another on February 29 when she received the Reserve Officers Association Minuteman Award for the "Citizen Who Has Contributed Most to National Security in These Times." It was the ROA's Mid-Winter Banquet and Military Ball and President Lyndon B. Johnson was to present the award to her at the banquet.

Recognizing the uncertainties of the schedule of a President, the ROA had arranged to have a back-up for him in the event that he could not attend. Senator Richard B. Russell of Georgia, Chairman of the Senate Armed Services Committee, happily agreed to stand by as the back-up. When Colonel John T. Carlton, Executive Director of ROA asked him, Senator Russell said that he would be honored to make the presentation to his very good friend. His respect for her was matched only by his affection. He called her "Sis." "You know," Senator Russell said, "she is just ornery enough that if she were a man she would make a hell of a good President!" The afternoon before the banquet it began snowing and Senator Russell, a victim of emphysema who needed to avoid exposure to damp atmosphere, checked with ROA as to whether Johnson would make the presentation that evening. The assurance from the White House staff was so strong that ROA told Senator Russell that he shouldn't come out; the President would make the presentation.

But when presentation time came that evening President Johnson was nowhere in sight. Not only that, he sent no message (although McNamara did) and no regrets. There was never at any time any word of explanation to the Senator or the ROA. Some observers felt it was because she had become a candidate for LBJ's job and the New Hampshire primary election was just a few days away. Others said it was because her speech had been critical of McNamara's whiz kids' derogation of the military, but that was not credible since the speech was not released before its delivery. Within the same week, it was noted, LBJ had made a point of attending functions honoring other women and speaking in praise of them. Whatever his reason, the wounding impression left was that LBJ had deliberately snubbed the Senator.

The next Presidential primary took place April 14 in Illinois. After the crushing defeat in New Hampshire the prospects in Illinois were indeed dim and grim. After all, Illinois was regarded as the exclusive political preserve of Goldwater. A group of Young Republicans led by Lewis V. Morgan, Illinois legislator, together with a group of very energetic and dynamic women led by Vi Dawson (Mrs. Murray Dawson) in separate efforts had obtained enough signers of primary petitions to place Senator Smith's name on the ballot.

The dedication of Vi Dawson's gals was unquestioned. They were for Margaret Chase Smith for President and for no one else. They were for her for President—and not just for Vice President. In contrast, Lew Morgan's boys were considerably ambivalent. Apparently they feared repercussions and reprisals from the Goldwater leaders, who dominated the Republican Illinois organization. They told the press that no one runs for Vice President and that they were really pushing Senator Smith for Vice President by getting her on the Illinois ballot for President. They protested that they were really not against Goldwater.

Everett Dirksen, Senate Republican Leader, was openly unhappy about Margaret Smith's candidacy in his own state of Illinois. Charles Percy and all other leading Illinois Republicans shied away from her candidacy.

There were other unfavorable straws in the wind. For example, liberal Democratic columnist Ralph McGill, former editor of the Atlanta *Constitution,* had observed in his nationally syndicated column that Senator Smith's Presidential candidacy had set the cause of women back several decades. Ironically, prior to the column the Senator and I had run into McGill at the Exeter Inn while campaigning in New Hampshire. McGill was dining with friends and when he saw the Senator he made a special point of speaking to her and introducing his friends. He seemed to be almost ostentatiously proud to know her. The political experts said that Margaret Smith would be lucky to get as much as 10 percent of the vote in Illinois and would likely fall far below that. Determined not to miss roll call votes in the Senate, the Senator could get away for only two weekends in Illinois. On those two she got up before dawn and campaigned until after midnight at coffee klatches, supermarkets, schools, women's clubs, on radio and TV talk shows making the most of every precious minute in the schedule that Lew Morgan's boys and Vi Dawson's gals had set for her. Her total campaign cost in Illinois was $85 as the plane fare one weekend was paid for by a women's Republican Club she addressed.

Whereas it was Lew Morgan's men who originally got her into the Illinois primary, it was actually Vi Dawson's women who provided the sustained effort and momentum for her candidacy and campaign. And what a job they did! When all the returns were in Senator Smith had scored a stunning moral victory. Instead of getting less than 10 percent of the vote she got 30 percent—a total of a quarter of a million votes. She had literally crashed Goldwaterland.*

Now perhaps the Oregon Secretary of State, Howell Appling, Jr., was having second thoughts about his earlier irrevocable re-

* Significance of Margaret's surprise showing was recognized that night by pro-Goldwater movie actor Efrem Zimbalist, Jr., in his introduction of Goldwater at a Long Beach (California) rally. He read what he called "a holiday gift list" to what he called "my Socialist masters." Newsmen said it included a remark about sending Senator Smith roses for her showing in the Illinois primary.

Zimbalist had just paid his Federal income tax and was presumably referring to the Federal Government. News reports claimed his remark was derogatory. He not only denied this publicly with the statement of "I couldn't because I think she's a very fine woman, a very fine Senator. I have much respect for her," but he repeated this in a personally penned letter to Senator Smith, which was answered saying she understood and inviting him to have lunch with her when he was next in Washington.

fusal to put Senator Smith on the ballot for the Oregon Presidential primary. Appling had stated that he didn't find any substantial advocacy of her candidacy and under Oregon law he could therefore refuse to put her name on the ballot. Yet, he had put Scranton and Romney on the ballot.

The only way to overcome such arbitrary refusal was through the petition route. And that's the way Margaret Smith got on the Oregon ballot. The successful petition drive was led by an Oregon Democrat, James B. Daniels, and an Oregon Republican, Al Phelps, both of Salem. The initial momentum that Daniels and Phelps gave to the Smith candidacy was then picked up by Leona T. Jensen's (Mrs. Harold B. Jensen) Oregon Business and Professional Women. But the effort was destined to severe limitations.

In the first place, though TV personality and telecaster Tom McCall (later to become Governor of Oregon) and others pledged their support, Governor Mark Hatfield displayed considerable coolness to her candidacy and spoke of Oregon Republican resentment of her failure to support Elmo Smith against Maurine Neuberger for the Senate. [Elmo Smith had never requested her support, and Senator Smith never gave her support to Mrs. Neuberger.] Some thought that Appling, who was Hatfield's appointee and successor as Oregon Secretary of State, was only reflecting Hatfield's wishes when he refused to put Senator Smith on the ballot.

The second limitation was geographic. Oregon was three thousand miles from Washington, too far to get to and still fulfill her duty of answering roll call votes. The third was money. The original hope of the pro-Smith supporters for organizing fell through when they were unable to raise enough money* to retain the public relations agency they wanted to handle the campaign. In the end result there was no real organization.

---

* What they lacked in money they more than compensated for with creativity. The Margaret Chase Smith campaign button originated by the Oregon Women became the prized campaign button of the 1964 election. Before the campaign was over, the bidding price for Rose-Signature campaign button was to reach $25.00.

As in New Hampshire she came in a disappointing fifth—but she did beat Scranton by a 2 to 1 margin. Scranton later was to become the principal opponent of Goldwater at the National Convention.

Although she entered only those primaries in New Hampshire, Illinois, and Oregon, Senator Smith received several thousand votes in the Texas, Massachusetts, and Pennsylvania primaries. Her usual position, outside of Illinois, was to follow Lodge, Goldwater, Rockefeller, and Nixon.

When she went to the Republican National Convention in San Francisco on July 12, 1964, she had only sixteen delegates pledged to her candidacy—fourteen from Maine, Vermont's George D. Aiken and North Dakota's John Rouzie. The entire Maine delegation was committed by a resolution passed at the Maine Republican State Convention.*

* Despite this total commitment, there had been rivalry between Goldwater and Rockefeller forces for second choice if and when Senator Smith withdrew. The Goldwater forces were headed by Cyril Joly, Jr., of Waterville, the Rockefeller forces were headed by First Congressional District Representative Stanley R. Tupper. Back in November, Tupper had called Senator Smith and asked if she would see him and Second Congressional District Representative Clifford G. McIntire. Tupper did most of the talking and, much to her surprise, strongly urged her to run for the Republican Presidential nomination.

Tupper contended that her candidacy would bring favorable publicity to Maine and help ease the tensions between the Goldwater and Rockefeller forces. Her response was that, regardless of what she decided, she felt he was obligated to support Rockefeller since Rockefeller had provided the major financing for Tupper's Congressional campaign. She would not expect Tupper to support her but would prefer that he remain loyal to Rockefeller. Ten days later the political column in the November 17, 1963, issue of the Portland *Sunday Telegram* reported that Tupper had remained silent about Senator Smith's candicacy and pictured him in political agony about the matter because of his loyalty to Rockefeller. "If Sen. Smith should run and if Tupper continued to remain firm for Rockefeller, Tupper's decision would have to stand as some sort of a monument to the strength of his personal convictions." It was fairly clear that the columnist had gotten his story from Tupper and apparently Tupper had not told the columnist that the Senator had urged him to stick with Rockefeller and not support her. Or if he had, the columnist had chosen to withhold the important truth. This column was followed up by an editorial in the same paper two days later. The editorial was titled "Despite Growing Political Heat Rep. Tupper Sticks to His Pledges" and called upon Maine people to tell Tupper that they "admired his courage and integrity." To set the record straight as far as she was concerned, Senator Smith sent a letter to Tupper on November 21, 1963, in which she stated:

When Senator Smith alighted from the TWA airliner early Sunday afternoon, July 12, 1963, at the San Francisco airport, she was welcomed by a large and enthusiastic* crowd waving Smith-for-President signs and banners, and a band playing "Hello, Maggie." Two women's groups had been buzzing all-out for her. Vi Dawson, National Chairman of the Smith-for-

---

Dear Stan:

I shall never forget how you and Cliff McIntire called on me on November 7, 1963 and asked to talk with me and in that talk how you and Cliff so warmly urged me to enter the Presidential preferential primaries. If I do, the urging that you and Cliff made will have been a factor in my decision. I have read with interest the Hansen column and the editorials of the Portland papers reporting that my possible candidacy has placed you in a political dilemma and that it would take monumental courage for you to continue your support of Governor Rockefeller.

As far as I am concerned personally, I want to do what I can to remove you from any such political dilemma. With vigor and warmth that I hope will match the vigor and warmth in which you urged me to enter the Presidential preferential primaries, I want to urge you to continue your support of Governor Rockefeller undiluted regardless of what my decision may ultimately be. For I deeply admire those who stay with their convictions and friends and I admire you for not forgetting the splendid and substantial support that Governor Rockefeller has given your congressional candidacies in 1960 and 1962.

Sincerely yours,
Margaret Chase Smith
United States Senator

Senator Smith released her letter to the press. A month later, on December 24, 1963, the political columnist of the Portland *Press Herald* and *Sunday Telegram,* in reporting that Tupper had been chosen by Rockefeller to be his New England campaign manager, also wrote: "Tupper made something resembling political history recently when, in an exchange of 'Dear Margaret' and 'Dear Stan' letters, he told GOP U. S. Sen. Margaret Chase Smith that he could not desert Rockefeller even though Mrs. Smith was considering running for President." Once again he had failed to tell the true story, that the Senator had told Tupper to support Rockefeller instead of her.

* According to Drew Pearson, this enthusiasm was not shared by everyone as he reported that the Convention Chairman, Kentucky Senator Thruston Morton (later to become Republican National Committee Chairman), was doing his best to belittle Margaret's candidacy and had fumingly snorted to friends in San Francisco: "Three people will be nominated for President— Goldwater, Scranton, and the G— D— Margaret Chase Smith." While Margaret had often had good reason to question Pearson's accuracy after experiencing his misrepresentations against her, this Pearson allegation had credibility in view of Morton's past snide comments against Margaret earlier that year in a hatchet story that Maxine Cheshire had written about Margaret in the *Saturday Evening Post.* Pearson claimed that Morton viewed Margaret as a potential rival for the Vice Presidential nomination.

President forces, and her group had rented a large house at 2430 Vallejo Street in San Francisco for headquarters and Marion Otsea, Chairman of the Smith California Committee, had set up a business campaign office in a downtown building, at 525 Market Street.

Marion Otsea's group concentrated on convention arrangements, especially on organizing the convention floor demonstration to follow Senator Aiken's nominating speech. Vi Dawson and her group concentrated on lining up delegates. They not only took their efforts to the convention floor but entertained energetically, if modestly, at the attractive large headquarters. They persuaded Mrs. Betty Horne of Longview, Washington, for example, not only to support Margaret Smith but to make a speech seconding her nomination.

It was abundantly clear that Goldwater had had the nomination wrapped up long before the convention. But through the Republican National Committee Chairman William E. Miller (whom he chose to be his Vice Presidential running mate), he also had a total vise on the convention arrangements. Miller had publicly expressed his disapproval of Margaret Chase Smith's entering the New Hampshire primary. It was no surprise therefore that Smith people had difficulty in getting access to the convention hall, the Cow Palace. Supporters of other candidates reported similar experiences.

The worst difficulty our forces encountered was when Mrs. Charlotte Logan and I went to the convention hall to distribute copies of the Aiken nominating speech to the press. Despite the official passes we presented, we were physically blocked from entering the convention hall. After being refused permission at several entrances, we finally forced our way through one. Later the convention officials tried to explain by claiming that counterfeit passes had been printed and strict security had had to be invoked. Margaret Smith not only broke the barrier for women by having her name placed in nomination for the Presidency, she also broke with the tradition requiring Presidential candidates to be absent when their nominating speeches are made. Instead she was seated in the Smith box in the Cow Palace throughout Senator Aiken's speech and the seconding speeches by Governor John Reed of Maine, Representative Frances P. Bolton of Ohio, John Rouzie (Chairman of the North Dakota Delegation), and Mrs. Betty Horne of Longview, Washington.

The Aiken speech was a monument to New England sincerity and elegant simplicity. This was what the Senator from Vermont said:

Mr. Chairman and Delegates:

I intend to nominate for President one of the most capable persons I have ever known and one with whom I have been associated in public service for twenty-four years.

I don't like to start a nominating speech with a confession, but the circumstances are compelling.

In introducing my candidate, I find myself in a most peculiar position; I am severely restricted in what I can offer for your support.

I can't promise you a cabinet job, an ambassador's appointment—or even a shot at a nice government contract.

I can't even offer you cigars or chewing gum.

For a while, it looked real promising.

I thought I could at least invite you all out for coffee because I knew my candidate was having checks and $10.00 and $1.00 bills and pennies sent her from most every State in the Union.

Pennies came from school children—and dollars from low income people who couldn't afford it.

Then there were some beautiful checks in three and four figures from real important business people.

The outlook was as rosy as a Pacific sunset as portrayed by the Chamber of Commerce.

You and I were going to have a wonderful time here in San Francisco.

Then do you know what happened?

Do you know what my candidate pulled on me?

She took every big check—every little check—every $10.00 bill—every $1.00 bill and every penny and sent them straight back to where they came from.

My candidate wants the nomination solely on her record and her qualifications for the job. As a result our transportation fund is busted. Our entertainment fund is shattered. Our demonstration wallet collapsed. Our conscience is intact.

And that's why I can't offer you any candy or cigars or chewing gum or even ask you all out for a cup of coffee.

The only thing in the world left for me to offer you for your support is the best managed government the United States ever had—a government headed by the best qualified person you ever voted for.

Before setting forth the qualifications of the candidate I shall shortly present to you, let it be distinctly understood that I am concerned solely with the nomination of one who is best qualified for the job and who can bring victory to our Party in November.

I am not making this nomination for the purpose of embarrassing or downgrading any other candidate.

I intend to support the nominee of this Convention next November.

What do we have a President for?

Certainly not to do just those things which you and I as individuals would like to have done.

Certainly not to run this country exactly as he or she would like to run it.

If that is the way we feel, we should promptly scrap our Constitution and become a monarchy.

Until we reach that state of political depravity, however, the President of the United States will be required to perform the duties of the office as set forth by our Constitution and to administer laws and carry out programs as laid down by the Congress.

In carrying out programs and administering laws as determined by the Congress, the President will necessarily use the great powers which originally were vested in the Congress but which have long since been delegated to the Executive Branch.

There are some Republicans who still insist that Congress rescind these delegations of authority.

Let us not kid ourselves, however.

The next President, whether Republican or Democrat, and

regardless of race, creed, color, or sex, is not going to recommend that Congress rescind the powers that have been delegated to the White House over the past century.

In view of this situation, it is far more important to elect a person of integrity and ability to the Presidency—one who owes allegiance to no special interests—either domestic or foreign—one who will conscientiously perform the duties of the office as prescribed by the Constitution—than it is to elect one on the premise that he or she may agree with our particular viewpoints.

I have definite ideas as to the qualifications our candidate for President should have.

I say unequivocally that the candidate I will propose most nearly meets that criteria.

1. A President should have integrity.

Whether dealing with foreign nations or the folks at home, integrity is a priceless asset.

My candidate stands ace-high in this respect.

2. A President should have ability.

Good intentions alone are not enough.

We don't want the floors of the White House paved with good intentions.

If my candidate does not have ability, then the forty-four universities and colleges that have awarded her degrees based solely on merit have been wrong.

3. A President should have had wide experience in government.

Well—if twenty-four years' experience on the roughest-toughest committees of the Congress—Defense—Space—Appropriations—Government Operations and Rules don't qualify my candidate then the other candidates whose names are being submitted to you cannot possibly be qualified for none of them can approach her record.

4. A President should have courage—courage to stand for the right when it may not be popular to do so—courage to stand for decency in the conduct of public affairs—courage to stand alone if necessary against formidable odds.

Does my candidate have this kind of courage?

I can refer you to several high ranking officers of the United

States Armed Forces who have learned from experience that she is ably qualified in this respect.

As a sincere testimonial to her courage the Reserve Officers Association has recently designated her as "Minute Man of the Year"—the first time that this great honor has ever been conferred upon a person of her sex.

5. A President should have common sense.

My candidate stands par-excellence in this respect.

Time and again I have watched her keep her head "when all about her were losing theirs" and blaming it on everyone but themselves.

She wants to get things done that ought to be done—and she wants them done right.

She does not panic when things don't go to suit her.

She just keeps on headed for her goal—which at this moment is the Republican nomination for the Presidency.

We need a candidate who does not panic in a crisis, not even a campaign crisis.

Nor should we support a candidate just because we are partial to any particular industry either at home or abroad.

We don't want an industry in the White House.

We want a living, capable, conscientious human being.

We want to nominate and elect a President who will promote the interests of our Nation both at home and abroad with impartial consideration for all.

We want a candidate who enjoys the confidence of people in all walks of life.

The one I shall nominate has demonstrated time and again that she "can walk with Kings nor lose the common touch."

She never forgets her own people and the glare of glory has never turned her head.

The record majorities which the people of her home State have given her with each passing election are eloquent testimony to this trait of her character.

Her conduct during this campaign has been rather unusual.

She has not neglected her work in the Senate to chase down delegates to this Convention.

The job she was elected to do has come first.

Running solely on her record and her qualifications for the

office, she has spent no money for advertising—has hired no paid workers—has made no promises—and will have nothing to do with the wheeling and dealing—the trading and raiding practices which I understand have sometimes been used in political campaigns.

I now ask you two questions:

Do you want the United States to have good government?

If you do—then vote for the candidate best qualified to give good government.

Do you want to win the November election?

If you do—then vote for the candidate who enjoys the confidence and respect of all people and who can get the votes necessary to win.

I am now proud to nominate that candidate—the Senior Senator from the Great Republican State of Maine—Senator Margaret Chase Smith.

While Senator Aiken was in the middle of his speech, Mrs. Donna Wright of San Francisco, the organizer and director of the floor demonstration that was to follow, was near apoplexy.

My husband was in the gallery (she was to write later) . . . and there were no Smith demonstrators to be seen in the entrance. He ran to the lobby and found our group trying to make their way through an enormous press of people and he shoved, pushed and prodded a path through to the arena entrance. The two boys came in, bewildered, with the letters, not knowing where to go, and my husband grabbed the cards and forced his way to the section of the gallery where Maine guests were sitting. Mr. Katz gave me a handful of extra tickets and I passed into the arena every nice-looking person with a Smith sign I could find in the lobby.

Then the miracle occurred. Somehow, the demonstrators and cheerleaders were on the floor of the arena, the band was playing "Drink a toast to dear old Maine," the cards were held up in the gallery (though it took some time to get them straight) and everyone was cheering and singing and the delegates were carrying Smith signs and the whole huge hall was having a good time.

An element we hadn't even considered came into play . . . sentiment, and respect and good wishes for a gallant lady. We had captured the audience in a genuine, spontaneous show of affection, sensed, just as much, from all reports, by individuals watching TV in their living rooms far from the electricity of the actual scene. Perhaps everyone was tired of the tension and strife of a bitter contest, perhaps they suddenly realized what Senator Smith had been trying to say was *for* something instead of *against* (which we had known all along, of course). The Cow Palace was singing "Boola, Boola," Senator Smith was beaming from her box, Marion was waving a rose around her head, my husband finally got "Hello, Maggie" [in individual large single letter signs] almost perfect and people smiled through their tears.

What happened after the floor demonstration and the seconding speeches was anticlimactic. In his desperate, frantic drive to stop the Goldwater steamroller, greatly frustrated by the on-again-off-again declarations of former President Eisenhower, Governor Scranton publicly stated that he would welcome Margaret Chase Smith as his Vice Presidential running mate.

A group of Air Force-minded visitors at the convention, who had warm feelings for both Goldwater and Smith, suggested to Goldwater forces that, as a gracious gesture to all women, Goldwater ask each of the delegations pledged to him to cast one vote for Margaret Chase Smith in honor of women nationally. The argument was made that by this gesture Goldwater could gain the votes of millions of American women—and at a very little cost of only a few delegates out of the more than eight hundred he claimed. They were curtly rebuffed.

The night of the voting Senator Smith left the convention

hall early in the roll call. When the first balloting had been completed, Barry Goldwater had won overwhelmingly with 883 votes. Margaret Smith received only 27 votes—but more than Henry Cabot Lodge, Jr., who had scored impressively in the primaries. And in the final recording of the vote, Margaret Smith came in second because the delegates for all other candidates permitted their votes to be shifted to Goldwater once he had won the nomination. Twenty-six of the 27 who had voted for Margaret Smith remained with her to the end. The only vote she lost was cast by the Massachusetts alternate for former Republican Speaker Joe Martin after Joe had retired for the night. The votes she got were 2 from Alaska, 14 from Maine, 1 from Massachusetts (former Republican Speaker of the House Joe Martin), 3 from North Dakota, 1 from Ohio, 5 from Vermont, and 1 from Washington. Drew Pearson wrote in his column:

Those few scattered votes for Senator Margaret Chase Smith outside her own Maine delegation were quietly lined up for her by three chivalrous Senate colleagues.

Senators John Williams of Delaware, Frank Carlson of Kansas, and George Aiken of Vermont decided it would be a shame for Mrs. Smith not to get a few courtesy votes after her ladylike campaign for President.

Unknown to her, they made a few quiet calls to delegates and persuaded them to cast their first complimentary ballot for the lady from Maine.

Since she received not a vote from Senator Williams' Delaware or Senator Carlson's Kansas, Senator Smith didn't really believe that they had made any effort in her behalf. In contrast, she knew that Senator Milton R. Young had been responsible for her three North Dakota votes—and he got no public credit.

Three thousand miles across the nation in New Bern, North

Carolina, the editor of the *Mirror* had perceived with sagacity, as well as Southern gallantry, the true significance of Senator Smith's candidacy. He wrote:

Harking back to the Republican National Convention in San Francisco, we hope it will be our good fortune to remember longest Senator Margaret Chase Smith. Some of the other folks there we won't mind forgetting, if such a thing is possible.

This distinguished woman never really had a chance to be her party's standard bearer, but the *Mirror* is glad she campaigned for the nation's highest office. It gave millions of Americans a televised glimpse of one of this country's great public servants.

At a gathering where true dignity was an oddity, just as it will be rather inconspicuous when the Democrats meet in Atlantic City, she managed to retain the graciousness and charm that has characterized not only her personal life but her career in Congress.

As true as the song the convention orchestra had played for her, Everything Had Come Up Roses.

Anti-ABM

"I never saw so many men so publicly woo one woman."

—Mike Mansfield
Senate Majority Leader
August 6, 1969

Members of the Armed Services committees of Congress have long been indiscriminately maligned as "tools" and "puppets" of the military-industrial complex. Liberal pacifists are particularly prone to consider any member of the committee guilty until proved innocent.* Such extremists ignore the individual records of the committee members. They draw no distinction between the contrasting positions of such doves as Ohio liberal Democrat Stephen Young (former Senator) and Iowa liberal Democrat Harold Hughes and such hawks as South Carolina conservative Republican Strom Thurmond and Arizona conservative Republican Barry Goldwater. They lump us all in the same bad bag.

In their attacks on the alleged warmongering puppets of the military-industrial complex, they conveniently ignore those instances of heated clashes between some of the committee members and the military brass. A prime example of this occurred in August of 1969, when eight of the eighteen members of the Senate Armed Services Committee voted against the Safeguard ABM (anti-ballistic-missile system). Despite our military backgrounds and affiliations† and despite our membership on the Armed Services Committee, we eight clearly went against the wishes of the military brass in voting against the Safeguard ABM.

For more than two years prior to this vote, I had expressed misgivings about the proposed anti-ballistic-missile system. In a Senate speech on March 21, 1967, I said:

It was with considerable reluctance that I joined the committee's approval of the authorization with respect to the deployment of an anti-ballistic-missile defense system. I can give no

* EDITOR'S NOTE: Typical of the opprobriums heaped on Senator Smith is what Jack and Gladys Sarda of Ellsworth, Maine, called her: "Top-killer . . . telling the world how to slaughter little people."
† Symington was the former first Secretary of the Air Force, Cannon a Major General in the Air Force Reserve, Young a Bronze Star decorated veteran, Inouye a Distinguished Service Cross decorated veteran, McIntyre a Bronze Star decorated retired Infantry Major, Brooke a Bronze Star decorated veteran, Schweiker a World War II aircraft carrier veteran, and myself a retired Lieutenant Colonel in the Air Force Reserve.

assurance that I will do so again next year . . . I am not
convinced that the ground placements of what may appear to be
Russia's anti-ballistic-missile defense system are what they seem
but rather they may be decoys of classic deception designed to
motivate us to a very costly defense system that may be obsolete
or become obsolete in the near future.

A year later I carried out my warning and voted against ABM
in the committee. On April 18, 1968, I explained:

But when the United States is relying upon the certainty of
devastating retaliation in order to deter an attack from the
Soviet Union, it makes little sense to me to deploy a ballistic-
missile defense system against Red China, which could have
over the next ten years, at least, only a small part of the
destructive power that the Soviet Union now possesses.

Despite this record of opposition, speculation persisted about
how I would vote when the roll was finally called on the Defense Procurement bill that contained the Safeguard ABM program. Neither opponents nor proponents of the Safeguard ABM
attempted to pressure me. Ken BeLieu of the White House staff
talked briefly with me but I made no commitment or sign of
one. After that the White House sought to reach me through the
ranking Republican on the Foreign Relations Committee, Senator
George D. Aiken.

One morning at nine-fifteen—and about fifteen minutes before he left Washington for Vermont—Senator Aiken called
and read to me the draft of a proposed compromise amendment
that the White House had given him. They had asked him to ask
me to present it later that morning at the Senate Armed Services
Committee executive meeting called to "mark up" and adopt
amendments to the Defense Procurement bill. Although the proposed amendment Aiken read to me seemed ambiguous, I wrote

it down and agreed to talk with Senators Stennis and Russell about it.

It appeared that the White House viewed the threat of defeat of the Safeguard ABM program as being sufficiently serious to warrant a move toward a compromise. Yet their proposed language did not strike me as a significant compromise. The ABM item in the bill was not taken up in the morning "mark-up" session but put over until afternoon. At the end of the morning session I asked Russell and Stennis to talk with me about the proposed White House compromise amendment. I read it to them and both stated they could not agree to it because of its ambiguity.

Consequently, I did not place the White House compromise amendment before the committee at the afternoon session. By a narrow margin the Safeguard ABM was left in the bill when voted on in the afternoon. I voted against it. After the session, I called Ken BeLieu at the White House and told him that Russell, Stennis, and I had all felt the language was too ambiguous. I read to him what Aiken had dictated to me over the telephone. BeLieu replied that somewhere in the transmission a serious discrepancy had entered because the White House was not willing to compromise, as in Aiken's amendment, to the point of barring further development of the ABM program.

This experience confirmed my reservations about the entire exercise. In the first place, it was odd that the White House would use the ranking Republican on the Foreign Relations Committee (a group openly opposed to the ABM and highly critical of the Armed Services Committee) as an intermediary to reach the ranking Republican on the Armed Services Committee. In the second place, it was poor to have waited until just an hour before the "mark-up" session to have the compromise relayed to me, leaving so little time for its consideration. And the fact that Senator Aiken had made the telephone call at the very last minute before he left for Vermont precluded any real chance for a realistic discussion as to exactly what the compromise proposed and meant. When Aiken returned to Washington, I told him of my subsequent talk with BeLieu and the disavowal of the language. At the request of the White House, Aiken continued to explore the possibilities of compromise. There were by now two proposed amendments: the Cooper-Hart and the McIntyre, the latter of which was more acceptable to the White House. Aiken made a Senate speech warning the White House that it would have to compromise or face defeat on the Safeguard ABM. The White House gave Aiken a redrafted proposed compromise. But the language of the redrafted compromise was so ambiguous no one would sponsor it. The White House even hedged about its participation. The result was that the whole assignment given Aiken by the White House ended up as an exercise in futility.

As the Senate debate on the ABM wound down and the voting drew near, I became more concerned about what seemed to be a significant inconsistency in the Cooper-Hart Amendment. Although it opposed deployment of the Safeguard ABM, it proposed to allocate more than three quarters of a billion dollars for development and research of the Safeguard ABM. This simply didn't make sense. Why would one propose to spend nearly a billion dollars to develop something on which he opposed deployment?

Yet no proposal had been brought forward which would give Senators the opportunity of voting against a cent for the Safeguard ABM. The alternatives the amendments permitted were either to vote for development of the Safeguard ABM or to vote for development *and* deployment of the Safeguard ABM. No opportunity was being given to vote against *both* development and deployment.

Because I was the top Republican on the Armed Services Committee, I had no desire to take the lead in opposing the Republican President. But I was willing to support any Senator who did and to vote for a "fish or cut bait" amendment. When it became clear that no one was going to take the lead, I told Bill to ask the Senate Legislative Counsel's office to draft an amendment.

Late in the afternoon of August 5 (the day before the vote on ABM) I rose on the Senate Floor and sent to the parliamentary desk for printing what I called my "fish or cut bait" amendment. It read:

> None of the funds authorized by this or any other Act may be used for carrying out, after the date of the enactment of this Act, any research, development, testing, evaluation, or procurement of the anti-ballistic-missile system known as the Safeguard system, or to carry out any research, development, testing, evaluation, or procurement of any part or component of such system.

I soon learned that both the opponents and proponents of the Safeguard ABM wondered what "Maggie" was up to. They thought I had some gimmick in my amendment. This attitude persisted with many throughout the entire consideration of the issue. My point was very simple and direct—I was opposed to spending a cent for the Safeguard ABM. In the Machiavellian world of Washington, simplicity and directness is so rare that it is suspect.

So that there would not be the slightest ambiguity or question about my amendment, early the next morning of August 6, I sent a letter to each of the ninety-nine other Senators stating:

August 6, 1969

Dear Senator:

I hope that you will give serious consideration to my Amendment No. 122 (a copy of which is attached) offered as a substitute to the Hart-Cooper Amendment No. 101.

My amendment is very simple as you can see from reading it—it proposes to bar any funds for the Safeguard ABM system whereas the Hart-Cooper Amendment would approve authorization of funds for research, development, testing, evaluation and normal procurement incident thereto.

I have no confidence in the Safeguard ABM system and if one

has no confidence in it then I cannot see the logic or justification in voting for research and development of it.

Furthermore, I think we should face up to the issue now of either being for or against the proposed Safeguard ABM system —instead of postponing the decision until next year or two or three years from now. The Hart-Cooper Amendment in supporting research and development on the Safeguard ABM system merely postpones the time of the decision and, if adopted now and every time this issue comes up, would result in having the issue annually debated without any clear decision resulting.

Finally, the adoption of my amendment would save a total of twelve and a half billion dollars. I shall detail this in my remarks on the Senate Floor this afternoon in support of my amendment.

Sincerely yours,
Margaret Chase Smith
United States Senator

The Senate opened its session on August 6 at 11 A.M., one hour earlier than usual. In the morning session, Tennessee Senator Albert Gore spoke in opposition to the Smith Amendment claiming that it might go even further than I had intended and adversely affect the Nike X advance development. He said that if my amendment could be limited to the Safeguard system and still allow research and development on other systems, the Cooper-Hart forces might then consider it.

His observations were made in a friendly and gentlemanly manner, but my private reactions were somewhat less than reciprocal. In the first place, I felt it was somewhat presumptuous to suggest that I had not thought my amendment through and that it might go further than I intended. Second, in making this observation it was Senator Gore who had failed to do his "homework" for the actual wording of my amendment was limited strictly to the Safeguard ABM system.

At 1:20 P.M. I rose to call up my "fish or cut bait" amendment, and after the Senate Reading Clerk read my amendment to the Senate, Senator Mansfield requested and obtained a recess from 1:24 P.M. to 1:55 P.M. After the recess, I began my speech:

Mr. President:

I am told that this morning my amendment was attacked on the claim that it went too far, for it would adversely affect the Nike X advance development.

Let me set the record straight. This is simply untrue. The adoption of my amendment will not affect the Nike X advance development. The bill has $141 million for Nike X under a separate account. This item was approved by our committee [Armed Services Committee] and has nothing to do with the Safeguard system.

In addition to the R. and D. for Nike X advance development, the Army seeks $3 million for anti-ballistic-missile activities in research and development funds at White Sands Missile Range. This also has nothing to do with Safeguard.

Mr. President, I offer this amendment in the nature of a substitute to the Hart-Cooper Amendment because I believe that the proposed Safeguard anti-ballistic-missile system is too vulnerable and too costly and would be a waste of resources at a time when we must carefully determine our national priorities.

Even the advocates of the Hart-Cooper Amendment have at length expounded on their opposition to the Safeguard ABM system. Yet, the Hart-Cooper Amendment is a partial approval of the Safeguard ABM system in that it proposes a compromise authorization for research, development, testing, evaluation, and normal procurement incident thereto for the Safeguard ABM system.

I don't approve of such a compromise and such authorization for the Safeguard ABM system. It would be a "foot-in-the-door" authorization for a system in which I have no confidence.

Why waste funds on research and development of a system in which you have no confidence? To do so is to beg the question.

Why not face the issue directly instead of obliquely? If you have no confidence in the Safeguard ABM system, then why vote for any kind of authorization for it in any manner?

Why vote for authorization of research and development of a system in which you have no confidence? Why vote to develop a system when you are opposed to deployment of such a system?

Mr. President, on the proposed ABM system, I find myself torn between the desire to grant to the President of the United States and the leader of my political party that which he feels is necessary and my own conscience that it is not only not necessary but would be an unwise application of resources.

The United States is the most resourceful nation in the world. But our resources are not unlimited. We must face up to the fact that there are limits and that those limits dictate a conscientious effort to establish priorities.

As I see it, the purpose and mission of the proposed ABM basically is deterrence—to deter Russia from a miscalculation of attacking the United States because we would have sufficient defenses for our missile sites.

To the contrary, I think offensive strength is the better deterrent and as such rates national security priority over the proposed ABM system. For what really deters Russia from attacking us is our offensive arsenal.

That is what the Soviets respect the most—that is what has stayed their hand during each confrontation starting with the first Berlin crisis on through the Cuban missile crisis—that is what has preserved the peace for two and a half decades—and it is that which is most likely to cause the Soviets to engage in meaningful talks on arms limitations.

I keep hoping that arms limitations talks will ultimately be productive—that the Soviets will be reasonable, sincere, and constructive—that we can bequeath a peaceful world to succeeding generations—that we can find accommodation with honor and security for each other and for the world.

But I am like the "show me" Missourian as I have watched the Soviets achieve a power status of first-class magnitude by developing devastating weapons in complete secrecy—boastfully parading them on so-called peaceful May Day repeatedly in great surprise to our best intelligence forces—and totally rejecting inspection procedures whether it be on the limited test ban or on nonproliferation of nuclear weapons.

And, Mr. President, I am convinced that the proposed Safeguard ABM system would be woefully inadequate against a massive Soviet attack on our country should the Russians decide to attack. Make no mistake about it, if the Russians decide to attack it will be a massive attack with full utilization of all of their devastating weapons on cities as well as missile sites.

There are those who seem to think that both the United States and Russia have reached a technological plateau and in this thinking tend to doubt the probability of the development of a system superior to the proposed ABM system.

I do not share this view. I do not think that either of the two countries has reached a technological plateau. Instead I think that technology is progressing so rapidly and that the state of the art is changing so swiftly that the proposed ABM will be obsolete and outmoded before it is ever put in place.

I don't want our nation and our people to have a 40 billion or 20 billion or even a 10 billion dollar obsolete white elephant ABM system on our hands.

I am without scientific knowledge, training, or ability. I certainly cannot speak with authority. But I certainly can speak with conviction—and I am convinced that the proposed ABM would be not only a tragic waste of money but even more tragically a self-deluding Maginot Line false sense of security.

Instead, I have greater confidence and faith in the ability of our scientists to develop a far more effective and far less costly system than the proposed ABM system.

I am sure that it is no breach of security when I say that I have great hopes that before too long a sufficiently powerful laser will be developed for the defense not only of our missile sites but as well of our people and our cities.

I have been dubious about the practicability of the proposed ABM system ever since it was first proposed. Frankly, it lacked credibility to me—both the system and the rationale for it.

I don't believe that we need have any fear of a nuclear attack on this country by Red China for many, many years. Red China simply doesn't have the capability to wage nuclear war against us and won't have for many, many years.

While I think the Russian Kremlin leaders—as differentiated from the Russian common man and woman—would destroy the United States without hesitancy if they thought it was to their advantage and they could do it without any great risk to Russia, I can't see the men in the Kremlin contemplating that now.

Why? Because I am sure that the increasing defiance of law and authority in the United States by growing dissent that has degenerated into violence and the open advocacy of, and militancy for, anarchy—that this trend is increasing the confidence of the men in the Kremlin that they, and their system of communism, can complete a Communist conquest of the United States without the necessity of firing a shot.

Why then should they devastate the resources of this nation with nuclear attack? Why would they want to have the tremendous problem of rehabilitating and reconstructing a nuclear-devastated country when they are growing so confident from trends here that their own advocates among Americans will ultimately deliver this country to them?

No, Mr. President, I simply can't buy the rationale of fear of the men in the Kremlin advanced in advocacy of the proposed ABM. I simply don't find it credible. And I have so told President Nixon.

For these reasons, I do not believe that we have to precipitously rush into a most dubious ABM system for fear that Russia is on the verge of attacking us—I do not believe that there is an imminent threat of such urgency as to preclude us from trying to develop a more effective and less costly system than the proposed ABM system within not too distant a future.

Reaching the decision that I have on the ABM has not been easy. As the ranking Republican on the Armed Services Committee, it is neither pleasant nor easy to oppose the Republican President on this issue.

In the past I opposed a Democratic President when he proposed the ABM.

I opposed him on the proposed thin system—on the Sentinel system—because I felt it would be obsolete before it could be put in place—and because I felt that the claim that it was for defense against Red China was not credible.

I have felt a personal obligation as the top Republican on the Committee on Armed Services to try to see my way to supporting the Republican President on this issue—and I have listened intently in trying to find the proposed Safeguard ABM system to be sufficiently improved over the Sentinel ABM system and sufficiently credible to change and support the leader of my own political party.

But I remain unconvinced—and I cannot see my way to change my position because it is now a Republican President making the proposal instead of a Democratic President.

I respect the sincerity of those who have opposed the President on some of his selections for high federal office and have successfully blocked him on those selections. I would hope that there would be a reciprocity of respect for my own sincerity in this ABM issue. I know that there is from President Nixon.

The more I study the history of the proposal of an ABM system the more evident becomes the lack of credibility and consistency of the rationale for it.

First, a thick ABM system was proposed on the basis of defending against Russia. Then when opposition developed to the proposed thick ABM because of its great cost, the shift was made to a thin ABM system on the basis of not defending against Russia but against Red China and on the rationale of cost effectiveness.

Thus, the first shift—from thick to thin—from defense against Russian attack to defense against Red Chinese attack.

Then sites were selected and plans started on the thin ABM sites in the defense of cities and population centers.

But then another rebellious tea party broke out in Massachusetts on the part of irate citizens of the locality of a proposed site in Massachusetts—and the political fat was in the fire.

And then came another shift in the theory and rationale of the ABM—the shift from the defense of cities and population centers to defense of the missile sites.

What has not been so apparent to many is another very decided shift—for now the talk in support of the proposed thin Safeguard ABM system is not for defense against Red China but rather for defense against Russia.

Thus, the rationale for an ABM system has made the full circle in shifting on the factor *of whom* it is proposed *to defend against,* for first it was the *thick* system to defend *against Russia,* then it shifted to the *thin Sentinel* system to defend *against Red China,* and now it is back to the *thin Safeguard* system to defend *against Russia.*

This shifting on *against whom to defend*—first Russia then Red China and then back to Russia—coupled with the shifting on *what to defend*—first the cities and population centers and now missile sites—not only taxes one's credulity but even challenges one's imagination as to what the next shift will be by the advocates of the ABM.

Mr. President, I have read that retaliatory action has been taken against some of us who oppose the ABM system. I find that difficult to believe because no such action against me has even been hinted. Instead, I have found President Nixon and members of his staff to be very patient and courteous and understanding about my opposition to the ABM.

On the other hand, Mr. President, it has been charged that opposition to the ABM is being used just to try to stop President Nixon. I think that is an unfair charge. In opposing the ABM, I am certainly not trying to stop President Nixon any more than are those in his own party who have opposed some of the administrative policies of his administration.

Mr. President, let me make it crystal clear that while I don't believe in the ABM, I do believe in America.

I do believe in our form of government—but I don't believe in the ABM.

I do believe in free enterprise—but I don't believe in the ABM.

I am for our American way of life—but I don't believe in the ABM.

The ABM is not an acid test of patriotism.

EDITOR'S NOTE:

This speech began what several members of the Washington press characterized as an unparalleled four-hour domination of the Senate by a single Senator. It was easily one of the most intense and dramatic sessions in the entire history of the Senate. One veteran of four decades of Senate service noted, "In all my years, I have never seen one Senator dominate the Senate Floor as long as she did. And to think that it would be the only woman in the one hundred Senators!"

At the height of the proceedings *Newsweek* reported Mike

Mansfield "cast an eye at his brethren hovering around Mrs. Smith's desk and said: 'I never saw so many men so publicly woo one woman.'"

By unanimous consent, debate on what was to be the first Smith Amendment was limited to an hour. It was not a particularly lively debate. The pro-ABM Senators were so confident that they could beat the amendment that they were not greatly concerned. In fact, a few like Senator Barry Goldwater chuckled about it. Goldwater said to me that Margaret had certainly put the anti-ABM forces on the spot with her "fish or cut bait" amendment. "Are you sure," he asked, "there wasn't a witch somewhere in Margaret's New England ancestry?"

The anti-ABM Senators favoring the Cooper-Hart Amendment actually were somewhat embarrassed by the direct logic of the Smith Amendment and used their time to sound out Senator Smith's willingness to consider a modification of her amendment. While several Senators on both sides of the issue were praising Senator Smith for her amendment [pro-ABM Senators Dole and Stevens and anti-ABM Senators Fulbright and Aiken], Senator Albert Gore strode over from the Democratic to the Republican side where I was standing near Senator Smith's desk. He took me by the arm, "Bill, let's talk for a minute." We stepped into the lobby corridor adjacent to the Senate Floor and Gore came to the point. "I think we can get behind Senator Smith's amendment if we can make some changes in the wording." "Senator, let us have a draft," I said.

Within a few minutes, Gore handed Senator Smith the suggested draft. She asked me what I thought about it. I read it and said, "Take it, Senator. It doesn't change your amendment one bit. They propose to make your amendment apply only to Safeguard and not to any other system. This is no change at all because your amendment applies only to Safeguard and not to any other system. It's just additional and repetitive words*—but I think this meaningless change gives them a chance to save face." Senator Smith was delighted with this development but carefully concealed her delight. [Later she laughed when *Time* magazine

---

* Additional language proposed by the Gore-Cooper-Hart forces said only that nothing contained therein should affect "any other" system.

said that the Cooper-Hart forces "sweet-talked" her into the second Smith Amendment.] Though she did consider it helpful because it emphasized and focused her opposition to the Safeguard ABM system rather than to all systems, she simply said that she was willing to accept the proposed "compromise" modification, and she asked me to tell Gore so.

When I had relayed the message, Gore then rose and addressed the presiding officer:

> Mr. President, I wonder if the distinguished senior Senator from Maine is agreeable to modifying her amendment as follows:
>
> On page 2, after the word "system," strike the period and insert a comma and the following words: "Provided that funds contained herein for research and development of radar and computer components of other weapons systems shall not be affected."?

Senator Smith replied:

> Mr. President, the Senator from Maine would be willing to accept the modification.

After a short colloquy among several Senators she then said:

> Mr. President, I ask unanimous consent that my amendment be modified as suggested by the distinguished Senator from Tennessee.

At this point, Goldwater's amusement over the "witchcraft" in the Smith Amendment evaporated. "I object," he said, and thereby blocked the modification for the time being. Senator Fulbright then made a parliamentary inquiry of "Would it be in order at a later date to offer the amendment with the modification the Senator from Maine has requested?" and the answer was in the affirmative. When Fulbright subsequently made the same unanimous consent Margaret had previously made, Stennis objected.

Just as emotions were reaching a peak, pro-ABM Senator John Sparkman presented the Right Honorable Horace Maybray King, the Speaker of the British House of Commons, and Senate Majority Leader Mansfield requested a brief suspension of debate.

While various members paid their respects to the British visitor, Senators Smith, Gore, Hart, Cooper, Symington, Fulbright, and Javits, together with Charlie Ferris of Majority Leader Mansfield's staff and Bill Miller of Senator Cooper's staff, huddled around a couch in the lobby-corridor off the Senate Floor. After a short exchange of views, I was summoned.

Senator Gore said, "Our concern is that it would bar research and development on *all* missile defense systems. That goes too far."

Senator Smith replied, "No, my opposition is centered solely on Safeguard, which I have no confidence in. I am agreeable to such *clarifying* language as you suggested in your note to me."

Javits said: "I'm disturbed by the word 'component'—whether it is so sweeping as to have a restrictive affect on the Sprint or Par systems because of the commonality of some components of the Safeguard with Sprint, Par, and other systems."

Symington said: "That troubles me as well. Is the Gore phraseology of 'component' too broad?"

They looked at me, expecting an answer. Uncomfortably surprised, I said, "I don't think so, for we have to be practical on the interpretation of 'component.' Such an objection could be extended to the argument that you couldn't even use a transistor from the Safeguard system in another system. I think this illustrates how practically the word 'component' would actually be interpreted."

By this time the courtesy welcome on the Senate Floor had

concluded and the Senate was ready to resume the ABM debate. The Senators returned to the Floor. Majority Leader Mansfield asked the presiding officer, Vice President Agnew, what the parliamentary situation was. The Vice President replied that it was a yea-and-nay roll call on the Smith Amendment.

An indication of the consensus agreement emerging from the lobby huddle came when Senator Symington asked, "After the vote on this amendment, will it be in order to offer another amendment?" The Vice President said it would be if the Smith Amendment were rejected. The roll was called, and the first Smith Amendment was defeated by the overwhelming margin of 89 to 11.* But this was just the beginning.

The Senate then returned to debate on the Cooper-Hart Amendment and during this time the draft of the second Smith Amendment containing the Gore-Cooper-Hart modification was polished up and copies were distributed. At this point Senator Smith arose to announce her second compromise that was to become the Senate's all-time cliff-hanger and set a record for the greatest number of votes cast in the history of the Senate. She said:

Mr. President. At the expiration of time on the Hart-Cooper Amendment I intend to offer another amendment, and for the information of the Senate I will read the amendment at this time. The amendment will be my original section 402, with an additional provision.

Sec. 402. None of the funds authorized by this or any other Act may be used for carrying out, after the date of this Act, any research, development, testing, evaluation, or procurement of the anti-ballistic-missile system known as the Safeguard system, or to carry out any research, development, testing, evaluation, or procurement of any part or component of such system: *Provided, That funds contained herein or elsewhere for*

---

* Only these ten other Senators supported the first Smith Amendment: Vermont's Aiken, Arkansas' Fulbright, Tennessee's Gore, Minnesota's McCarthy, South Dakota's McGovern, Maine's Muskie, Wisconsin's Nelson, Connecticut's Ribicoff, and Ohio's Saxbe and Young.

*research, development, test and evaluation of components, and
related procurement, of any other advanced anti-ballistic-missile
system or other weapons systems shall not be affected.*

Senator Cooper arose to say, "I have decided her [second]
amendment, in a different way, but as precisely and more clearly
accomplishes the purpose of our amendment." Senator Smith
replied, "The observations I made on my original amendment
apply to this amendment, for this amendment merely clarifies
my original amendment."
Senator Javits added:

   This does not mean that if Safeguard has a transistor that
we cannot deal with that transistor in another system, or a
weapon, or a Sprint, or a Par, or anything else that happens
to be in the Safeguard system.

The pro-ABM Senators claimed the modification was no dif-
ferent from the original Smith Amendment. Texas Senator
Tower insisted that the modification "acutally changes nothing."
Senate Dean Georgia Senator Richard B. Russell said:

   I congratulate the distinguished Senator from Maine. If she
succeeds in having her amendment adopted in its present form,
she will have carried the original amendment, or it will have
that very effect. There cannot be any possible question about
that.

Javits, replying for the anti-ABM forces, protested that "the
interpretations are substantive." To which Senator Smith carefully and precisely replied:

Mr. President, the proof that there is a substantial difference between my original amendment and this new amendment as proposed is that the latter has been accepted by the sponsors of the Cooper-Hart amendment.

As far as she was concerned, the substantive difference was in the clarification of her amendment.

Pro-ABM Kansas Senator Dole (later to become Republican National Committee Chairman) asked, "Do I understand that her present substitute is for the same purpose, to prohibit funds for Safeguard research or development?" To which Senator Smith answered with her repeated point, "Of the Safeguard, that is correct."

Barry Goldwater asked sarcastically whether the name could be changed from Safeguard to "Rightguard" or "Outguard," to which Senator Smith sweetly said she would not answer "yes" or "no."

Pro-ABM Senator John C. Stennis of Mississippi and Chairman of the Senate Armed Services Committee shouted:

It is a legislative monstrosity . . . every word that was in the first Smith Amendment about Safeguard is in this amendment. Senators who have been saying they are for research for Safeguard and for this amendment are going to have awfully red faces and they are going to be trying to get out of that situation. That is why I say it is tragic. It is compounded tragedy.

The only uncommitted Senators were Delaware's John J. Williams and New Mexico's Clinton Anderson. As the debate time began to run out, Senator Fulbright crossed the Floor and whispered to Senator Smith, "Margaret, Clint Anderson is with you and his vote may put your amendment over the top."

Immediately after that, Senator Anderson arrived at her desk and said, "Margaret, I'm with you. Do you need any more time on this? If you do, I'll get Mike Mansfield to give it to you." Margaret thanked him and said she didn't need any more time.

And immediately after that, pro-ABM Senator Jackson, who is perhaps Anderson's closest friend in the Senate (Jackson married a secretary of Anderson's), went over to Anderson's desk and was seen talking very earnestly with him. Watching these walks across the Senate Floor—Fulbright to Smith, Anderson to Smith, and then Jackson to Anderson—was like watching the last two minutes of a tied basketball game. It was these final walks and talks that were to decide the ultimate legislative fate of Safeguard.

Finally the roll was called and it ended in a 50 to 50 tie. This was Senate history—one of the extremely rare times of a tie vote with all members voting and the first tie vote with one hundred Senators voting. The Vice President voted against the second Smith Amendment making the final tally 51 to 50 and the largest total vote in the history of the Senate.*

Then came the roll call vote on the Cooper-Hart Amendment. Senator Smith had said again and again during the debate that she was opposed to it. She was against it simply because she was opposed to spending a cent for the Safeguard ABM and the Cooper-Hart Amendment proposed to spend nearly a billion dollars for development and research on Safeguard. Yet, when she voted against it, a surprising number of persons accused her of reversing herself. She was pilloried by much of the liberal press. One ultra-liberal Washington TV commentator went so far as to accuse her of duplicity.

Even the astute Rhode Island Democratic Senator John Pastore, a pro-ABM Senator and opponent of the Cooper-Hart Amendment, told me a few weeks later she had voted against the Cooper-Hart Amendment because she thought she had been betrayed. When I pointed out that she had said repeatedly she

---

* The Vice President need not have voted because a tie vote is treated as a defeat and rejection by the Senate rules. Had either Senator Williams or Senator Anderson voted for the second Smith Amendment, it would have carried 51 to 49, eliminating a tie and the right of the Vice President to cast a vote. But both Anderson and Williams voted against the second Smith Amendment.

was opposed to spending a cent for Safeguard, Pastore refused to grant credibility to what she had said.

In contrast, the authors of the Cooper-Hart Amendment graciously defended her, giving her credit for voting consistently even though it was against their amendment. Senator Cooper said, "Her position was consistent because our amendment did permit research on the Safeguard system. She is consistent, courageous, independent, and very influential." Senator Hart said, "I certainly have no reason to believe she was voting other than what her convictions told her to do. We didn't expect her support. We took her position at face value. I can ascribe no roundabout motivation to her. After all, she almost knocked out the whole program." Perhaps the fairest and most objective evaluation by any publication came from *Newsweek*, the liberal weekly magazine. It characterized her actions as that of "one unblinkingly logical lady" with the "utterly consistent argument that Safeguard—if it is indeed evil—shouldn't have any funds at all."

The most incisively accurate analysis appeared in the monthly magazine *Air Force* (pro-ABM) in which senior editor Claude Witze wrote:

Then there was the lady, Republican Senator Margaret Chase Smith of Maine, who was torn between her anti-Safeguard convictions and what she said was "a personal obligation as the top Republican on the Committee on Armed Services to try to see my way to supporting the Republican President on this issue."

She was opposed to Safeguard because she has no confidence in it. She said the system lacks credibility and that the rationale for it is inconsistent.

There were Senators who put up a good argument in contradiction to Mrs. Smith, but there was no Senator to challenge her cool logic. She offered a "fish-or-cut-bait amendment" . . . she faced strenuous courting by her less straightforward friends . . . She voted against it [Cooper-Hart Amendment], and

there is no man in the Senate ready to quarrel with her logic
or her intellectual honesty.

The Senator's favorite summary and evaluation of her speech
was written by conservative columnist Holmes Alexander, pro-
ABM and a no-nonsense journalist. He wrote:

The U. S. Senate isn't a gentlemen's club, just a genteel
club, for the most part. Margaret Chase Smith, R-Maine, is
the reason why.

For most of her tenure, Sen. Smith has been the lone lady
member, and it is her lady-likeness which counts the most.
Not only is she beautiful and bright at 71, but she has the
relentless logic of womanhood at its finest and she inspires a
chivalry that keeps 99 gentlemen genteel.

When the Senate's debate on the Safeguard ABM reached
its climax, Aug. 6–7, she was the star, and the men only
players by comparison. "Maggie's exercise in futility," said
somebody in the too-noisy gallery, as time approached to vote
on her amendment which would have abolished Safeguard and
spent the money on general research for "another" ABM.

This wasn't an altogether sensible idea, and it perished 89–11
in the voting, but Sen. Smith wasn't finished. She accepted
modifying language, by Senators Gore and Case, and tried
another amendment which lost by a tie vote, 50–50, but her
ultimate good sense came through in her main speech if not
in the countdown.

Unlike others who voted with her, Mrs. Smith did not "trust
the Russians." To the contrary, she didn't believe that Safeguard
would stop Russian missiles, but she did believe that fear of
America's offensive weapons would do so, and that a better
ABM could be developed by use of laser beams.

It was in her estimate of Soviet psychology that Mrs. Smith
surpassed all other members in sensibility. She made mincemeat
of male arguments which came before and after. Only "our
offensive arsenal," she said, "has restrained the Soviets."

Nothing else but respect for American nuclear might "has

stayed their hand" at every confrontation from Berlin to Cuba. If "the Russian Kremlin leaders" (she gave no names) could advantageously get away with attack, they would let loose "all their devastating weapons on cities as well as missile sites."

Mrs. Smith demolished the argument, by Sen. Ted Kennedy and others, that upcoming arms-talks with Russia could make Safeguard and other weapons unnecessary. The Soviet Union had achieved great-power status among nations "by developing devastating weapons in great secrecy."

The USSR had celebrated so-called peaceful May Days, year after year, by "boastfully parading" arms which our intelligence forces have failed to anticipate. Russia has consistently refused inspection procedures on both the nuclear treaties with the U.S.

Sen. Smith's psychoanalysis of Soviet Russia now hit its high point. The Kremlin leaders, although without conscience or remorse, had other reasons for not launching an attack. She said that "dissent . . . violence . . . anarchy . . ." in the U.S. was a reason why the Russians wouldn't shoot their missiles at us.

Those men in the Kremlin, she said, had "confidence" that they can complete "a Communist conquest of the United States without firing a shot." So why should the Kremlin leaders destroy American resources which they "avidly covet" when it appeared that "Americans would ultimately deliver this country to them."

This part of Sen. Smith's speech, the part that made it so exceptional, went largely unreported in the press. Her anti-Safeguard amendment, which so nearly won, got most of the play. But her ferocious feminine instinct on Soviet mentality, and American social vulnerability to communism, was where she shone the brightest.

That was Maggie Smith's finest hour.

The press account that amused the Senator the most was by the Scripps-Howard war correspondent and military writer Jim G. Lucas. Back in 1953 before the Armed Services Committee vote on Jimmy Stewart, Lucas had written in his column that

the Senator was going to get clobbered, that the committee would
overwhelmingly approve of Stewart. The result had been exactly
opposite.

With this past history in mind, she smiled now as she read
Lucas' piece of August 7, 1969:

Finally they produced a compromise . . . After that, there
was much talk about what it really said, what it all meant,
and who had said what. The Senator from Maine kept her
cool. Tempers flared briefly between a couple of members—
"You said I was absurd," Sen. Tower yelled at Sen. Stuart
Symington, D-Mo.—but the Senator from Maine continued to
smile.

The trouble, Sen. Goldwater snorted, was that there isn't
another ABM system in the works. Sen. Richard B. Russell,
D-Ga., said Mrs. Smith was "too smart a legislator not to
know that." Mrs. Smith seemed, at times, to agree they were
right, but by now it no longer mattered.

. . . "Margaret Chase Smith is a first-class Senator," Sen.
Mike Mansfield, D-Mont., an ABM opponent, said later. "She
has a mind of her own."

Someone else put it differently.

"Maggie foxed them again."

Four months later she was still opposed to spending a cent
for Safeguard. Senator Cooper came to her office on Saturday
morning, December 13, 1969, to talk about the Safeguard
item in the Defense Appropriations Bill scheduled for a Senate
vote the next Monday. He told her that he had talked with
Majority Leader Mike Mansfield and told him that she, Cooper,
and Hart were thinking about offering an amendment to knock
the Safeguard funds out of the Defense Appropriations Bill. He
reported that Mansfield had said that was fine, that he had encouraged them to get on with it.

During that Saturday morning conference, a long distance call
was relayed to Senator Cooper. His mother had had a stroke. He

left at once for Kentucky, and the following Monday Senator Smith offered the anti-Safeguard amendment.

Her amendment was defeated 49 to 36, but she was not surprised at the outcome. Her only surprise was in the number of defections from the 50 to 50 vote on August 6. The most surprising defection was that of Mike Mansfield, since only two days before Cooper had reported that Mansfield had urged Cooper to offer the amendment with Senator Smith. Other defections were Aiken of Vermont, Burdick of North Dakota, McIntyre of New Hampshire, and Pearson of Kansas.*

Although the liberal anti-Safeguard press had pilloried Senator Smith for her vote against the Cooper-Hart Amendment, it made no criticism of these five Senators who reversed their actions on the Safeguard appropriations. Nor did the anti-ABM Washington TV commentator accuse these five of the duplicity he had so freely ascribed to Senator Smith.

She herself did not criticize any of them. They changed their votes because the Safeguard authorization had been approved even though they had voted against it, and she accepted their explanations.

Although he voted against her December 15 anti-ABM amendment, it was not long before Senator Mansfield was paying tribute to Senator Smith's ESP. On February 4, 1970, he called the Senate's attention to her prediction of another shift in the rationale for supporting ABM. He said:

> Last year, the President, quite properly in my judgment, announced that the Sentinel system was being abandoned because it could not be made to work to defend cities against a hypothetical attack of Soviet warheads and because he would not "buy" the contention of its value for that purpose against a hypothetical attack of Chinese warheads. Yet, this year it is proposed that Safeguard be extended to include defense of cities against precisely such an attack from Chinese sources. It

* Nine anti-ABM Senators either were absent or gave live pairs, thus accounting for the fourteen difference between the August 6 and December 15 votes.

is disturbing to find the facts stating one conclusion one year and the same facts stating the opposite the next. A true credibility gap does, indeed, open up when, each year for four years, these changing rationales are presented for the same system. As the distinguished Senator from Maine (Mrs. Smith) so aptly stated last year:

"This shifting on against whom to defend—first Russia then Red China then back to Russia—coupled with the shifting of what to defend—first the cities and population centers and now the missile sites—not only taxes one's credulity but even challenges one's imagination as to what the next shift will be by the advocates of the ABM."

I fear that the "next shift" of which the distinguished Senator from Maine spoke about is about to be presented.

Having shown how well Senator Smith's speech had worn with time, Mansfield made reference to the developments at the two ABM sites, one in his own state at Malmstrom Air Force Base, Montana, and the other in the state of ABM-opponent Quentin Burdick at Grand Forks, North Dakota. Nine months after the Mansfield tribute to her, Margaret made a visit to these two Safeguard sites to try to discover some reason that she had been wrong in opposing Safeguard.

What she saw and what she heard only confirmed her original doubts. The Safeguard programs at these two sites looked more like WPA make-work programs and population relocation movements than true missile defense. The briefers at these two sites did not speak with conviction or enthusiasm for the programs.

They spoke more in terms of community development and expansion than in terms of national defense.

She came away all the more convinced that Safeguard would be a waste of billions of dollars at best and another boondoggle at worst. Concurrently she was receiving reports that tremendous strides had been made on the development of a potential laser defense against missiles. The chances for developing lasers powerful enough to project power at required distances had never been brighter.

She still believes a laser defense will be developed sooner than most are willing to admit and that (without the nuclear radiation fallout of the Safeguard system) it will be a cleaner and much less expensive defense.

Declaration of Conscience II

JUNE 1, 1970

"Once again, you have said in your own quiet, concise, and persuasive manner what many of us have been thinking and all too few have been able to clearly articulate."

—Hubert Humphrey
June 3, 1970

"It was indeed fitting and timely that you should speak out as you did on the Twentieth Anniversary of your 'Declaration of Conscience.' Your counsel of reasoned judgment was needed then, and is needed now. I thank you."

—Richard M. Nixon
June 5, 1970

Ever since my statement on June 1, 1950, denouncing McCarthyism without using the word or referring by name to the Senator, I have repeatedly received requests, pleas, demands to make another Declaration of Conscience. The contention that "it is time to make another Declaration of Conscience" has come from persons on both extreme ends of the ideological spectrum and practically every shading in the middle.

Yet, in many of these instances, those asking had an axe to grind and clearly wanted to use me to advance their own subjective views and goals.

Worthy as many of the requests have been, I declined them. In the first place, I believe that frequency of expression—like an excess of currency—inescapably dilutes its value and effectiveness. Frequency tends to lessen credibility. In the second place, a statement does not have real meaning and validity unless I am moved to make it, rather than prodded by someone else.

For twenty years after the Declaration of Conscience, I was tempted on occasion to make such a second Declaration but I did not until June 1, 1970. What was there that was so different, so sufficiently motivating to cause me to do in 1970 what I had declined to do in the intervening nineteen years? Some slight motivation may have come from the date itself—the twentieth anniversary of the first Declaration. But basically, my utterance was a reaction to a long accumulation of growing diseases in the body politic, diseases threatening literally to destroy the fundamental concepts and values that had made the United States the freest and greatest nation in history. To me, in 1950, the Communist threat of "confuse, divide, and conquer" was real—but the McCarthy blunderbuss-shotgun approach ultimately was acting to help and serve the Communist design of conquest.

I saw our Nation survive the disease of McCarthyism. But a decade after my first Declaration, there were symptoms of another illness beginning to take hold. The disease this time was unlimited and crass pragmatism—the creed that the end justifies the means. While there was much of this element in McCarthyism, in this new outbreak, ironically, it was more subtle yet more pervading. In fact, it had a sanction and credibility that McCarthyism never even remotely approached. Such respectability came from the eager acceptance of crass pragmatism in avant-garde form by famous leaders of the intellectual community, the academic field, as well as the "jet set," the cultured theater, the arena of sports, the hallowed halls of theology, the military profession—and perhaps foremost, government and politics.

I have given several speeches, echoing the eloquence of Charles H. Brower, the champion crusader of "The Square." In a December 23, 1964, recording for an RCA album for release in 1965, I paid tribute to The Square in my own words but with a dominance and emphasis on denunciation of pragmatism:

> In today's growing, but tragic, emphasis on materialism, we find a perversion of the values of things in life as we once knew them. For example, the creed once taught children as they grew up was that the most important thing was not in whether you won or lost the game but rather in "how you played the game."
>
> That high level attitude that stresses the moral side no longer predominates in this age of pragmatic materialism that increasingly worships the opposite creed that "the end justifies the means" or the attitude of get what you can in any way, manner, or means that you can.
>
> This perversion of values has even prostituted our semantics, for the meaning of once revered and honored words has even been changed in this glorification of pragmatism. The word "character" used to have an honorable meaning for it indicated intelligence with heart and a high sense of ethics—it meant courage of one's convictions. Its connotation was determination, integrity, responsibility, and honor.
>
> But today we hear it used increasingly in a derogatory sense. For many of us will refer to an eccentric or a person who is abnormal or strange as a "character." The "character" is

equated with an "oddball"—or he is equated with another formerly honored word that has now been perverted in today's pragmatic lingo—the word "square."

The dictionary definitions of the word "square" include: "According with ordinary justice; fair; just; equitable; honest; accurately adjusted"; and "Having debt and credit balanced; even; settled."

When you were "on the square" you were acting in an honest and fair manner. You had paid your debts. You were honest. You were fair.

But what is a "square" today? He's the fellow who has pride in playing a fair game—instead of being interested only in the result. He's the fellow who is laughed at because he refuses to take the short cut of cheating or to short-change his fellow man. He's the eager beaver who gives everything he does the "old college try"—who believes the sin is the dishonest act not just in getting caught and not in trying to get away with something dishonest.

He's the fellow who makes his lazy fellow workers mad because he volunteers, excels, puts forth that little extra effort, and is genuinely interested in his job and his responsibility. He's the fellow whose interest is in doing the best job he can instead of the pragmatic interest of only holding a job.

He's the fellow with feeling whose spine tingles, whose heart beats faster with pride when he hears the song of his alma mater or the national anthem and when he stands at attention as the flag unfurls. He's the fellow willing to get "involved" in emotional defense of principles instead of hiding behind a "cool and cozy" silence.

But he's the fellow who is so derogated these days by the sophisticates, who deride the things he stands for, that too many of us remain mutes who do not speak out in defense of the principles he stands for because we fear that if we do we too will be called "squares."

He's the prime victim of today's pragmatic materialism. And he is a continuing target of those who debase our fundamental moral principles. Tragically he is a dying breed, and when the last of his breed has passed on, then so will the moral decay of our country and our civilization have become complete, and the triumph of the pragmatist over the "character" and the "square" have become total.

I was deeply disturbed by the youthful adulation of openly immoral movie stars, people glamorized by the news media for their flaunting of heretofore widely accepted moral codes. Such codes made for the protection of the family as an institution and for individual dignity and privacy. The actions of such performers were widely sanctioned under the guise of the new morality and the new sexuality; they were said to be the really beautiful people with the real honesty to do their thing. They were becoming examples for the younger generation to follow.

To me, they were prime examples of the creed of unlimited pragmatism: get whatever you want whatever way you want to regardless of how amoral, ruthless, or unfair the means.

I was disturbed also by the similarly selfish pragmatism of the "beautiful people" of the jet set, their open flaunting of their wealth and defiance of moral codes, but even more so by the glamour in which the news media cloaked them. Culture idols of the younger generation. Emulate them and you reach the peaks of highest society.

I was disturbed with the hero worship of boxing champions with repeated crime convictions. Emulate them and become champion of the world. I was disturbed with football champions who commercialized and exploited their alleged sex behavior. Emulate them and you command all the wealth, power, and happiness that anyone could dream of. I held priceless the derogatory observation of a Green Bay pro footballer, Jerry Kramer, when the New York Jets won their championship victory in 1969. He called it "a body blow to clean living."

I was troubled by the growing trend of military leaders who prostituted their principles by selling their silence for one or two more years' extension of power and postponement of forced retirement—and who suddenly, after their retirement, found their tongues, their consciences, their principles, and their publication capability. The example to younger officers was clear: trade your principles and silence for promotion and retention.

I was troubled not only by widespread cheating in the academic world but even more by the growing acceptance of it as part of education—and by the sophistry of the academic leaders' attitude toward it. Yes, it was no more than an exercise or implementation of the pragmatic code that the end justifies the means and get whatever you can regardless of how you do it. I was surprised at the number of academicians who defended "pragmatism."

I was distressed by high ranking prelates and theologians who used their churches and pulpits as springboards for sensationalism and for exotic, personalized revisions of theology both for the monetary gains of commercialism and egoistic publicity. Inescapably, they undermined the credibility of the church with the younger generation.

Perhaps most of all, I was unhappy about the unlimited new pragmatism within my own field of government and politics. Increasing numbers of emerging leaders in the Legislative and Executive branches of the government were becoming symbols and personifications of this ugly practice. They not only showed the youth of our country how to use raw power or money and position to ruthlessly destroy anything in their path toward the pinnacle of power, but they encouraged them to follow and imitate their crusades of pragmatism to extenuate their own seizure of power. The extent to which they were successful in selling this image of ruthless revolution could be seen in the manner in which their youthful followers aped their gestures, their tonal inflections, and their physical appearance.

In the Senate itself, I saw the mushrooming of the practice of "moonlighting" in which growing numbers of Senators had little time for the Senate or their other official duties because of heavy schedules of high-paid lectures and deliberate building of their national images. Being a Senator to them was not a dedicated career but only the pragmatic means to an end— outside the Senate. One example of this was a Senator who publicly derided attendance of the Senate and staying on the job.

He said that any Senator who answered 85 percent or more of the roll call votes simply wasn't doing his job—that instead of being present to vote on legislation, the Senators should be traveling throughout the country making speeches. I wondered what had happened to the old concept that Senators were elected to legislate—to debate and vote on legislation. Here in my own arena, the United States Senate, was unlimited pragmatism in its rawest, crudest form.

The seeds for disillusionment, disrespect, disgust, resentment, and ultimately revolution were not only planted by leaders in the various fields, but they were cultivated and nurtured, consciously and unconsciously, by them. It is no wonder what followed. Vietnam did not cause it. Vietnam was only a convenient rallying point and a useful excuse for the extremism of the revolt that exploded into murder, arson, assault, and violent trespass. It is no wonder that a President was literally forced to evacuate the White House rather than face a re-election campaign.

Given a mandate to get us out of Vietnam—actually on "either-or-else" ultimatum by the electorate—the new President responded by reversing the previous policy of combat involvement and escalation and started bringing the boys back home. This was not enough for the extremists. It was not enough for crassly pragmatic politicians, who had supported Presidents Kennedy and Johnson on getting us combat-involved and escalated and suddenly attacked President Nixon for failing to get us out completely. They deliberately fanned the fires of dissension and revolt. They deliberately accelerated the polarization of our people to further their own political ambitions. And they were given extremely active and extended accommodation by the news media, particularly the television networks.

The excesses of irresponsible pragmatism helped produce and then proliferate polarization.

It was then completely understandable to me that President Nixon would defend himself and that Vice President Agnew, long a target of ridicule by the news media, would go to the defense of President Nixon. At first I approved the effective defense made, even the virulent criticism by the Vice President of the television networks. I felt that many of his remarks were justified and felt that the prejudices of the telecasts were obvious—and from the first public reaction so did a great majority of Americans.

I admired the courage of ABC-TV commentator Howard K. Smith in defending the Vice President and in agreeing with him on his criticism of the TV networks and commentators. I agreed with Mr. Smith's critical analyses against the extremists of the left and against the intellectuals who advocated and defended resort to violence. He was not an extreme Rightist. This was a TV network commentator who has stood up against Joe McCarthy and the extremists of the Right when I had, twenty years ago.

Yet, after a while, I had to conclude that Vice President Agnew, after making his point extremely well, had overreacted to the shrill overreaction of the TV networks and commentators to his valid criticism of them. I felt that he had used words, however justified they might be, that were better not said. Better left unsaid because they were intensifying the polarization of our people as much as the words of extreme Leftists and the TV networks and commentators were. Understandable as President Nixon's use of the word "bums" was—and even though it was meant only to apply to those "burn, baby, burn" extremists of violence—it was unfortunate. Its ambiguity was seized upon by his critics with the false claim that he had impugned all students. It was something better not said for, however unintentional, it contributed to the growing split.

Then came Kent State on May 4, 1970. That shock convinced me that it was truly time to speak. So I told Bill Lewis to start working on a statement and to key it back to my first Declaration twenty years past. I set June 1, 1970, as the date to read it in the United States Senate.

At this time I was in constant and extreme pain in my right hip. The pain was almost unbearable and Bill said that the strain was showing in my face. I made a concurrent decision to have a second hip operation (the previous one having been on my left hip in 1968) some time after making my second Declaration and tentatively planned to enter the Columbia-Presbyterian Hospital in New York on the weekend of July 4.

The day after Kent State, a group of striking college students in Maine, headed by the President of the student body at Colby College, released to the press a telegram the group reported it was sending to me. It called upon me to "return home and address yourself to the people whom you represent." It was more of a demand than an invitation, something similar to a command performance. As for my obligation to report to my constituents, it was amusing that the telegraphed demand was headed up by the President of the Colby student body, who was not a resident of Maine but rather of Massachusetts. In fact, 90 percent of the Colby students were non-Maine residents. The telegram was never delivered. We got notice of it in the newspapers and did respond.

The time set for the command performance was Sunday afternoon, May 10. The spokesman for the striking students was told by Bill Lewis that I could not make it on Sunday afternoon because of previous commitments but would be willing to do so either on Friday or Saturday afternoon.

The student spokesman demanded that I cancel my Sunday commitment and insisted that I had to give them first priority. Lewis responded that they had their choice of Friday or Saturday. If they accepted neither, that was their decision and responsibility. Senator Smith, he said, would not surrender to their demand for Sunday. The student spokesman said that they would accept Saturday.*

I stood on the steps of the Colby Library before an estimated crowd of two thousand students (newspaper crowd estimates are notoriously inflated) and faced taunts, invectives, and obscenities for an hour and a half. The pain in my right hip was

* EDITOR'S NOTE: Later we learned that the students paid for a chartered plane to fly Senator Muskie to meet with them on Sunday. This was in keeping with the contrast of their treatment of the two Senators: warm praise for Senator Muskie obviously because he attacked Nixon on Vietnam and insults for Senator Smith because she defended President Nixon and most specifically on the Cambodian incursion.

intense. I said very frankly that I was there at their request, that I was not there to make a speech or to lecture, that instead I was there to listen to them and to try to answer their questions, however much they might disagree.

The situation was tense but was kept under relatively good order. They calculated to embarrass me by producing a young retired army lieutenant (from Bowdoin College) who had been injured in Laos. (Later, some at Colby attempted to blame Bowdoin for the discourtesies to me.) Three times during the hour-and-a-half confrontation, it was suggested to Bill Lewis that the questioning be terminated—first by the President of Colby, second by their public relations officer, and finally by the Colby student President presiding. To each of the three approaches, Bill replied that "Senator Smith is here for as long as they want to confront and challenge her." That was the way I wanted it.

It was perhaps the most unpleasant experience of my entire public service career. At one time Colby College was one of the places I most enjoyed visiting. The faculty was friendly, as were the students. But time brought changes. A campaign was mounted on the Colby campus in 1954 to run a member of the faculty against me for United States Senator, a history professor who had invited me to speak to his classes, praising my work as public service at its best. The Dean of Women at Colby had advocated my defeat in an address to the Girls State on the Colby campus. A Colby student hurling obscenities at me during the confrontation had been financed in his schooling by a Colby trustee, a sincere friend of mine. (Later, with much chagrin, this Colby trustee apologized for the boy's behavior.)*

The discourtesies of some of the striking students from sixteen Maine colleges assembling on the Colby campus for the con-

---

* EDITOR'S NOTE: While Margaret Smith has been awarded sixty-seven honorary degrees by institutions from Maine to Florida to California to Canada, Colby has the distinction of being the only one to award her an honorary *master's* degree. The discrepancy between that degree and the sixty-six doctorates is undoubtedly explained by Colby's failure to perceive Margaret Chase Smith's future potential at the time of awarding her an honorary master's, a true rarity in honorary degrees.

frontation had nothing to do with my decision to make a second Declaration of Conscience. But the shock of that experience did affect some of the language I ultimately used. The experience brought home to me, as nothing else had, the threateningly high intensity of the polarization. I had been troubled but now I observed to friends that one could not deeply sense the intensity of the division unless personally experiencing it. Unpleasant as it was, I found it valuable because I could speak from experience, rather than from what I had merely read or heard.

On returning to the Washington office on Monday, I told Bill Lewis I would like to talk with Howard K. Smith. His position in his TV commentaries had been parallel to my thinking—just as it had been twenty years before on Joe McCarthy and his tactics. The next day, Howard K. Smith accepted my invitation to lunch and the time was set for Friday, May 15.

The day before, came the Jackson State killings of May 14. At lunch I told Howard K. Smith that I had decided to make a second Declaration of Conscience on June 1, two weeks from then. I related my growing concern, the contrast between 1950 when I had denounced the attempted repression by extreme Rightists and now 1970 when my concern was about the anarchism of the extreme Leftists.

Mr. Smith expressed agreement with my ideas, with the decision to make a second Declaration, and with the timing. I asked him if he would give us some written suggestions for the second Declaration. His response was that an editorial in the *Wall Street Journal* was the best expression he had seen and recommended it as better than anything he could suggest. His response was not only extremely helpful because of the excellence of the editorial, but it was discreet and wise. It precluded his commenting on television about wording he might have suggested.

The drafting centered around the wording of the first Declaration with the flavor of the *Wall Street Journal* editorial added. I considered the second Declaration to be, in essence, an updating of the first. No one else was consulted on it. The actual drafting of the second Declaration was done only by me and Bill Lewis.

Though I did not disclose in advance that I was going to make the first Declaration, this time we announced that I would made a statement. I did not disclose the contents or tone of the second Declaration, however, prior to the actual delivery.

The closest I came to an advance revelation of the contents was on the morning NBC-TV "Today" show on June 1, 1970. Our advance notice had prompted the Washington correspondent of the "Today" program, Bill Monroe, to ask me to do the guest spot that morning. Most of the discussion between us in that appearance related to the first Declaration of twenty years past, why I had made it then, my relations with Joe McCarthy, and how I viewed the national scene twenty years later.

I said that the threatening extremism in 1950 was from the far Right, in 1970 it was from the far Left, and I pointed out that extremism produced not only violent reactions but a tendency, among the great moderate majority of Americans to draw back in disgust into their mental shells and not speak up. After the interview was completed in Washington, Hugh Downs, "Today's" man-in-charge, at that time, in a post-interview commentary in New York, discounted the fears that I expressed for 1970. Many viewers felt that Downs had literally put me down.*

That afternoon, June 1, 1970, I made my second Declaration of Conscience, by saying:

Twenty years ago on this June First date at this same desk I spoke about the then serious national condition with a state-

---

* EDITOR'S NOTE: If Senator Smith felt that, in this instance, a man had gotten in the last word, or that Downs had "put her down" and should have given an opportunity to answer his observations, she never said so and never complained. She did not comment on the matter. Yet she gave some indication. She said that she was confident that the "Today" show's newscaster, Frank Blair, was in agreement with her concern because of a very forceful commencement address he had given the year before at Nasson College in Springvale, Maine, when he and Senator Smith had received honorary degrees.

ment known as the "Declaration of Conscience." We had a national sickness then from which we recovered. We have a national sickness now from which I pray we will recover.

I would like to recall portions of that statement today because they have application now twenty years later.

I said of the then national condition, "It is a national feeling of fear and frustration that could result in national suicide and the end of everything that we Americans hold dear." Surely that is the situation today.

I said then, "I speak as briefly as possible because too much harm has already been done with irresponsible words of bitterness and selfish political opportunism." That is not only the situation today, but it is even worse for irresponsible words have exploded into trespass, violence, arson, and killings.

I said then, "I think that it is high time for the United States Senate and its members to do some soul searching—for us to weigh our consciences—on the manner in which we are performing our duty to the people of the United States—on the manner in which we are using or abusing our individual powers and privileges."

That applies today. But I would add this to it—expanded application to the people themselves, whether they be students or construction workers, whether they be on or off campus.

I said then, "Those of us who shout the loudest about Americanism in making character assassinations are all too frequently those who, by our own words and acts, ignore some of the basic principles of Americanism—

The right to criticize;
The right to hold unpopular beliefs;
The right to protest;
The right to independent thought."

That applies today—and it includes the right to dissent against dissenters.

I said then, "The American people are sick and tired of being afraid to speak their minds lest they be politically smeared . . . Freedom of speech is not what it used to be in America. It has been so abused by some that it is not exercised by others."

That applies today to both sides. It is typified by the girl student at Colby College who wrote me, "I am striking with my heart against the fighting in Cambodia but I am intimidated by those who scream protests and clench their fists and cannot listen to people who oppose their views."

I said then, "Today our country is being psychologically divided by the confusion and the suspicions that are bred in the United States Senate to spread like cancerous tentacles of 'know nothing, suspect everything' attitudes."

That applies today—but it must be expanded to the people themselves. Twenty years ago it was the anti-intellectuals who were most guilty of "know nothing" attitudes. Today too many of the militant intellectuals are equally as guilty of "hear nothing" attitudes of refusing to listen while demanding communication.

I said then, "I don't like the way the Senate has been made a rendezvous for vilification, for selfish political gain at the sacrifice of individual reputations and national unity."

That applies today. But I would add that equally I don't like the way the campus has been made a rendezvous for obscenity, for trespass, for violence, for arson, and for killing.

I said then, "I am not proud of the way we smear outsiders from the Floor of the Senate and hide behind the cloak of congressional immunity and still place ourselves beyond criticism on the Floor of the Senate."

Today I would add to that—I am not proud of the way in which too many militants resort to the illegalities of trespass, violence, and arson and, in doing so, claim for themselves a special immunity from the law with the allegation that such acts are justified because they have a political connotation with a professed cause.

I said then, "As a United States Senator, I am not proud of the way in which the Senate has been made a publicity platform for irresponsible sensationalism."

Today I would add that I am not proud of the way in which our national television networks and campuses have been made publicity platforms for irresponsible sensationalism—nor am I proud of the countercriticism against the networks and the campuses that has gone beyond the bounds of reasonableness and propriety and fanned, instead of drenching, the fires of division.

I have admired much of the candid and justified defense

of our government in reply to the news media and the militant dissenters—but some of the defense has been too extreme and unfair and too repetitive and thus impaired the effectiveness of the previous admirable and justified defense.

I said twenty years ago, "As an American, I am shocked at the way Republicans and Democrats alike are playing directly into the Communist design of 'confuse, divide, and conquer.'" Today I am shocked at the way too many Americans are so doing.

I spoke as I did twenty years ago because of what I considered to be the great threat from the radical right—the threat of a Government of repression.

I speak today because of what I consider to be the great threat from the radical left that advocates and practices violence and defiance of the law—again, the threat of the ultimate result of a reaction of repression.

The President denies that we are in a revolution. There are many who would disagree with such appraisal. Anarchy may seem nearer to many of us than it really is.

But of one thing I am sure. The excessiveness of overreactions on both sides is a clear and present danger to American democracy.

That danger is ultimately from the political right even though it is initially spawned by the antidemocratic arrogance and nihilism from the political extreme left.

Extremism bent upon polarization of our people is increasingly forcing upon the American people the narrow choice between anarchy and repression.

And make no mistake about it, if that narrow choice has to be made, the American people, even if with reluctance and misgiving, will choose repression.

For an overwhelming majority of Americans believe that:

Trespass is trespass—whether on the campus or off. Violence is violence—whether on the campus or off. Arson is arson—whether on the campus or off. Killing is killing—whether on the campus or off.

The campus cannot degenerate into a privileged sanctuary for obscenity, trespass, violence, arson, and killing with special immunity for participants in such acts.

Criminal acts, active or by negligence, cannot be condoned

or excused because of panic, whether the offender be a policeman, a national guardsman, a student, or one of us in this legislative body.

Ironically, the excesses of dissent on the extreme left can result in repression of dissent. For repression is preferable to anarchy and nihilism to most Americans.

Yet, excesses on the extreme right, such as those twenty years ago, can mute our national conscience.

As was the case twenty years ago when the Senate was silenced and politically intimidated by one of its members, so today many Americans are intimidated and made mute by the emotional violence of the extreme left. Constructive discussion on the subject is becoming increasingly difficult of attainment.

It is time that the great center of our people, those who reject the violence and unreasonableness of both the extreme right and the extreme left, searched their consciences, mustered their moral and physical courage, shed their intimidated silence, and declared their consciences.

It is time that with dignity, firmness and friendliness, they reason with, rather than capitulate to, the extremists on both sides—at all levels—and caution that their patience ends at the border of violence and anarchy that threatens our American democracy.

EDITOR'S NOTE:

That evening the American Newspaper Women's Club had a long-planned testimonial dinner honoring Senator Smith. Esther Van Wagoner Tufty, President of the club and head of the Tufty News Bureau (known in Washington as "The Duchess," an affectionate nickname), some months before had arranged such a dinner honoring the Senator's long service in Congress. Tributes were paid to her by Howard K. Smith, Senators John Stennis and Hugh Scott, and Defense Secretary Melvin Laird. Although not a large dinner, with an attendance of about

350, it was one of the warmest gatherings that most anyone could remember in Washington. There had been some difference of opinion among club members over the date for the dinner. There were even at that date some pro-McCarthy members who did not like June 1 for the very reason that it was the twentieth anniversary of the Declaration of Conscience. They pressed for June 3 as the date, giving as an excuse that June 1 was too soon after Memorial Day and too many Senators would not have returned from the holiday weekend in time to attend the dinner. One of them observed that the June 1 date might be embarrassing to President Nixon because he had been a supporter of Joe McCarthy and this might cause him not to attend. But The Duchess held out for June 1 and after Margaret Smith had made her speech that afternoon The Duchess was elated that she had stood firm.

An interesting call came a few days before the dinner from the Washington *Post* gossip columnist Maxine Cheshire, whose unfriendliness to Senator Smith is well known in the city. Mrs. Cheshire told me that she had been informed that Senator Smith had expressed the hope that President Nixon would not be invited because of his tie with Joe McCarthy. Mrs. Cheshire wanted confirmation. It was clear to me that a pro-McCarthy club member opposing the June 1 date was the person who had given this story to Mrs. Cheshire.

I said that the report was completely false, adding that, "The only one who raised that question was _____." I was fairly confident that this would squelch the story that Cheshire was planning because it would indicate that the club member had planted the story with Cheshire. She never wrote the story.

The reaction to the second Declaration was overwhelmingly favorable—both within the Senate and outside, from Democrats as well as Republicans, from the press and news media of liberal and of conservative views. Praise for her speech in the Senate ranged from liberal Democrat Edward Kennedy to conservative Republican John Williams. Outside the Senate the spectrum of the praise ran from Walter Lippmann to Richard M. Nixon.

Lippmann, whom she had consulted prior to her 1950 Declaration, with his wife Helen, sent a telegram stating, "Proud of you again." President Nixon wrote her:

> It was indeed fitting and timely that you should speak out as you did on the Twentieth Anniversary of your "Declaration of Conscience." Your counsel of reasoned judgment was needed then, and is needed now. I thank you.

From California the star of the TV program "Bonanza" Lorne Greene, expressed his admiration with "I salute you for your stands of the past, and your present courage in speaking out against the nihilism of the left *and* right."

From Hubert Humphrey came:

> Once again, you have said in your own quiet, concise, and persuasive manner what many of us have been thinking and all too few have been able to clearly articulate.
>
> I was asked just today in a student audience question period if I agreed with your analysis, and I was proud to say that I agreed with you on what you had to say twenty years ago, and I fully agree with what you had to say today.

Editorial comment was widespread and overwhelmingly favorable, both in newspapers and magazines and on television and radio. The mail was heavier and more favorable than it had been on the first Declaration twenty years before.

The reaction of the national weekly magazines was interesting by contrast. *Newsweek* sent Sam Shaffer to me, and I gave him nearly two hours. They didn't print a word on the speech. In sharp contrast, *Time* had a commendatory block piece quoting at length from the speech—and *United States News & World Report* had a special section reproducing the speech in full.

Criticism of the new Declaration was relatively slight. Some of the Right were unhappy that Senator Smith had raised the prospect of the Right reacting with repression to the anarchy of the Left. A few of these pointed to a speech by FBI Director J. Edgar Hoover given not long after Senator Smith's second Declaration in which he said:

> People do not always say what they mean, sometimes intentionally . . . Much of the talk about repression comes from those involved in or in sympathy with revolutionary violence on our campus and on our streets . . . Some people imply that our choice may be between anarchy and repression. Indeed, it is not . . .

These critics of Senator Smith could make a good case that Mr. Hoover was attacking her by rather direct identification in words, if not by name. If he was, then surely there was just as much flak against Margaret from the Left. For some accused her of "threatening" them with repression in her speech. A few wrote obscene letters, as did some of her critics on the Right.

Both Senator Smith and her speech were ridiculed by Washington *Evening Star* columnist David Braaten in his June 4, 1970, column. Whatever the reaction might have been to Braaten's ridicule of Senator Smith, it had to be admitted that his prophetic assignment of her to a wheel chair was quite accurate, for a month later she was confined to a wheel chair. But this was a relatively easy future projection on his part since it had been known that she was suffering intense hip pain. It was no surprise when a month later she underwent total hip replacement surgery that did put her in a wheel chair —for about a week.

Margaret Chase Smith is just as human as anybody else, just as appreciative of a pat on the back as anyone else, and just as sensitive to criticism as anyone else. But more important to her than praise or condemnation was whether her second Declaration had made a contribution to defusing the dynamite, to slowing the polarization of our people, and to calming the national temper.

A friend observed to her, "Margaret, you have a reputation of being a woman of few words. They say you can pack a lot of message and meaning into a few words. Once you took an official twenty-five-hundred word statement of the Republican National Committee on Republican Principles and boiled it down to only eighty-nine words and it was accepted. If you could boil your second Declaration message to the American people down to a minimum of words, what would they be?"

With a twinkle in her eyes, Senator Smith replied, "Just two words—'Cool it!' "

The real test then was whether it had had any cooling effect on highly polarized people and groups. How could one tell? How could one gauge? There was no sure way.

But there were straws in the wind. Perhaps the most impressive indication was from the New York woman attending the commencement exercises of Adelphi University in Long Island, New York, where Senator Smith gave the commencement address. The woman went up to her and said with great feeling, "Senator Smith, I want to say God bless you for your speech in the Senate a few days ago. You restored communications in my family. My daughter and I have started talking to each other again. For too long we have failed to communicate."

This gave the Senator the best answer she could ask for. She only hoped that there were many such cases. Perhaps there were. University officials had been concerned that there might be an angry and unfortunate demonstration at the commencement exercises. There was not the slightest trace of such.

At the National War College in Washington, D.C., during a Defense Strategy Seminar for Reserve officers from all over the Nation, a lecturer gave further evidence of the beneficial effect of the speech. The lecturer was a high official of the Federal Bureau of Investigation who cannot be identified by name because of the non-attribution policy of the National War College. He traced the development, organization, operations, and financing of the youth and student revolutionary groups of the SDS, Black Panthers, Weathermen, and others. In the question-and-answer period, he was asked about the present status of the student revolutionary movement. His answer was that he thought it had reached its peak in intensity and violence and was on the downgrade and cooling off considerably. He was asked when he thought that cooling-off change came. His answer was that the first break came after Senator Margaret Chase Smith's June 1, 1970, speech.

The lecturer said that the FBI got clear soundings from throughout the Nation after her speech that the extremists on both sides had started to calm down. He praised Senator Smith for having hit the nail on the head about the ultimate danger of repressive reaction to the anarchists if they didn't cool off. He felt she had been effective not only because of the validity of her message but because of her rare credibility with colleges, universities, and students.

Such praise from such a highly informed, qualified, and sophisticated official of the very FBI division investigating and studying the problem was an impressive answer to the question of whether Margaret's second Declaration had had any effect. It could also be interpreted as a refutation to those who had interpreted J. Edgar Hoover's speech as critical of Senator Smith.

Each American can best judge for himself or herself and recall what the conditions were before and after the Smith speech of June 1, 1970. Each can make his or her own comparison of the rate of campus violence, killings, arson, trespass, disorders, or demonstrations before and after that speech—and form his or her own judgment as to its effect.

On June 2, 1970, the day after the second Declaration, Leo Cherne, Chairman of the Executive Committee of Freedom House, wrote Senator Smith of his unbounded admiration for the speech, as well as the officers of Freedom House. He said that her speech and her philosophy and actions dating back to the days of McCarthyism greatly paralleled the aims and efforts of Freedom House against extremism for many years. He asked her to accept the Chairmanship of the Board of Freedom House "as another opportunity to nurse our 'national sickness.'"

At first Senator Smith was hesitant to accept, even though greatly honored, because of her heavy official workload and her scheduled surgery. But then her mail on the speech developed a heavy overtone of challenge from students to do something about the words in her speech. They wanted to know what she was going to do to implement her words with action. They pledged to do what they could—but they wanted her to meet them at least halfway.

Then she went into the hospital at Harkness Pavilion of Columbia-Presbyterian Hospital in New York on July 4 for surgery on her right hip. Surgery and hospitalization required three weeks. During that time she received heavy mail from throughout the United States, telling her to get well and back to the Senate soon because she was badly needed there.

She returned to the Senate at the end of July. At a press conference on August 18, 1970, her acceptance of the Freedom House Chairmanship was announced. She said that she had agreed to become Chairman of the organization that had been formed to fight political extremism because in doing so she was very specifically accepting the challenge that young Americans had made to her to back up her talk. In addition, she joined in 1971 with the Student National Education Association in its efforts to fight polarization.

Cynics question that any real value comes out of speeches—arguing that they really don't produce results or have any effect. They particularly hold speeches made in the Senate in this view. But speeches do have some results. There is some cause and effect. They are not always made in vain—nor in vanity.

Like the other speeches of Senator Margaret Chase Smith related in this book, her second Declaration of Conscience of June 1, 1970, had one other very specific result. It prompted

Doubleday to renew efforts to get a book by Senator Smith. This time that effort succeeded because Margaret Smith had concluded that there should be a book to show what leads up to the making of a speech or a public appearance and the consequences of such speech. That is what this book attempts to do.

"This I Believe"

EDITOR'S NOTE:
In January of 1953, Senator Smith was asked to make a statement for "This I Believe," a daily radio series and weekly newspaper feature. The program and series presented "the personal philosophies of thoughtful men and women in all walks of life." It was produced by the distinguished commentator Edward P. Morgan and the star of the radio series program was the famous Edward R. Murrow. These two, together with Ward Wheelock, the principal promoter and underwriter of the series, constituted the Editorial Board of the project.

After writing her statement, Senator Smith sent it to Mr. Morgan on February 7. A week later he replied, "I can say without hesitation or qualification that yours is one of the very best scripts we have ever received." He asked that she make a recording of the statement at her "earliest convenience."

After the broadcast on Murrow's radio program, her statement was incorporated in a book, *This I Believe,* published in 1953 by Hamish Hamilton, Ltd., of London and edited by Morgan. This book contained statements of fifty British leaders and fifty American leaders. In the following year her statement appeared in an American edition published by Simon and Schuster and edited by Raymond Gram Swing.

"This I Believe" also opened a friendly and productive association with Edward R. Murrow. In May of 1954 when Senator Smith was campaigning against Joe McCarthy's proxy candidate, Robert L. Jones, Murrow and his partner and producer of the CBS-TV prize-winning "See It Now" program, Fred W. Friendly, sent their camera-sound team to Maine to cover both candidates.

The presentation of the films on "See It Now" revealed so devastatingly Jones's striking similarity to McCarthy—in facial expressions, tonal inflections, gestures, mannerisms, and subject matter—there was no need for editorial comment.

Subsequently, in the fall of 1954 and spring of 1955, Senator Smith was to become a star on "See It Now." Several of her conferences with such world leaders as Churchill, Mendès-France, Adenauer, Nasser, Chiang Kai-shek, Franco, Nehru,

U Nu, and Magsaysay were shown on the program. On April 19, 1955, at the Sixteenth Annual Awards Dinner of the Overseas Press Club of America at the Waldorf-Astoria Hotel in New York, she accepted the "Best Consistent Television Presentation of Foreign Affairs" Award to the program on behalf of Ed Murrow and Fred Friendly.

Because no political and ideological storm swirled around her statement of "This I Believe," it is not as well known as the first Declaration of Conscience. It is the speech that she has repeated the most, however. The occasions for its repetition have been mostly commencement addresses at universities and colleges. They have been frequent, for Senator Smith has received honorary degrees from sixty-seven universities and colleges from Canada to California, from Maine to Florida. Only President Herbert Hoover ever received more.

It is her favorite statement. And if there is any one statement or speech that best sums up all of her others, this is it.

THIS I BELIEVE

Many nights I go home from the office or the Senate Floor tired and discouraged. There's lots of glory and prestige and limelight for a United States Senator that the public sees. But there's just as much grief and harassment and discouragement that the public doesn't see.

Of course, like everyone else I went into public service and politics with my eyes wide open. I knew that any public official is fair game for slander and smear and carping criticism. I knew that ingratitude was to be expected.

I knew that fair weather friends would turn on me when they felt I no longer served their purposes. I knew that I would be called all sorts of names from crook on down.

I should have known that chances were good that I would

even be accused of being a traitor to my country. These things I knew. But I never knew how vicious they could get and how deeply they could cut.

It is these things I think of when I'm tired and discouraged—and when I wonder if being a Senator is worth all that I put into it. These are the times when I consider quitting public life and retreating to the comforts and luxury of private life.

But these times have always been the very times when I became all the more convinced that all the sorrow, abuse, harassment, and vilification was not too high a price or sacrifice to pay.

For it is then that I ask myself, "What am I doing this for?" I realize that I am doing it because I believe in certain things—things without which life wouldn't mean much to me.

This I do believe—that life has a real purpose—that God has assigned to each human being a role in life—that each of us has a purposeful task—that our individual roles are all different but that each of us has the same obligation to do the best he can.

I believe that every human being I come in contact with has a right to courtesy and consideration from me. I believe that I should not ask or expect from anyone else that which I am not willing to grant or do myself.

I believe that I should be able to take anything that I can give out. I believe that every living person has the right to criticize constructively, the right honestly to hold unpopular beliefs, the right to protest orderly, the right of independent thought.

I believe that no one has a right to own our souls except God.

I believe that freedom of speech should not be so abused by some that it is not exercised by others because of fear of smear. But I do believe that we should not permit tolerance to degenerate into indifference. I believe that people should never get so indifferent, cynical, and sophisticated that they don't get shocked into action.

I believe that we should not forget how to disagree agreeably and how to criticize constructively. I believe with all my heart that we must not become a nation of mental mutes blindly following demagogues. I believe that we should never become mental mutes with our voices silenced because of fear of criticism of what we might say.

I believe that in our constant search for security we can never gain any peace of mind until we secure our own soul. And this I do believe above all, especially in my times of greater discouragement, *that I must believe*—that I must believe in my fellow men—that I must believe in myself—that I must believe in God—if life is to have any meaning.

Margaret Chase Smith

Appendices

APPENDIX

ANSWER TO A SMEAR

MARGARET SMITH'S ANSWER
May 21, 1948

I was in business before I entered Congress. And as a business woman, I respected the principle that real success cannot be gained by running down your competition. I have respected this principle in politics—and particularly in this campaign—and I have not made one word of criticism of my opponents. I had hoped my opponents would respect this principle.

But the campaign has reached the smear stage. My opponents have resorted to the distribution of anonymous printed lie sheets. As anyone knows, an anonymous letter is not worth the paper that it is written on. The writer of such a letter, who does not have the courage to identify himself to those charges which he cannot prove, is nothing less than contemptible. These smear sheets betray the desperation of my opponents.

But I refuse to stoop to the smear tactics that my opposition has chosen. I have refused to pursue and participate in the charges of State administration mismanagement, of which we have all been reading so much in the papers lately, laid to Governors, past and present. I have refused to attack either Governor Hildreth or Governor Sewall or Mr. Beverage because I am campaigning on my record—not on any mistakes that they might or might not have made.

The smear charges that are being made against me, through these anonymous circulars being distributed through the State, are so ridiculous and so patently a pack of lies that they do not warrant the dignity of recognition.

But lest someone might possibly misinterpret silence on my part, I am going to answer the smears. First, let us take the smear sheet that is composed of only one page. I have been told that a relative of one of the candidates is using this sheet to try to charge that I am a puppet of the CIO—that that is the real purpose of the distribution of the sheet.

This is easy to answer. I voted for the Taft-Hartley Bill and the CIO has called upon its members to make an all-out effort to defeat every congressman or congresswoman who voted for the Taft-Hartley Bill. In addition to this, the CIO specifically endorsed my opponent in 1944. My opponents are actually insulting your intelligence when they think that you will believe such an evident ridiculous misrepresentation that I am a tool of the CIO.

An indication of the inaccuracy of this sheet that they are putting out is that it states that Congressman Carl Vinson resigned from Congress in 1946. I know that Mr. Vinson did not resign for he was the Chairman of my committee, the House Naval Affairs Committee, and so remained throughout 1946—and is still in Congress.

What the distributors of this smear sheet fail to tell you is that the latest CIO scoresheet on congressional voting stated that in 1947 I voted *against* the CIO ten out of twelve times.

Now let us take the second smear-Smith paper that is being circulated —it is even bigger and more impressive for it is three pages of mis-representations—in fact it is such a masterpiece of deception that I believe its anonymous author must have had "radical" training from his evident adeptness at fabricating lies and spinning half-truths.

He saves the best for the last. So let's turn to page three of the smear paper and his punch conclusion that infers that I am un-American.

Let me answer his charges that I am un-American, first generally, and second specifically. In the first place, there have been twenty votes during the eight years that I have served in Congress that involved the House Un-American Activities Committee. Of these twenty times, I have voted to support, uphold, and continue the Un-American Activities Committee sixteen times. Only in four instances did I disagree with the committee and I offer no excuses for those four times. If you examine the Congressional Record you will find that there are several Republicans who have differed with that committee at times.

But after all, I supported the committee 80 percent of the time. I supported the committee on February 11, 1941, March 11, 1942, April 28, 1942, February 10, 1943, February 18, 1943, January 26, 1944, February 27, 1946, March 28, 1946, April 16, 1946, May 13, 1946, August 1, 1946, February 18, 1947, March 24, 1947, April 22, 1947, November 24, 1947, and May 14, 1948. On those occasions, Mr. Marcantonio, whom the smear writer charges I voted with "nearly 50 percent of the time," voted the opposite way from the way I voted. Who does the smear writer think he's fooling?

The smear writer points out that on June 26, 1946, I voted against the committee's proposal to bring contempt proceedings against one Corliss Lamont. But he fails to tell you that Congressman Hale of Portland voted the same way—and that not a single member of the Maine delegation voted for the committee on this issue. (See page 7600 of the Congressional Record.)

The smear writer states that on May 17, 1946, I voted to "attempt to prevent the Un-American Activities Committee from obtaining a $75,000,000 appropriation." This time he went a little too far in his twisted exaggerations—for $75 million is just a little too much for a congressional committee to spend. According to his figures, that would be enough to "run the business of the State of Maine for over" three years.

This statement of the smear writer is another evidence of the inaccuracies of this three-page smear sheet—for the amount sought was only one thousandth of the amount stated by the smear writer—only $75,000. I voted against the $75,000 and I have no apologies for I felt that the work that would require the $75,000 could be more effectively and efficiently done by our FBI—and certainly I don't have to make any excuses for the FBI. (See page 5224 of the Record.)

The smear writer points out that on January 3, 1945, I voted against making the committee a standing committee of the House. What he does not say is that many Republicans, including Congressman Clare Boothe Luce, joined me in voting this way. What he does not point out is that we voted this way because only a short time before the Congress had enacted the Legislative Reorganization Act which delegated investigating functions to regular committees instead of creating special investigating committees. (See page 15 of the Record.)

Now let's take the smear writer's charges under the section he titles "Appropriation and Expenditure of Public Funds." In the first paragraph, he points out that on February 20, 1947, I voted against the proposed $6,000,000,000 cut in the President's proposed budget.

What he fails to point out is that the Congress never did approve the proposed budget cut—that the House and Senate never agreed on the amount of the cut—that I voted against the House proposal to cut by $6,000,000,000 because I favored the more realistic Senate cut of $4,500,000,000—that I favored a smaller cut because I didn't want to see the Air Force funds slashed by one billion dollars as the $6,000,000,-000 cut would have required.

What he fails to point out is that my view on this was vindicated recently when both the House and the Senate overwhelmingly voted to increase the funds for the Air Force—by almost one billion dollars.

In the second paragraph, the smear writer points out that on April 30,

1947, I voted against the proposed $150,000,000 cut in foreign relief. What he fails to point out is that Congressman Charles Eaton, the Republican Chairman of the House Foreign Affairs Committee, also voted against the proposed $150,000,000 cut. (See page 4420 of the Record.)

I offer no apologies for that vote because certainly the Chairman of the Foreign Affairs Committee is the best informed on such a matter as foreign relief—that's what we have committees for—to specialize. I talked with him before I voted and he urged me to vote the way I did.

In the third paragraph, the smear writer attacks me for voting on February 14, 1946, for an $1,854,000 appropriation for OPA. What he does not tell you is that Congressman Hale voted the same way that I did—what he fails to tell you is that not a single member of the Maine delegation in the House voted differently from me. (See page 1323 of the Record.)

In the fourth paragraph of this section, the smear writer points out that on October 18, 1945, I voted against a rescission of $52,650,000 and against the return of United States Employment Service to the States. What he fails to tell you is that Congressman Hale voted the same way that I did—that a majority of the Maine delegation in the House voted the way I did. (See page 9818 of the Record.)

In the fifth paragraph, the smear writer points out that on March 10, 1944, I voted against the proposed $7,500,000 cut in war housing appropriations. What he fails to tell you is that Congressman Pehr G. Holmes (Massachusetts), the then highest ranking Republican member of the Public Buildings and Grounds Committee—the committee having jurisdiction over such legislation—that Congressman Holmes voted against the cut and the same way that I did—that my vote was in keeping with that of the cognizant Republican committee leadership.

What the smear writer also fails to mention is the critical lack of housing today—and how much more critical it would be if we did not have the houses that that $7,500,000 built.

In the opening section of the paper, the smear writer attempts to show under the title "In Support of the Administration and in Opposition to Her Own Party" that I have been a traitor to the Republican Party. Let me answer that generally and specifically.

First, I would call the smear writer's attention to the official statement of the Honorable Joseph W. Martin, Jr., the Republican Speaker of the House, who wrote me as follows:

> Your loyalty and patriotism have made possible the building of a Republican record which I believe will restore sanity in our government.

And I would call the smear writer's attention to the statement of the House Republican Whip, Congressman Leslie C. Arends—whose job it is to round up the party votes on legislation. Of my record, he said:
Our party benefited by your ready response to every call for action.

Specifically, first the smear writer raises the question about my vote against the proposed $6,000,000,000 budget cut. I have already answered that as he raised the same question in the first paragraph of the section "Appropriation and Expenditure of Public Funds."

In the second paragraph, the smear writer points out that on January 29, 1946, I voted against returning the United States Employment Service to the States. What he fails to point out is that Congressman Richard J. Welch, then the highest ranking Republican on the House Labor Committee—the committee which had cognizance over this matter—voted the same way I did. What he fails to tell you is that my vote was in keeping with that of the cognizant Republican committee leadership. (See page 547 of the Record.)

In the third paragraph, the smear writer points out that on May 26, 1945, I voted for the bill to grant the President authority to declare a 50 percent tariff reduction. What he fails to tell you is that I voted with Congressmen Hale and Fellows to recommit the bill. (See page 5165 of the Record.)

In the fourth paragraph, the smear writer charges me with preventing political opportunism by voting on June 7, 1944, to delay the date of a congressional investigation of Pearl Harbor. What he fails to tell you is that I voted the same way that the present Republican Chairman of the House Armed Services Committee voted (Congressman W. G. Andrews)—that we along with many other Republicans felt that politics should be out during the war and that the Pearl Harbor investigation should be delayed until such time as it would not make revelations that our enemies could use to advantage—such as the working of our radar and other secret devices. (See page 5476 of the Record.)

In the fifth paragraph of this section, the smear writer points out that on January 25, 1944, I voted against the proposed $650,000,000 cut on the UNRRA appropriation. This he offers as evidence that I opposed my own party, the Republican Party.

This time he hit the jackpot—but for me rather than my opponents. For if I was betraying the Republican Party by my vote against the cut, so was the present Republican Speaker of the House Joseph W. Martin, Jr., for he voted the same way that I did and against the cut—so was Congressman Charles Eaton, the present Republican Chairman of the House Foreign Affairs Committee, for he voted the same way I did and against the cut—so was the greatest Republican proponent of economy and saving, Congressman John Taber, the present Republican Chairman of the House Appropriations Committee, for he voted the same way that I did and against the cut—and last but not least, so was the present Chairman of the Republican National Committee, the then Congressman B. Carroll Reece, for he voted the same way that I did and against the cut. (See page 694 of the Record.)

Yes, if my vote was a betrayal of the Republican Party—then the present Republican Speaker of the House, the present Republican Chairman of the House Foreign Affairs Committee, the present Republican Chairman of the House Appropriations Committee, and the present Chairman of the Republican National Committee all betrayed their party—for they all voted the same way I did.

The smear writer concludes his allegations that I have opposed my own party by pointing out that in "July, 1943" (the record voting date was July 1, 1943) I voted to continue the National Youth Administration. What he fails to tell you is that the entire Maine Congressional delegation joined me in support of this NYA vote— Congressmen Hale and Fellows (see page 6969 of the Record), and Senators White and Brewster on July 3 (see page 7089 of the Record). Yes, the entire Maine delegation voted the same way that I did— for continuation of the NYA. Senator Brewster took the floor in support of the NYA. In fact, Senator White made one of the most important speeches of his entire career on the Senate Floor in favor of the NYA. (See pages 6595 and 7344 of the Record.)

Now for the smear writer's summary of my voting record in the 76th, 77th, 78th, 79th, and 80th Congresses. First, he says that I cast 71 votes against my party. Next, he says that I voted 107 times with Representative Marcantonio and that I am 44.2 percent with Representative Marcantonio.

In the first place, it is to be pointed out that those 71 votes he picks include those instances where the present Republican Speaker of the House; the present Republican Chairman of the House Appropriations Committee; the present Republican Chairman of the House Foreign Affairs Committee; the present Republican Chairman of the House Armed Services Committee; the present Republican Chairman of the House Public Lands Committee; the Majority Leader of the Senate, Senator Wallace White; the Junior Senator from Maine, Senator Owen Brewster; Congressman Robert Hale of the First Maine Congressional District; and Congressman Frank Fellows of the Third Maine Congressional District; and the present Chairman of the Republican National Committee when he was a member of Congress—where this imposing array of Republican leaders voted the same way that I did. Yes, in some instances where the entire Maine delegation voted the same way that I did.

In the second place, the smear writer's statistics are hard to reconcile or understand. He says a "record vote on 242 measures." So how he got only 242 record votes I can't understand for during the time that I have been in Congress from 1940 to now there have been more than 1500 record votes.

He says that I cast 71 votes—or 29.3 percent of his hand-picked 242 votes—in opposition to my party. If he were going to pick only 242 of more than 1500 recorded votes for his analysis, he should have gone all the way and picked just 1 vote so that he could say that according to his standards he could misrepresent I had voted 100 percent of the time against my party—or 1 out of 1. He could have used the NYA vote where he said I voted against the party—yes, where the entire Maine delegation voted as I did.

The ridiculous nature of his analysis is evident from the fact that in so many voting instances he picked, my vote was the same as that of top Republican leaders.

But taking his 71 hand-picked votes, which I think we can assume is the maximum number of black marks that he has against me in view of the character of his attack on me—taking those 71 in a total of at least 1500 recorded votes during my time in Congress, would show that by his own standards I failed to vote with my party only 4.7 percent of the time—that I had voted with my party 95.3 percent of the time.

I would say that was fairly good for as I remember during my school days anything 90 percent or over was marked A and anything 95 percent or over was marked A plus. So that my Republican report card grade would be A plus—and even Speaker Joseph Martin or Appropriations Chairman John Taber would not be given a grade of 100 percent by this smear writer.

The 107 times that he said that I voted the same as Marcantonio would be only 7 percent of the time—and according to the votes picked by the smear writer even Speaker Joseph Martin and Chairman John Taber occasionally vote the same as Mr. Marcantonio.

If he had tried any harder, this smear writer couldn't have picked better instances to show how the Republican leaders vote the same way I do. It is no wonder that the smear writer was too ashamed and afraid to put his name on the smear sheet.

VOTING RECORD OF REPRESENTATIVE MARGARET C. SMITH
in
Seven Sessions of the 76th, 77th, 78th, 79th, and 80th Congresses

SUMMARY: In the record vote on 242 measures:

Representative Smith cast 71 votes—or 29.3 percent—in opposition to the majority of her own Republican Party; Representative Smith cast 107 votes—or 44.2 percent—with Representative Vito Marcantonio of New York.

Analysis of all votes cast indicates that Representative Smith gave her support, in opposition to her own party, to many important measures sponsored by the Democratic Administration, bearing on Government operation and economy, consistently opposed machinery for Congressional investigation of un-Americanism, and always in company with Representative Marcantonio—supported the demands of the CIO, voting for the CIO in eleven out of twelve instances. Typical examples of Representative Smith's voting record follow:

In Support of the Administration
And in Opposition to Her Own Party

One Republican vote was cast in support of the Administration— cast in an effort to stop a $6,000,000,000 cut in the Truman budget. That one Republican vote was given by Representative Smith. (Feb. 20, 1947)

The Republican majority moved for the return of the public employment service to the States, in the name of economy and efficiency. The Administration insisted upon Federal operation until June 30, 1947. Representative Smith voted against the majority. (Jan. 29, 1946) She lost.

The President requested authority to declare a 50 percent tariff reduction. This Maine representative voted with the Administration. (May 26, 1945)

The Administration—seeking to delay prosecution of those responsible for the Pearl Harbor catastrophe until after elections—was supported by Representative Smith. (June 7, 1944) Her vote helped to make that politically important delay possible.

A saving of $650,000,000 was at stake, in the cost of this Country's participation in UNRRA. Representative Smith joined the majority of the Democratic Representatives in voting against the saving. (Jan. 25, 1944)

An effort was made to continue the life of the National Youth Administration, at a cost of $45,000,000—an amount sufficient to run the business of the State of Maine for over two years. Representative Smith voted for the NYA. She was defeated. (July, 1943)

Appropriation and Expenditure of Public Funds

Nearly two thirds of all members of the House of Representatives voted for a $6,000,000,000 cut in President Truman's budget. Representative Smith supported the President. She was defeated. (Feb. 20, 1947)

A saving of $150,000,000 in expense for foreign relief was the objective of the Republican majority on April 30, 1947. Representative Smith opposed the saving. She lost.

An extra $1,854,000 was expended on the OPA (Feb. 14, 1946)—with the help of this Maine Representative—although the members of her own party argued that the money would promote inflation and be spent on OPA propaganda. (Such adverse votes were cast by Representative Smith to the same end.)

A few Representatives—among them Smith of Maine—attempted to prevent consideration of the Rescission Bill, with the return of more than $52,650,000 in war appropriations at stake. The attempt failed, and at the same time Representative Smith voted against return of the employment offices to the States. (Oct. 18, 1945)

Even though a large number of war housing units already built were still unoccupied, Representative Smith voted against a proposed cut of $7,500,000 in war housing appropriations. She was successful. (March 10, 1944)

Investigation of un-Americanism

The record shows that nearly 50 percent of the time, Representative Smith's voting was identical with that of Representative Vito Marcantonio of New York. Most frequently the two Representatives were counted in a small minority in opposition to efforts made to strengthen Congressional investigations of disloyalty.

On June 26, 1946, this Representative from Maine joined a minority of both parties in an effort to block a charge of contempt against Corliss Lamont. Lamont, Chairman of the "National Council of America-Soviet Friendship," refused to produce his organization's records for the inspection of the Un-American Activities Committee. The House voted overwhelmingly to bring contempt proceedings.

Representative Smith was numbered among a handful of Congressmen—a minority of both parties—in an attempt to prevent the Un-American Activities Committee from obtaining a $75,000,000 appropriation. (May 17, 1946)

Early in the 79th Congress, this Maine Representative was counted with a handful of Congressmen—again a minority of both parties—who tried to kill an appropriation for expenses of the Un-American Activities Committee.

At the opening of the 79th Congress, Representative Smith voted—along with Administration forces—to prevent the Un-American Activities Committee from becoming a standing committee of the House, with more power to investigate communism.

APPENDIX

MEDICAL RESEARCH

SENATOR MARGARET CHASE SMITH
HIP OPERATION

The operation performed on Senator Smith's right hip has been medically described as "total hip replacement surgery" and "low friction arthroplasty." The procedure was developed in Great Britain in 1960 by a Doctor John Charnley. It involves the severance and removal of a segment of a center bone structure of the hip complex and replacement with a plastic cup socket in the upper hip joint and a stainless steel bar in the lower femur joint. The bar has a round head that contour-fits into the plastic cup socket. Lubrication for free movement of the bar in the socket is provided by the natural fluid of the body.

The plastic cup socket and the stainless steel bar were cemented to the respective bone segments with a fast-setting epoxy-like cement named Surgical Simplex P and/or Surgical Simplex P Radiopaque which, because of the definitions of the Federal Food, Drug and Cosmetic Act, has been classified as a new drug. Critical in the operative process is the very limited time in which the cement can be mixed and applied since it is fast-drying and fast-setting cement.

This cement is not available generally, as its use is restricted to certain investigators and clinical studies with the cement must be performed before it can be approved for general use. Consequently, Senator Smith had to sign a waiver to absolve the operating physicians, their attendants, the manufacturer of the cement, and others who might be involved in the investigation, of any blame and to renounce any rights to damages because of any unfavorable outcome from the use of the cement in the operation.

It is the cement element of the operation which barred the same type operation on Senator Smith's left hip on August 6, 1968. While the cement had been used in Great Britain for nearly eight years at that time with great success, the Food and Drug Administration did not feel that a sufficient time had elapsed to fully test the cement and had withheld authorization for the use of the cement and thus operation of the Charnley operative procedure in this country.

About six months after the operation on Senator Smith's left hip in 1968, the Food and Drug Administration gave approval to two operating teams to use the Charnley procedure and the cement. One of the two teams was that headed by Doctor Frank E. Stinchfield of the Columbia-Presbyterian Medical Center, 168th Street and Fort Washington Avenue, New York City, who has performed the operations on both of Senator Smith's hips. A member of the Stinchfield team is Doctor Nasseroddin Eftekhar, who studied under Doctor Charnley for several years in Great Britain.

The procedure used in the surgery on Senator Smith's left hip in 1968 was the Smith Pedersen arthroplasty developed by the doctor of that name at the Massachusetts General Hospital in Boston. Among the basic differences between the two operative procedures is that the Charnley operation provides (1) quicker recovery, (2) less hospitalization, (3) far less disruption of the muscle complex, and (4) no therapy or exercise requirement.

The surgery on Senator Smith's right hip was performed on July 8, 1970, and she took her first steps one week later on July 15, 1970. She was released from the hospital on July 24, 1970, and returned to her office on part-time schedule (restricted activity for several weeks for internal healing of surgery and adjustment) on July 27, 1970. In contrast, in the 1968 operation Senator Smith's left hip and leg were in a cast for a week and Senator Smith was in traction for a month and three months' hospitalization and over six months of intensive therapy were required.

The only therapy in which Senator Smith then engaged in was walking in four feet of warm water daily for a few minutes. While this was beneficial to accelerating the recovery rate and adjustment in connection with recent surgery on the right hip, its value was greater as therapy for the left hip. For two years the right hip carried the greater load and then the greater load shifted to the left hip.

Following the operation in 1968 and release from the hospital, Senator Smith had her therapy at the Walter Reed Medical Center. Such therapy included swimming and walking in the heated pool there as well as the discipline of monitored therapy exercises under the supervision of Doctor Walter Metz. Inasmuch as the only therapy required following the 1970 operation was walking in four feet of water in a heated pool, Senator Smith relented on her long policy of declining to use the pool facilities of the Senate. For a period of several weeks she walked for a few minutes in the 88-degree Senate pool every morning starting at nine o'clock. This was an hour before the regular opening time of the Senate pool.

On August 25, 1971, Senator Smith underwent her third hip surgery. This time it was on the left hip on which the Smith Pedersen arthroplasty had been done in 1968. This time the Stinchfield-Eftekhar surgery team performed the Charnley "total hip replacement surgery" as had been done on the right hip the year before. This eliminated the need for therapy and exercises for the left hip. Less than three weeks later Senator Smith had returned to her full Senate schedule and made a major Senate speech on September 15, 1971.

The extensive news coverage on Senator Smith's Charnley "total hip replacement" operation has prompted a flood of inquiring mail from persons throughout the Nation suffering from hip ailments. Senator Smith finds great gratification in the fact that many persons suffering from similar severe hip pain have originally learned of this new operative procedure as a result of the news coverage on her surgery and have gained courage to make the decision to have the same surgery for themselves. She feels that indirectly she may be the cause of great relief from pain and suffering to many people throughout the Nation—and feels that this is probably the greatest benefit and gain that has come out of her own personal physical adversity.

In answer to the many inquiries—many of which are actually requests for reassurance and advice on whether to have the surgery performed—Senator Smith reports that until now the surgery has been a tremendous success not only in the fact that she has had absolutely no pain since the operations but as well in the fact that she has made excellent and rapid progress to total recovery and complete independence from walking aids. She cautions, however, that while she is optimistic and confident for the future, she has her fingers crossed.

APPENDICES

GENERALS IN RETREAT

APPENDIX A

May 9, 1957

Honorable Richard B. Russell, Chairman
Armed Services Committee
United States Senate
Washington, D.C.

My dear Mr. Chairman:

I have examined the transcript of the hearing on the Air Force Reserve General nominations and the penciled changes made personally by General O'Donnell. While I have no objection to affording witnesses an opportunity to make grammatical corrections and revisions which do not change the meaning and purport of their testimony before the Committee, I cannot agree to a wholesale rewriting of his testimony by a witness.

For that reason, I am disturbed with the penciled changes that General O'Donnell has made of his testimony and desires to be made for the printed copy. I am disturbed both at the quantity and the quality of his penciled changes. I am disturbed at both the character and the extent of his attempted changes. I do not believe that General O'Donnell should be permitted to make some statements in public and before the press and then attempt to reverse those statements privately and have completely reversed answers in the printed edition of the hearing.

General O'Donnell went even so far as on at least three occasions of his answers to my questions to state flatly that I was incorrect in my statements and to give the press and the public the impression that I was making misrepresentations or did not know what I was talking about—and then to attempt privately through penciled changes to reverse answers in those instances where I was stating the truth and the fact and I knew what I was talking about and in contrast it was General O'Donnell, who, by his contradiction of my statements, was guilty of misrepresentations himself or apparently didn't know what he was talking about. This is a sad commentary that the Chief of Personnel of the Air Force would know less about his business in these particular respects than I did.

For example, on page fifty-four of the transcript, I asked General O'Donnell in reference to Colonel Stewart being rated as only a pilot (instead of Command Pilot or Senior Pilot) although his mobilization assignment is Deputy Director of Operations of the Strategic Air Command, "Is it not a fact that the overwhelming number of rated Reserve General officers are either Command Pilots or Senior Pilots?" and to this General O'Donnell answered with a vigorous and unequivocal denial saying, "Oh, no. Definitely not." Yet, in his penciled changes he has stricken out that answer and substituted for it a complete reversal with the answer of "Yes."

This is not a small matter. As Chief of Personnel, and as a Command Pilot himself, he should have known better. Instead he had not the slightest doubt in his answer in the public hearings and in the impression that he gave to the press and the persons in the hearing room that I was making an incorrect statement or did not know what I was talking about.

My question was particularly relevant because it went to the matter of Colonel Stewart's qualifications to be Deputy Director of Operations of the Strategic Air Command. Clearly a Command Pilot should have such a mobilization assignment instead of a man with only the rating of Pilot. The records of the Air Force show that I was absolutely right in stating that the overwhelming number of rated Reserve Generals in the Air Force are either Command Pilots or Senior Pilots and not just Pilots—for the Air Force records show that there are twenty-one rated Air Force Reserve Generals and that of this number eighteen are Command Pilots or Senior Pilots and only three are just Pilots—an overwhelming ratio of six to one.

Another illustration of General O'Donnell's attempted changes to reverse privately the answer he gave to the Committee in public hearing is found at page fourteen of the transcript where I was summarizing the "lack of participation" record of Brigadier General Smith who has been nominated for Major General. At that page, General O'Donnell took issue with my statement that General Smith

has had no fifteen-duty tour since 1950. General O'Donnell took
issue with my statement and gave the impression that I was making
a misrepresentation or did not know what I was talking about as
he said, "Senator Smith, he met the minimum requirements for
retention, year of 1956, in serving from the tenth to the thirty-first
of December."

Yet, he now privately makes a penciled notation striking his
statement out and saying that it is incorrect. On the same page it
will be seen that I gave him a chance to correct himself and that
I extended to him the courtesy of accepting his word when I said,
"I do not see that it does, in this record, but of course you know."
To which General O'Donnell publicly replied, "To 31 December
1956." but which reply he now privately seeks to have stricken from
the printed and public record and in his penciled notation he crossed
a line through this answer.

General O'Donnell should have known. He is the Chief of Personnel of the Air Force. He represented at great length that he
knew General Smith's record. He should have known more about
it than I did but he didn't for the Air Force records show that I
was right and General O'Donnell wrong on this point. There is no
excuse for this for it was the Air Force who selected General
O'Donnell to represent it before the Committee and to provide the
information and the answers. The Committee did not select or ask
for General O'Donnell to be the witness before it on these matters.

My question was extremely relevant because of the fact that
General Smith holds a Training "D" category under which all that
is required of him is that he do a fifteen-day tour each year and
nothing else and that if he does not he must be discharged. The
Air Force records show that he has not yet met that requirement.

Another illustration of General O'Donnell's highly questionable
character of changes of his testimony is that on page twenty-seven
of the transcript. I was summarizing the record on Colonel Montgomery in his resignation from the Regular Air Force and in using
the Reserve to come in the back door to get the retirement pay
credit that he would have otherwise lost by his resignation. This
was a point of relevancy as it showed how the Regular establishment
was using the Reserve in this instance. That it was a point of
interest is attested to by the fact that later Senator Stennis very
pointedly questioned General O'Donnell on this.

I made the statement of "I think the record should show at
this point that after Colonel Montgomery resigned, had he not
been appointed in the Reserve component, he would not have

been eligible for any future retirement benefits of any kind." At that point General O'Donnell interrupted me and stated, "That is incorrect, Senator." It was a flat, unequivocal, and unqualified statement on his part stating categorically that I had made an incorrect statement—thus giving the impression that I had made a misrepresentation or did not know what I was talking about.

Yet, now General O'Donnell privately by his penciled changes proposes that his public contradiction of me be qualified by revising his answer to read, "That is incorrect, *in a sense,* Senator." The fact is that my statement is correct—and is correct in every sense and not incorrect in any sense. For on page forty-six in answer to my further questions on this point, General O'Donnell said, "If he resigned, then he has no rights." And again on page forty-seven, I asked, "Am I correct if he had resigned and he had not received the appointment, he would have had nothing?" and General O'Donnell answered, "Nothing." And again in information submitted subsequent to the hearing, the Air Force states, "If General Montgomery had resigned and received no retirement or appointment, he would have had no retirement rights."

There are several other instances of penciled changes made by General O'Donnell which change the meaning instead of merely the form of his public answers. I will not burden you with them but should you have the time to examine all of his changes, I think you would find them disturbing. So much for the quality and character of the changes General O'Donnell seeks privately to make of his public answers.

Now let us take a look at the quantity and extent of his changes. The transcript is one hundred four pages in length. Of those one hundred four pages, General O'Donnell made statements and gave answers on eighty-three pages. Now the eighty-three pages on which General O'Donnell gave answers and made statements, he now seeks privately to change his answers and statements on sixty-two pages—in other words, he seeks to change his answers and testimony on about three-fourths of the pages on which his answers and statements appear and he leaves unchanged only about one-fourth or twenty-one pages. If that is not literally a wholesale rewriting of one's testimony, I don't know what is.

How does this wholesale change compare with what the other Air Force witness, General Hall, did to his testimony? The contrast is very interesting. General Hall gave answers and testimony on thirteen pages. He had only one change on one page and no changes on the remaining twelve pages of his testimony. And in contrast to General O'Donnell's revisions, General Hall's sole change was only on form and not on substance and did not change the meaning of his answer. He merely struck out a meaningless few words. Interestingly enough, General Hall made no attempt to change his testimony in the instance where he was shown later by my questioning to have been inaccurate.

Of the sixty-two pages on which General O'Donnell seeks to change his answers, forty-three pages are on answers to questions that I asked him. In contrast, there were only six pages of his answers to me that he left unchanged. In other words, he changed his answers to me at the rate of more than six out of every seven pages.

On three pages Senator Barrett questioned General O'Donnell with respect to the financial aspects of Colonel Montgomery's retirement from the Regular Air Force and his appointment in the Reserve. General O'Donnell seeks to change his answers on all three of these pages.

On six of the pages that Senator Stennis questioned General O'Donnell about Regular Air Force officers being able to resign and by going into the Reserve to finally get as much retirement pay as Regulars not resigning but serving thirty full years and about the extent to which the nominees had earned points, General O'Donnell seeks to change his answers on five pages—leaving only one page unchanged.

In response to the leading questions of Senator Symington, General O'Donnell's rate of testimony changes is not nearly so high as the above cited instances. For on twelve of the twenty-one pages on which General O'Donnell gave answers to Senator Symington's questions, General O'Donnell seeks no changes. Of the nine pages that he does seek changes on, the only material changes are on only two pages. This relatively low rate of change in quantity and character on his answers to Senator Symington's leading questions is in sharp contrast to the extensive manner in which he seeks to change his answers to my not-so-leading questions.

Because of the extent and character of the penciled changes that General O'Donnell has privately made to his public answers and statements to the Committee and members of the Committee, I cannot agree to such a wholesale rewriting of the true record.

Instead it seems to me that the more honest action in keeping with the integrity of the Senate Armed Services Committee at least, if not the integrity of the Air Force, would be for General O'Donnell to list his penciled changes in his answers in a letter to the

Chairman requesting that such letter be placed in the hearing record for the purpose of making changes and extensions to his answers and statements and to let the original transcript stand in its true, pure, and unadulterated form. This will give General O'Donnell a full opportunity to make his changes and extensions without adulterating the hearing record of the Committee.

Sincerely yours,
Margaret Chase Smith, U.S.S.

Mr. President, I opposed the Montgomery and Stewart nominations but I did not oppose any of the other nominations because I did not feel that it was fair to block nominees Herndon and Bradshaw who had excellent records of long participation in the Air Force Reserve. I am certainly not enthusiastic about the Reserve participation records of nominees Henebry, Smith, Alison, Larson, Stiles, Potts, and De Brier. But their records were not to be put in the same class with those of Montgomery and Stewart. And I could not conclude that they, too, should be rejected merely because Montgomery and Stewart had been.

The member of the committee who opposed me in this matter expressed his feeling that fairness to all parties concerned required that my statement to the committee should be printed and made public. I am happy to comply with his expressed feeling and desire in this regard, and so I now submit the text of my statement made yesterday morning to the committee, and ask that it be printed in the Record.

There being no objection, the statement was ordered to be printed in the Record, as follows:

Mr. Chairman, I have gone into these nominations very deeply and were I to make a full presentation of the objectionable matters about them it would take three hours of the time of the committee. I shall not impose upon the committee, but rather limit my statement to a few minutes. If the committee should want my full statement on any of the nominees I shall be happy to give it.

To get these nominations in proper perspective, we must first look at the record of the Air Force itself on these nominations. It is a record of repeated and direct misrepresentations to the committee, a record of extensive false testimony on these nominations, a record of attempts to make a wholesale rewriting of the transcript of the hearing before it was printed.

General O'Donnell sought to change his answers on sixty-two of the eighty-three pages of his testimony—on forty-three of the forty-nine he gave in answers to my questions. General O'Donnell gave false testimony with respect to the J. B. Montgomery nomination: General O'Donnell gave false testimony with respect to the James Stewart nomination: General O'Donnell gave false testimony with respect to the Robert Smith nomination: General O'Donnell gave false testimony with respect to the John R. Alison nomination: General O'Donnell gave false testimony on the John Henebry nomination: General O'Donnell gave false information on the Jess Larson nomination.

For example, at page 34 of the hearing record General O'Donnell gave false testimony in challenging my observation that after Montgomery resigned from the Regular Air Force he would not have been eligible for any retirement benefits if he had not then been commissioned in the Reserve. He interrupted me with the flat statement of "That is incorrect, Senator." Yet later at page 79 the Air Force retracted this misrepresentation made by General O'Donnell and admitted that my statement was true and accurate.

At page 45 in connection with the Stewart nomination I asked if it were not true that an overwhelming number of rated Reserve Air Force generals were either command pilots or senior pilots instead of having the lowest rating of just pilot like Stewart. General O'Donnell's answer was an unequivocal and vigorous "Oh, no. Definitely not." Yet later General O'Donnell tried to have the transcript changed so that his answer would read "Yes" instead of "Oh, no. Definitely not." And the Air Force so requested that change in its letter of correction at page 80 of the hearing in the appendix. Information subsequently submitted by the Air Force revealed that there are twenty-one rated Air Force Reserve generals and that nineteen of that number are either command pilots or senior pilots and that only two hold the lowest rating of mere pilot (see p. 46).

At page 28 of the hearing when I observed that Brigadier General Robert J. Smith at that time had had no fifteen-day active duty training tour since 1950, General O'Donnell gave directly false testimony to the committee and challenged my observation by stating flatly that General Smith served on duty from the tenth to the thirty-first of December 1956. When I said that the record did not show that, General O'Donnell repeated and persisted in this false testimony and misrepresentation to the committee. Yet, the truth is that my observation was truthful and accurate. The Air Force records show that General Smith was not on duty at any time during the period of December 10 to 31 of 1956—and that he had not performed, at the time of the hearing, a fifteen-day tour since 1950. Later General O'Donnell sought to have stricken from the printed hearing record this false testimony that he had given. The correction was later made in the Air Force letter of correction in the appendix of the hearing at page 79.

At pages 51 and 52 Senator Stennis asked for the names of the nominees who had served more than the annual minimum of fifteen days since 1954 and on page 52 General O'Donnell submitted a list stating "The following officers who are up for promotion have had more than the fifteen days' active duty per year since 1954"; and included in that list was Colonel Alison. Again in this instance General O'Donnell gave false testimony and information to the committee for Colonel Alison did not have fifteen days' active duty in 1954 but rather had only three partial days in 1954 and actually was in the inactive Reserve until May 15, 1955 (see p. 24 of the hearing).

At page 60 of the hearing General O'Donnell testified that no waivers had been granted to any of the nominees. Yet, although General Henebry's training category "A" requires not only an annual fifteen-day tour of active training but also a minimum of forty-eight inactive duty training periods annually. General Henebry did not get in forty-eight inactive duty training periods in any year—in fact, he didn't get in any such inactive duty training periods in the fiscal year 1957 just ended. Yet, at page 59 of the hearing General O'Donnell testified that all nominees had met the minimum requirements. Obviously, his testimony with respect to General Henebry in this regard was false.

At page 20 of the hearing the Air Force, through General O'Donnell, represented that Colonel Jess Larson had a training category "A". Because I knew that this could not be true since Colonel Larson is not a pilot or rated officer, I asked pointedly at page 54 about this. Air Force representatives failed to correct this false information when I asked about it and they were content to leave the committee with the false impression that Colonel Larson did have a training category "A" assignment when he did not. They did not correct this false information until over three weeks after the hearing and only after I had pressed the point (see pp. 55 and 56).

Mr. Chairman, there are several other misrepresentations made by the Air Force and its representatives in this matter. I shall not burden the committee with a recital of them for I feel they would be merely cumulative in effect and I think that these enumerated should sufficiently and impressively demonstrate that the Air Force record in this matter before the committee has clearly been one of disregard for truth, disregard for accuracy, and disregard for encouragement of active participation in the Air Force Reserve.

I now turn to the specific nominations. First, I say that the records of nominees Herndon and Bradshaw are excellent and that their nominations should be approved without hesitancy by the committee.

But from that point on there are substantial questions in increasingly serious degree about the rest of the nominees. Colonel Larson was in the Air Force Reserve less than five years before he was nominated for brigadier general. Colonels De Brier, Potts, and Stiles have deficiencies in their records of Reserve participation.

General Henebry failed to perform a fifteen-day tour in retention years 1953, 1954, and 1956—and failed to meet his training category "A" requirement of forty-eight inactive duty training periods in retention year 1957—not only not getting in the required number but failing to get a single period of inactive duty training. General Smith failed to perform a fifteen-day tour from 1950 until the very last minute of retention year 1957, just barely getting in under the deadline for that year. Colonel Alison earned only six points in nine years from 1946 to May 1955 and became active in the Air Force Reserve only when given an assignment that carried the authorized rank of brigadier general.

The worst two cases of the eleven nominations are those of Colonel Montgomery and Colonel Stewart.

There has been much false publicity about Colonel Stewart and the qualifications claimed for him. It has been claimed that he has trained actively with the Reserve every year. That claim was proved false at page 44 of the hearing. It has been claimed that he is the first pilot of a B-52. That claim was proved false at page 45 of the hearing. It has been claimed that he could fly a B-52 anywhere in the world. That claim was proved false at the hearing.

In fact, the real truth was established at the hearing—that Colonel Stewart is not current or qualified on any military aircraft (see p. 45). Instead of being a command pilot or senior pilot as the overwhelming number of rated Air Force Reserve generals are, he has the lowest rating of mere pilot.

Instead of having trained actively every year with the Reserve, he didn't start training until a year ago in July—the first time that he did a fifteen-day tour since the end of World War II—the first time in eleven years. In fact, his participation record in the Reserve until last year was only nine days in eleven years.

What's more, even though his mobilization assignment is Deputy Director of Operations of the Strategic Air Command—literally the No. 3 job in SAC importance if war comes—the very bare minimum of participation is to be required of him in the future—the minimum of only fifteen days—nothing else.

For he has a training category "D" in this most important mobilization assignment. Now what is the basis for such a low minimum training category "D"? The Air Force provided the answer to this at pages 54 and 71 of the hearing with the statement of: "These individuals are considered proficient in their Air Force specialty by virtue of their recent release from active military service or maintain their proficiency through their normal civilian pursuits."

Stewart was released from active military service in 1945—twelve years ago. Obviously that is not a recent release.

Stewart's normal civilian pursuit is that of motion-picture actor. Obviously he can't maintain his proficiency for Deputy Director of Operations of the Strategic Air Command by being a motion-picture actor.

Past national presidents of the Reserve Officers Association have complained bitterly to me that the Stewart nomination was destructive to the morale of the Air Force Reserve.

The worst case in my opinion is that of the John B. Montgomery nomination, for here is a record of a nominee showing practically no interest in the Reserve—a nominee who for nearly sixteen months after he was commissioned in the Reserve did not lift his finger for participation in the Reserve—a nominee, who in over two years, in over twenty-six months, has put in a total of only fifteen days in the Air Force Reserve—a nominee with the least participation of all of the nominees in the Air Force Reserve—a nominee who has been in the Air Force Reserve only a little over two years.

Here is a case where a regular officer used the Air Force Reserve to get what he couldn't get in the regular establishment— who left the Regular Air Force, after being refused retirement as a regular major general, to take a high-paying civilian job—but who, by taking advantage of a slip and loophole in the law, will be able to get just as much retirement pay as his contemporaries who stay in the Regular Air Force on duty 365 days a year while Montgomery is not on duty in some years a single day in the year—a nominee who is having his cake in the form of abandonment of the Regular Air Force for a plush job in private industry but who is also eating his cake by using the Air Force Reserve to get, at the age of fifty-three, the maximum retirement pay of 75 percent of the base pay of a major general on a shocking minimum of participation in Reserve training duty with the Air Force.

The Montgomery case has become not only a symbolic case of a destructive blow to Air Force reservists who see in it a way for regulars to use the Reserve to their personal advantage—but also to the regulars themselves who see one of their contemporaries abandon the Regular Air Force for a plush job in industry and still get just as much retirement pay as those contemporaries who remain faithful to the Air Force and stay on the job 365 days a year for thirty years. I know because I have had one- and two-star Regular generals who served under and with Montgomery come to me and complain about the Montgomery nomination. They say that the Montgomery nomination is literally an invitation to all Regular

Air Force generals to resign from the Regular Air Force to accept
high-paying civilian jobs and then be commissioned in the Air
Force Reserve and use it for minimum participation and the easy
way to get the maximum retirement pay with the least possible
service.

In fact, the Montgomery case is so bad that in an unguarded
moment even General O'Donnell at page 39 of the hearing stated:
". . . I have been in the personnel business for four years over
there, and that is the first time an action like this has been taken,
and I don't anticipate any in the future because of this."

Mr. Chairman and members of the committee, I say that the
committee should make sure of this—that the committee should
serve notice on the Air Force and all Regular Air Force generals
that the Montgomery nomination is not an invitation for them to
abandon the Air Force for plush civilian jobs and use the Air Force
Reserve to get the most retirement pay for the least service—by
rejecting the Montgomery nomination now and serving notice on
the Air Force and Colonel Montgomery that if he is to be made a
general in the Air Force Reserve he is going to have to give a little
more of his time—that there is no justification for making him a
general in the Air Force Reserve on only fifteen days' activity in the
Air Force Reserve.

APPENDIX

NUCLEAR CREDIBILITY

One may well ask why the Soviets suddenly took the pretext of Berlin to demand that the status of the city be changed—willingly or by force. One may ask, too, why the situation in Berlin, which for sixteen years seemed tolerable to them, and which they themselves created with the United States and Great Britain at the Potsdam conference—at which France was not present—*now, suddenly, seems intolerable.* One may ask why they are suddenly coupling their demands with frightful threats. One may ask whether anyone really believes that the German Federal Republic, as it is, is today a threat to Russia. One may ask whether there is any Russian who believes this, since the Kremlin claims that they are in a position to crush totally and immediately, with bombs equivalent apparently to over one hundred million tons of TNT, anyone who lifts a hand against the Communist world.

There is in all this welter of imprecations and cries organized by the Soviets so much that is arbitrary and artificial that one is led to attribute it either to the premeditated unleashing of wild ambitions or regard it as an attempt to conceal great difficulties. The second hypothesis seems to me the more plausible because, despite the constraint, isolation, and violent acts to which the Communists have shackled the countries under their yoke, and despite certain collective successes which they have achieved by (exerting pressure?) on the majority of their subjects, in fact, communism's shortcomings, its defiances, its domestic failures, and on top of it all, its character of inhuman oppression, are being felt more and more by the elite and the masses.

The Communists are less and less able to delude and to curb. And then also the satellites, which the Soviet regime holds under its laws, are experiencing more and more, because of national feelings, all that is cruel in the annexation which they have suffered.

Thus, one can understand that in these conditions the Soviets consider the Berlin Affair an appropriate occasion for distracting the attention of their own people and others. And, in fact, with Berlin where it is, it will be relatively easy for them to demonstrate on the spot, that the restrictive measures which they have taken have for them limited risks.

And then, they may think that the United States, England, and France will allow themselves to slide into discouragement, into resignation, and thus the withdrawal of these three powers would be a hard blow to the Atlantic alliance. Moreover, the whole world would be shown that the totalitarian regime—the totalitarian camp—is decidedly the stronger in the face of an uncertain and divided West.

But, to be precise, this is not true. Of course the Soviets have at their disposal terrible nuclear arms, but the West has formidable ones too. If a world conflict were to break out, the use of these forces of destruction would doubtless bring in its wake, in particular, the complete overthrow of Russia and of countries under the Communist yoke. What is the use of ruling over dead men? And, moreover, the rule would itself be finished, for in such a disaster the backbone of the regime would be broken as well—the backbone of a regime which rules only with an authoritarian apparatus and the police, with everything rigidly planned and implacably enforced. This the Soviet leaders know in spite of all their boasting.

The Western powers have, then, no reason for not considering the Soviet moves with a clear eye and a firm heart.

It is true, I repeat, that locally, in Berlin, the act of force which would be involved might provoke, might procure for the Soviets certain advantages, since it would obviously be difficult for the Western powers to act from a distance on the territory and in the air of the former German capital. However, the West could answer very well on the seas and in the skies crossed by Soviet ships and planes, and this would be far from their bases. This poor exchange would undoubtedly not end to the advantage of the Soviets. In short, if the latter wants to reduce the positions and cut the communications of the Allies in Berlin by force, the Allies must maintain their positions and their communications by force. Certainly one thing leads to another, as they say, and if all this leads to a multiplication of the hostile acts of the Soviets, acts which must be answered, it may end in general war. But it would be because the Soviets deliberately wished it, and in that case any preliminary retreat by the West would only have served to enfeeble and divide it without preventing the outcome.

At a certain point in facing the threats of an ambitious imperialism, any retreat has the effect of overexciting the aggressor, or encouraging him to double his pressure, and, finally, facilitates and hastens his attack. In summation, the Western powers have at present no better means of serving world peace than remaining firm and direct.

APPENDIX

NUCLEAR TEST BAN TREATY

Congressional Record—Senate—
September 19, 1963

Mrs. SMITH. Mr. President, on September 16, 1963, I raised certain questions with respect to the wording of the nuclear test ban treaty. Very promptly and voluntarily and without prompting or request from me, the Secretary of State sent to me the answers of the Legal Adviser of the State Department to those questions.

Because I believe the Members of the Senate will be interested in those answers, I ask unanimous consent that the letter of the Secretary of State to me, dated September 18, 1963, and the memorandum of the State Department Legal Adviser, dated September 17, 1963, be printed at this point in the body of the Record.

There being no objection, the letters were ordered to be printed in the Record, as follows:

Hon. Margaret Chase Smith,
U. S. Senate.

Dear Senator Smith: The questions concerning the language of the test ban treaty that you raised during the debate in the Senate Monday, and are printed at page 16204 of the Congressional Record for September 16, were called to my attention yesterday morning. I asked the Legal Adviser of the Department to prepare a memorandum dealing with these questions. I am pleased to send you that memorandum which represents the position of the executive branch on these points of law. I am also sending a copy of the memorandum to Senator Fulbright.

Sincerely yours, Dean Rusk

September 17, 1963

Memorandum for the Secretary.

From: The Legal Adviser.

Subject: Questions raised by Senator Smith concerning the test ban treaty.

You have asked me to prepare a memorandum responsive to the questions raised by Senator Smith concerning the language of the test ban treaty and printed at page 16204 of the Congressional Record for September 16, 1963. Senator Smith had grouped her questions under Roman numeral headings. For convenience, the same format is adopted here.

I

The first three questions raised by Senator Smith relate to the phrase, in article I, "at any place under its jurisdiction or control." This phrase was inserted in article I by the United States to qualify the obligation of parties "to prohibit" and "to prevent" nuclear tests in the three environments. Without this qualifying phrase, parties to the treaty would have been obligated to prohibit and prevent all nuclear explosions prescribed by the treaty, no matter where they occurred or by whom they were conducted. A party obviously could not prohibit or prevent a nuclear test explosion unless it had either jurisdiction or control over the carrying out of the explosion. For this reason, the obligation was limited to tests occurring "at any place under its jurisdiction or control."

For the purposes of the test ban treaty, a party is considered to have temporary control over any place in which it conducts a nuclear test explosion during the time that the explosion is being conducted. Each control is distinguished in the treaty from jurisdiction by the use of the disjunctive "or." It was precisely to avoid the problems to which Senator Smith calls attention that the words "or control" were inserted in article I.

Thus, the answer to Senator Smith's first question is that a party could not justify carrying out a nuclear explosion in the atmosphere above an uninhabited island not claimed by it. Although the explosion would not occur at a place under the jurisdiction of the party conducting the explosion it would occur at a place under its control for the purposes of article I. Such an explosion would also violate paragraph 2 of article I which prohibits parties from "causing, encouraging, or in any way participating in" the carrying out of the proscribed explosions "anywhere." This is one of a number of cases in which the obligations imposed by the two paragraphs overlap.

Similarly with respect to Senator Smith's second question, any party conducting a nuclear weapon test in outer space would be considered to have temporary control over the place in outer space where the test was conducted, although it would not have jurisdiction over outer space or any portion thereof. Such a party would also have control over the area on earth from which it directed the explosion.

The same analysis applies to Senator Smith's third question. For the purposes of article I, any party conducting a nuclear weapon test explosion in the high seas would be considered to have temporary control over that portion of the high seas. An opinion of the legal adviser, dealing in part with the high seas, is attached.

Senator Smith's fourth question is:

"4. Does the ban on any other nuclear explosion prevent us from operating atomic energy plants for the production of electricity, the steamship *Savannah,* or any atomic submarine, all of which are operated by means of controlled atomic explosions?"

The answer is "No." An explosion is the release of large quantities of energy in a very short period of time—on the order of a few millionths of a second. Nuclear power reactors such as those for producing electricity or propelling steamships or submarines release energy comparatively slowly—over periods of many hours, weeks, or months. No explosions take place within the meaning of the treaty. Chairman Seaborg told the Senate Committee on Foreign Relations:

"The treaty will, of course, not inhibit the peaceful uses in any of the fields that do not have to do with nuclear explosives; that is, the field of civilian nuclear power, and the use of nuclear energy for propulsion and auxiliary power in space and the use of isotopes in medicine and industry and research, and so forth" (p. 239, hearings).

Senator Smith's fifth question is:

"5. Will we be branded as a violator of the treaty if we have an accidental explosion at one of our atomic energy plants?"

The answer is "No." The obligations of the treaty are concerned with the intentional conduct of the parties. It could not reasonably be maintained that a party had "carried out," "caused," "encouraged," or "participated in" a nuclear explosion if the explosion occurred by accident. Nor could the obligation to "prevent" and "prohibit" nuclear explosions be violated by an accidental explosion occurring against the will of the party and despite its best efforts to prevent it.

II

The analysis of the first three questions under Roman numeral I above applies in large measure to the two questions raised under Roman numeral II. As noted earlier, paragraphs 1 and 2 of article I of the treaty overlap to some extent. Paragraph 2 of article I is intended in part to prevent a party from giving assistance to another nation in carrying out the proscribed tests, and thus doing indirectly what paragraph 1 would prohibit it from doing directly. However, by virtue of the words "causing" and "in any way participating in"—deliberately chosen because of their broad scope—paragraph 2 also outlaws direct action by the parties. To use Senator Smith's examples, the Soviet Union would be prohibited both by paragraph 1 and by paragraph 2 from carrying out an atmospheric explosion anywhere. It would also be prohibited by paragraph 2 from "causing, encouraging, or in any way participating in" a nuclear explosion by the Communist Chinese regime in the atmosphere above Mainland China. Paragraph 2 is not limited by the phrase "under any place under its jurisdiction or control" because it does not obligate the parties "to prohibit" or "to prevent" nuclear weapon tests, as does paragraph 1.

III

With respect to Senator Smith's final question, an opinion of the Legal Adviser of August 12 was prepared on this point. It concludes that the United States would not be compelled to wait three months before resuming nuclear weapons tests if the Soviet Union violated its obligations under the treaty. A copy of that opinion is attached. The President's letter of September 11 to Senators Mansfield and Dirksen also points out that the "United States retains the right to resume atmospheric testing forthwith if the Soviet Union should conduct tests in violation of the treaty."

Abram Chayes.

Mrs. SMITH. Mr. President, I wish to make very brief observations and comments on the answers of the Legal Adviser of the State Department.

I

The answers to, and observations concerning, the first three questions under the heading "I" depend for their validity upon the parties to the treaty being in agreement with the Legal Adviser's views concerning the meaning of the term "control," as used in paragraph 1 of article I of the treaty. The term "control" is not defined in the treaty and the doctrine of temporary control with respect to outer space and the high seas expressed by the Legal Adviser appears to be novel. It is reassuring to know that the Legal Adviser believes that paragraph 2 of article I of the treaty, which does not contain the term "at any place under its jurisdiction or control," would apply with respect to explosions of the type dealt with by the first three questions.

The answers to, and observations concerning, questions 4 and 5 under the heading "I" likewise are dependent for their validity upon the parties to the treaty being in agreement with the Legal Adviser's view that the term "any other nuclear explosion" does not include either the process by which heat is obtained from fissionable material in a nuclear reactor or an accidental nuclear explosion.

II

As indicated before, it is reassuring to know that the Legal Adviser construes paragraph 2 of article I of the treaty to be applicable with respect to both direct and indirect acts of the parties to the treaty and is therefore not compelled to rely upon any questionable definition of the term "control," as used in paragraph 1 of article I, for the purpose of finding that explosions over unclaimed territory, in outer space, and under the high seas are barred by the treaty.

III

In connection with the question which was posed under this heading, it is assumed that the President's statement in his letter of September 11 to Senators Mansfield and Dirksen that the "United States retains the right to resume atmospheric testing forthwith if the Soviet Union should conduct tests in violation of the treaty" means that we are prepared under those circumstances to have others brand us as a treaty violator and that we would not feel compelled to follow the procedure adopted with respect to our denunciation of the extradition treaty with Greece— see page 4, opinion of the Legal Adviser of the State Department, dated August 12, 1963, with respect to the right of the United States to withdraw from the nuclear test ban treaty in the event of violation by another party.

October 20, 1963

Mrs. Smith. Mr. President, this morning I received from the Secretary of Defense answers of the General Counsel of the Department of Defense to the legal questions I raised in the Senate on September 16, 1963, on the wording of the nuclear test ban treaty. Because of their striking similarity to answers of the Legal Adviser of the State Department, which I placed in the Record yesterday. I shall not comment on these answers of the chief legal officer of the Defense Department but rather will observe that the comments I made yesterday on the answers of the State Department's Legal Adviser apply equally to these which I now ask unanimous request be placed in the body of the Record at this point.

There being no objection, the answers were ordered to be printed in the Record, as follows:

ANSWERS BY THE GENERAL COUNSEL OF THE DEPARTMENT OF DEFENSE TO LEGAL QUESTIONS RAISED BY THE WORDING OF THE NUCLEAR TEST BAN TREATY

I

Question 1: Could a party to the treaty carry out a nuclear explosion in the atmosphere above an uninhabited island not claimed by it and justify its action upon the ground that the explosion did not occur at a place under its jurisdiction or control?

Answer: No. The words "at any place under its jurisdiction or control" in the first paragraph of article I of the treaty apply only to that paragraph and are necessary as a legal matter since a party to the treaty would have no authority to prohibit or to prevent nuclear explosions at places not under its jurisdiction or control and accordingly would not be able to fulfill any treaty obligation to prohibit or to prevent nuclear explosions at such places. It should be noted, however, that a party would be construed temporarily to have control over any place where it conducted a test, and therefore paragraph 1 would prohibit a party from conducting a test in the circumstances hypothesized. In any event, the second paragraph of article I prohibits a party, itself, from conducting a nuclear test in the three environments anywhere.

Question 2: What nuclear explosions in outer space are banned by this paragraph in view of the fact that outer space, and particularly the more remote regions thereof, is not considered to be within the jurisdiction or control of any nation? If Russia explodes a nuclear device in outer space and we claim that such action is prohibited by this paragraph, are we placed in a position where we must simultaneously admit that Russia has jurisdiction over or controls the particular region of outer space in which the explosion occurs?

Answer: No. As was the case in question 1, a party is prohibited by paragraph 2 from conducting tests in the three environments without regard to the question of "jurisdiction or control," and by paragraph 1 by virtue of the temporary control.

Question 3: Would a nuclear explosion underwater in the middle of the Pacific Ocean be barred by this paragraph in view of the fact that the high seas are not considered by nations to be within the control or jurisdiction of any particular nation?

Answer: Yes. Such a test would be barred by article I for the reasons given in answers 1 and 2.

Question 4: Does the ban on "any other nuclear explosion" prevent us from operating atomic energy plants for the production of electricity, the steamship *Savannah,* or any atomic submarine, all of which are operated by means of controlled atomic explosions?

Answer: No. Atomic energy reactors, which release energy slowly, do not produce a nuclear explosion within the meaning of the treaty.

Question 5: Will we be branded as a violator of the treaty if we have an accidental explosion at one of our atomic energy plants?

Answer: No. An accidental explosion of one of our atomic energy plants would not constitute a violation of the treaty; the treaty is aimed at intentional acts.

II

Question 1: Does paragraph 2 apply to direct acts of the parties or only to indirect acts of the parties? For example, does it apply to a nuclear explosion by Russia in the atmosphere above Russian soil or is it intended to apply only to such a situation as a nuclear explosion by the Communist Chinese regime in the atmosphere above China which is caused, encouraged, or participated in by Russia?

Answer: Paragraph 2 of article I is intended to bar a party from conducting tests itself in the three environments (direct acts) and from giving materials for use in nuclear weapons, or information relating to their design or manufacture to any other state whether or not a party, if that state was engaged in, or proposed to engage in, nuclear weapons tests in the three environments (indirect acts).

Question 2: If paragraph 2 does apply to direct acts of the parties, how do you resolve the conflict between its provisions, which are not limited by the phrase "at any place under its jurisdiction or control," and the provisions of paragraph 1, which are limited by such phrase?

Answer: As shown by the answer to the preceding questions, there is no conflict between the provisions of paragraphs 1 and 2. The two paragraphs overlap to some extent. The words "jurisdiction or control" do not limit paragraph 2 because paragraph 2 does not impose an obligation to prohibit or to prevent.

III

Question: If the United States decides to withdraw from the treaty because it has irrefutable evidence that Russia has violated it, would we not be compelled to wait three months before resuming nuclear testing unless we were willing to risk being branded as treaty violators?

Answer: It is clear under international law that the United States would not be compelled by the treaty to wait three months before resuming nuclear testing if Russia violates the treaty.

———

Department of Defense,
Washington, September 19, 1963.

Hon. Margaret Chase Smith,
U. S. Senate,
Washington, D.C.

Dear Senator Smith:

As I explained to you over the telephone last evening, I am extremely sorry that I did not see your letter of September 10 relative to the sixteen questions on the test ban and I am particularly sorry that I did not see or sign the outgoing letter.

I agree with the answers to your questions given by Secretary Rusk, and I am in full agreement with the statements made by the President in his letter to Senators Mansfield and Dirksen—some of which deal with matters raised by your questions. Nevertheless, I would like to take this opportunity to offer some further comment on a few of the questions which you posed on September 9. Specifically, I refer to your questions 2, 9, and 11.

Your second question was: "Are we reasonably confident and secure in the knowledge that our ballistic-missile retaliatory second strike force will survive and operate in a nuclear environment?" This is of course a very important matter. You have the information concerning missile-site survivability contained in my earlier remarks, referred to by Secretary Rusk. I would like to add a few comments on the ability of our missiles to penetrate enemy defenses.

Present penetration capability, as you know, depends upon saturation of defenses—upon numbers of weapons, decoy design, salvo techniques, and nuclear technology. The limited test ban treaty does not affect the first three of these factors. It is relevant only to the last of them. Ballistic-missile re-entry vehicles and warheads are susceptible to both blast and radiation. The latter can be tested sufficiently underground. Although blast cannot be tested underground, we have information from which to extrapolate blast effect and are able to build around uncertainties. Furthermore, we have every reason to believe that the Soviet Union has had no more experience in the testing of relevant blast effects than have we.

Because of the extremely large number of U.S. missiles and penetration aids available for saturating Soviet defense, I am confident that, in any event, sufficient U.S. striking power not only can survive attack but can penetrate to destroy the Soviet Union.

In your ninth question, you asked: "Can we, in fact, maintain an adequate readiness to test in those prohibited environments in the event the treaty should suddenly be abrogated?" You are familiar with the testimony on this point and with Deputy Secretary Gilpatric's letter to Senator Russell, in which he dealt with the Joint Chiefs of Staff safeguard (c). I am convinced that we can maintain a state of readiness such that we will be ready to perform proof tests within two months, development tests within three months, and (by a year from now) effects tests within six months. We are, now, improving test support facilities, which include preparation and maintenance of off-continent support bases and test sites. We are obtaining diagnostic aircraft, instrumented ships and aircraft, weapon drop aircraft, and sampler and other support aircraft; and we are preparing operating bases on Johnston Island and in the Hawaiian area. Also, the Atomic Energy Commission and Department of Defense test organization is being kept strong and ready.

Your eleventh question was: "Will we be restrained from ever determining feasibility, developing and deploying any defense whatever against ballistic-missile attack?" In my testimony, I addressed this point quite fully, but two points are worth repeating: First, we should bear in mind that, while an anti-ballistic-missile system might be very important, it is unrealistic to expect any foreseeable anti-ballistic-missile system to be effective enough to save a nation from great harm in the event it is attacked. Second, the nonnuclear aspects (capacity for decoy discrimination, traffic-handling capacity, reaction speed, and missile performance) dominate the problem of developing an effective anti-ballistic-missile system. The nuclear aspects involved are warhead development and the nuclear effects problems of self-kill and blackout. The treaty, as you are aware, has no bearing on the nonnuclear features. Warhead development can continue through underground testing, and some of the important questions of self-kill can also be resolved by underground testing. Questions relating to blast, as in the case of incoming warhead kill, referred to on the previous page, cannot be solved by underground tests, but we have information from which to extrapolate blast effect and are able to build around uncertainties. And atmospheric testing would be needed to provide either side further understanding of the blackout phenomenon—a phenomenon which has been probed in different ways, with what I believe to be comparable success, by both the United States and U.S.S.R. We believe that our latest atmospheric tests revealed the approximate limits of the blackout problem. If the anti-ballistic-missile problems unaffected by this treaty could be resolved, the uncertainties caused by gaps in our understanding of blackout could be circumvented through conservative design. Those responsible for the U.S. anti-ballistic-missile program believe that the Nike-X system can be developed and deployed without further atmospheric testing. Moreover, it is their judgment and the judgment of those responsible for making intelligence estimates on Soviet capabilities that our efforts in developing an anti-ballistic-missile system are comparable, if not superior, to those of the Soviets.

I note that on September 16 you asked eight legal questions about the treaty. I asked my General Counsel to prepare answers to the questions. His answers are attached for your information.

If I can be of further assistance to you, please let me know.

Sincerely, Robert S. McNamara,
Secretary of Defense.

Mrs. SMITH. I also ask unanimous consent to place in the body of the Record at this point the answers submitted by the Secretary of State and the Secretary of Defense to the sixteen questions I raised in the Senate on September 10, 1963.

There being no objection, the answers were ordered to be printed in the Record, as follows:

The Secretary of State,
Washington, September 18, 1963.

Hon. Margaret Chase Smith,
U. S. Senate.

Dear Senator Smith:

In answer to your letter to me dated September 10, I am pleased to enclose a memorandum prepared at my request responding to the 16 questions on the test ban treaty which you asked in your address to the Senate on September 9. I hope the enclosure will prove helpful to you.

Sincerely yours, Dean Rusk.

RESPONSE TO SIXTEEN QUESTIONS ON THE TEST BAN
TREATY ASKED BY SENATOR SMITH

1. Has the Soviet Union, through its most recent atmospheric test series, now achieved a nuclear advantage over the United States of a military or scientific significance?

In his message transmitting the treaty to the Senate, the President said: "According to a comprehensive report prepared by the responsible agencies of Government for the National Security Council, the tests conducted by both the Soviet Union and the United States since President Eisenhower first proposed this kind of treaty in 1959 have not resulted in any substantial alteration in the strategic balance. In 1959 our relative nuclear position was strong enough to make a limited test ban desirable, and it remains so today."

See also the statement of Secretary McNamara at pages 97–109 of the hearings before the Committee on Foreign Relations and his statement at page 191, where he concluded that "The Soviet tests of 1961–62 definitely did not reverse the superiority of the United States in the technology of strategic nuclear warheads."

Attention is also called to the testimony on this topic by Mr. McCone before the Committee on Foreign Relations in executive session.

2. Are we reasonably confident and secure in the knowledge that our ballistic-missile retaliatory second strike force will survive and operate in a nuclear environment?

Testimony by Secretary McNamara in support of his conclusion that "The U.S. strategic missile force is designed to survive, and it will survive," appears at pages 102–3 of the hearings before the Committee on Foreign Relations. Additional testimony to the same effect is referred to at pages 17–18 of the report of the Committee on Foreign Relations.

3. In seeking to slow down the arms race as a purported advantage of this treaty, will we adopt nuclear parity as the basis for deterring thermonuclear war rather than nuclear superiority?

As Secretary Rusk testified before the Committee on Foreign Relations on August 12, 1963:

"I believe that the United States must maintain in its own security interests a very large overall nuclear superiority with respect to the Soviet Union. This involves primarily the capacity to demonstrate that regardless of who strikes first, the United States will be in a position effectively to destroy an aggressor." (Hearings, p. 45.)

Secretary McNamara testified as follows on August 13:

"The United States has nuclear superiority. We are determined to maintain that superiority.

"I regard as essential to our national security the maintenance of a military posture such that we can absorb any initial surprise attack and strike back with sufficient power to destroy the aggressor." (Hearings, p. 98.)

And AEC Chairman Seaborg testified as follows on August 14: "I feel convinced that we can maintain our overall nuclear weapons superiority over the Soviet Union for a longer period under this nuclear test ban treaty than would be the case in the absence of the treaty." (Hearings, page 221.)

4. Will the treaty, as claimed, prevent the proliferation of nuclear weapons when France and Red China refuse to be bound and when underground testing is sanctioned for all nations whether they sign or not?

In his message of August 8, 1963, transmitting the test ban treaty to the Senate, the President wrote:

"While it cannot wholly prevent the spread of nuclear arms to nations not now possessing them, it prohibits assistance to testing in these environments by others; it will be signed by many other potential testers; and it is thus an important wedge in our effort to 'get the genie back in the bottle.'"

Over a hundred nations—including everyone, except France and the Chinese Communists, which appears to have any serious prospect of becoming a nuclear power—have now either signed the treaty or indicated publicly that they would do so. Each of these signatories is not only undertaking to deny itself the right to conduct tests in three or four possible environments, but also agreeing not to cause, encourage, or in any way participate in such tests by others. Moreover, the treaty will prevent any power—whether a signatory or not —from receiving such help or encouragement from any signatory. Secretary McNamara indicated some of the effects of these restrictions when he said:

"With testing limited to the underground environment, the potential cost of a nuclear weapons development program would increase sharply for all signatory states. And, since testing underground is not only more costly but also more difficult and time consuming, the proposed treaty would retard progress in weapons development in cases where the added cost and other factors were not sufficient to preclude it altogether." (Hearings, page 108.)

Reference is also made to pages 976–77 of the hearings before the Committee on Foreign Relations; page 20 of the report of that committee; and the testimony of Secretary Rusk before that committee in executive session on August 28, 1963.

5. How is one to define or interpret that which shall constitute an

underground test within the meaning of article I, section 1, sub-section (a) of the treaty?

The views of Secretary Rusk on this question are set forth at pages 34–35 and 44 of the hearings before the Committee on Foreign Relations, excerpts from which are quoted at page 22 of the report of that committee. See also the testimony quoted in response to the eighth question, below.

6. Do we possess the capability to detect all nuclear detonations occurring in the three environments prohibited by the treaty?

The agreed statement of the Joint Chiefs of Staff at page 274 of the hearings dealt with this question as follows:

"The dangers of detection and the cost and difficulty of testing in outer space would tend to impose severe restrictions upon such clandestine testing. Other clandestine tests in the atmosphere or underwater, depending on their size, would involve a fairly high probability of detection by our conventional intelligence or our atomic energy detection system."

This conclusion is supported by the information with respect to our detection system brought out by Mr. McCone and Dr. Northrup in executive session. Your attention is also called to the following point made by the President in his letter to Senator Mansfield and Senator Dirksen appearing at page 15915 of the Congressional Record for September 11, 1963:

"Our facilities for the detection of possible violations of this treaty will be expanded and improved as required to increase our assurance against clandestine violation by others."

7. Can any significant advances in nuclear technology be achieved by clandestine testing in those three environments at yields which may possibly be below our ability to detect?

The conclusion of the Joint Chiefs of Staff with respect to clandestine testing appears at page 274 of the hearings, immediately following the testimony quoted above with respect to the probability that such tests could be detected:

"Moreover, the Joint Chiefs of Staff consider the resulting progress which the Soviets might make clandestinely to be a relatively minor factor in relation to the overall present and probable balance of military strength if adequate safeguards are maintained."

This conclusion is supported not only by the other expert testimony specifically referred to at page 18 of the report of the Committee on Foreign Relations, but also by the testimony of Mr. McCone and Dr. Northrup before that committee in executive session.

8. Will we be able to differentiate between a shallow underground

explosion and an atmospheric burst detonated close to the surface of the earth?

It is believed that the testimony of Dr. Harold Brown in the printed hearings before the Committee on Foreign Relations is responsive to this question:

"A third type of clandestine tests which might be tried is surface bursts or very near surface bursts. These are very detectable." (Hearings, p. 535.)

"From the technical point of view, I think what I can say is that any test, any large test, that is not underground will be detected as not being underground . . . I would view a test that put most of its energy into the atmosphere as an atmospheric test and it would be detected as such, and so I would assume, as the Secretary of Defense said, that a clearly atmospheric test is illegal, even if there is a foot of dirt over it. But from the technical point of view, I have said all I can say on an expert basis." (Hearings, p. 551.)

For more detailed information with respect to our detection capabilities, see the testimony of Mr. McCone and Dr. Northrup before the Committee on Foreign Relations in executive session.

9. Can we, in fact, maintain an adequate readiness to test in those prohibited environments in the event the treaty should suddenly be abrogated?

The director of the Los Alamos Scientific Laboratory testified as follows on this point at page 582 of the hearings before the Committee on Foreign Relations:

"I believe, with a reasonable expenditure, it could be possible to resume the airdrop type of nuclear atmospheric test almost immediately upon notice to proceed provided current normal preparations are continued and somewhat amplified."

In addition to the other testimony on this point summarized at pages 18–20 of the report of the Committee on Foreign Relations, attention is called to the letter dated August 23, 1963, from the Deputy Secretary of Defense to Senator Russell set forth at pages 16084–86 of the Congressional Record for September 13, 1963.

10. Will our scientific laboratories and the interest of our scientists deteriorate under a treaty which permits only underground testing?

The Director of the Los Alamos Scientific Laboratory testified as follows at page 582 of the hearings:

"If we do, indeed, vigorously prepare for atmospheric test resumption; if we do, indeed, continue an active program of underground testing, then I believe that the Los Alamos Scientific Laboratory can maintain a vigorous, enthusiastic, and productive group of scientists engaged in weapon development.

"We have met this challenge, and harder, before when we did not test at all for the three years after 1958."

Other reassuring testimony on this point (excerpts from which appear at pages 19–20 of the report of the Committee on Foreign Relations) was given by Chairman Seaborg and by a former director of the Lawrence Radiation Laboratory. For the plans to implement Secretary McNamara's pledge to "maintain the vitality of our weapons laboratories," see the letter from the Deputy Secretary of Defense to Senator Russell set forth at pages 16084–86 of the Congressional Record for September 13, 1963.

11. Will we be restrained from ever determining feasibility, developing and deploying any defense whatever against ballistic missile attack?

In concluding his testimony on this subject at pages 103–4 of the hearings before the Committee on Foreign Relations, Secretary McNamara said: "Thus, with or without a test ban, we could proceed with the development of an ABM system." Other testimony on this question is referred to at pages 12–15 of the report of the Committee on Foreign Relations.

As for deployment, Secretary Rusk pointed out at page 28 of the hearings: "There is nothing here that interferes with . . . the deployment of nuclear weapons."

12. Will this treaty permit the Soviet Union to achieve equality in the low-yield tactical weapons where it is generally acknowledged that we have an advantage and yet preclude us from ever achieving equality in the high-yield weapon where the Soviet Union is unquestionably superior?

Secretary McNamara testified that:

"There is no question in my mind but that without a test ban the Soviets would be able to advance more rapidly and at lesser cost in the field of tactical nuclear weapon technology than they will be able to under the test ban." (Hearings, p. 152.)

As for high-yield weapons, reference is made to Dr. Teller's statement (quoted at p. 11 of the report of the Committee on Foreign Relations) that: "It is not clear to me that these very big yields will result in a substantial advantage for the Russians . . . In evaluating the consequences of the test ban, I do not place very great importance on the lead which the Russians enjoy in this particular field"; to his similar testimony at pages 470–71 of the hearings before that committee; and to the other testimony on this subject referred to at pages 10–11 of the report of that committee.

13. To what extent can we satisfy, through underground testing,

the military and scientific requirements which were to have been investigated by atmospheric tests planned for next year?

A number of possible test objectives by the United States are listed at page 6 of the interim report of the Preparedness Investigating Subcommittee issued on September 9, 1963. The extent to which certain of these objectives can be met by underground testing or otherwise compensated for was discussed by Dr. Howard Brown at pages 557 et seq. of the hearings before the Committee on Foreign Relations. Questions as to the significance of a number of the listed test objectives are discussed at pages 10–18 of the report of the Committee on Foreign Relations and in Chairman Seaborg's testimony at pages 207–8 of the hearings before that committee, which he concluded by pointing out that "where there are limitations on our testing program, there are also limitations on the Soviets and on the other signatories."

14. What is the human tolerance for radioactivity and what is the truth about the danger of atmospheric contamination, even at previous rates of testing, in causing genetic damage and leukemia to the living and yet unborn?

The difficulties of giving any precise answer to this question have been brought out not only in the test ban hearings before the Committee on Foreign Relations, but also, much more fully, by the hearings on "Fallout, Radiation Standards, and Countermeasures" before the Subcommittee on Research, Development, and Radiation of the Joint Committee on Atomic Energy. For a fairly succinct statement of these difficulties and of the probabilities of genetic and somatic effects from fallout from nuclear weapons tests conducted through 1961, see the report of the Federal Radiation Council printed at pages 403 et seq. of the printed hearings before that subcommittee conducted in June 1963, which includes the following statements:

"Much available evidence indicates that any radiation is potentially harmful . . . It is virtually certain that genetic effects can be produced by even the lowest dosages. These effects in children of exposed parents and all future generations may be of many kinds, ranging from minor defects too small to be noticed to severe disease and death.

"Estimates of two kinds of somatic effects, leukemia and bone cancer, are given in table III. As mentioned earlier, it is not known whether or not there is a threshold dose below which these diseases are not produced."

When asked whether the radioactive fallout from the unrestricted testing which could occur if the treaty were rejected was a matter of concern, former AEC Commissioner Libby replied:

"Yes, sir. We ought to consider it was one of the factors involved, one of the important factors."

Some additional materials on the subject appear at pages 15670–75 of the Congressional Record for September 9, 1963.

15. What will be the effect of ratification upon our Plowshare program—a project designed to deepen harbors, dig tunnels and canals, or otherwise cause beneficial changes to the topography through controlled and contained nuclear explosions?

AEC Chairman Seaborg's statement on this subject, appearing at pages 210–11 of the hearings before the Committee on Foreign Relations, included the following:

"Device development and the program for scientific studies planned for the immediate plowshare program can clearly proceed under the terms of the treaty. This is also true of applications for mining and water resource developments which would be carried out deep underground and involve the release of very little, if any, radio-activity.

"In the excavation application, however, some radioactivity will reach the atmosphere and a careful determination will have to be made that a given project is permissible."

In addition to the other testimony on this point referred to at pages 20–21 of the Report of the Committee on Foreign Relations, attention is called to the following paragraph of the President's letter to Senator Mansfield and Senator Dirksen (quoted at page 15915 of the Congressional Record for September 11, 1963):

"The United States will diligently pursue its programs for the further development of nuclear explosives for peaceful purposes by underground tests within the terms of the treaty, and as and when such developments make possible constructive uses of atmospheric nuclear explosions for peaceful purposes, the United States will seek international agreement under the treaty to permit such explosions."

16. Will the participation of East Germany in this treaty constitute even so much as a tacit, implied, or suggestive recognition of that Communist regime as a sovereign national entity?

No. The reasons for this answer are indicated at pages 14–18 of the printed hearings before the Committee on Foreign Relations. The President re-emphasized this answer in his letter to Senator Mansfield and Senator Dirksen printed at page 15915 of the Congressional Record for September 11, 1963.

Mrs. SMITH. I shall comment briefly on these answers together with the answers given by the President of the United States and by the

able and distinguished junior Senator from Alabama [Mr. Sparkman].
I group all four sets of answers because of their similarity and their
various obvious coordination in preparation and presentation.

I would first take note of that statement of Senator Sparkman that:
> There are no single factual answers available to most of the
> questions posed. There are only speculative answers, but answers
> with high probabilities.

This was the predicate for the detailed statement of Senator Sparkman.
It set the tone for his answers to my questions. It was the foundation
and keystone of his detailed answers.

Any structure is no firmer than its foundation, than its footings.
And I do not find the foundation and footings for Senator Sparkman's
answers to have the degree of reassurance and confidence that I had
hoped for. He observes that "there are only speculative answers." I
had hoped for far more than speculation on this matter which so
seriously involves our national security.

My questions were an attempt to resolve the widespread conflict of
opinion and disagreement among the military specialists and nuclear
scientists over the probable military consequences to us if the treaty is
ratified. Clearly, answers that are only "speculative" do not resolve
that conflict. Nor does the contention that foreign policy or international
political considerations outweigh the military disadvantages.

I am disappointed in the suggestion made by some proponents of the
treaty that the only way in which the appropriate data can be acquired
is to engage in an all-out nuclear war with the Soviet Union. This is
defeatist talk. This is dangerous extremism.

Surely it is not unreasonable for a Senator to request some reasonable
degree of factual assurance that our reliance upon a complicated
ballistic-missile, second-strike force is not misplaced before being called
upon to support a treaty which will so restrict our freedom of action
that we may never be able to gain such requisite factual assurance.

Nor do I think that it is in the interest of constructive debate in
which light, rather than heat, is sought to resort in answers to questions
by implying that if a Senator will only take the time to read the
testimony of a witness he will find the absolute truth. This is no more
constructive that to imply that a Senator's thinking has been misled by
the testimony of a witness, particularly if the party making the implication himself is relying upon opinion, as distinguished from facts, in
offering his speculative answers.

I am deeply appreciative of the answers offered by Senator Sparkman,
Secretary Rusk, Secretary McNamara, and President Kennedy. They are
helpful. But they do not remove doubts. They only partially answer
questions—they only partially resolve doubts. They fall far short of
making an ironclad, airtight case for ratification of the treaty. They are

no more convincing to me than the arguments thus far made against ratification of the treaty.

My more detailed observations with respect to some, but not all of the answers submitted to the questions follow.

Question 1. We are certain of the Russian advantage in the high-yield weapon. Its possession by the Russians is of military significance to the United States—even though we still apparently cannot decide whether we want them in our own arsenal—in its impact upon increasing even more the uncertainties or suspected vulnerabilities in our ballistic-missile systems—whether that of launch sites or penetrating warheads over target. The blast and thermal effects were lightly touched upon but nothing was said of the probable radiation and electromagnetic phenomena associated with such a high nuclear yield. Dr. Brown does not believe that the Soviet high-yield shots were instrumented for effects data but one has to assume that whatever knowledge they gained of blast, thermal and radiation effects, it is 100 percent greater than ours and this disparity will be perpetuated once atmospheric testing is denied to us by treaty ratification.

Question 2. The survivability of a second strike force through "mix" or variety of back-up systems has merit. The theory is that if the land-based missile force should happen to be unexpectedly vulnerable to particular effects phenomena, the Polaris system or the B-52s will not be.

Yet, each has its peculiar uncertainties and vulnerabilities whether in deployment of the system or in the operation of the system. Warhead testing under dynamic conditions of reentry is as fully important as electromagnetic pulse testing for determining actual hardness of launch sites. In the absence of knowledge of what one is trying to harden against, it seems that "designing around" the unknowns is a catchy phrase which has been given too much prominence in the debate.

Question 3. Nuclear superiority for deterrence must be measured both quantitatively in terms of deployed weapons systems and qualitatively in terms of superior scientific knowledge manifesting itself in superior weapon design. The treaty will still permit further quantitative deployment of weapons systems, but its ratification will acknowledge Soviet superiority in critically important areas of nuclear technology having military qualitative significance.

Question 4. The treaty will not prevent the spread. Secretary Rusk and Mr. William Foster said that a comprehensive ban would prevent the spread of nuclear weapons but it should have the effect of retarding the rate at which other nations, apart from France and Red China, might have otherwise acquired a nuclear capability.

Question 5. Secretary Rusk and Dr. Brown would view an explosion which, although within the legal letter of the treaty, releases most of its energy into the atmosphere as a treaty violation. "Underground" has not been sufficiently defined.

Questions 6 and 7. The worry here is the fact that we cannot detect low kiloton yields in the atmosphere. According to Dr. Teller, exposure of radars and communications devices and other electronic gear could upset the nuclear balance, although these are nonnuclear devices, in discovering ways to make them operate efficiently in a nuclear environment, that is, overcoming blackout for example.

Question 8. Question 8 is related to the definition of underground. If, as is contended, we will abrogate the treaty upon detecting a test which, though shallowly buried and the radioactivity from which is confined to Soviet territorial boundaries, then there would be no need to differentiate. One can, however, visualize some heated arguments arising over the contention by the Soviets that they conformed to the letter of the treaty in whatever they did. Differentiation then, between shallow burial and atmospheric, is important.

Question 9. One can accept the data given as to time periods of readiness for different types of tests. The question is whether they are acceptable from the standpoint of national security in the face of another sudden abrogation by the Soviets. We are told that this is a large risk.

Question 10. Both laboratories and scientists deteriorated under the moratorium for lack of any testing. If the other disadvantages inherent in the treaty can be accepted, it would seem that permitted underground testing, if vigorously implemented, should prevent deterioration in nuclear weapons research.

Question 11. The discussion of an anti-ballistic-missile defense has been confined to systems of the Nike-Zeus and Nike-X type. It may well come to pass in the years ahead that an effective ballistic-missile defense will take the form of maintaining above one's country a highly charged atmosphere of rays omitted by enhanced radiation devices which will exploit the vulnerabilities and uncertainties in warhead design of penetrating re-entry vehicles. Discrimination of warhead from decoy, traffic handling, reaction and radar blackout are problems which would be eliminated by this concept and it is one of the unresolved questions concerning the sophisticated nature of the Soviets recent tests and their sudden willingness to sign the treaty.

Question 12. True, without a treaty, the Soviets could overtake our alleged advantage in low-yield weapons more readily. The answers do not mention the fact that the U.S. position in high-yield weapons and knowledge of their effects is committed to inferiority in comparison to the Soviets.

Question 13. The chart appearing on page 6 of the Preparedness

Subcommittee's report, while more far reaching than just next year's planned test, more accurately answers the question.

Question 14. Elsewhere in the debate other facts, figures, statistical studies, and opinion have appeared. The truth of the matter is—we do not know. My question was designed to emphasize in the debate that the propagandized emotionalism on this point is so highly exaggerated.

Question 15. Plowshare, despite claims to the contrary, is generally prohibited by the treaty and the administration has admitted that it must be negotiated out. Senator Sparkman properly introduced as part of his answer, President Kennedy's letter of September 10, 1963.

Question 16. The excerpt from the testimony of Secretary Rusk appearing on page 7 of the Foreign Relations Committee report and the State Department answer are that the answer is no and that even when asserting privileges of participating and voting on amendments, and so forth, we would reserve the right to object.

APPENDIX

CLOSURE OF KITTERY-POTSMOUTH
NAVAL SHIPYARD

November 20, 1964

I am deeply concerned with the announced closings, phase-outs, and curtailments on military establishments in Maine. This is a very serious blow to the workers and economy of Maine. The Federal Government has a very serious obligation to do everything it can to assist Maine workers and Maine communities. I have complete confidence that Maine people and Maine communities can meet this very serious economic challenge as well as did the workers and the community of Presque Isle.

I know that the people of Maine do not ask that a military facility be continued merely for the benefit of the local economy if the mission for that facility has ceased. I know that all that Maine citizens ask for and expect is fair, just, and equal treatment with the citizens of other states in the absorption of this economic impact.

I took this position when the Presque Isle Air Force Base was closed in 1961, being the first United States Senator to speak in the Senate and state my acceptance of this closing on the basis of the principles set forth above.

But on a per capita basis, I doubt if any other state has been singled out for such an economic blow as has been the State of Maine. At least my present impression is that Maine is shouldering an inordinate share of the military cutback.

In fairness to the Secretary of Defense, I want to acknowledge that we all must face change and that the technological changes in our weapons system and national security have indicated that some of the changes were ultimately inevitable. In this bad news for Maine, I am at least grateful that the closing of the Kittery-Portsmouth Naval Shipyard will be gradual and not abrupt—and that we have been given almost four years' notice on the phase-out closing of the Dow Air Force Base.

I am grateful that the scheduled reduction at Loring Air Force Base will be no greater than an indicated 17 percent cutback in the next two years. We should not be surprised at the action on the Topsham Air Force Base in view of the drastic changes in our Air Defense system. The only real surprise is that it is coming this soon.

And it should be acknowledged that the Secretary of Defense has very carefully set forth impressive logic with respect to his actions.

But there are aspects that are very disturbing and raise doubts and suspicions as to the action taken. In the first place, the timing of the announcement is highly suspect. Why was this withheld from the people? Why was it not given to them sooner? Why was the timing just two weeks after the election?

The Secretary of Defense has denied that there were any political implications in the decisions as to which bases and facilities would be cut back. I am willing to accept his word on this—but I would certainly be less than honest if I did not say that I cannot accept any claim that the timing of the announcement was not politically motivated and controlled. The timing in itself casts a political cloud over the announcement.

Nearly a year ago I made a speech in the Senate on December 16, 1963, in which I reported that I had been told that there would be no closings of Government naval shipyards until after the 1964 election. Time has proved that report amazingly accurate.

I also reported that a Government official of full authority had informed me that the Kittery-Portsmouth Naval Shipyard was on its way to being closed and that it was merely a matter of time without indicating when that closing might come. I reported this because I felt that I had an obligation to give the truth to the people at the shipyard and in the Kittery-Portsmouth area so that they could plan accordingly.

I recall very vividly not only of how official denials were made but how I was pilloried with accusations of being reckless and irresponsible and even of deliberately calculating to panic the workers in the shipyard —of the claims by my critics that my warning that the Kittery-Portsmouth Shipyard was on its way to being closed was completely false.

My informant was the highest authority in the land—the President of the United States—and the truth of his statement to me has now been established some two weeks after the 1964 election. I am truly grateful that he warned me. I am truly grateful that I was thus able to warn the people of the Kittery-Portsmouth area almost a year in advance of the finally announced gradual closing of this shipyard.

In that Senate speech of a year ago on December 16, 1963, I also called for an investigation by the Senate Preparedness Investigating Subcommittee on possible shipyard closings. Previously to that time I had called for Senatorial investigations. It is interesting that some of my caustic critics who then opposed Senatorial investigation are now calling for a Senatorial investigation.

While an investigation by the Senate Preparedness Investigating Subcommittee was promised, it never got off the ground and the Defense Department and the Department of the Navy never gave the subcommittee any meaningful information. Consequently, I had no choice but to have an investigation made on my own.

That investigation has produced some rather startling facts that are contradictory to the justifications given by the Secretary of Defense for the decision to close the Kittery-Portsmouth Naval Shipyard. I shall disclose those facts and make a detailed statement early next week.

The announcement on Dow Air Force Base is a distinct surprise to me because earlier this year I had a conference at the Dow Air Force Base with the commanding officers there and was told in answer to my direct and specific questions that there was no question on the future of Dow Air Force Base because there was a definite and stable five-year fund scheduled for the base.

I shall closely analyze the announced actions and question the Department of Defense on them and I am gratified that at long last I have been joined by others in calling for a Senatorial investigation. From what information I already have, I am certain that some of those closings cannot be justified. And I shall press for as much information as possible.

But to hold out any hope to the people in the affected areas of Maine that we can get these decisions reversed would just simply not be being honest with them and would only get their hopes up falsely—just as their hopes were falsely raised that the shipyard would not be closed by those who attacked my warning of nearly a year ago.

If nothing else, the very timing of the announcement within two weeks after the election is the clearest indication that it will be practically impossible to get any reversals of decisions regardless of how hard we press, how much we investigate, and even however impelling, unanswerable, and impressive the facts and logic we can marshal against these decisions.

Index